CHILDREN'S ETHNIC SOCIALIZATION

OTHER RECENT VOLUMES IN THE
SAGE FOCUS EDITIONS

CHILDREN'S ETHNIC SOCIALIZATION

Pluralism and Development

Edited by

Jean S. Phinney
Mary Jane Rotheram

Published in Cooperation with the
Society for Research in Child Development

SAGE PUBLICATIONS
The International Professional Publishers
Newbury Park   London   New Delhi

The study group on which this book was based was funded by the foundation for Child Development, which is a private foundation that makes grants to educational, charitable institutions. Its main interests are in research, advocacy, and public information projects and service experiments in New York City that help translate theoretical knowledge about children at risk into policies and practices that affect their daily lives.

For information address:

SAGE Publications, Inc.
2455 Teller Road
Newbury Park, California 91320

SAGE Publications Ltd.
6 Bonhill Street
London EC2A 4PU
United Kingdom

SAGE Publications India Pvt. Ltd.
M-32 Market
Greater Kailash I
New Delhi 110 048 India

Printed in the United States of America

Library of Congress Cataloging-in-Publication Data

Main entry under title:

Children's ethnic socialization.

(Sage focus editions ; v. 81)
Bibliography: p.
1. Ethnicity in children—United States—Addresses, essays, lectures. 2. Children of minorities—United States—Addresses, essays, lectures. 3. Socialization—Addresses, essays, lectures. I. Phinney, Jean S. II. Rotheram, Mary Jane.
GN495.6.C48   1986   305.2'3   86-1971
ISBN 0-8039-2815-7
ISBN 0-8039-2816-5 (pbk.)

92 93 94 10 9 8 7 6 5

Contents

Preface

In today's increasingly diverse world, ethnicity has a dramatic impact on the developing child. The "melting pot" concept—a single culture resulting from the blending of different ethnic groups—has given way to pluralism—the recognition and acceptance of differences among groups. Most children, whether from majority or minority ethnic groups, have contact with groups other than their own and must learn to live with ethnic diversity. How do children respond to and deal with the differences among groups in both the observable characteristics and the less obvious values and norms? How do children come to understand the meaning of their own and others' ethnic group membership? How does the impact of ethnicity change with development? These are some of the questions that this book addresses. As the ethnic group balance of Western countries changes, it is essential for all those who work with children to understand the impact of differences among ethnic groups in their socialization practices, values and norms, and attitudes toward their own and other groups. Such understanding is particularly important for members of the majority culture, who have in the past been insulated by numbers from having to deal with these issues, but who can no longer ignore ethnicity.

Aspects of ethnicity have been studied by anthropologists, sociologists, psychologists, and sociolinguists. The focus of such work generally has been on entire cultures, on group processes and attitude formation related to ethnicity, or on ethnic identity, and studies have dealt largely with adult populations. Developmental psychologists have examined early ethnic awareness in children, but generally have shown only limited interest in studying ethnicity throughout childhood and adolescence. The leading journals in developmental psychology and the recent *Handbook of Child Psychology* (Mussen, 1983) reveal little current research dealing with ethnicity. However, some researchers, particularly those from minority groups or from geographic areas where ethnicity is highly salient, are addressing the complex issues related to children and ethnicity in pluralistic societies. The goal of this book is to present an integrated review of that work for students, researchers, and professionals concerned with children. It is based on research in a number of Western countries, including the United States, Canada, Mexico, Australia, and New Zealand; it does not attempt to address these issues in developing countries.

7

The book derives from a study group for which funds were obtained from the Society for Research in Child Development by Mary Jane Rotheram. The group, consisting of researchers interested in children and ethnicity, met in January 1984 to exchange theoretical and empirical perspectives on this topic. Papers presented to the group have been rewritten completely for the book and new material has been added. Our goal is to present the reader with an understanding of both the theoretical background and the recent research on children's ethnic socialization. The focus of the book is on the social impact of ethnicity and does not deal with issues such as academic achievement or integration per se. The majority of the chapters are by developmental and social psychologists, but the fields of education and sociolinguistics are represented also.

The chapters are written at a level that assumes some undergraduate background in the social sciences but no advanced training. The book is intended primarily for upper-division and graduate students, professors, and researchers in the fields of developmental and social psychology, education, and ethnic studies, and could be used for courses dealing with cultural diversity, psychology of minorities, multicultural education, and intercultural communication. In addition, it provides a reference source for professionals, or those training to be professionals, in education, counseling, health care, social work, or community service.

The book begins with an introduction and overview of the topic, including definitions used throughout the book. The chapter also examines the various perspectives from which the study of ethnicity is approached in children.

The remainder of the book deals with the impact of ethnicity across the development of the child. The first part focuses on the preschool and early elementary-age child. During these years, ethnicity affects the child primarily through the immediate environment of family, peers, and school, although the existing social structure also influences awareness and attitudes. Research with children at this age has dealt mainly with children's developing awareness and attitudes about their own and other ethnic groups, and their ability to label themselves and others as to ethnic group membership. During middle childhood, as their understanding of the world increases, minority children in particular are faced with realization of the lower status, power, and economic resources of their ethnic group. The special problems associated with minority status for children are addressed in the second part of the book in chapters written by minority group researchers. As they approach and enter adolescence and face the development of a personal identity, children begin to deal more consciously with ethnicity and to be increasingly influenced by the wider culture. The third part of the book examines ethnicity in this broader context. The final part of the book discusses methodological issues in the study of ethnicity and examines themes and implications emerging from the book.

In summary, in order to provide a variety of readers with an understanding of the issues related to ethnic socialization, the book presents a clarification of concepts and definitions in the field and a thorough review of the relevant research. By integrating existing knowledge within a developmental framework, the book provides a basis both for future research and for applications to all aspects of a child's life that are affected by ethnicity.

—Jean S. Phinney
Mary Jane Rotheram

Introduction:
Definitions and Perspectives in the Study
of Children's Ethnic Socialization

MARY JANE ROTHERAM
JEAN S. PHINNEY

A child whose parents immigrated to the United States from Mexico before he was born lives in a White neighborhood, speaks fluent English, and considers himself to be just like the children with whom he plays. However, when he goes to school he is labeled "Hispanic" because of his Spanish surname and dark skin. As he gets older he is asked, "What are you?" He may answer "Mexican American," "Chicano," or "Latino." Occasionally he is asked, "Can you speak English?"

A Black child grows up in a Black community in the United States, secure in the feeling that he is loved and accepted. But from television, magazines, and picture books he sees that all the most successful, powerful people are White. Even Santa Claus, who gives out all the presents, is White. When asked whether he would prefer to be Black or White, he says White.

An Asian girl whose family recently has arrived from Vietnam attends a primarily White school. She studies hard and takes special English classes. Soon she is speaking English well, getting good grades in school, and translating for her parents. From her White friends she learns the latest fads in clothing and popular music. She begins to spend more time with her friends and studies less. Her parents worry that she is losing her culture.

An 8-year-old boy whose parents were Aborigines in the outback migrates with this family to a major city in Australia. He dislikes the changes in his way of life. The language and the customs are strange and the people unfriendly. He feels uncomfortable at school and in his neighborhood. He longs to return home, but attends city schools until he is 16. When he finally returns to the outback, he again finds himself uncomfortable in the same way that the city was once uncomfortable. Has he lost his identity as an Aborigine?

What does their ethnicity mean to each of these children? How do they see themselves and how do others see them in relation to their ethnic group membership? How will their understandings of their own and other groups change as they grow older and as society itself changes? These are the types of questions addressed by this book.

This book is about children's ethnic socialization, that is, the ways in which ethnic group membership affects development. *Ethnic socialization* refers to the developmental processes by which children acquire the behaviors, perceptions, values, and attitudes of an ethnic group, and come to see themselves and others as members of such groups. Research in this area contributes to the understanding of developmental processes that shape children's self-concept and self-esteem, their attitudes and behaviors toward their own and other groups, as well as the way they are evaluated by others. Understanding such processes may suggest methods of facilitating a child's personal development and promoting positive cross-ethnic interactions.

In discussing ethnic socialization a variety of terms have been used, such as *ethnicity, ethnic identity, ethnic self-identification, ethnic awareness,* and *ethnic attitudes.* There has been little consistency in the field of ethnic research as to the definitions of these basic concepts. In this chapter, theoretical perspectives and current usage of these terms are reviewed in order to clarify their meaning. It is hoped that such clarification will promote consistent usage of these terms among those writing on this topic.

Ethnicity and Ethnic Groups

An *ethnic group* has been defined by Shibutani and Kwan (1965) as "those who conceive of themselves as alike by virtue of their common ancestry, real or fictitious, and who are so regarded by others." However, ethnicity is more than ancestry, race, religion, or national origin. It patterns our thinking, feelings, and behavior in both obvious and subtle ways (McGoldrick, Pearce, & Giordano, 1982). Ethnicity includes group patterns of values, social customs, perceptions, behavioral roles, language usage, and rules of social interactions that group members share (Barth, 1969; Ogbu, 1981). These group patterns occur with and without awareness (Kochman, this volume).

The boundaries of ethnic groups often are not clear. Group members may label themselves differently from the way an observer labels them. For example, the use of "Spanish surname" as a criteria for Hispanic children has little validity, because Blacks, Whites, and Asians can have Spanish names. Obgu (1974) documents the substantial proportion of children who label themselves in a way different from their official classification in public schools.

The term *ethnic group* generally has been used to refer to minority groups within a larger culture. Wagley and Harris (1958) assert that ethnic groups are subordinated segments of a complex state that are characterized by traits held in low esteem by the dominant group. Carlos and Padilla (1974) include social distance from a dominant group, pride in one's group, and generational and geographic proximity to the traditional ethnic group as characteristics of an ethnic group. By specifying ethnic pride (Barrera, 1980; Garcia, 1982), these authors are pointing to psychological processes occurring among ethnic group members that result from their lower status and power.

In contrast, it can be argued from a broader, less ethnocentric perspective that not only minority groups but also the dominant groups in a country, such as White Americans in the United States, are ethnic groups. In Canada, both English- and French-speaking populations are considered ethnic groups. If ethnic groups are conceptualized in this way, the distinctive characteristics of each group can be examined and understood in their own terms, rather than as deviations from the "norm" of the dominant culture. Furthermore, the study of ethnic groups on their own terms allows the examination of within-group differences that have been ignored when groups have been compared only to a dominant culture (Buriel, 1982).

In this book the term *ethnic group* is used to apply to any collection of people who call themselves an ethnic group and who see themselves sharing common attributes. Being a minority in numbers and/or status is not a prerequisite of being defined as an "ethnic group." However, when ethnicity and minority status co-occur, predictable social psychological processes occur both within the group and between the group and the majority culture. Therefore, we review below models proposed for the relationships among ethnic groups within a culture.

Three models for the relationship between the minority and the majority group have been proposed: assimilation, acculturation, and pluralism (Padilla, 1980). *Assimilation* describes a situation in which the minority ethnic group gradually loses its distinctiveness and becomes part of the majority group. This can result from either a rejection of the minority group by the dominant group (which in turn forces the minority group to acquire majority norms) or an acceptance by the minority group of the dominant group's norms and a rejection of its own group norms. This term emerged with the characterization of America as the great "melting pot."

Acculturation or *accommodation* implies an acceptance of both one's own group and another group; through contact, conflict, and finally adaptation, elements of each ethnic group are included in the culture. This occurs at both personal and group levels.

Pluralism implies the maintenance of separate norms, customs, values, and possibly language by different groups within a culture; the result is a hetereogeneous culture consisting of a number of distinct groups.

All of theses models suggest the evolution of ethnic groups within a culture. In ethnically heterogeneous societies these processes will be occurring with several ethnic groups simultaneously, with the process proceeding along different lines with different groups. The group and the broader culture are evolving simultaneously, as reflected in the "Black is beautiful" and "Brown power" movements.

The specific content of ethnic group norms will affect the relationship of the minority group to the majority group and the impact of ethnicity on the child. If one's group patterns are similar to the dominant culture, one's ethnicity is likely to be rewarded by others more often than an ethnic pattern that is highly dissimilar to that of the dominant culture. For example, Asians have been referred to as the model minority in the United States and have been suggested as a model for other groups to emulate because of their achievement orientation (Sue & Wagner, 1973).

There are, however, predictable consequences to being a minority in numbers within a group. The early experiments of Asch (1956) demonstrated how having a minority opinion leads persons to deny their own views and to conform to the group norms. In business or task groups, the minority member is seen as representing all members of his or her group. Although these processes clearly occur among adults, they have not been investigated systematically in children. The finding that minority group children show a preference for dolls similar to the dominant group rather than dolls "like themselves" is one example of the impact of minority status.

Ethnic Identity

Broadly speaking, *ethnic identity* refers to one's sense of belonging to an ethnic group and the part of one's thinking, perceptions, feelings, and behavior that is due to ethnic group membership. Ethnic identity is distinguished from ethnicity in that *ethnicity* refers to group patterns and *ethnic identity* refers to the individual's acquisition of group patterns. Ethnic identity is conceptually and functionally separate from one's personal identity as an individual, even though the two may reciprocally influence each other.

The Components of Ethnic Identity

Ethnic identity is a broad concept that includes many components: ethnic awareness (the understanding of one's own and other groups), ethnic self-identification (the label used for one's own group), ethnic attitudes (feelings about own and other groups), and ethnic behaviors (behavior patterns specific to an ethnic group). The term *ethnic identity* has been used variously in the literature to refer to all of these components, alone or in combination. Researchers frequently have limited their focus to a single component. Only recently have there been attempts to study the way thoughts, attitudes, and behaviors reciprocally influence each other (Meichenbaum, 1983; Zajonc, 1980). For example, a child's level of cognitive functioning affects ethnic attitudes and understanding of ethnicity, as well as the relationship between cognitions and attitudes (Aboud & Skerry, 1983; Clark, Hocevar, & Dembo, 1980; Semaj, 1980; Spencer, 1982). In addition, a child's reaction to ethnic stimuli will vary depending on whether the cues are affective, perceptual, or cognitive (Aboud, 1984; Ramsey, this volume). Thus, although we discuss components of ethnic identity separately, it is important to keep in mind that they interact in complex and not well-understood ways.

Approaches to the Study of
Children's Ethnic Identity

A number of different theoretical and empirical approaches have been used in the study of ethnic identity. Psychoanalysts focus on the developmentally linked affective ties to one's group that motivate a person to become similar to others of one's group (Diaz-Guerrero, 1955; Freud, 1918). Erikson (1968) outlines identity as an evolving sense of the individual that is expressed differently at each developmental period, but that is rooted in one's culture. Cognitive developmental psychologists study the child's increasing ability to discriminate, differentiate, and integrate ethnic stimuli and experience (Aboud, 1977; Katz, 1973a; Kohlberg, 1976). Social psychologists examine processes of social comparison between oneself and others (Detweiller, 1979; Hewstone, Jaspars, & Lalljee, 1982; Lambert & Tucker, 1972; Tajfel, 1973). Anthropologists and ethnographers focus on descriptions of common behavior patterns within a culture or ethnic group. Sociolinguists study identity as the acquisition of communication patterns or styles that are common to a group (Giles, 1977; Gumperz, 1982a; Heller, this volume).

Developmental Models of Ethnic Identity

Although researchers of each of the above orientations have addressed the issue of group membership in relation to a person's identity, researchers from the cognitive developmental orientation have generated the most empirically based theories of ethnic identity development in children. Aboud (1977), Goodman (1964), Katz (1976), and Porter (1971) have proposed stage models to explain the acquisition of ethnic identity and attitudes in children. These stages are outlined and summarized on Table I.1 in a comparative fashion.

Although these models vary slightly, each of the investigators assumes a developmental model of change, describing an age-related progression in the ability to perceive, process, and interpret racial or ethnic stimuli, which leads to the establishment of ethnic identity. In this book, Katz's and Aboud's chapters reflect most clearly this developmental perspective.

TABLE I.1

Stages in the Development of Ethnic or Racial Concepts and Attitudes

Goodman (1964)	Porter (1971)	Katz (1976)	Aboud (1977)
		Early observation of cues (0-3)	
Ethnic awareness (3-4)	Awareness of color differences (3)	Formation of rudimentary concepts (1-4)	Unawareness of ethnic affiliation
		Conceptual differentiation	
	Incipient racial attitudes (4)		Awareness of groups leading to social comparison
		Recognition of the irrevocability of cues	
Ethnic orientation (4-8)	Strong social preferences with reasons (5)	Consolidation of group concepts (5-7)	Awareness of group affiliation
		Perceptual elaboration	
		Cognitive elaboration	
Attitude crystallization (8-10)		Attitude crystallization (8-10)	Curiosity about other groups

NOTE: Numbers in parentheses are approximate ages.

Children initially learn from others what group they belong to; however, as they get older, they become aware of options in the extent to which they behave as and consider themselves to be members of an ethnic group. Some Mexican American adolescents stop speaking Spanish, associate mainly with Anglo-Americans, and think of themselves as White, and others retain the language and customs of their parents and consider themselves Hispanic. To deal with changes in identity beyond childhood, a four-stage model has been proposed by Cross (1978) and Thomas (1971), based on the Black experience: (1) pre-encounter, a stage in which Blackness has little salience, especially in political and economic terms; (2) encounter, involving realization of the status of Blacks in the United States; (3) immersion in one's ethnic group, with high emotional intensity; and (4) internalization, a stage of consolidation of personal and group identity. In contrast to the models shown in Table I. 1, Cross suggests a process of ego development rather than the acquisition of the concept of ethnicity.

One's developing sense of ethnic identity is influenced both by how others see one (ascribed criteria) and by the extent to which one feels and acts like a group member (performance criteria). Ascribed criteria are likely to be more important when ethnicity is marked by very apparent physical characteristics, such as skin color and facial features. Thus a dark-skinned Black is likely to be considered clearly Black by most people who meet him or her. However, among those who know them, some Blacks are more "Black" than others, and some are in fact considered to be "White." The term *Oreo* has been used to refer to those who are "Black on the outside and White on the inside"; that is, they think and behave more like Whites than like Blacks. Other minority groups have similar terms for group members who, in spite of outward appearance, identify with the dominant White group: "coconuts" (for Mexican Americans, who are brown on the outside . . .), "bananas" (for Asians), and "apples" (for American Indians).

The Changing Nature and Salience of Ethnic Identity

The importance and meaning of ethnic identity varies with the specific context and with changes in the social milieu and will be more salient in some situations than in others. Children's exposure to situations in which they are aware of their ethnicity will vary depending on their status as minority or majority group members, as well as on the degree of ethnic homogeneity or heterogeneity in their daily activities. For example, ethnicity is likely to be more salient for one White child in a class of 20 Black peers than for the same child in a predominantly White classroom.

In addition, ethnic identity changes with the shifting sociocultural milieu (Diaz-Guerrero, 1982a). For example, both in the United States and New Zealand the political movements of the 1960s and 1970s significantly affected the data on ethnic identity and preference (Banks, 1976; Vaughan, 1978a). Prior to 1974 Black children in the United States were more likely to choose White dolls and have negative self-esteem. Since 1974 and parallel with the "Black is beautiful" movement, Black children are less apt to show this tendency.

Ethnic Awareness

Ethnic awareness is the child's understanding of own and other ethnic groups. Awareness involves knowledge about ethnic groups, their critical attributes, characteristics, history, and customs, as well as the difference between oneself and others. It changes with experience, exposure to new information, and developing cognitive abilities. With awareness comes children's acquisition of the ability to label themselves accurately as to ethnic group. This ability we term *ethnic self-identification;* it is discussed as a separate topic below. Long before children come to label themselves as members of an ethnic group, they are becoming aware, perceptually and cognitively, of ethnic stimuli, as Katz (this volume) discusses. Initial awareness is likely to be based largely on obvious perceptual cues (especially skin color), language, or customs (distinctive food, holidays).

The actual information acquired about other groups is highly dependent on the amount and the kind of contact a child has with other groups (Hallinan, 1982; Helson, 1964; LeVine & Campbell, 1972; Longshore, 1982). Children who live in multiethnic neighborhoods and attend integrated schools will have a much greater awareness of the characteristics of other groups than those who live in homogeneous neighborhoods.

An additional critical factor in the study of ethnic awareness is the child's status as a minority or majority group member (Goodman, 1964). Although minority children inevitably are aware of the dominant culture, both through the media and through personal experience, majority children largely can ignore the minority culture if not exposed to it in integrated schools and neighborhoods. The differences in behavioral norms, expectations, values, and behavior patterns that distinguish groups are less frequently recognized by Whites because most of their contacts are with other Whites, or their contacts with non-Whites are in contexts in which White norms prevail. Thus many majority group children are not even aware that they belong to an ethnic group.

Although ethnic awareness is conceptualized as a cognitive component of one's ethnic identity, it is inevitably connected with affective or evaluative aspects. Thus, as Vaughan (this volume) points out, children's increasing awareness of group differences leads to a more accurate self-identification and also to greater acceptance of one's own group. Thus awareness is linked both to self-identification and to ethnic attitudes.

Ethnic Self-Identification

Along with the awareness of ethnic cues comes the knowledge of oneself as a member of an ethnic group. *Self-identification* refers to children's acquisition of the accurate and consistent use of an ethnic label, based on the perception and conception of themselves as belonging to an ethnic group. Research in this area assumes that children can be objectively and accurately assigned to a particular group, and can then be tested for the accuracy of the label they apply to themselves. Although this assumption may be applicable to young children, who can be considered to belong to their parents' ethnic group, it does not take into account the lack of precision in ethnic group boundaries or the subjective nature of ethnic identity in older children, as discussed above. Thus the term *self-*

identification should be understood as referring to children's use of the ethnic label that others would apply to them.

Self-identification typically is assessed in young children by presenting them with pictures or dolls representing various ethnic groups and having them select the one that is most like themselves. To identify themselves, children must be able to recognize their group, perceive similarity between themselves and others, know the label, and apply the label consistently over time regardless of confusing stimulus cues (Aboud, this volume). The problems associated with measurement of self-identification and the confusion surrounding interpretation of results are discussed by many of the authors in this book. The aspect of this concept that has generated the most confusion and controversy is that of misidentification.

Misidentification or Race Dissonance

For very young children, responses to identification tasks typically are random, showing no awareness of ethnicity. However, once responses begin to show consistency, some children, particularly those from minority groups, tend to choose the "wrong" stimulus; for example, some Black children choose a White doll as most like themselves. This is a paradox in that minority children are likely to be confronted with their ethnicity at an earlier age and in a more dramatic fashion, and are consistently more aware of ethnic differences (Goodman, 1964; Lasker, 1929). A wide variety of interpretations of this phenomenon are presented in the chapters of this book. Essentially, it is not clear whether children really think they belong to another group, would like to belong to another group, or simply admire the other group because of its higher status in the culture.

Cross (this volume) makes fundamental distinctions among personal identity, one's self-concept, and reference group orientation (the group that one admires or uses as a comparison group). Several authors point to the mutually exclusive and simultaneous demands presented to Black children (McAdoo, 1977): (1) Be like Whites and (2) be Black and be proud of it. In such a context, it is not surprising that children show hesitancy in expressing a cultural identity that is not valued by the dominant culture.

Thus in interpreting research in this area it is important to examine carefully the specific measures used. Increasingly, researchers rely on a network of techniques, and distinguish among awareness, preference, and identification (Aboud, 1980; Garcia, 1982; Semaj, 1976, 1980; Spencer, 1982, 1984a).

Relationship to Social Cognition

Assessment of self-identification is contingent upon the acquisition of language. Ethnic self-identification is an aspect of self-understanding, and the process of defining oneself evolves concomitantly with the knowledge of others, one's relationship to others, and the ability to verbalize this (Damon & Hart, 1982; Lewis & Brooks, 1975). Lewis has suggested that gender, familiarity, and age are dimensions that underlie social cognition; ethnicity may be a fourth dimension. However, as has been noted, affect plays a role in the process as well.

Ethnic Attitudes

Ethnic attitudes are characteristic ways of responding to ethnicity, your own and others, that may have either a positive or negative valence. The research on attitudes has focused on the developmental or social psychological factors contributing to the existence of "good" (positively valenced) or "poor" (negatively valenced) ethnic attitudes. This research includes the two most controversial aspects of children's ethnic socialization: children's preferences or liking for their own or another ethnic group, and their negative attitudes toward other groups (that is, prejudice).

Children's Feelings About
Their Own Ethnic Group

Ethnic attitudes in children have been assessed primarily with dolls or pictures in a manner similar to self-identification, but with questions such as, Which doll is nicest? Which would you like to be? Which would you like to play with? As with the identification research, Black children have tended to show a preference for White figures. However, the research has been questioned for methodological reasons, and the findings have given rise to many diverse interpretations. There are methodological problems in the use of a doll to represent an ethnic group in which appearance is assumed to be the basis of similarity. Forced choices limit statistical variance and raise issues of reliability and validity (Aboud & Skerry, 1984). The effects vary with ethnic groups, that is, cross-ethnic preference choices are more frequent among some minority groups than others (Fu, Hinkle, & Korslund, 1983; Vaughan, 1964b).

Even preference measures that are more sophisticated, assess across several domains, and use continuous rating scales rather than forced choice are difficult to interpret. Findings vary with age, cohort, and situational variables. It is clear in any case that preference tests are not measures of ethnic identity, as has sometimes been implied. In this volume, Cross and Vaughan, based on work with two different ethnic groups in different countries, argue that the results of preference studies reflect the fact that minority children must develop bicultural competence, that is, skills to succeed both in the majority culture and in their own group.

Feelings Toward Other Groups:
Stereotypes and Prejudices

Like other aspects of ethnicity, attitudes toward other ethnic groups are studied in different ways by different academic disciplines. Developmental psychologists, focusing on age-related changes, have shown that ethnic attitudes become more integrated and differentiated with age (Katz, 1976). Ramsey (this volume) shows how children's level of cognitive understanding influences the way their experiences are interpreted and lead to attitudes toward other groups.

It is not clear whether attitudes become more or less positive with age. Proshansky (1966) points out that although results may show older children to be less prejudiced, this finding indicates primarily that they know the socially correct attitudes; in fact, their own ingroup preferences tend to increase with age. Brand, Ruiz, and Padilla (1974) conclude that attitudes are formed very early: "Once prejudices are formed, either positive or negative, they tend to increase with age." This is supported by Williams and Morland (1979), whose research shows that age is not a variable of major importance in ethnic preferences. Early socialization experiences, then, are critical to the determination of ethnic attitudes. In addition to age-related changes, Jenkins (1982) reports that cross-ethnic attitudes are becoming more positive with each succeeding cohort of White children.

Researchers with a psychoanalytic orientation focus on personality types, and see negative attitudes as being determined by early childhood experience, especially the parent-child relationship. Children who show less acceptance of other groups tend to be more constricted, cynical, and suspicious, and less secure than children who are more tolerant (Adorno, Frenkel-Brunswik, Levinson, & Sanford, 1950; Gouch, Harris, Martin, & Edwards, 1972). Prejudiced children are more likely to be moralistic, to dichotomize the world, to externalize conflict, and to have a high need for definiteness (Allport, 1954). These characteristics emerge from families in which the children feel a great deal of ambivalence toward their parents and foreshadow an authoritarian personality in adults.

In contrast, social psychologists focus on group processes that influence prejudicial attitudes. A variety of situational factors such as proximity, frequency of contact, ethnic balance, density, heterogeneity of the population, and the degree of vertical mobility within a society influence cross-ethnic attitudes (LeVine & Campbell, 1972). The relationship between ethnic identity and attitudes is suggested by work discussed by Rosenthal (this volume), showing that adolescents who are secure in their own identity are less apt to have negative attitudes toward other groups.

Ethnic Patterns

The existence of differences in attitudinal, affective, and behavioral patterns across cultures has been well documented (Whiting & Whiting, 1975). Classic works, such as Benedict's (1934) *Patterns of Culture,* describe underlying themes that characterize and distinguish Native American cultures. A similar approach has been used more recently by scholars in international relations who attempt to describe cultural differences in social behavior in order to minimize misunderstanding among people who work and travel in foreign countries (Hofsted, 1984; Landis & Brislin, 1983; Stewart, 1972). This theory describes American cultural patterns in contrast to non-Western cultures, and identifies aspects of behavior that distinguish Americans from non-Westerners. Thus, for example, Americans tend to be individualistic and independent, and non-Westerners are oriented toward kinship ties and group cohesion.

These differences are not random, but are organized and interdependent within the gestalt of a particular culture (Ogbu, 1982). Anthropologists provide rich qualitative descriptions of how these patterns interact in a coherent framework within each culture (Benedict, 1934). Psychologists and sociologists have attempted to quantify these differences in order to understand cross-cultural and subcultural differences (Forgas, 1979; Triandis, 1971). Efforts by these researchers to specify ethnic group differences in an organized fashion have focused on dimensions that underlie differences in behavior across ethnic groups (Hofstede, 1984).

A number of writers have proposed explanations for the origins of dimensions of difference. An empirical approach is taken by Forgas (1979), who argues that dimensions emerge statistically from analysis of situations. He demonstrates the existence of similar dimensions from research in a variety of settings and countries by researchers employing very diverse methodologies and analytic techniques.

An alternative approach suggests that the dimensions reflect common human dilemmas. Spiegel (1982) has argued that each culture must resolve basic questions about the nature of the human predicament, that is, why abilities and resources are not equally distributed, whether people are basically good or evil, and what our relationship should be toward other people. Berry (in Triandis & Berry, 1980) asserts that there is a universal domain of behaviors but great diversity in the functional equivalence of these behaviors across cultures. He suggests that dimensions may be understood broadly as ways of organizing or handling social situations that are common to all cultures. For example, authority figures exist in all cultures, but there are differences in who is considered an authority, as well as in how one behaves in interaction with authorities. Attitudes, and hence behaviors, toward authority figures vary across a range from extreme deference to a feeling of personal, if not political, equality.

These dimensions reflect consistencies in the type of social rules held by ethnic group members. Each dimension cuts across interpersonal issues in a variety of situational contexts and is predictive of social rules (Argyle, Furnham, & Graham, 1981). These rules are implicit (Goffman, 1974), but are evident in that behaviors repeatedly occur that are consistent with the rules. An ethnic group's social rules reflect different positions on the dimensions that structure interpersonal interaction. These rules then predict behaviors within specific situations. Thus researchers can begin by analyzing behaviors across settings in order to understand social rules and then specify dimensions, or vice versa, from dimensions to rules and then behaviors.

There have been a variety of attempts from researchers with widely differing goals to identify and specify these dimensions (Lonner, 1980). Such efforts have focused on very different constructs, such as national character (Inkeles & Levinson, 1969), motivational constructs (McClelland, 1968), values (Spiegel, 1982), or attitudes toward work (Hofstede, 1984). In spite of different goals and methodologies, a high degree of consistency emerges from this work. Although it has been suggested that there are as many as 21 different dimensions of cultural difference (Triandis & Brislin, 1984), most writers feel that there are from 3 to 5 major dimensions that distinguish cultures. Although different terms may be used, similar concepts recur throughout the literature. From an examination of this literature, we suggest 4 dimensions that are central to differentiating the social behaviors of cultural groups: (1) an orientation toward group affiliation and interdependence versus an individual orientation emphasizing independence and competition, (2) an active, achievement-oriented style versus a passive, accepting style, (3) authoritarianism and the acceptance of hierarchical relationships versus egalitarianism, and (4) an expressive, overt, personal style of communication versus a restrained, impersonal, and formal style. These four dimensions are shown in Table I.2. Our terms are listed at the top and the terms that other writers have used for similar concepts are shown below. Additional dimensions identified by other writers are shown in a note below the table. Given the diversity of the methodologies, ethnic groups, settings, and goals of the writers, the amount of agreement is impressive.

Children learn the behavior patterns that derive from these dimensions. According to the perspective of symbolic interactionism (Mead, 1934), children begin to understand that meaning of specific acts in their culture and to structure their world with reference to these meanings. The interpetations that children give to situations in turn influence their behavior.

Much of the early research describing the behavior of ethnic minorities used middle-class White American behavior as the norm, and saw minority values and behavior patterns as deviant or deficient (Howard & Scott, 1981). In contrast, the approach to the study of ethnic group differences based on underlying dimensions allows one to examine such differences from a universal rather than an ethnocentric perspective. Relatively little research has specifically examined differences in children's behavior in terms of the dimensions described above. A notable exception is the work of Whiting and Whiting (1975). These researchers observed the frequency of twelve different behaviors in children from six cultures. Analyzing the frequency of these behaviors using multidimensional scaling, they identified two dimensions: (1) nurturance and responsibility in contrast to dominance and dependence, and (2) reprimands and assaults versus sociability and intimacy. Although there is little other research that

TABLE I.2

Dimensions of Cultural Differences

Reference	Individual- versus Group-oriented	Active versus Passive	Authoritarian versus Egalitarian	Expressive versus Restrained
Burger, 1973[a]	social organization: independence versus interdependence	time: precise versus casual; environmental control–high versus low	communication–respectful, polite versus egalitarian, informal	cognition versus effect versus psychomotion
Diaz-Guerrero, 1975	interdependence versus autonomy	active versus passive	affiliative obedience versus self-assertion	
Hofstede, 1984	individualism	masculinity	power distance	uncertainty avoidance
Inkeles & Levinson, 1954[b]	inner versus outer directed		authoritarian versus egalitarian	expression versus inhibition of affect
McClelland, 1961	need for affiliation	need for achievement	need for power	
Parsons & Shils, 1951	self-orientation versus collectivity	ascription versus achievement		affectivity versus affective neutrality
Spiegel, 1982[c]	individual, collateral, lineal	doing, being, becoming; present, past, future		
Triandis et al., 1972[d]	associative versus dissociative		superordinate versus subordinate	intimate versus formal

NOTE: Other dimensions noted: (a) Goodness versus badness of human nature; (b) other primary dilemmas such as control of aggression and self-esteem; (c) humans as good, neutral, or evil; (d) overt versus covert.

specifically identifies dimensions with children, there is a large body of research describing cross-cultural and subcultural variations in children's behavior. This research is reviewed in Chapter 10.

Only gradually through the media and direct contact do children learn that some of their behaviors, which to them are the only way to behave in a given situation, are in fact "ethnic." Although children become aware very early of the more obvious ethnic cues (language, skin color, and so on), as discussed above, they may not realize until adulthood, if then, that they think and behave differently in certain situations from members of other ethnic groups. In integrated school settings children may be exposed to other groups and their characteristic patterns. This awareness of differences leads to the possibility of conscious choice, either to emphasize one's own distinctive patterns, as when English-speaking Welsh subjects broaden their Welsh accent when speaking to native English speakers (Giles, 1977), or to adopt the patterns of another group. The group that one chooses consciously to imitate has been referred to as one's *reference group*. It is not clear at what age children begin to be able to choose which ethnic patterns they will adopt, that is, which reference group they have.

Bicultural Competence

Children raised in a pluralistic society may, to some degree, be "bicultural," or even "multicultural," that is, acquire the norms, attitudes, and behavior patterns of their own and another, or perhaps several other, ethnic groups. Biculturalism occurs most typically with minority children, but the concept may apply to majority group children who have contact with a minority group, or to two minority groups that interact. For example, Black and Hispanic children in an integrated school may acquire bicultural competence. The term *bicultural identity* has been used in reference to such children, but its meaning varies widely. It can mean bicultural competence, that is, the ability to function in two different cultures by switching between two sets of values and attitudes. It is also used to describe individuals who are between two cultures, showing some attributes of each. This latter definition is discussed further in Chapter 10. However, children cannot have a bicultural self-identification; that is, they cannot simultaneously label themselves as belonging to two different groups (except perhaps children from mixed marriages). Therefore, in this volume we refer to *bilcultural competence* rather than to *bicultural identity*.

There is disagreement in the literature as to whether biculturalism has a positive or negative effect on development. It has been presumed by some writers that conflict is the inevitable result from the forced choice every minority person must make between his or her own culture and the dominant culture (Stonequist, 1935, 1964). This conflict or replacement model sees minority children as being required to replace their own set of ethnic behaviors and norms with another. As long as the individual is midway between two groups, he or she would have a diffuse identity. This is associated with insecurity, anxiety, increased emotionality, distrust, hostility, and defensiveness (Child, 1943; Goodman, 1964; Lewin, 1948; Mussen, 1953; Paz, 1961; Stevenson & Stewart, 1958).

More recently, however, the concept of bicultural or multicultural competence has become the goal in socializing non-White children in the United States (Ramirez, 1977; Ramirez & Castenada, 1974; Ramirez & Price-Williams, 1974). In a flexibility or synthesis model, children raised in two cultures are seen as demonstrating greater role flexibility, flexibility in cognitive style, adaptability, and creativity. The norms of both cultural groups are assimilated and available to be used by the child, depending on the demand of the situational context. Rather than presenting it as a liability, current theories emphasize the benefits of socialization to more than one cultural group's norms (Fitzgerald, 1971; McFee, 1968; Ramirez & Castenada, 1974). Some writers suggest that children with bicultural competence can be expected to have higher self-esteem, greater understanding, and higher achievement than others (Ramirez, 1983). In this book, Rosenthal demonstrates that the impact and outcome of exposure to two cultures depend on a variety of factors, such as the attitudes of the majority culture, the strengths and institutional completeness of the minority group, and individual factors within the family and child. Cross (this volume) suggests that Black children are raised to be bicultural, because they must be able to get along in both Black and White cultures.

Perspectives in Research on Ethnic Socialization

The topics discussed above represent aspects of the broad area of children's ethnic socialization. A complete understanding results only from considering the way these aspects interact and influence each other, but each aspect is most easily studied separately. Researchers examining the issue typically are selective in their focus and approach. It is therefore important in reading and evaluating research to be aware of both the possible perspectives on a topic and the approach used by a particular researcher. An examination of research on children's ethnic socialization reveals a number of different perspectives in the way the topic is studied: (1) the level at which it is addressed (individual, family, community, or larger social group); (2) the viewpoint adopted (observer versus child); (3) the assumptions regarding change (age or developmental processes, group processes, or secular trends); (4) the methodology used (psychometric measures, naturalistic observations, ethnographic methods); (5) the actual groups studied; and (6) the goals of the research.

(1) Levels. The impact of the ethnic group membership on the child is the focus of this book. However, the child is affected by the family, the community, and the broader culture. Typically, researchers from different academic disciplines focus on different levels. Anthropologists study phenomena at the level of cultural groups; sociologists and sociolinguists examine social groups and communities; and developmental psychologists focus on the individual person. An understanding of the interactive influences at each level is essential for understanding the impact of ethnicity on the individual child.

(2) Viewpoint. A child's designation as an ethnic group member is often a function of the perspective assumed, that is, that of the child or of an observer.

Ogbu (1974) has demonstrated that children are frequently mislabeled in school census. In South America ethnicity is based not on blood lines but on skin color. This destroys the notion that there are "objective" means of determining one's ethnicity. Each researcher of children's ethnic socialization is a participant in the process under investigation. This must be remembered in defining terms, adopting labels for groups (for example, White Americans often are referred to as Anglos by Hispanic, outlining developmental processes, and interpreting data; that is, whose criteria are being adopted?

(3) Assumptions regarding change. Changes in children's ethnic identity, awareness, and attitudes occur as a result of developmental changes as well as of variation in the sociocultural milieu, cohort groups, generation (among immigrants), and the interaction among these influences. Researchers focus on different aspects of this process, and their assumptions about the nature of change are relevant to the interpretation of data on ethnic socialization. Cognitive developmental psychologists assume that there are predictable qualitative shifts with age in the child's ability to process information about the world (Damon & Hart, 1982; Katz, 1976). These developmental changes lead to a reorientation of the child's ethnic awareness, attitudes, and identity with each developmental stage (Ramsey, this volume). Typically the child's developing cognitive abilities are seen as the critical factor leading to differences in feelings and behaviors (Piaget & Weil, 1951). More recently, the interactive nature of social and emotional experiences with evolving cognitive capacities is being emphasized.

Social psychologists identify group processes that affect ethnic socialization. For example, cognitive dissonance might lead members of a minority group to minimize the importance of being accepted by Whites (Banks, 1972). In general, children are assumed to be influenced by the same group processes that have been found to influence adults.

Historical sociocultural changes are recognized as an important influence by most researchers concerned with ethnicity, but their effects have been studied less systematically. Riegel (1976) presents a conceptual model of the interaction of the historical sociocultural milieu, individual factors, and the physical environment, as these forces interface to form unique patterns of development for each generation, each ethnic group, and each individual. Little empirical work has been done in this area, but Ogbu's (1974, 1981, 1982) work suggests a beginning.

(4) Methodology. Diverse methodologies have been used to study ethnic socialization, ranging from quantitative, empirical work in structured settings with predetermined questions to ethnographic descriptions of naturally occurring behavior (Schofield, this volume). These differing methodologies reflect differences in fundamental assumptions among the researchers. In ethnographic methodologies the researcher is a participant in the action being investigated. Basic concepts are seen as being defined by the persons being studied, as in Kochman's (this volume) examination of what Blacks themselves consider to be ethnic markers. In contrast, quantitative methodologies are more likely to set

specific objective criteria for the variables being studied and evaluated, as in Aboud's (this volume) definition of an ethnic group and criteria for self-identification.

(5) Actual groups studied. Until recently most ethnic research has been on Black and White children (Milner, 1983). But with increasing ethnic diversity, more research has been emerging on Hispanic and Asian children within the United States, and ethnic research in other countries has been increasing (Hofstede, 1984). As other ethnic groups are studied, we become aware of the limitations of research based on one group. For example, Hwang and Morland (1981) found that the widely discussed finding that majority children prefer and/or identify with the majority culture is true only in societies that are stratified and where there is not ethnic heterogeneity among members of the society. Aboud (1977), working with ethnic groups in Canada, found that physical appearance often is not the most critical discriminator of ethnicity. Salient ethnic features vary with populations (Driedger, 1976; Giles, Taylor, Lambert, & Albert, 1976). In addition, the age at which children recognize salient ethnic characteristics varies with ethnic groups. Black and White children recognize their own groups in advance of American Indians, Chinese, and French Americans. The type of impact that the race of experimenters will make varies as a function of the ethnic group studied. For example, in working with Cubans and Chinese, Campbell (1981) found that cross-ethnic experimenters were more likely to elicit positive self-references than same-ethnic experimenters, a finding not consistent with the research on Black-White relations in the United States. Research with Hispanics in the United States indicates that within-group differences are often as important as between-group variations (Buriel & Vasquez, 1982). In addition, when studying Mexican Americans, the generation of the immigrant is important to understanding patterns of assimilation and acculturation (Buriel, 1982). When more than two groups are contrasted, Hispanic groups have been found to have more positive cross-ethnic attitudes than either White or Black groups and less of an outgroup orientation (Fu, Hinkle, & Korslund, 1983). Researchers are attempting to expand the range of groups studied to recognize the differences among groups and yet look for generalizations that may apply across groups in order to determine the impact of ethnicity on children.

(6)Values in research. The goals of researchers generally are stated as an attempt to understand a phenomenon. Historically, however, investigators and policymakers have interpreted research on ethnic groups in an evaluative fashion. There is a "good" or "competent" fashion in which to develop an ethnic identity and "good" cross-ethnic attitudes. The definitions of *good* arise from sociopolitical systems, not objective, data-based conclusions.

The early research on ethnicity conducted by psychoanalysts demonstrates these biases. Early researchers attempted to remedy prejudice against minorities and low achievement scores of Black children in schools. The type of empirical questions raised, the context within which the research was conducted, and the interpetation of results reflected the sociocultural milieu of the times. Ryan (1971) labeled this "victim blaming," that is, identifying the deficits of Black children, rather than assessing social, economic, political, or cultural factors that generate these problems (Howard & Scott, 1981).

The chapters in this book reflect assumptions regarding positive and negative aspects of ethnic identity and attitudes. Spencer, Aboud, Cross, and Katz define healthy ethnic identity and cross-ethnic attitudes as being those in which you feel good about yourself, but are also positive toward other ethnic groups. Cross, in fact, defines a developmental progression of healthy minority group members who pass through a series of developmental stages until they finally feel positive about themselves—just slightly more positive than they feel about other ethnic groups. Even if researchers are not attempting to encourage positive ethnic attitudes, others, such as policymakers and educators, will interpret or use their results for their own purposes. In the area of ethnic research it is virtually impossible to conduct research that does not have evaluative implications.

In summary, research on ethnic socialization has been conducted from a variety of perspectives, each of which contributes to our understanding of certain aspects of the topic. However, in order to gain a broad and balanced understanding of ethnic socialization, it is important to bring together the varied approaches: (1) Not only the individual child, but the influence of family, community, and societal factors must be considered. (2) The perspective from which the topic is approached, that of the participant or the observer, determines the definition of ethnic terms. (3) Along with developmental changes that occur with age, there are important cohort differences based on changing social and historical forces. (4) The precise findings of quantitative research can be enriched with qualitative studies, and vice versa. (5) Studying a variety of ethnic groups in different contexts allows for a clearer understanding of their similarities and differences, in terms of their effects on the developing child. (6) Research on ethnicity will inevitably have evaluative implications, in spite of efforts to avoid bias and ethnocentrism.

PART I

Ethnicity and the Young Child: Awareness, Attitudes, and Self-Identification

The first part of this book examines the impact of ethnicity in early and middle childhood. During these years the foundation is laid for children's understanding of and attitudes toward their own and other ethnic groups. The questions addressed here concern children's awareness of the characteristics of ethnic groups and their understanding of their own ethnic group membership. How early do children know which ethnic group they belong to (ethnic self-identification) and how can this knowledge be assessed? Which ethnic attributes are critical in children's understanding of their own and others' ethnic group membership? Why do some minority children appear to make an inaccurate choice as to their own group membership (misidentification, or race dissonance)?

These questions are complex and can be addressed from a variety of perspectives. In these chapters, the level of analysis is primarily the individual child, and the focus is on developmental changes. However, group processes and the characteristics of the society also affect development in the early years, even without the child's awareness. The viewpoint taken here is that of observers who assign children to an ethnic group on the basis of external criteria, rather than in terms of children's subjective sense of group membership. The methodology reported in these chapters is primarily quantitative, involving precise measures of children's ability and preference in choosing ethnically related stimuli; but qualitative methods are also discussed. Previous research on these issues generally has been carried out with Black and White children, in which the differences in physical characteristics are most apparent to children. These chapters deal with a number of other groups as well, such as Asian, Mexican American, or Maori children, in which the physical differences are less clear to young children and their reactions may depend more on other attributes, such as language, clothing, or customs.

Given these perspectives, each chapter provides a specific focus that contributes to our understanding of early ethnic socialization. Aboud presents a detailed review of both the measurement issues and the findings of recent research on ethnic self-identification and attitudes in young and preadolescent children. She notes that no one measure provides an adequate assessment of these concepts. The various measures that have been used differ in reliability as well as conceptual requirements; accurate responses to self-identification tasks emerge at different ages depending on the measure used. Self-identification depends on awareness of critical attributes that define an ethnic group. However, critical attributes vary by ethnic group and differ in salience; thus self-identification tasks are not comparable across groups. Ethnic attitudes, Aboud suggests, precede identification in young children. Later, as perceptual and cognitive processes lead to children's understanding of their similarity or dissimilarity to others, children categorize themselves more accurately and show increased preference for their own group.

Ramsey examines many of the same issues with a different methodology. Using open-ended interviews in addition to semistructured tasks, she shows how young children's understanding of ethnicity depends on their level of cognitive development. Children's categories are more inconsistent, undifferentiated, and concrete than adults. As they assimilate information observed or heard about ethnic groups, children overgeneralize and think in terms of absolutes. They have an inadequate understanding of the causes and permanence of ethnic differences. Their thinking is often suffused with and determined by feelings, either their own or those inferred from the remarks of adults; thus children's comments about other groups may appear to be prejudiced. Yet children's behavior is not bound by their expressed opinions, and they are likely to act in a way that is at odds with their attitudes. Therefore, children's responses to measures of identification and preference cannot be interpreted in the same way as adult responses; rather, they must be considered with reference to the child's developmental level.

The interrelationship between affective and cognitive processes, noted by both Aboud and Ramsey, is discussed further by Vaughan from a social psychological perspective. He incorporates the two processes into a model of ethnic identification and shows that such a model needs to be expanded to include group processes. Simply being a member of a group inclines children to favor that group over others. However, the processes of intergroup comparison operate differently for minority children and vary with age and social change.

Using data from his own work in New Zealand, Vaughan shows how the early misidentification of Maori children gives way to more accurate identification and more positive own-group attitudes both with increasing age and with shifts in the cultural milieu; for example, the social changes accompanying the "Brown power" movement.

In the last chapter in this section, Katz discusses and integrates the concepts and findings presented in the first three chapters, and examines the extent to which the questions posed above have been answered. She suggests five issues that remain to be addressed. First, researchers should broaden the developmental age range over which ethnic identification is studied, both upward and downward. Second, the importance of ethnicity relative to other social cues needs to be examined. Third, the relationship between ethnic identity and other components of identity formation, such as sex-role identity, is not clear. Fourth, more information is needed on how children obtain information about ethnic groups other than their own. Finally, we need to understand better how to use the information that has been gathered regarding ethnic socialization to maximize children's positive attitudes toward their own and other ethnic groups.

1

The Development of
Ethnic Self-Identification and Attitudes

FRANCES E. ABOUD

This chapter presents a developmental and social psychological approach to the study of ethnic identity and attitudes. As developmental phenomena, ethnic identity and attitudes are examined with a focus on the individual in the process of acquiring a self-definition and a set of likes and dislikes about ethnic groups. The development of identity and attitudes is conceived of as proceeding from rudimentary forms of identity and attitudes to fully developed adult forms. The adult forms can be defined in terms of the characteristics they possess. Children's identity and attitudes are precursors of adult forms that serve the same functions but have a simpler structure. Consequently, a child's response to ethnic groups may meet some, but not all, of the criteria required by the definition of the adult form. The development of identity and attitudes can be traced as children gradually acquire the adult criteria. In order to examine the development of identity and attitudes, this chapter reviews research on preadolescent children since 1965 plus a few of the pioneer works. (For research conducted before that date, see Brand, Ruiz, & Padilla, 1974.) The review is presented in three sections: ethnic self-identification, attitudes toward own group and other groups, and the relation between identity and attitudes.

Identification of Self

Definitions and Procedures

Ethnic self-identification is the sense of oneself as a member of an ethnic group, possessing attributes common to that ethnic group.

Because the term *identity* can include both the self as an active agent as well as the self as the object of one's knowledge and evaluation (Rosenberg, 1979), the term *identification* will be used for the latter aspect. *Ethnic self-identification,* then, refers to the description of oneself in terms of a critical ethnic attribute, that is, an attribute that defines rather than merely describes the ethnic group. Although only one attribute is necessary to meet the criterion of identification, the description of several attributes may indicate a stronger identification. Two other features of self-description could be considered secondary criteria: (1) describing oneself as distinctive from members of different ethnic groups, and (2) understanding the sameness and continuity of one's ethnic attribute.

What are the critical attributes required for ethnic self-identification? They would be those for which a consensus emerge if members of that ethnic group were asked: What are the most important things about being X, so important that without them one could not be X? Attributes might include ancestry or parentage, national or religious background, language, skin color, and the group's label. Describing oneself in terms of one of these critical attributes would be the first criterion for saying that an ethnic identification had been made. The second criterion is that this attribute be perceived as distinguishing one from members of other ethnic groups. Clearly certain attributes are shared by several groups; but if only shared attributes are used to describe oneself, the identification would be to both groups. Thus the attribute or combination of attributes must be specific to that ethnic group. The third criterion is that one's ethnicity be seen to remain constant, that is, to be both consistent across changes in the context, and to be continuous over time. If one's ethnic identification changes as a result of changes in clothing, language, or age, then it is not constant. These three criteria appear in the conceptual and empirical literature on self and gender identity in children (for example, Erikson, 1968; Mohr, 1978; Rosenberg, 1979; Slaby & Frey, 1975). They are less common in the ethnic identity research.

The typical procedure to measure ethnic identification in children is to ask about perceived similarity in appearance (Clark & Clark, 1947). The child is told to select from a set of visual stimuli (pictures or dolls) the one who "looks most like you." Pointing to a peer of the same ethnic group as the child constitutes a correct response. By correct, we usually mean the ethnic group(s) of the parents. This is often assumed by the tester, though in some cases it is not a single or simple affiliation (see the discussion of biculturalism and misidentification). Although the question inquires about appearance similarity, neither ethnicity nor appearance necessarily underlies the child's response. Comparable results have been obtained when no attribute is specified, as in the question, "Who is most similar to you?" (Aboud, 1977; Rosenthal, 1974). When asked why they chose a particular person, Whites mentioned, in order of frequency, inferred behavior, appearance, ethnic label, and language (Aboud, 1977). This implies that an ethnic feature of appearance is not always the most salient attribute forming the basis of perceived similarity even when the question specifies "looks." It may not be the most salient attribute associated with ethnicities other than perhaps Blacks and Whites (Kircher & Furby, 1971). The advantages of this measure are that pictorial stimuli are good elicitors of self-identification and that similarity is one way to tap the perception of common attributes. However, to be a good measure of ethnic identification an attribute associated with the ethnicity must form the basis of the similarity judgment.

Other measures based on more cognitive processes include categorization, labeling, and matched self-ethnic descriptions. Categorization requires the child to put into one pile pictures of people who belong to the same ethnic group. Usually pictures of other persons are to be categorized (Vaughan, 1963a), but it is also possible to include a photo or stick figure of the child to measure self-identification (Aboud, 1984). If the self-stimulus is placed in the correct pile, ethnic self-identification is accurate.

Labeling one's own ethnicity is another cognitive measure. Pointing to pictures of one ethnic member at a time, the examiner provides the appropriate ethnic label (X) and then asks the child, "Are you X?" If the child says yes to his or her own label and no to the others, the self-identification is accurate. Misidentification involves saying yes to only one label but the wrong one. Saying yes to many labels implies a lack of understanding of the concept of ethnicity. Saying no to all the labels implies that the child has no ethnic identification in terms of the label but may identify with other critical ethnic attributes. A variation of this technique is to ask the child to describe him or herself and to note whether ethnicity is mentioned (McGuire, McGuire, Child, & Fujioka, 1978). If it is not mentioned, ethnicity may be known but is not salient. The latter is therefore not a good measure of ethnic identification on its own.

Matching self- and ethnic descriptions is another cognitive index, one used by Lambert and Tucker (1972). The procedure involves self-ratings along a number of bipolar adjectives from the semantic differential.

These ratings are then matched against the children's descriptions of their own and another ethnic group. If self-ratings match own group more than other group ratings, the child is said to possess an ethnic identification. By itself, this measure would tell us nothing about the child's knowledge of belonging to that group, but it does indicate possessing attributes in common with the group. Unfortunately, researchers have tended to use evaluative attributes, turning this into a measure of attitudes.

The procedures discussed so far measure the first criterion of ethnic identification, namely, describing oneself in terms of one critical ethnic attribute (appearance, belonging, label). The perceptual measure of similarity appears to evoke accurate responses before the cognitive measures of categorization, labeling, and matched descriptions (Aboud, 1980; Vaughan, 1963a). This is consistent with the development of identification generally in that perceived features are salient before inferred internal features (Rosenberg, 1979). Ethnic identification may be a cumulative process in which a number of ethnic attributes are gradually added to one's self-description. Children who describe at least one critical ethnic attribute may be said to possess a rudimentary ethnic identification.

Describing oneself as distinctive from other ethnic groups is an important criterion but less frequently measured. The question here is, "Who is different from you?" When asked why the selected peer was different, children mentioned behavior, ethnicity, and appearance (Aboud, 1977). Ethnicity was mentioned more often as a different feature than as a similar feature.

Ethnic constancy includes two components: consistency or sameness despite superficial change, and continuity over time. Procedures for assessing the sense of consistency and continuity of one's ethnicity are parallel to those used to determine gender constancy (Aboud, 1984; Aboud & Skerry, 1983; Semaj, 1980). The questions for consistency propose a superficial alteration of one's ethnic features and ask if one would still be one's present ethnicity. For example, one might ask a White child, "If you dressed in Eskimo clothes, would you be Eskimo or White?" and to a Black child, "If you wore a blond wig, would you be White or Black?" Maintaining one's ethnicity despite the clothing or hair change indicates consistency. Continuity is assessed by asking, "How long have you been White?" and "Ten years from now what will your ethnicity be?" Data for ethnic continuity have not yet been reported. The data for ethnic consistency indicate that it does not emerge until 8 years of age (Aboud & Skerry, 1983; Semaj, 1980). Using a slightly different procedure, Vaughan (1963a) found a disruption of ethnic identification when clothing was not consistently available as a cue; accurate categorization without the clothing cue emerged at 10 years only. Correct ethnic identification may be labile until the child develops a conception of ethnicity as unchangeable (Aboud, 1984).

The procedure best suited to incorporate the three criteria of ethnic identification would be one similar to Slaby and Frey's (1975) assessment of gender identity. A preliminary measure of recognition would ensure that children recognize ethnic members when given the label. The main procedure would include several questions to make sure that each criterion was being met reliably rather than by chance, and would cover perceived similarity, labeling, continuity, and consistency. Photos of children from several ethnic groups are placed in front of the child. To assess recognition, the examiner asks, "Who is Black? Who is White? Who is Chicano? Who is Indian?" To assess perceived similarity, one would describe the critical ethnic attribute (skin color, language, ancestry) of each stimulus person and ask "Who is like you? Who is different from you?" To assess degree of similarity, one could use a continuous rating scale as in Aboud and Mitchell (1977), and ask children "How similar is X to you?" The label questions are, "What are you: a Black? a White?" requesting a yes or no answer to each. The rejected labels would be checked by asking "Are you a (rejected label)?" Finally the continuity and consistency questions are as stated previously.

Age and Ethnic Status Differences

The two variables of age and ethnic status will be used to organize a review of empirical findings based on these measures. Accuracy in recognition, which may be included as a preliminary measure, depends on perceptual factors. Recognition of White and Black persons develops at 3 to 4 years of age. For Black and White children, recognizing one's own group members reaches an asymptote soon after this age (Clark & Clark, 1947; Epstein, Krupat & Obudho, 1976; Hraba & Grant, 1970; Weiland & Coughlin, 1979), and recognizing other group's members continues to develop up to the age of 7 (Ballard, 1976; Fox & Jordan, 1973; George & Hoppe, 1979; Goldstein, Koopman, & Goldstein, 1979; Rice, Ruiz, & Padilla, 1974). For all children, recognition of other minorities such as Chicano, Chinese, and Amerindian emerges later and reaches asymptote around 8 years (Fox & Jordan, 1973; George &

Hoppe, 1979; Rice et al., 1974; Rosenthal, 1974). Presumably, the features salient to children such as skin color and hair type (Kircher & Furby, 1971) do not allow them to distinguish these latter three groups from others until a later age.

In response to the question, "Who looks most like you?" most Black and White children choose a member of their own group by 5 years (Clark & Clark, 1947; Greenwald & Oppenheim, 1968; Morland, 1966; Rice, Ruiz & Padilla, 1974). There is also improvement beyond this age, reaching asymptote around 9 years (Aboud, 1980; Clark & Clark, 1947; Epstein, Krupat & Obudho, 1976; Fox & Jordan, 1973; Genesee, Tucker & Lambert, 1978; George & Hoppe, 1979; Lambert & Klineberg, 1967; Rosenthal, 1974; Williams & Morland, 1976). Others have found lower perceived own-group similarity among Blacks (Clark & Clark, 1947; Crooks, 1970; Rohrer, 1977), Amerindians (Aboud, 1977; Hunsberger, 1978; Rosenthal, 1974), Chicanos (Rohrer, 1977), and Chinese Americans (Fox & Jordan, 1973).

In response to the question, "Who is most different from you?" 4- and 5-year-old White, Black, Amerindian, and Chinese Canadians are reported to have chosen an other group member with frequencies greater than 80% (Aboud, 1977, 1980). Perceived dissimilarity also increases with age (Aboud & Mitchell, 1977; Genesee, Tucker, & Lambert 1978). Perceived own-group similarity correlates positively with other-group dissimilarity (Aboud, 1980). These two indices therefore demonstrate an age-related increase in perceptual differentiation that reflects a distinctive ethnic identification.

Categorization and labeling were performed accurately by White, Black, Amerindian, and Chinese children only at 7 years (Aboud, 1977, 1980; Ballard, 1976; Spencer, 1982; Stevenson & Stewart, 1958; Vaughan, 1963a), and only after perceived own group similarity had developed. The younger children claimed to be none of the five ethnic labels offered; apparently they lacked familiarity with the labels or an understanding about ethnic categories.

Children's developing recognition that their ethnicity remains constant across time and superficial changes is not well documented. Aboud (1984) asked children about the constancy of other groups. Not until 7 years of age did children say that ethnicity was unchangeable, that an Italian Canadian could not become an Indian, and that he was still an Italian Canadian even after he dressed in Indian clothes. Constancy of one's own ethnicity may develop somewhat later. Black children under 10 years thought that a Black would be a White person if he used White makeup or put on a blond wig (Semaj, 1980). Similarly, most Jewish children from 6 to 8 years said they were Eskimo when they saw a photograph of themselves in Eskimo clothing taken previously (Aboud & Skerry, 1983). Those who said they were still Jewish possessed two salient ethnic cognitions. One was the cognition that Jewishness was essential to being themselves (without it they would not be themselves) and a second cognition was about an internal attribute such as a belief or preference possessed by Jews.

Critical Evaluation of Procedures

Four features of the typical procedures are problematic: the use of a doll to represent an ethnic group, appearance as the basis of similarity, forced choices, and reliability and validity.

One criticism of the early doll studies was that the dark-skinned dolls did not represent Blacks adequately, and so one could not expect children to identify with them (Greenwald & Oppenheim, 1968). Although the use of dolls may minimize fear of retaliation, and therefore elicit more negative feelings than real persons, dolls are not appropriate stimuli for self-identification because they do not accurately represent members of an ethnic group. Photographs are better in that they are accurate and allow for some variation in features. Averaging across the similarity ratings made toward several representatives of each ethnic group incorporates this response to variation.

It became apparent when reviewing the literature that appearance is not always the appropriate critical attribute to present to children when requesting them to make an ethnic identification. Many young minority children did not recognize their own group from appearance alone. To determine the critical attribute, one would have to ask children what X group is that other groups are not. From a multidimensional scaling of dissimilarity judgments (Aboud & Christian, 1979), and from responses to the questions "Could you be an X (for example, Eskimo or French Canadian) and still be yourself? Why?" we discerned a variety of attributes. English and French Canadians were defined in terms of their language; Blacks in terms of skin and hair; Chinese in terms of eyes, food, and language; and Indians in terms of possessions and activities. These were not merely descriptive attributes; they were critical in the sense that they defined what a person must be in order to belong to that group.

Forced-choice techniques also pose a problem. They require the selection of one stimulus and rejection of others. For example, in response to the question, "Who looks most like you?" the subject must pick only one person. Although some identifications are all-or-none phenomena (for example, label), perceived similarity is not. One may be more or less similar to many people. Knowing the degree of similarity is useful when assessing bicultural or dual identities and when examining the relation between identity and attitude. The degree of perceived similarity to nonchosen groups can be determined using a concrete continuous rating scale in which each target person is judged independently (Aboud & Mitchell, 1977).

The reliability and validity of several identity measures were examined by Ballard (1976). Among 3- to 7-year-old Black and White children, reliability over a two-week period was only .35 on a recognition task, .10 on a perceived similarity task using dolls or photos, .65 on a color similarity task (color a drawing the color you are), .62 on a categorization task, and .85 on a labeling task. The earliest emerging measures of recognition and perceived similarity were the most unreliable. Ballard did not determine whether or not recognition and similarity emerged before categorization and labeling, but he did note that they correlated only .20 to .39 and that responses to all measures improved with age. Rather than blaming the tests for lack of convergence, we might consider each to be measuring a step toward mature identification. Guttman scalograms are one way of determining the order of acquisition of judgments, and thus the sequence of tests in terms of their difficulty.

Issues to be Resolved

What does bicultural identity mean? Bicultural identity refers to an identification of oneself with two ethnic groups. Many children accept two group identities, for example, those whose parents have different ethnicities (Aellen & Lambert, 1969), or children in special language or cultural programs. Particularly in the early grades, English Canadian children attending an entirely French school rated themselves most similar to English Canadians and only slightly less so to French Canadians. These children initially thought that language was an important basis of similarity; because they spoke French, went to a French school, and played with French-speaking classmates, they considered themselves similar to French Canadians, as indeed they were. Older children weighted nonlinguistic attributes more heavily when making their similarity judgments. By third grade they did not differ from their monolingual counterparts attending an English school (Genesee et al., 1978). A comparable form of bilingual identity was reported in Franco-American children living in Maine. Children in the traditional English school said they resembled English speakers more than French speakers; whereas those in a bilingual French-English program rated themselves similar to both French and English speakers (Lambert et al., 1975). The language spoken at school also affected the identity of children from mixed ethnic backgrounds in Aellen & Lambert (1969). The purpose in describing these results is to point out that measures should allow for the separate identification with more than one ethnic group.

What does misidentification mean? Many minority children appear to identify with an ethnic group other than their actual one. By actual, we mean the ethnic group(s) of their parents. Misidentification usually is found with the perceived similarity measure in that some minority children say they are most similar to a White doll or photo. It has not been found with the label measure; that is, children rarely say yes to a label not descriptive of themselves and no to their own group label.

Given appropriate stimulus persons, why do some minority children say they look most like a White person? The question may be a poor one because it assumes that skin color and hair type are the salient attributes. Although these attributes may be salient when judging others (Kircher & Furby, 1971), they may be less salient when judging oneself. In addition, some children may infer other qualities of the stimulus persons, such as behavior and mood. Minority children may then say that they look like Whites because they can act like them, be happy and successful like them, or play the same games. In fact, Cross (this volume) suggests that minority children are raised to identify with both their own and the majority culture because such a bicultural identity is functional.

Misidentification may also be a reflection of attitudes. Children who say they are most similar to Whites often prefer Whites over their own group. Until 6 years of age, Black children believed that they could become a White child if they really wanted to (Semaj, 1980). This belief appears to be characteristic of all children under 6 years. It would seem, then, that desire determines identification until cognitions about the permanence of ethnicity develop.

With all these interpretations, one might ask why it is worthwhile to designate an identification as accurate or inaccurate. First, it allows the researcher to specify attainment of the concept of own-group similarity, which matches an objective judgment of similarity. Second, it draws our attention to factors other than objective ethnic membership that might influence a child's identification, factors such as language spoken, peer and parent pressure, salient goals, and values. These factors are relevant to our understanding of ethnic identity during adolescence and adulthood when a malleable identity is functional for maintaining one's affiliation with diverse groups (friends, work colleagues, and family).

Attitude to One's Own Group and Other Groups

Definition and Procedures

An ethnic attitude generally is defined as an organized predisposition to respond in a favorable or unfavorable manner toward people from different ethnic groups. For a reaction to be considered an attitude, it must be evaluative, and it must be an organized predisposition elicited by the person's ethnicity.

The evaluative aspect may take many forms. In addition to varying from positive to negative, the response varies in intensity from very favorable to very unfavorable. An organized predisposition is more difficult to describe. Psychologists tend to endow predispositions with the properties of traits, namely, stability over time and consistency across situations (Allport, 1954). It is debatable as to how much stability and consistency are necessary to qualify as a trait, given that a variety of factors may cause the individual to deviate from the predisposition. Finally, by saying that the predisposition must be organized, we mean that the predisposition be unified, or that its many forms interrelate.

A number of problems arise when one attempts to operationalize this definition of an attitude, and these problems are compounded when measuring a child's attitude. For this reason, it becomes useful to talk about rudimentary attitudes that are clear precursors. For example, before children are able to conceptualize a group, they may evaluate members of a group similarly without being aware of their group affiliation. Furthermore, children's predispositions are less organized and less stable than an adult's (Ramsey, this volume). Attitudes may also change with age as a function of experience and cognitive development.

The attitude tests used with children fall into three format categories: forced-choice questions, multiple-item tests, and continuous rating scales. In a forced-choice question format (Clark & Clark, 1947), the child chooses one doll or photo in answer to questions about play preference and evaluation, for example, Which would you like to play with? Which looks bad? The child must choose one of two or three dolls, and the sample frequency of selecting a particular doll is statistically compared with chance levels of 50% or 33% respectively. The multiple-item tests of Williams and Morland (1976) or Katz and Zalk (1978) require the child to choose which child fits a series of positive and negative descriptions, for example, Who is a happy child? Who will win a trophy? Who will be reprimanded by the teacher? These tests assess favorability in many forms in response to many contexts. Thus they have the advantage of determining whether or not the child possesses a unified and consistent attitude toward an ethnic group. The weakness is that rejection of one group is confounded with acceptance of the other.

Continuous rating scales (for example, Aboud & Mitchell, 1977; Genesee et al., 1978; Verna, 1981) provide many response alternatives along a positive-negative dimension. Children evaluate each ethnic member separately by locating him or her on a scale ranging from like to dislike. The advantage of this technique is that attitudes to different ethnic groups are assessed independently; the disadvantage is that the context and form of favorability are not varied.

Combining the strong features of each format would result in a measure more closely satisfying the criteria of an attitude. Multiple items are needed to determine unity and consistency across the various forms of favorability. Several members of each ethnic group would be judged to provide a measure of generality. If each member were judged separately along a continuous rating scale, then independent scores indicating the intensity would be available.

Age and Ethnic Status Differences

By integrating the results of studies of children from many ethnic groups at different ages, it is possible to plot the course of development and to compare the responses of majority and minority children.

White children's attitudes toward their own group. White children have consistently expressed favorable attitudes toward their own group at 4 years of age (Asher & Allen, 1969; Clark, Hocevar, & Dembo, 1980; Crooks, 1970; Greenwald & Oppenheim, 1968; Hraba & Grant, 1970; Kircher & Furby, 1971; Morland, 1966). Younger children do not express a consistent preference (Clark et al., 1980; Kircher & Furby,

1971). Attitudes continue to be positive in 5-, 6-, and 7-year-olds (Aboud, 1977; Asher & Allen, 1969; Clark et al., 1980; Crooks, 1970; Fox & Jordan, 1973; Greenwald & Oppenheim, 1968; Hraba & Grant, 1970; Kircher & Furby, 1971; Klein, Levine & Charry, 1979; Morland, 1966; Rice et al., 1974; Williams, Best & Boswell, 1975; Williams & Morland, 1976). Studies of White children above the age of 7 or 8 years sometimes find a decline in own group preference (Asher & Allen, 1969; Clark et al., 1980; Davidson, 1976; Katz & Zalk, 1978; Rice et al., 1974; Williams et al., 1975; Zinser, Rich, & Bailey, 1981). Others reported no change in own group attitudes during these years (Epstein, Krupat, & Obudho, 1976; Genesee at al., 1978; George & Hoppe, 1979; Katz, Sohn, & Zalk, 1975). The decline is somewhat controversial in that it may be provoked by factors that enhance social desirability concerns such as the presence of another group tester (Clark et al., 1980) or awareness that prejudice is undesirable (Katz et al., 1975).

Minority children's attitudes toward their own group. The data on Blacks' attitudes toward their own group are variable. Banks(1976) reviewed 21 studies of Blacks between 3 and 8 years of age. There were 16 additional studies found in the literature bringing the distribution up to date as follows: 27% reported a significant proportion of Blacks showing a preference for their own group (Aboud, 1980; Fox & Jordan, 1973; LeVine & Ruiz, 1978; Semaj, 1980; Spencer, 1982; Ward & Braun, 1972); 16% found White preference (Crooks, 1970; Davey & Mullin, 1980; Moore, 1976; Rice et al., 1974; Rohrer, 1977); and 57% showed no preference (Branch & Newcombe, 1980; Greenwald & Oppenheim, 1968; Klein et al., 1979; Moore, 1976; Rohrer, 1977). The nonpreference results can be interpreted in several ways depending on whether they are based on an analysis of individual scores or group frequencies. Individual scores on a multiple-response test could indeed reflect nonpreference if the intensity of liking was neutral or half the items were pro-Black and half pro-White (Aboud, 1980; Williams & Morland, 1976). Switches in choice in the latter test reflect liking for both groups equally rather than neutrality (Hraba, 1972). In contrast, group frequencies that do not differ from chance may reflect nonconsensus among the children rather than nonpreference. In other words, each half of the sample may be expressing strong but opposite preferences.

Analyses of age effects among Black children indicate either an increase in Black preference (Asher & Allen, 1969; Fox & Jordan, 1973; Hraba & Grant, 1970; Semaj, 1980; Spencer, 1982) or no change (Aboud, 1980; Epstein et al., 1976; Katz et al., 1975; Williams et al.,

1975). No studies reported a decrease in own group preference, but there was a trend in that direction from 8 to 11 years in Semaj's (1980) study. It seems appropriate at this point to examine some variables that might explain the differences among Black children. The role of two factors will be discussed briefly: social values and the salience of between-group differences. These two factors provide a useful, parsimonious way to integrate numerous other social and psychological factors.

Social values refer to the positive or negative valence placed on certain qualities by groups of people. The preference of minority children for Whites over their own group may reflect the positive value that Whites place on being White. However, since the civil rights movement of the 1960s, many Black communities have tried to strengthen pro-Black values and attitudes. Barnes (1980) has documented the relationship among community, parent, and child attitudes. He found that the political activity and beliefs of parents differed as a function of their SES. Furthermore, children held more pro-Black attitudes if their parents were active and believed in promoting the Black cause. This finding received some support from Branch and Newcombe's (1980) data, and may be the case even for Black children who have been adopted by White parents with pro-Black values (Womack & Fulton, 1981). Self-esteem also may determine whether one accepts majority or minority values. Using an experimental design, Moscovici and Paicheler (1978) found that people assigned to a minority group did not show own group favoritism unless their self-esteem had previously been enhanced. Those with higher self-esteem generalized their positive self attitude to their own group.

Salience refers in particular to the prominence of group differences. According to Katz et al. (1975), between-group differences are salient in highly prejudiced children but also remain more salient for Blacks than for Whites from 8 to 12 years of age. The salience of within-group differences is higher in less prejudiced children but tends to remain lower in Blacks than in Whites from 8 to 12 years. The salience of between-group differences is enhanced by emphasis on physical attributes, such as skin color, rather than internal attributes, such as personality, and by the distinctiveness of one's ethnicity. Presumably, Black children become more aware of their distinctiveness with entry into broader social networks at integrated schools. However, in integrated schools, an increase in Black preference is often noted in younger children, whereas a decrease appears in older children (Goldstein, Koopman, & Goldstein, 1979, Rohrer, 1977; Stephan, 1978). The factor of group salience may be a promising link between certain social psychological variables and prejudice.

Non-Black minority children from Amerindian, Chicano, and Chinese backgrounds express even less preference for their own groups. Only 15% of the studies reported an own-group preference in Amerindians (Aboud, 1977) and older Chicanos (Rice et al., 1974). Of the remaining studies, half indicated a White preference (Aboud, 1977; George & Hoppe, 1979; Hunsberger, 1978; Rosenthal, 1974; Weiland & Coughlin, 1979), and half showed no preference (Fox & Jordan, 1973; Rice et al., 1974). An increase with age in Chicanos' own-group preference was reported by Rice et al. (1974).

White children's attitudes toward other groups. Although attitudes toward other ethnic groups are confounded in most studies with the response to one's own group, it is useful to describe the results separately. By comparing results from the confounding forced-choice technique with those from independent measures, we find that other group attitudes appear less extreme when expressed independently from own group attitudes. Furthermore, not all groups are evaluated the converse of one's own; certain groups are liked more than others.

White children typically hold negative attitudes toward other groups from 4 years of age (Asher & Allen, 1969; Cantor, 1972; Crooks, 1970; Fox & Jordan, 1973; George & Hoppe, 1979; Greenwald & Oppenheim, 1968; Hraba & Grant, 1970; Katz et al., 1975; Kircher & Furby, 1971; Morland 1966; Rice et al., 1974; Williams & Morland, 1976). Most of these studies used the forced-choice or multiple-item technique. Studies of White children using continuous rating scales find only moderately negative attitudes toward peers from different ethnic, national, and linguistic groups (Aboud, 1977, 1980; Aboud & Mitchell, 1977; Genesee et al., 1978).

Some studies show a continuation of negative attitudes up to 12 years of age (Katz et al., 1975). However, many others find that prejudice declines after 7 years (Aboud, 1980; Clark et al., 1980; Davidson, 1976; Fox & Jordan, 1973; Kalin, 1979; Williams et al, 1975; Zinser et al., 1981). For example, in one study the proportion of children rejecting a Black dropped from 64% at 7 years to 34% at 9 years and 19% at 11 years (George & Hoppe, 1979). One explanation for this decline is that White children become more familiar with other ethnic groups as they grow older (Friedman, 1980). However, integrated schooling by itself does not reduce Whites' prejudice (Stephan, 1978). If exposure forces the child to focus on individuals rather than groups, it can promote more positive attitudes (Katz & Zalk, 1978).

A second explanation for the decline in negative attitudes is that older children are more sensitive to social issues. When tested by a Black examiner or when the measure transparently assesses prejudice, older children express socially desirable attitudes toward Blacks (Clark et al., 1980; Friedman, 1980; Katz et al., 1975). However, Davidson (1976) cites data to demonstrate that social sensitivity reflects developing cognitions about morality. This implies that prejudice declines with the development of mature social cognitions.

Minority children's attitudes toward other groups. As reported earlier, 27% of the Black samples expressed negative attitudes toward Whites. The remainder showed no consensus or were pro-White. Negative attitudes generally remained high up to 12 years (Epstein et al., 1976; Katz et al., 1975) but in one study they declined (Aboud, 1980). Pro-White attitudes often neutralized or became anti-White with age (Asher & Allen, 1969; Davey & Mullin, 1980; Fox & Jordan, 1973; Semaj, 1980). In short, positive attitudes toward other groups apparently do not develop in Blacks the way they do in Whites. It may be unfair to compare the two groups because their initial attitudes are not uniformly negative. Likewise, the predominant preference for Whites among Chicanos, Chinese, and Amerindians remains high throughout middle childhood, but at the expense of developing positive attitudes toward their own group.

Critical Evaluation of Procedures

Two problems complicate the definition of an attitude and its operationalization. One is the separation of a predisposition from its response, given that factors other than predisposition might determine how attitudes are expressed. One such factor is the need to express socially desirable attitudes, particularly in the presence of an other-group examiner. A second problem is the generalizability of the response to all members of a particular ethnic group and to many contexts. This can be seen in the low correlations that have been found between scores on different attitude measures (Katz et al., 1975; Katz & Zalk, 1978). It could mean that children's attitudes are not organized or that certain measures are better than others at assessing real attitudes. These problems will be discussed shortly in relation to the issue of validity.

The forced-choice format may exaggerate pro-anti biases more than continuous ratings. Although the unchosen stimulus may evoke a slightly less intense response than the chosen one, it receives a zero score. Furthermore, the analysis of forced choices produces group frequencies that often are interpreted as if they were individual scores. That is, frequencies that do not differ from chance are interpreted as nonpreference, though in reality the children may be expressing strong but opposite preferences. Finally, forced choices confound attitudes toward another group with attitudes toward one's own group. Presumably, the more salient group will be responded to first and will thereby determine the attitude score recorded for the nonselected group. One might argue, then, that forced choices do not reflect true variation in the intensity of attitudes. Other-group attitudes, in particular, may be less intensely negative when measured with continuous rating scales (Aboud & Mitchell, 1977; Genesee et al., 1978; Verna, 1982).

Reliability and validity are two important psychometric properties of a good attitude test. Moderate group reliability over a one-year-period of time has been reported for only two measures, the Preschool Racial Attitude Measure (Williams & Morland, 1976) and the Katz-Zalk Projective Prejudice Test (Katz & Zalk, 1978). Given the possibility that attitudes change with age, we should approach the issue of stability with caution.

Validity is a more difficult problem. Convergent validity is demonstrated when a number of meaningfully related measures produce correlated scores. Katz et al. (1975) found only low correlations among the following tests: Projective Prejudice Test, General Intolerance Test, Dogmatism Scale, and Social Distance. This indicates that children do not possess an organized network of attitudes toward ethnic groups; variations in the form and context of evaluation produce different results. The low correlations also indicate that intolerance and dogmatism do not underlie prejudice in children.

Criterial validity is determined by correlating an attitude with its related behavior. However, measures of adult attitudes often do not relate to behavior, largely because of the simplicity of the measure and personality variables of the respondents (see Jackson & Paunonen, 1980). Scores based on aggregated responses to items varying in context and form correlate more highly with behavior than do single item scores. In addition, individuals who use social cues in the setting to guide their behavior show less attitude-behavior consistency than those who use internal beliefs and attitudes (Snyder, 1974). Children may express variable responses not because the measure is poor but because they use contextual cues rather than internal states to guide their response.

In search of more behavioral measures, many researchers have turned to the use of friendship measures in place of attitude tests (St. John & Lewis, 1975; Schofield & Francis, 1982; Singleton & Asher, 1979). It is questionable that friendship is a more valid index of attitudes than a test is. Two studies compared play preferences with friendship choice (Davey & Mullin, 1980; Hraba & Grant, 1970). They found that other-group peers were more frequently regarded as friends than as preferred playmates. The choice of a friend, however, is determined by more than simply one's attitude to that person's ethnicity; also important are attributes such as common interests, and the proportion of each ethnic group in the classroom. Friendship choice is therefore not a substitute for a good test of attitudes.

A problem related to the validity of most attitude measures is their transparent purpose. The objection is that subjects inhibit their expression of prejudice to appear socially desirable. Older children in particular may be aware of which attitudes are socially approved. This awareness may account for the decline in prejudice among White children over 7 years (Katz et al., 1975). At issue is whether or not children have altered their responses or their underlying predisposition toward other groups (Davidson, 1976). Some researchers have found that prejudice is lower in the presence of an other-group examiner than a same-group examiner (Clark et al., 1980; Corenblum & Wilson, 1982; Friedman, 1980; Katz, 1973; Katz et al., 1975; Katz & Zalk, 1974). Although children may temporarily alter their response to avoid disapproval, the presence of an other-group examiner may also activate longer term ethnic and moral cognitions about prejudice. Also certain measures may be more influenced by social desirability than others. For example, social desirability affects responses to a forced-choice test more than to a Social Distance Scale (Friedman, 1980; Verna, 1982).

A final problem with most procedures is that they assess attitudes toward only two ethnic groups. Because of this limitation, children appear to like one group and dislike the other. This has led to the conclusion, perhaps erroneous, that Whites are more rejecting of other groups than minority children (Brand et al., 1974). In fact children may like more than one ethnic group and may dislike more than one (Aboud, 1980; Aboud & Mitchell, 1977; Genesee et al., 1978; George & Hoppe, 1979). This conclusion is inconsistent with the dichotomy of an ingroup and an outgroup, and calls for further examination of what perceived qualities of a group make them likable or dislikable. Two such qualities emerging from the literature are conflict (Sherif & Sherif, 1969) and dissimilarity (LeVine & Campbell, 1972). Only the latter has received systematic research attention. Groups who are perceived as different from oneself may be disliked for a number of reasons, the most likely being that dissimilar people are assumed to hold different values and beliefs. To the extent that people seek validation of their beliefs from other people, dissimilar groups will be avoided. Children may react more intensely to disagreement than adults. Children from 5 to 9 years in Aboud's (1980) study were unable to reconcile the different ethnic preferences that they and an other-group member expressed; they did not know that they and their partner could agree to disagree. Thus the consequences of perceived dissimilarity are striking for the child.

Issues to Be Resolved

What is the relation between attitudes toward own group and other groups? The term ethnocentrism refers to an exaggerated preference for one's own group and concomitant dislike of other groups (LeVine & Campbell, 1972). The term not only describes a phenomenon but gives rise to a theory of attitude development. The theory basically proposes that negative attitudes toward others stem from a need to maintain self-esteem by projecting one's own negative attributes on to others. It is not clear whether strong liking for one's own group is always associated with strong dislike of other groups, or if all possible combinations of own group and other group attitudes exist. Forced-choice techniques do not answer this question adequately. Two studies using independent measures (Aboud, 1980; Semaj, 1980) confirmed that the more children liked their own group, the more they disliked the others.

However, correlations reveal nothing about the level of like or dislike. To correlate inversely, a highly positive own-group value could be associated either with a highly negative other-group value or with a neutral other-group value. The latter combination was found by Aboud (1980) and Semaj (1980). In other words, child were generally more positive about their own group than they were negative about the other groups. It is doubtful whether or not we would call this ethnocentrism. Application of this term therefore requires an assessment of both the relation and the level of own-group and other-group attitudes.

How negative must an attitude be to be called prejudice? Most researchers avoid this issue by reporting results in terms of significant differences between groups of children. However, a difference could mean that one group was more unprejudiced than the other, that one was more prejudiced than the other, or that one was prejudiced and the other not. At the other extreme are those who assume that choosing an other-group member as "the bad one" is a sign of prejudice. This may be an unwarranted judgment. If questioned further as to how bad, children may rate the other group as 4 out of 10 (10 being very bad) and their own group as 2 out of 10. Would we want to call this prejudice?

In the literature, we find two approaches to resolving this issue. One is that of Williams, Best, and Boswell (1975) who divide scores into three categories: pro-White/anti-Black bias, no bias, and pro-Black/anti-White bias. Unfortunately the range of scores falling into each category is somewhat arbitrary and changeable (Williams & Morland, 1976), and there is no empirical basis for choosing the division point between unbiased and biased. The second approach, that of Katz et al. (1975), is to examine differences in the perceptual bias of high and low scorers on an attitude test. The authors thereby establish strong validation for the two extreme categories of scores, but not for the middle, residual category. Furthermore, no division points are given for the categories, leading one to assume that the authors do not want to set fixed categories for their test scores.

In summary, to determine what is a prejudiced response, prejudice must first be defined in terms of the intensity of a negative response. Therefore, it is important to use a multiple-item test or a continuous rating scale, rather than a forced-choice procedure. Division points must be set for different categories of prejudice, for example, prejudiced and unprejudiced. Finally, one must validate these categories through the usual procedure for establishing criterial validity. Criterial validation results may reveal that childhood prejudice has a different meaning from adult prejudice, that is, it may reflect perceptual and cognitive limitations of development rather than the individual's personality.

Relation between Identity and Attitudes

Identity is often confused with attitude. Tajfel (1978), for example, defined social identity as the part of self-concept derived from membership in a group together with the value and emotional significance attached to it. The measurement of a favorable attitude toward a group is often taken as an index of identification with that group. However, the two are conceptually different and require separate measures. Only by measuring identity and attitudes independently is it possible to examine their relation.

In the first section of this chapter, a mature ethnic identification was defined as describing oneself in terms of common group attributes that are distinctive from others and are constant. Maturity is associated not only with having a realistic identification, but also with having a secure identification, in which one is aware of one's own group membership yet free to adopt attributes, beliefs, and attitudes more frequently associated with an other group (Block, 1973). That is, a secure identity is not threatened by holding seemingly incompatible attitudes about other groups, nor by behaving in line with individual needs when these are seemingly incompatible with characteristics of one's group. A realistic and secure identity allows for what I would consider mature attitudes: favorable predispositions toward all ethnic groups with perhaps a preference for one's own, and an emphasis on attitudes toward individuals rather than groups. Similar qualities were used by Cross (1980) to describe one of the last stages of Black identity, internalization. In this sense, mature identity and attitudes appear to be related.

To examine the relation between identification and attitudes at each step of development is an ambitious project. One would first want to describe, as I have previously, the progression of identity development and the attitudes that correspond to each stage. Second, one would want to demonstrate that the two correlate or appear in a reliable sequence of development. Third, it would be important to find out whether or not they are necessarily related, perhaps because of a common underlying process.

Three developmental theories will be selectively considered while formulating an integrative view of the relation between identification and attitude. The first is Katz's (1976) social-cognitive model of attitude acquisition. Katz claims that a rudimentary concept of an ethnic group develops around 3 years of age and includes all three components of attitude, perception, and cognition. Later steps involve the integration of these components and then their elaboration. Elaboration in particular has an effect on identification and attitude. Around 5 to 8 years of age, children elaborate on group differences. From 8 to 12 years, group differences become less salient and individual differences become more so (at least for White children). Also, group differences tend to be more salient to highly prejudiced children, whereas individual differences are more salient for less prejudiced children. This suggests a possible relation between identification and attitude. If group features are salient when identifying other people, then they also may be salient when identifying oneself. The salience of one's own ethnic identity appears to be related directly to positive own-group and negative other-group attitudes. The salience of an individualized identity appears to be associated with more neutral group attitudes.

The second theory is Zajonc's (1980) theory of preferences. Zajonc proposed that affective, perceptual, and cognitive systems may operate independently of one another. One's affective reaction to a person (for example, preference) is immediate, inevitable, and intense; it may be based on minimal perception and cognition of the person; and its retrieval occurs without effort. There are three implications of this theory for the development of ethnic identification and attitudes. One is that preferences for ethnic persons may develop before perceptions of similarity and before categorization or labeling. The second is that preferences are difficult to change because they are experienced intensely, made with confidence, and recalled easily. Third, the judged similarity or dissimilarity between two persons may be based on preference rather than on perceptual or cognitive information. This would suggest that attitudes develop independently of the perceptual and cognitive processes of identity formation. Furthermore, the affectively based differentiation between ethnic groups (liking one and disliking the other) may take place before the members are perceived as belonging to a group, that is, before between-group differences and within-group similarities become salient.

Although Zajonc's theory deals well with the prepotency of affect, he says little about the relative strengths of perceptual and cognitive processes. This distinction has been made by Flavell (1977) and other cognitive developmentalists who place the development of perceptual structures ahead of cognitive ones. The transition from preoperational to concrete operational functioning around 7 years signals the change from perceptual to cognitive dominance. For example, 8-year-old children not only attend to observable features but also can infer personality traits. They understand the invariance of a person's identity despite transformations in appearance. This theory in conjunction with Zajonc's would propose an overlapping sequence of development from affective to perceptual to cognitive processes. Each develops ahead of the following process in the sense of becoming more differentiated, elaborated, and integrated. That is, attitudinal responses to ethnic groups may become differentiated before perceptions of similarity and dissimilarity, which in turn precede cognitions about similar and dissimilar attributes.

The third theory relevant to this discussion is Block's (1973) theory of sex-role development. The stages of sex-role development consist of preoccupations first with oneself and one's satisfaction, second with social rules, and finally with one's own personally adjusted set of principles. This sequence from self to social to individual focus of attention is found in moral development as well (Kohlberg, 1976). Applied to the ethnic domain, the first stage involves a preoccupation with self-identification and self-evaluation. Own-group members are identified with and liked to the extent that they possess resources to satisfy one's needs (Gottfried & Gottfried, 1974). Likewise, other-group members are seen mainly as individuals who are identified with and liked for the same reasons. The second stage is characterized by a preoccupation with oneself as a group member. One identifies with and likes the group one belongs to. Other-group members are seen mainly in terms of their belonging to a different group. Social rules determine how one reacts to each group. The third stage involves an emphasis on oneself and others as individuals again, but now with a more differentiated perspective. One identifies with many social groups and in terms of many personal attributes regardless of their seeming incompatibility. That is, one may identify with own-group members because they possess the same ethnic background but identify with other-group members who hold the same political beliefs. Attitudes toward people are based on their individual dispositions rather than their group membership. Not everyone develops to this stage of ethnic identity and attitude, just as not everyone develops an androgynous sex role.

This sequence applies most clearly to majority children who initially acquire an identification with their own group rather than another group. It seems to apply equally well to the development of a new identity in initially pro-White Blacks. Cross (1980) describes five stages of Black identity, three of which—pre-encounter, immersion, and internalization—correspond to Block's (1973). The pre-encounter stage entails White identification and preference. The encounter stage is distinctive to minority identification and is the turning point from being pro-White to pro-own group. Cross describes the catalyst as "a shocking personal or social event," for example, a vivid experience of being discriminated against. The immersion stage is characterized by a high level of Black identification and glorification along with the devaluation of Whites. In the internalization stage, one identifies with Blacks

internally and more confidently; attitudes toward Whites as a group become less negative and friendship with a White individual is possible. Presumably this description could apply to any minority person who initially identifies with and prefers Whites, and to child as well as to adult development.

With regard to the relation between identification and attitude, the Block (1973) and Cross (1980) models suggest a shift from focusing on oneself, to groups, and finally to individuals. This sequence of development is supported by research on moral (Kohlberg, 1976) and sex-role development (Block, 1973) and by Katz et al.'s (1975) work on the shift from group to individual differentiation.

The theories of Zajonc (1980) and Flavell (1977) indicate that the relation between identification and attitude change as first affective, then perceptual, and finally cognitive processes predominate. The sequence implies that in the early years attitudes precede and determine identification because of the belief that one can be what one wants to be. The prepotency of attitudes is evident most strikingly in young children who misidentify themselves. To the extent that all young children believe they can be whatever ethnicity they want to be, their attitude will determine whether they make the correct or incorrect identification.

Later, perceptual and cognitive processes of identification determine attitudes. The domination of cognitive processes of identification can be seen in Tajfel's (1978) research findings. Students are told that they belong to one of two groups on the basis of a random coin toss or similarity in preferences. Regardless of the meaninglessness of group assignment, students allocate more resources to their own group than to the other group and prefer their own group (Turner, 1978; Vaughan, 1978b). However, drawing attention to the subject's individuality reduced own-group preference (Turner, 1978). Also drawing attention to the group's small numbers increased other-group preference, though minority preference was restored by enhancing the individual's self-esteem. Thus cognitive categorization determined preferences, and conditions that reduced one's reliance on the group categorization also reduced the initial bias. A similar relation was found between perceptual categorization and attitudes in studies conducted by Katz et al. (1975) and Katz and Zalk (1978).

Although extensive descriptive data on identity and attitudes have been reported, few researchers have examined their relation using correlations or Guttman scalograms. These statistical techniques have been used in two studies in which the data reveal the following sequence:

own-group preference, perceived own-group similarity, perceived similarity or dissimilarity of others, and finally categorization and labeling (Aboud, 1980; Vaughan, 1963a). The development of mature social and ethnic cognitions such as ethnic constancy may precede the neutralization of early ethnic biases found in White children (Clark et al., 1980; Davidson, 1976).

These results are intriguing but weak in comparison to the corresponding theories. One is left with the feeling of a schism between conceptual and empirical work on ethnic identity and attitudes. In the past, once a technique was found to measure these two constructs, researchers collected descriptive data. They rarely stopped to reevaluate their procedures in relation to the definition or their design in relation to a theoretical issue. However, a few researchers represent exceptions; they have thrust the field forward by pioneering new measures, by examining the relation between measures, and by using sophisticated experimental designs and statistical techniques. As these innovations become available and standardized across cultures, the field of ethnic socialization will gain a much needed boost.

2

Young Children's Thinking
About Ethnic Differences

PATRICIA G. RAMSEY

"The best way to predict whether a person will harbor hostile attitudes . . . is to find out how he understands the intergroup situation" (Tajfel, 1981, p. 130). As we examine elements of children's ethnic socialization such as identity and intergroup attitudes, it is important to consider the cognitive aspects of children's responses to ethnic differences. To gain an understanding of children's thinking one must explore the informational content of children's perceptions and ideas as well as the processes by which they construct their social knowledge.

These investigations require a more qualitative kind of data than often is yielded in traditional measures of ethnic socialization. Many methods of assessing children's ethnic identities and cross-group perceptions, attitudes, and behaviors have used a forced-choice format. As pointed out by Aboud (this volume), these tasks often elicit yes/no or all/none responses that fail to distinguish between mild and strong preferences or different degrees and dimensions of ethnic identity. Many yield virtually no information as to the ideas and cognitive processes that contribute to particular choices. In contrast, this chapter focuses on classroom observations and studies that have used open-ended tasks and clinical interviews to elicit information about the thinking related to ethnicity of preschool and early elementary school children.

The characteristics of ethnic diversity that children notice and their ideas about the causes and implications of these differences are reflections of their level of thinking. Young children, described by

Piaget as "preoperational," live in a concrete and static world, and rely mainly on immediate information to organize their experiences. They cannot mentally manipulate information and are unable to see events from multiple points of view.

This chapter focuses on four dimensions of young children's thinking about ethnicity. Tajfel (1981) has identified three cognitive processes that are particularly relevant to ethnic socialization: categorization, assimilation of information, and the search for coherence. In addition, children's understanding of causality and conservation affects their thinking about ethnicity.

Categorization. The formation of categories enables people to simplify information by organizing a wide variety of facts into a limited number of classifications. The criteria, flexibility, and emotional tone of various categories form a lens through which children perceive and store social information. Because racial and cultural differences are important factors in defining groups, it is important to understand the way in which they serve as organizing schemas for children's categorization of people.

Assimilation. The assimilation of ethnic information refers to the process by which children absorb overt and covert beliefs and attitudes that prevail in their social environment. In the case of ethnicity, this process influences both the informational and evaluative content of children's conceptions of people. Although categorization defines the shape of children's perceptions, assimilation of values and norms provides their content (Tajfel, 1981).

Search for coherence. The search for coherence is the attempt to deal with new situations in a manner that is consistent with one's beliefs and self-image. According to Tajfel (1981), people often attribute their changing relationships with a particular group or the circumstances of a group to inherent characterological traits of that group. Young children are more bound in the immediate environment and are therefore less concerned about the consistency of their beliefs over time and the congruence between statements and actions. However, they do begin to integrate prevailing beliefs about group characteristics and to resist information that challenges their assumptions. By studying ways in which young children define and create their own sense of coherence, we learn about the relative importance of different kinds of information and experience in their learning about ethnicity.

Causality and conservation. Children's conceptions of causality and conservation determine how they relate events and consequences across change. Although most of the work on this aspect of cognition has examined children's understanding of physical phenomena (Piaget, 1960), it is relevant to children's ideas about the origin and stability of ethnic differences.

Perception and Categorization
of Ethnic Differences

Studies of children's classification skills suggest that children as young as 3 and 4 years old can create meaningful categories (for example, cats are distinguished from toys) and even superordinate groups of objects (for instance, a cat and a dog are placed in a group of animals, but a train is not; Rosch, Mervis, Gray, Johnson, & Boyes-Braem, 1976). In the Rosch et al. study, some children were able also to generate labels for their groups, but their verbal explanations were less often correct than their nonverbal actions.

From many studies about children's racial classification abilities (for example, Clark & Clark, 1947; Stevenson & Stewart, 1958; Williams & Morland, 1976), it is evident that children as young as 3 can classify and identify people by whether they are Black or White (most studies have included only these two groups), and ability in racial classification increases during the preoperational years (3 to 6). However, these studies do not provide information about the salience of these categories in children's perceptions or the ways that children conceptualize them.

Salience of Race
in Children's Categories

In a recent series of interviews (Ramsey, 1982, 1983), children aged 3 to 5 were presented with a series of three photographs. In each array, there was a different distribution of gender and race (for example, Black boy, Asian boy, Black girl) and children were asked to select two children out of the three that "go together." In these studies, as is generally true, children primarily relied on concrete information to construct their categories of objects. Groups generally were formed along visible traits such as skin color, gender, hair, and clothing. The subjects used race most frequently, gender the next most frequently, and clothing least often.

However, in their answers to questions about the reasons for their groupings, children often mentioned small details that did not relate to race or gender. In other words, although race and gender seemed to exert some influence on children's categorizations, they were not the factors that children necessarily mentioned. This finding may reflect the pattern found by Rosch et al. (1976), that children's nonverbal performance in classification of physical objects usually exceeds their verbal reasoning about their categories. Alternatively, children may be reluctant to mention race explicitly as a subject that is considered taboo.

In addition, the salience of race varies across tasks. In the same study children were asked to describe photographs of their classmates and unknown peers. They often listed details of the photographs such as clothing, hair style, facial expressions, and (in the case of familiar children) activities that a particular child did, rather than larger categories such as gender or race. However, when children were asked to say who was different from them, they often explicitly used race as a defining factor. This pattern suggests that salience may be related to whether one is focusing on similarities or differences. Semaj (1981) found similar variations in racial salience with elementary school children.

Stimulus objects also may influence the salience of race. Van Parys (1983) found that with a similar population of children, gender was more salient than race. In the Ramsey (1982, 1983) studies, colored photographs of children's faces were shown; in the Van Parys (1983) study, black-white drawings of full bodies were used. It is likely that the latter presented the children with more gender clues (stature and clothing) whereas the former displayed more racial cues (skin tones and facial structures).

In short, the salience of race varies across situations. At times, children may be consciously reacting to it, at other instances, race may be more subconscious or not relevant at all. Thus the assumption that children's forced choices reflect their feelings about racial differences may not necessarily be correct. In Gestalt terminology, race may shift from figure to ground to figure in young children's perceptual fields.

Earlier studies found that racial classification ability differed across groups and regions (Williams & Morland, 1976). Salience likewise shows some variation between sociocultural groups (Ramsey, 1983). In the categorization tasks, Black middle-class children, who were a clear minority in their community, more consistently used race in all the categorization tasks than did their White classmates. However, in a more equally balanced working-class community, the White children and Black children used race with the same frequency. In this community, where there were some intergroup tensions, both groups mentioned race more than did the middle-class sample. Interestingly, in the balanced community, the children who least frequently classified by race were the offspring of recent (Black and White) immigrants to this country. This finding suggests that the larger sociocultural context, as well as the composition of one's immediate neighborhood or classroom, exerts an influence.

Formation of Racial and Cultural Concepts

When young children are beginning to form their concepts of racial and cultural differences, they often make associations that are neither conventional nor obviously functional. Such associations frequently strike adults as inaccurate and sometimes are interpreted as evidence of prejudice. However, it is clear that they often reflect children's efforts to assimilate new information into their existing cognitive structures. For example, young White children often describe Blacks as "chocolate." For adults, chocolate and skin are in completely different categories. However, children make associations based on color alone. Preschool children often refer to "brown people" as opposed to Black people. They are labeling according to their experience in the physical world. In a recent interview, a Black child described her own eyes as "balls" and an Asian classmate's as "lines." She borrowed words from her knowledge of the physical environment, rather than more conventional terms.

In some cases, children actually redefine their existing categories to accommodate these discrepant pieces of information. When a White 3-year-old was looking at a photograph of a Black child, he declared, "His teeth are different!" Then he looked again, seemed puzzled and hesitantly said, "No, his skin is different." Visually, the contrast between the white teeth and brown skin was more prominent and therefore the first feature that the child noticed. However, when he tried to consider how the teeth varied from his own, then he had to reorganize his perception (Ramsey, 1983). The following dialogue also illustrates this process.

S [a White 4-year-old, looking back and forth between Ms. F, a White teacher, and Ms. T, a Black teacher]: Hey, Ms. F, you are the same color as Ms. D. [another White teacher who was not in sight]!

Ms. F: Do you see anyone else that color?

S: [shakes her head no, then stares at the other children—all White—and slowly nods yes].

Here the child was shifting her perceptions related to skin color as that characteristic became more prominent in her perceptual field.

Most studies of children's classification of others have focused on fairly obvious physical differences such as gender, race, and age. Less is known about children's formation of culturally related concepts and categories. However, some anecdotal evidence suggests that children notice concrete manifestations of cultural diversity such as clothing, foods, and eating and, as with racial differences, they try to assimilate this information into their existing schemas.

Recently I overheard a 4-year-old child express amazement at the sight of "those men in skirts" at a St. Patrick's Day Parade. Exposure to cultural diversity often presents the child with conflicting categories. In this example, the young child was trying to reconcile men wearing clothing that he associated with women. He did not question whether or not the people he saw were men; he was secure enough in his knowledge about how men and women differ so that his gender categories were not confused by this discrepant information. However, the child was clearly perplexed. An explanation that the men were dressed that way because they were "Irish" would not have contributed much to the child's understanding. However, demonstrating to the child through his own experience some of the advantages of kilts over trousers when walking through wet grass might have helped the child integrate this new information into a category of "clothes that people wear for different kinds of work (or weather)."

Children sometimes form associations that incorporate cultural features, although they lack coherent concepts about the nature of cultural differences. When non-Asian children see photographs of Asian children, they often say "they eat with those 'stick things.'" When asked about why some people eat with chopsticks, they often cannot answer at all or reply in a way that suggests that their ideas about cultural differences are vague and undifferentiated associations rather than coherent concepts. Several children have explained that people eat with chopsticks "because they speak Spanish" (or French or English, rarely Chinese). In other words, unfamiliar behaviors are linked together, but not related in a meaningful and stable way.

**Transductive Reasoning
and Class Inclusion**

Although preoperational children are able to form basic categories, they are unable to reason about categorical hierarchies. In a series of studies of children's concepts of class inclusion, Inhelder and Piaget (1964) found that children were unable to categorize by two variables simultaneously and therefore could not understand the relationships between superordinate and subordinate groups. As a result, they often overgeneralize and use transductive reasoning. After one altercation with one of his two Black classmates, a 5-year-old White child told his mother that "brown people always fight." This child linked two concrete pieces of information, the fight and his opponent's skin color, and assumed that people who are alike in one respect must be similar in all respects. He was unable to consider at that time that he also had fights with White classmates and that there was a Black child with whom he did not fight. He was unable to see that the dispute was only a subgroup within a group of many interactions with his Black classmates.

In another example of transductive reasoning, one child said that Chinese people always ate in restaurants. When asked whether or not the Chinese people would still eat in restaurants under various circumstances, she insisted that all Chinese people would eat there at all meals, including breakfast. Her only contact with any Chinese American people had been in a Chinese restaurant; she had concluded with perfect transductive reasoning that all people who were Chinese must always eat in restaurants. She was unable to think simultaneously of Chinese people as eating both at restaurants and at home, even though she was able to see that she herself ate at restaurants sometimes, but not all the time.

These examples illustrate the distinction between generalizations made by young children, who are unable to coordinate commonalities and exceptions, and attitudes of adults, who willingly ignore evidence that contradicts their negative assumptions about particular groups. That is not to suggest that young children who make these generalizations may not grow up to be prejudiced, but at this stage their perceptions must be analyzed as reflections of their cognitive abilities.

Because they cannot think in terms of class inclusion, children often over apply ethnically related labels. In a recent study of White children's responses to photographs of Black and Asian American children (Ramsey, 1985), the subjects frequently assumed that both groups were the same because they were "not-White." Sometimes they described both groups as "Chinese" with the Chinese children being described as "a little Chinese" and the Black children as "a lot Chinese." Other children made the distinction between the "Black-ish people" (Chinese) and the "real Black people." In some cases, children expanded the categories to become a catchall for all unfamiliar people. One child started by saying that Chinese children were Japanese. Then, he started labeling the Black children as Japanese. By the end of the interview, he was referring to all children that he did not know as Japanese. Thus when young children identify themselves as members of a particular group or state preferences related to different groups, their definitions may not coincide with conventional categories and may not be consistently applied.

Children's reliance on tangible factors to delineate categories means that cultural and national differentiations are often too abstract for young children to comprehend. According to Tajfel (1981), children at the age of 6 are able to categorize photographs as being own nationality or not-own nationality. However, Lambert and Klineberg (1967) found that 6- and 7-year-olds had only a vague idea about their own and other countries. Also because children do not think in terms of class inclusion, they cannot understand the concentric relationships among town, region, country, continent, and world. In their 1951 study, Piaget and Weil found that children before the age of 9 could not describe themselves as both "Genevan" and "Swiss." These concepts are confusing not only because of the multiple memberships; in addition, the idea of being defined as a member of a group by the abstract characteristic of location is particularly difficult for children to comprehend.

In conclusion, children's categories are more inconsistent undifferentiated, concrete, and idiosyncratic than adult classification schemes. By understanding the distinctive ways in which children organize social information, investigators will be able to interpret children's comments about ethnic differences more accurately.

Assimilation of Ethnic Information

Tajfel's second cognitive function related to ethnic attitudes is assimilation, the process by which people absorb information from their environment. Because Piaget's work is a major focus of this chapter, it is important to point out that Tajfel's use of the word *assimilation* differs from Piaget's definition. For Piaget, *assimilation* means that information is adapted to fit a person's preset notions of meaning. In Tajfel's work and in this chapter, *assimilation* means the influence of external information on one's existing perceptions and developing concepts.

Much of what is assimilated is neither taught nor learned in a conscious manner. Children learn about attitudes and values in subtle ways through vocal inflections, body language, and the absence of certain groups in their environment. The message, though subtle, is often pervasive. Tajfel points out that socially sanctioned beliefs about other groups of people tend to be learned from people who all share the same opinion. Therefore children are less likely to be exposed to contrasting points of view. As a result, "'bad' and 'good' . . . become incontrovertible statements of fact not different in their mode of assimilation from, for example, 'large' or 'small'" (Tajfel, 1981, p. 135).

This assimilation process is most evident in children's evaluative concepts of various groups and the development of their own group identity. Children are exposed to overt and covert expressions of social expectations and the relative status of various groups. The people whom they see (or do not see) among their parents' friends, in their neighborhoods, and in the media convey information about who is valued and who is not. They also learn about their own group and begin to absorb the expectations and behaviors associated with that group.

Evaluations of Groups

It is of particular importance to understand the ways in which children understand and integrate evaluative information about their own and other groups. It has been well documented that even at a young age, children's affective reactions to their own and other groups often reflect those of the social environment (for example, Goodman, 1964; Morland, 1962).

The influence of the social environment is highlighted when responses are compared across diverse groups. In a recent study (Ramsey, 1983), members of a low-income group made many more cross-racial pejorative remarks than a middle-class group. The negative comments often explicitly reflected certain environmental tensions. One White child from a low-income family declared that "I'm gonna kick the Black people out of the workplace!" Although it is doubtful that he knew what a workplace was, his comments reflected some of the economic bases of negative cross-group attitudes. One could argue that he was merely expressing an association that he had learned from adults. However, he did elaborate with some vehemence by describing how he would "kick them" and "punch them." He also generalized from this statement by saying that he would not let Black children into his school. He was assimilating the adult attitudes and beginning to apply them to his more immediate situation.

One negative statement often made by White and Asian American children about Blacks is that they do not like the colors brown and black. Although some writers claim that this aversion reflects a universal fear of the darkness (Williams & Morland, 1976), it also suggests that children assimilate and apply covert as well as overt social messages. In our society, the colors black and brown are often either avoided or used in a negative connotation (for example, "black lie"). Conversely, white and light colors have many positive associations. Even children who have not been exposed to explicitly negative attitudes about darker-skinned people may still have absorbed the prevailing aversion to dark colors and applied it to their perceptions of people with darker skin.

This prevailing antipathy towards darker skin illustrates Tajfel's (1981) point that many minority group children feel a conflict between a positive group identity and prevailing negative social attitudes. Several Black children (Ramsey, 1982) disparaged the relatively darker skin tones of their classmates or other peers. As one Black 4-year-old girl said, "I like brown people, but not real, real black people."

Friendship Patterns

Assimilated attitudes exert a more subtle, yet discernible, influence on children's preferences. In many studies (for example, Asher, Singleton & Taylor, 1982; Ramsey, 1983) children show some same race preference in choosing friends from known classmates and from pictures of unfamiliar peers (although it is usually a secondary consideration to gender). Although children often give nonracial reasons for their choices (he or she "is nicer," "looks friendly," and so on), their actual choices reflect a certain degree of same-race preference. Some children are more explicit; one Black child stated, "I don't like White people." When pressed to explain why they do not like a particular group, children often cannot provide any reasons or give nonsense answers. However, some children explain why they would want a particular unknown child as a friend by showing how that child is similar to them (for example, "She gots long hair like me"). Implied in these responses is the notion that similarity is a basis for friendship. If children look for similarities as an indication as to whether or not someone will be a friend, then obvious physical differences may limit that possibility.

Behavioral Norms

Very early in life, children learn to expect certain kinds of behaviors as they assimilate the social rules and mores of their families and communities (Longstreet, 1978). When confronted with an event or action that violates one of these, children are often perplexed, repulsed, and/or angry. In one kindergarten class, a teacher heard several children calling a child from India "garbage head" because of the unfamiliar smell of the coconut oil that he had on his hair. For children who had grown up with an emphasis on "clean," shampooed hair, the unfamiliar custom of oiling one's hair was associated with being dirty. In another classroom, a teacher noticed that an American child and an Israeli child (both aged 2. 5) were engaged in a dispute over whether or not the milk bottle should be on the table with "dinner." Although the Israeli child could not explain or even comprehend the kosher laws related to eating, her rule that milk should not be part of the dinner was clearly in conflict with the expectations of her American classmate.

Young children also learn nuances of social interaction that often differ between ethnic groups. The use of body language, the pace of conversations, and the acceptable entry behaviors are a few of the many dimensions that can vary among different ethnic groups (Longstreet, 1978). As discussed by Rotheram and Phinney (this volume), children develop expectations of how members of their own group interact and, in mixed settings, how other groups will react to certain situations. These stylistic differences can be a source of social discomfort and wariness, which, rather than consciously formed preferences, may be a factor in the increasing ethnic cleavage in the schools (Schofield, 1981). A Black kindergartener who complained that his White classmates always "get me into trouble with the teacher" may be expressing this same discomfort at an earlier stage.

The Role of Affect in
Assimilation of Information

Information that is emotionally arousing has a greater impact on children's ideas than neutral events (Kosslyn & Kagan, 1981). As an example, Native Americans usually are described by children in terms of violence that reflect the images of them that prevail in the media. Both Black and White children started talking about "karate chops" when they saw pictures of Chinese American children (Ramsey, 1982, 1985). One White kindergartener reported in an interview that "the Black kids are always bad, they don't listen to the teacher and have to go to the office." Here she was selectively paying attention to the dramatic events that occurred in the classroom and associating them with one group.

The other information that she had (that is, all the White children who got into trouble and the Black ones who did not) was superseded by a few dramatic events. As discussed by Allport (1954), affectively laden assumptions make it difficult for people to attend to and recall contradictory information. The child, just described was unable, even with some suggestions from the interviewer, to name any Black children who were not usually in trouble.

In conclusion, children assimilate ethnically related attitudes, preferences, and social expectations at an early age. Cognitively, they function in a world of absolutes and overgeneralizations that make them more receptive to global stereotyped and prejudicial comments of adults. Children are particularly "caught" by affect-laden comments or events. However, as we see in the next section, their behavior is not as "driven" by these sweeping assumptions as one might suppose.

Contradictions and the Search for Coherence

As people try to organize the vast amount of information in their environments, there is a strong motivation to simplify it (Rosch et al., 1976). People strive to make intergroup relationships predictable by engaging in a process that Tajfel (1981) refers to as the "search for coherence." For example, it is easier to dismiss all welfare recipients as "too lazy to work" than it is to understand the wide range of situations that create the need for public assistance.

Overgeneralization

Young children, like adults, try to construct their ideas and integrate new information in ways that will make the world meaningful and predictable. They frequently reduce the complexity of information by forming global assumptions and thinking in absolute rather than relative terms. In describing classmates (Ramsey, 1982), children frequently spoke in very strong terms about their peers' "bad" behavior. Although they often could think of only a single incident to support their claims, they would frequently (and vehemently) state that a certain child was always bad. Even with more neutral content, children have a hard time entertaining exceptions to their assumptions, as demonstrated by the child who insisted that all Chinese people always ate in restaurants. Contradictory information is difficult for them to integrate, as they see the extremes and not the range of differences and individual variations.

In their search for coherence, people often suppress individual variations to support group generalizations. This phenomenon is particularly true for children because they can focus only on one attribute at a time. Katz (1973a) found that Black children had more trouble distinguishing pink-tan shades on faces and White children had more difficulty in discriminating among brown shades. In interviews in which children saw photographs of their classmates (Ramsey, 1982, 1983), subjects frequently had greater difficulty remembering the names of their cross-race classmates than their same-race ones. White children also often mislabeled the gender of Asian children (Ramsey, 1985). Here, children, distracted by racial differences, were not able to perceive individual differences. However, a distinction must be made between adults who willfully assume that "they're all alike" and children who can only process one attribute at a time.

Inconsistencies

Although young children make generalizations about groups, they do not necessarily extend their beliefs over time and across situations. Because their thinking is situation-bound, there are often inconsistencies between their statements at different times and between their expressed ideas and their actions. Their evaluative reactions are likewise variable. For example, Porter (1971) found that some children who made negative comments about cross-racial people in interviews, were observed shortly afterwards playing with their cross-racial classmates. Their perceptions about the group did not necessarily influence their attraction to particular people in the immediate situation.

Thus children are not bothered by what adults see as contradictions. For instance, the child who declared that all Black people should be kicked out of the workplace later in the same interview selected a Black child as his best friend. When this discrepancy was pointed out to him, he immediately replied "Oh she's brown, not black!" Here the child had created a distinction between the "Black people" that he had heard described by adults and the brown children that he actually saw and played with every day. In short, children's global categorizations and rigid expectations are more easily overcome by immediate experiences than adults' attitudes are.

Situational versus
Inherent Characteristics

Adults frequently explain a group's circumstances as a result of inherent characteristics of a particular group. This way of organizing information enables adults to ignore the disparities within the social environment and the complexities that typify the interaction between social groups. Although young children often reduce the environment to its simplest concepts, they are more likely to attribute misfortune to the environment than to people's characters. In a task in which children saw a picture of a boy running away from a dog, Ross (1981) found that younger children (ages 5 to 7) more frequently explained that the dog was fierce; the older children (age 9 to 11) described the boy as timid and scared. Young children develop an early ability to empathize with others and often fuse their own reactions with those of other people. As children get older, they are more likely to "blame the victim." In a third-grade classroom, children discussing why some people had more money than others felt that poor people were lazy. Preschoolers, when asked the same question, thought that people had been robbed or had their houses burnt.

In conclusion, although young children think in absolute and generalized terms that characterize the adult search for coherence, they are less bound by the need to be consistent. While they show evidence of beginning to learn prevailing assumptions about group characteristics, they are more attentive to situational information and are freer to respond to situations in ways contrary to their verbalized assumptions.

Causality and Conservation in
Children's Thinking about Ethnic Differences

As children develop their concepts about ethnic differences, their ideas about the origins of various characteristics follow a developmental sequence that is correlated with their understanding of physical phenomena such as conceptions of causality and conservation of matter (Clark, Hocevar, & Dembo, 1980).

Conceptions of Causality

According to Piaget (1960), preoperational children are psychological, phenomenistic, and finalistic in their explanations of causal relationships. The stages of children's ideas about origins of ethnic differences identified by Clark et al. (1980) illustrate this type of thinking. At level one, children attribute the differences to the actions of supernatural or powerful others ("God made him that way" or "The doctor painted her"). Children assume that these beings act on the basis of their own wishes or motivations (for example, "The doctor wanted her that way" or "God ran out of the regular blood, so He made her Chinese"). This stage is similar to Piaget's description of young children who attribute all physical changes to psychological motivation (for example, "The sun comes up because it wants to"). At the second level, children use arbitrary causality ("She's bad"), similar to Piaget's phenomenistic causality in which two unrelated perceptions are assumed to have a causal relationship. Next children have inaccurate physical explanations ("They didn't get their suntans yet" or "He was born in Africa"), which are similar to Piaget's participation relation in which two events that have some commonalities appear to be causally related. As children approach the concrete operational stage, they begin to understand (although they cannot provide a reason) that "people are born that way."

At these early levels, both Black and White children often assume that everyone started off White and then something happened to some people and they became Black (Ramsey, 1982). As children try to understand these differences, they may notice more physical changes that go from light to dark than dark to light (for example, white paper is painted by darker paint). The major dark to light transformation that children see involves cleaning off dirt, which may further reinforce some children's association of darkness and dirt. One White child, watching his Black classmate wash fingerpaint off her hands, told the teacher, "She's going to have to wash real hard to get all that brown off." This notion that people with darker skin are changed or flawed White people, may contribute to some of the aversive comments about darker skin expressed by both Black and White children.

Conservation

Preoperational children confuse changes in state with changes in quantity. In one of the classic conservation tasks, they see two identical balls of clay. When one is rolled into a sausage, young children assume that it is bigger because it is longer. Nor are they able to mentally reverse the process that they just observed to understand that if rolled back into a ball it would be the same as before.

In a similar fashion, children do not conserve ethnic characteristics. Because they often equate skin color differences with temporary change (tanned or painted skin), children frequently assume that people can change their color (for example, "They better get that paint off by Christmas"). Several Black children have shown interviewers their lighter colored palm as proof that they were lighter once and can "get pink" at some future time. Children do not see ethnicity as unchangeable until they are 7 or 8 (Aboud, this volume).

Recently a group of White 4-year-olds were washing a Black doll. As they started the task they generally agreed that the doll would get lighter as they washed it. One girl seemed less sure and said with some hesitation that the doll might not change color. However, later in conversation she said that the reason it would not get lighter was because the paint had been on it for a very long time. In other words, it was only more permanent paint, not an inherent trait of the doll. As the children washed the doll, they noticed that it in fact became darker with the wetness. By the end of the washing session, the children were expressing some uncertainty about whether or not the doll would ever get lighter. Here the children's assumptions about color change were being challenged by a very immediate experience.

Conservation of Identity

Although children often assume that people in general can change skin color, their responses to the question if they themselves might change seem to reflect differences in group status. The Black children often said that they could change if they stayed out of the sun. They also talked about taking their skin off and frequently tugged at it to show how they might do that. A few Black children assumed that if they changed clothes with the White interviewer they would become White. Goodman (1964) quoted a Black child talking about washing her skin very hard in order to get the brown off.

In contrast, the White children interviewed by the author vehemently denied that their own skin could become brown. The same child who was certain that Black children were only temporarily brown, was often the one who was most certain that his or her own skin would not change.

Interestingly, children feel that their identity can change with the acquisition of different cultural traditions and artifacts. Aboud (this volume) reports that young children quite readily believe that they will be Eskimos when they are dressed in Eskimo clothing.

Just as in conservation tasks, children cannot simultaneously maintain their own identity and see themselves dressed as someone else. As any observer of young children can attest, preschool children easily shift from role to role in a very convincing manner. More work needs to be done on young children's ideas in this area. For example, it would be interesting to examine children's ideas about the effects of assuming different cultural artifacts (for example, clothing, foods, eating utensils) versus actually changing one's physical attributes (that is, skin color and facial structure).

Conclusion

Early ethnic socialization has a clear cognitive component. Although affective processes often influence what children remember and integrate from various experiences, their level of cognitive development determines the ways in which they process that information.

Children's dependence on concrete information, their tendency to categorize on that basis, and their inability to consider information from multiple perspectives means that their responses to many questions cannot be interpreted in the same ways as adult responses. Furthermore, children are often inconsistent in their responses across different situations. Studies in ethnic socialization always should include multiple tests, such as perceptual, preference, and behavioral measures, in order to see how children generalize and apply their ideas. In particular, clinical interviews may help researchers to understand more clearly how children themselves see the connections among the many aspects of their ethnic identities and attitudes.

This kind of information is particularly valuable for designing educational programs to promote positive ethnic identities and cross-group appreciation and respect. By understanding the ways that children perceive and process ethnically related information, adults who work with children can create experiences that will effectively challenge the attitudes that children absorb from their social environments. Also, by being aware of the ways in which children react to discrepant information, teachers can learn how to present unfamiliar material to children in ways that will enable them to empathize and identify with a broad range of people.

3

A Social Psychological Model
of Ethnic Identity Development

GRAHAM M. VAUGHAN

The basic proposition in this chapter is that a social psychological analysis can both help to understand the nature of ethnic identity development and to reconcile some diverging views in the literature. This analysis reviews a cognitive model, proceeds to incorporate an affective component, and then argues that the social structure surrounding the child plays an essential role in the development of ethnic identity.

Most of the early studies of ethnic identity required children to select the one that looked most like themselves from pictures and dolls that had differing ethnic cues. Responses to such tests were thought to indicate what the children actually thought they were, that is, their ethnic self-identification. Research in the 1940s and 1950s (for example, Goodman, 1952/1964; Landreth & Johnson, 1953; Morland, 1958; Stevenson & Stewart, 1958) reported that Black children responding to such questions selected White pictures and dolls as looking like themselves.

There are difficulties confronting clear inferences from such findings. A first problem is cognitive: How well do young children know what they look like? A second problem is affective: What do young children want to look like? Do young Blacks, for example, wish do look White? A third problem is methodological: The test materials may lack construct validity, that is, dolls and pictures may not signify real people (Brand, Ruiz, & Padilla, 1974; Katz & Zalk, 1974). A fourth problem is

73

statistical: Analyses of own-group and other-group choices across self-identification studies may not show a trend departing from chance expectation (Banks, 1976).

Although these issues are important, the thrust of a social psychological model of ethnic identity development embraces the older studies in an historical context. The earlier researchers seemed unaware that the way in which ethnic identity develops in a minority group child may be quite different from that for a child from a majority. The probability of such a difference would follow from a lack of symmetry in the status and power relationships between a minority group and a majority group. Furthermore, these relationships may alter in a given community or across different time periods.

Before proceeding further, some terms to be used will be clarified. *Ethnic identity* refers to the person's sense of self defined by membership in an ethnic group. *Personal identity* and *social identity* can also be distinguished; the former derives from a sense of self based on interpersonal comparisons and the latter from group membership. Because one's group membership is multiple, we can speak of ethnic identity, gender identity, political identity, and so on. The term *self-identification* is a construct thought to be tapped when children are asked who they think they are. Finally, the term *ethnic attitude* refers to a child's tendency to prefer members from a particular ethnic group or to attribute favorable characteristics to them.

The Individual Psychological Model

This model of ethnic identity development is a traditional approach to socialization that is centered on the child. Whereas from a behavioristic viewpoint children respond to external reinforcers, from a cognitive one children actively process information, including information about people and interpersonal relationships. The cognitive view is implicit in the more modern research referred to in this section.

The earliest studies dealing with ethnic identity in children immediately laid bare a fundamental conflict: White children, it appeared, "liked to be White," but so did Black children. Technically, own-group identification occurred in White but not in Black children. A model restricted to an explanation in terms of cognitive factors has difficulty in handling these data.

The individual psychological model allows for both cognitive and affective information processing. The child can discriminate between people on the basis of ethnic cues and classify them into categories with ethnic labels. At the same time, the child has self-awareness: By making self-other comparisons, self-knowledge accrues in terms of ethnic grouping, and hence ethnic identity develops. These ideas are incorporated in Figure 3.1.

Cognitive Processes

It may seem obvious today that cognitive processes underlie ethnic identity and attitude development, but such has not always been the case. At the close of the 19th century it was not uncommon to explain outgroup rejection as a derivative of "consciousness of kind" or of "dislike of the unlike" (Klineberg, 1940). Humans, like animals, were thought to possess a biologically controlled (that is, instinctive) fear of strangers and an innate sense of race. (These writers did not consider instances in which curiosity of the strange or novel lead to approach responses; see Berlyne, 1960.) By the 1920s, however, Lasker's (1929) research suggested that Whites had no innate prejudice toward Blacks; he argued that prejudice developed from a child's unfavorable contact with an outgroup.

Early American studies. Studies in the 1930s were the first to go to the source—children themselves. Horowitz (1939) used line drawings to represent Black and White children. Clark and Clark used the same drawings in their first works (1939a, 1939b), but introduced Black and White dolls in a later study (1947). Several other picture and doll studies followed, with a conflict in results and interpretation. Clark and Clark (1950) reported a "high" level of ethnic awareness at 7 years of age, and Goodman (1952/1964) at 4 years of age. A problem here is to define levels of awareness.

Authors also disagreed about differences in awareness between Black and White children. In terms of self-identification, some indicated earlier awareness in Blacks (Goodman, 1952/1964; Horowitz, 1936) and others in Whites (Landreth & Johnson, 1953; Morland, 1958; Stevenson & Stewart, 1958). As we shall see, this conflict can largely be resolved by addressing the question, what do young children *want* to look like? Asking a child which of a set of stimulus figures "looks like you" is not purely a cognitive (objective, intellectual) problem. The very question involves the issue of self-worth, and has a fundamentally affective basis.

These early studies were nevertheless theoretically important in demonstrating that children's responses varied with age, that there was a developmental trend, and that race awareness was not developed fully at birth. They were also practically important, because they contributed to

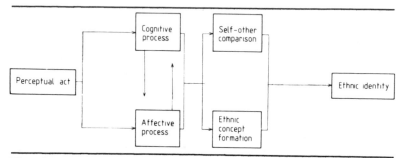

Figure 3.1:   An individual-psychological model of ethnic identity development.

the 1954 United States Supreme Court decision that racial segregation in American schools violated an equal protection clause of the United States Constitution (see Introduction by Clark, in Goodman, 1964).

New Zealand studies. In the research that I conducted in the 1960s, I assumed that ethnic awareness developed over a period of years, and that any one test instrument will, at best, measure only some of its facets. Primary goals were to examine, in a non-American setting, young children's sensitivity to ethnic difference, grouping, and identity; and their ethnic stereotyping and preference.

The subjects were Maori (Polynesian) and Pakeha (Caucasian) children. Both Maori and Pakeha interviewers were used, and, in one study, they tested other-race as well as own-race subjects. This interviewer manipulation tested the extent to which a child may attend to the racial characteristics of the tester as well as those of the materials. This check is one that has been surprisingly neglected in most of the developmental studies carried out.

The first studies (Vaughan, 1963a, 1963b, 1964a, & 1964b) tested children in the 4 to 12 years age range. Ten tests were developed from picture and doll materials—seven as awareness tests and three as attitude tests. The pictures were lifelike, black-and-white pen drawings of the upper torsos of Polynesian and Caucasian figures, with artistic attention focused on facial features. Two sets of dolls (male and female) were flat mannequin figures with detachable body portions, with skin surfaces colored either pink or brown; hair color was black, but the eyes had no color cues. Another set of female dolls were three dimensional, made from the same mold, some being pink-skinned and blue-eyed, and others brown-skinned and brown-eyed; all had black hair. One of the brown-skinned dolls was dressed in traditional Maori costume, and the others wore everyday dresses.

Considered together, the tests involved a variety of cues: facial characteristics in black and white tones, skin color without eye color, and skin color with eye color. Activities required of the children were

(1) *Self-identification.* The question was "Which one looks like you?" There were two tests, one with pictures and one with mannequin dolls.
(2) *Discrimination.* The question was "Which one of these is different from the other two?" The two tests were three-element oddity tasks, in which two elements were the "same" and one was "different." One test used pictures and the other three-dimensional dolls.
(3) *Assembly.* The instruction was "Put these together to make 2 little boys/girls." There were 12 jumbled body parts that could be assembled to make up 2 children, one pink-skinned and one brown-skinned.
(4) *Classification.* The question was "What kind of doll is this?" There were two tests. In one, there was a brown-skinned, three-dimensional doll in an everyday dress, and in the other a similar doll in Maori costume.

At least one of these four activities was present in each of seven awareness tests used by Vaughan (1963a, 1964a). The results are shown in Figure 3.2, and indicate the earliest age at which the number of "correct" responses departs from chance. Two crucial points emerged:

(1) In Pakeha children the development of awareness of ethnic differences and of ethnic identity followed an order through the seven tests, as in a Guttman scale. Self-identification tests ("Which one looks like you?") were mastered first. Discrimination tests (picture and doll discrimination, doll assembly) were mastered next. The last were the classification tests (requiring the verbal response of "Maori" or "Pakeha").
(2) In Maori children the pattern was nearly identical, with one notable exception: on self-identification tests, they did not identify with own-group figures until they were much older, at 9 to 10 years compared with 4 to 5 years for Pakehas.

The notion of orderly cognitive development of ethnic identity appears not to have been reported in earlier work, nor attended to again until Aboud's research (Aboud, 1980; Aboud & Skerry, 1984). Still, the results were consistent with other cognitive developmental research dealing with conceptual thinking (see Kendler, 1961). It had been shown that children could group individual instances of everyday objects into classes and respond to them in terms of their class membership rather than their uniqueness (for example, Bruner, Goodnow, & Austin, 1956). The term *social categorization* is now used to refer to the case in which

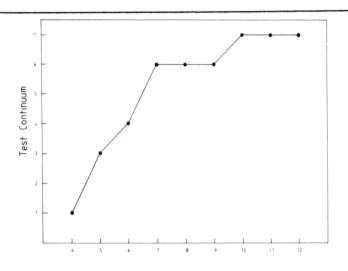

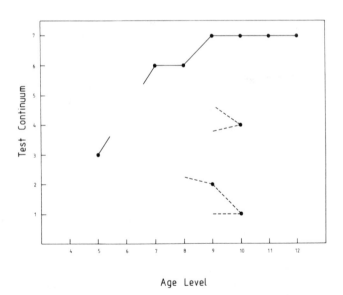

Age Level

Notes: Top: Pakeha; bottom: Maori. Tests 1 and 2 were self-identification; tests 3-5 were discrimination and assembly tasks; tests 6 and 7, classification.

Figure 3.2: Development of test mastery through seven tests of awareness of ethnic identity and differences.

the elements are people. The significance of social categorization was not explored for several years (Eiser & Stroebe, 1972; Tajfel, 1970).

My (1963a) study of Pakeha children treated ethnic identity as a special case of concept formation. Another feature of this work acquired extra meaning following the publication of American and Canadian results. I noted that Pakeha children younger than 10 years were more likely to label a brown-skinned doll as "Maori" when it was dressed in traditional Maori costume. Clearly, characteristics that define perceived ethnic grouping are subject to variation. The New Zealand data show that such variation can be a function of age. It also can be a function of other characteristics; McGuire, McGuire, Child, and Fujioka (1978) have argued that salience of ethnicity can vary according to the relative size of the ethnic minority ingroup. Aboud and Skerry (1983) showed that, in 5- to 8-year-olds, consistency of self-concept in terms of internal attributes (for example, traits) emerged later than consistency of self-concepts in terms of external attributes (for example, appearance).

The data pointing to "delayed" own-race identification in Maori children (Vaughan, 1964a) were comparable to some studies of young American Blacks. Theoretically more important, however, was the link between this trend in self-identification and preference on attitude tests, described below. This link demonstrates the need to incorporate an affective process in an otherwise purely cognitive account.

Affective Processes

Others also have found it necessary to refer to both cognitive and affective processes when articulating the nature of ethnic identity development. However, are these processes parallel or do they interact?. Piaget and Weil (1951) argued for a dualism underlying national identity development, based on cognitive and affective elements that were "parallel and isomorphous." Milner (1983) has underlined Piaget's rationality, even in this duality; the child learns not only facts about other national groups but also dispositions toward them. In this view, affect is a response to awareness of the facts.

Both this sense of rationality and the notion of parallel development have been challenged (Johnson, Middleton & Tajfel, 1970; Tajfel & Jahoda, 1966). Tajfel and Jahoda showed that 6- and 7-year-old children's preferences for national outgroups did not correlate with their factual information about these groups. The Johnson et al. study indicated that 7- to 11-year-olds had the highest level of factual information about national outgroups that were either most liked or most disliked, and that some facts were acquired as propaganda after an initial prejudice was already formed. Horowitz (1940) had already noted that a generalized prejudice can precede "techniques of differentiation" between outgroups.

Landreth and Johnson (1953) distinguished two processes. Their subjects were White (upper and lower SES) and Black (lower SES) children at 3 and 5 years of age. The task was a picture inset series in which it was possible to match figures by skin color. Spontaneous comments showed clear SES differences. The theoretical point is the authors' call for two processes: "Young children of parents engaged in professions perceive skin color in cognitive terms, children of parents engaged in semi-skilled occupations perceive it in affective terms" (Landreth & Johnson, 1953, p. 78).

The model in Figure 3.1 allows for an interaction between cognitive and affective processes, even though in research one can make a conceptual and a methodological distinction between tests of ethnic awareness (as if they tap only cognitive processes) and tests of ethnic attitudes (as if they tap only affective processes; Aboud, this volume; Vaughan, 1963a, 1964a, 1964b). If parallelism exists at all, it is only in the sense that affect in very young children might be applied inaccurately. For example, a child could respond evaluatively to an ethnic term describing an outgroup, such as "They are bad," without knowing clearly which members of a community belong to that group.

Consider now the New Zealand research, in which there were three tests of attitudes. In one, the child selects a doll, ostensibly as a gift for another child. There are two dolls, dressed identically, differing in skin and eye color. In another, the child selects a playmate from line drawings of Maoris and Pakehas. In a third test, the child allocates a series of evaluative stereotypes to either a Maori or Pakeha line drawing. Averaged data across the three attitude tests are shown in Figure 3.4 (below). These results show that Maori children up to 10 years of age preferred or favored other-race figures. These children also identify with other-race figures, as shown by their choices on the two self-identification tests.

Doubts about the efficacy of any self-identification test as a measure of ethnic awareness have been voiced by Porter (1971, p. 23):

> The Clarks' [later] doll-play study remedied a defect in both their earlier work and the Ruth Horowitz investigations, since they specifically asked the child to identify the "Negro," "Colored," and "White" doll rather than drawing inferences about level of awareness from the youngster's correctness of racial self-identification. Racial self-identification is a poor measure of awareness for Black children . . . who are highly aware of racial differences [and] may identify as White because they dislike their racial status.

In this sense, a self-identification test becomes an attitude test for young children. For children from an ethnic minority, the response to the question, "Which one looks like you?" will often be "incorrect." The point has crucial significance for the model of ethnic identity offered here. For the young child, sense of self defined in ethnic terms is as much a question of what one *wishes* to look like as what one *actually* looks like. Young children are sensitive to the existing social structure, to the nature of majority-minority relationships, and to existing privilege. Thus self-identification test data do not allow us to conclude that Black children in America, or Maori children in New Zealand, actually believe that they have white skins. Rather, the test situation probably allows children to fantasize.

In New Zealand research, an increase with age was found in the intercorrelations of the three attitude tests (doll preference, picture-playmate preference, stereotype attribution). For both Maori and Pakeha children, the correlations increased from about .25 at 4 to 8 years to about .48 at 9 to 12 years (Vaughan, 1964b). Such an increase with age in attitude response consistency has been reported before (Horowitz, 1940). A problem in assessing test reliability lies in contrasting data from younger and older age samples. With young children, lack of consistency may indicate not only that test behaviors are discrete but also that the construct itself is not yet integrated.

A further problem is that a test may be construed differently by majority and minority group children. Younger New Zealand children of both ethnic groups preferred white dolls, most often referring to color as a reason. Older children preferred brown dolls; when asked why, Maoris were either noncommittal or referred to color, although Pakehas referred to the doll's novelty. Clearly, the older Pakeha children did not see the test in ethnic terms.

A final result is worth noting. Of the three attitude tests, the one most obviously evaluative was the stereotypes test, involving positive or negative attribution to Maori or to Pakeha figures. This test correlated .36 (for Pakehas) and .60 (for Maoris) with the doll preference test, further evidence that the latter more directly tapped an affective component for the Maori group.

Summary

It is clear that two components, one cognitive and one affective, play a crucial role in ethnic identity development. A cognitive component is required to account for the child's capacity to organize information about ethnic cues. However, the child also is attempting evaluations, however primitive, of ethnic groups. It is clear that self-identification tests require the child to deal with how the self is evaluated by the ethnic cues provided. Whatever the answer, it is likely to match the child's response to tests of ethnic attitude.

The Social Psychological Model

The model of ethnic identity development presented above is rooted in individual psychological processes and is limited in not treating the individual as part of a social system. Social psychology, as a discipline, has always experienced difficulty in finding a level of discourse between a concrete (psychological) and a more abstract (sociological) one. The social psychological model put forward in this section incorporates both the individual and the social structure, each providing inputs to psychological processes.

The elements are shown in Figure 3.3. Those involving the perceptual act, cognitive process, and affective process are retained. The essential differences between this model and the individual model are

(a) The existing social structure appears as an input via path b.
(b) Two levels of dealing with persons are distinguished, one as individuals and the other as individuals in categories.
(c) The person uses both interpersonal and intergroup comparisons that promote two identities, one personal and the other social. The output is now shown as self-concept, which stresses that we are ultimately dealing with an integrated human being, and that ethnic identity is but part of self. For this reason the term "ethnic" does not appear, indicating that we have here a general model which, for example, could also be used to deal with gender identity. (Katz, 1983, has discussed some parallels between race and gender identity.)

Before dealing with the roles of social categorization and of the social structure, attention is given briefly to the inclusion of path a_1. The development of a personal identity has been treated extensively by Festinger (1954). His theory of social comparison argues that the individual "uses" others not only to provide a context for thoughts, feelings, and actions, but also to provide a locus for self. He proposed that one actively checks the validity of attributes and actions by constant comparisons with others. Personal identity derives from such comparisons.

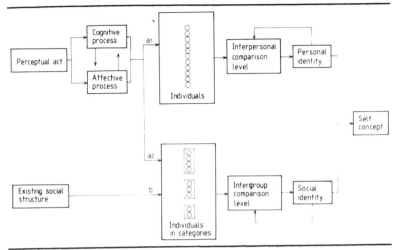

Figure 3.3: A social-psychological model of ethnic identity development.

Some attributes with potential ethnic significance, such as skin color, could be learned in this way, and could conceivably come to acquire a purely individual meaning. It is debatable, however, whether or not such learning plays an important role in understanding ethnic identity formation. The concept of interpersonal comparisons implies aspects of self-concept that are personalized rather than group defined. The importance of this distinction in the field of ethnic identity has been clearly enunciated by Cross (this volume). Dispute over the existence of negative self-esteem in Blacks, he argues, derives in good measure from a failure to distinguish (in both theory and method) between the concepts of "personal identity" and "reference group orientation." The former deals with "universal behavioral indices and/or internal states," which can be found among individuals in any group; the latter deals instead with an individual's orientation to own group as compared to other group. Cross's notion of reference group orientation fits well with the output of paths a_2 and b in Figure 3.3 discussed below.

As noted earlier, social categorization is the process whereby individual people are rendered functionally equivalent and responded to in terms of class membership rather than uniqueness. Allport (1954) was aware of the importance of this process and of its connection with stereotyping and prejudice: Social categories can be practical, gross and oversimplified, emotional and irrational.

Path a_2 in Figure 3.3 suggests that it is natural for the individual to classify people into groups. People may be shorter or taller, younger or older, male or female, and so on. The capacity for categorizing has been dealt with extensively by other authors (for example, Doise, 1976; Eiser & Stroebe, 1972), but it was Tajfel (1978) more than any other who saw the implications of this process for the development of *social identity*, and the need for a concept of *intergroup comparison* as a theoretical adjunct. The ease with which social categories are both formed and put to use was demonstrated by Tajfel (1970) within a research paradigm now known as the "minimal intergroup situation" (see Brewer, 1979). In this study, adolescent boys were divided randomly into two groups, supposedly on the basis of their preferences for artwork. When later given the opportunity to allocate rewards to ingroup and outgroup members they showed a high degree of ingroup bias. Not only did they give larger rewards to ingroup recipients, but they also tended to maximize the difference in reward size in favor of the ingroup.

Vaughan, Tajfel, and Williams (1981) extended these findings to girls as well as boys, and at younger (7- and 11-year-olds) age levels. Vaughan et al.'s findings demonstrate that the relatively simple act of creating two groups can be sufficient to trigger ingroup bias. A child could choose one of three outcomes when allocating coins indicated by numerals: (a) ingroup, 3, outgroup, 4; (b) ingroup, 2, outgroup, 2; or (c) ingroup, 1, outgroup, 0. Our results show that the child most often chooses (c), the smallest of the rewards available to an ingroup member, but the only choice favoring ingroup over outgroup. This strategy, when pursued across trials, is referred to as *maximum difference*. It is a strategy of relative gain rather than absolute gain, and is consistent with a separation between groups.

According to Tajfel, accentuating perceived intergroup differences helps to focus the unique attributes of ingroup membership, thereby defining one's social identity. In the present model, I also use the terms *interpersonal comparison* and *intergroup comparison*. The former is the process whereby self-concept is developed by comparisons with selected others' beliefs, attitudes, emotional states, and so on. The latter term is an intergroup analogue: the individual's self-concept is defined by attributes of ingroup rather than outgroup members.

An enhanced (positive) self-concept should follow particularly when a majority group member makes an intergroup comparison with one from a minority. A diminished (negative) self-concept could follow when it is the minority group member who makes the comparison. If we accept that all people basically wish to think well of themselves, that is, strive toward a positive self-image, then members of minorities who suffer from being underprivileged are in quandary. One viable alternative is for such minorities to change the nature of the ingroup relationship. Tajfel refers to this process as *social change,* a term which will be amplified below.

The foregoing discussion has been presented largely in the light of the individual's tendency to organize a world into groups. Ingroup bias in the laboratory is the analogue of real-life discrimination. Ethnic cues provide one such basis for discriminatory acts. Considerations of real-life settings bring us to consideration of path b (Figure 3.3), which indicates that a social structure precedes the existence of any given individual. However, the question can still be asked: Should the nature of social acts be determined at an individual or at a societal level of analysis?

> In the way that it is usually presented, this is a chicken-and-egg problem. . . . It is not a substantive, empirical problem, but a conceptual one. Our very terminology encourages us to conceive of "individual" and 'society' as separate and static entities, rather than as inseparable aspects of one complex and constantly changing set of interrelationships. It is fairly easy to see that 'society' is an abstraction and that it is composed of innumerable human beings, thinking, feeling, and behaving. It is a less familiar thought that 'the individual,' too, is something more than a human organism. We mean an organism that has already learned much in social relationships, and has absorbed ways of thinking, feeling, and behaving from other people who constitute "society." (Mennel, 1974, pp. 7-9)

In relation to ethnic identity development, we infer that the child enters an environment in which the relations between ingroup and relevant others are already specified. As we have seen, the perceptual act may lead a child (by path a_2) to divide people into groups on the basis of skin color. Similarly, the hint of a label, such as blue or red group, and of one's membership, likewise triggers an inevitable social-categorical sequence. The likelihood that the child will construct social categories in an idiosyncratic way is reduced by the existing categories and intergroup relations already structured and recognized by the community.

The tendency for young Pakeha (Vaughan, 1963a) and Maori children (Vaughan, 1964a) to identify with Pakeha figures, and to favor them (Vaughan, 1964b), reflects the children's early awareness of an existing social structure—one that they cannot influence. For Maori children, the Pakeha group serves temporarily as a positive reference source, because the ingroup cannot. In Cross's terms, these children, like many young American Blacks, have a reference group orientation toward the outgroup. The level of comparison is intergroup, and because the young Maori's social identity *qua* Maori is not contributing satisfactorily to self-concept, the orientation is toward the outgroup. (Various writers have dealt with difficulties in ethnic relations in New Zealand that detracted from Maori self-respect during the period in question; see Vaughan, 1972.)

The developmental sequence for older Maori children, however, shows a shift toward ingroup orientation. This points to the ultimate power of the social structure, and society's decree that the growing Polynesian child is "Maori." As a member of a disadvantaged ethnic minority, the Maori child has a limited number of intergroup comparison options: (a) accept an inferior social identity, and an unsatisfactory element in the self-concept; (b) be part of a social movement that challenges the legitimacy of the status quo, and improves the lot of the inferior group; or (c) avoid damaging comparisons by emphasizing unique characteristics of one's group (for example, language) and/or introducing new ones (for example, a new 'language'). Options (b) and (c) provide ways of removing inferiority and contributing positively to self-concept, and social psychologists are paying more attention to such solutions (for example, Lemaine, 1974; Ryan & Giles, 1982; Tajfel, 1978).

The input from the existing social structure in Figure 3.3 should not be construed as a static entity, because society is subject to alteration. Changes in the existing social structure can mean a change in input via path b that may alter either the categories or the relationships between the categories with which the individual must deal. For example, abolition of slavery in the United States presented an enormous problem in restructuring the perception of Black-White relationships, not only for Whites but also for Blacks.

Data from the New Zealand studies are relevant to the issue of change over time. Analyses from both my own (Vaughan, 1978a, 1978b) and other Maori-Pakeha studies afford comparisons of samples from four different parts of New Zealand and in different time periods. Young Maoris reacted quite differently to ethnic awareness and attitude tests in terms of whether they were drawn from rural or urban communities, and whether they had been tested in the early or late 60s. The rise of the

American Black power movement was known in New Zealand toward the end of that decade (Vaughan, 1972), where there was a parallel, though less aggressive, Brown power movement. Furthermore, Maoris had become predominantly urban rather than a rural people, and were now striving in a job market formerly dominated by Pakehas. Along with this urban shift, Maoris sacrificed their traditional extended-family living style, and their language all but disappeared.

Analysis of the test data indicated that these changes in the social structure were reflected in the way children perceived Maori-Pakeha relationships. For comparative purposes, results from the attitude tests averaged across four studies are shown in Figure 3.4. Age is one axis and shows a gross developmental trend. Pakeha subjects showed greatest ingroup preference in the middle years, with a falloff in this effect in older children. A mirror image effect is seen in Maori children, with outgroup preference yielding to ingroup preference with age.

This relatively simple developmental picture, however, interacts with social change. Figure 3.5 recasts the data of Figure 3.4 so that age is replaced by a social-change axis. The four studies are separated in terms of their region and year. Region A and B are both rural, and C and D are urban. Only D was carried out in the late 1960s, by which time the Brown power movement in New Zealand had commenced. Considering region and time as factors that can each affect the nature of an intergroup relationship, the studies can be conceptualized as samples across social change. The term *static* suggests status quo and entrenchment; *fluid* implies open to being challenged or restructured. The data in Figure 3.5 show that children were significantly affected in their intergroup choices by the context (region and time) in which they were tested.

The age trend in Figure 3.4 is retained in Figure 3.5 within each of the four samples shown by the arrows. The latter represent pairs of means from younger and older subjects. The outcome, therefore, is an interaction between age and social change. In terms of the model in Figure 3.3, the input change in path b carries through the system as a change in perceived intergroup relations. When an intergroup comparison is made, ingroup choice by Maoris contributes more favorably, as a function of social change, to their social (in this case, ethnic) identity. This ultimately enhances an aspect of each individual's self-concept.

This treatment suggests that a historical consideration can reduce the problem of conflict across decades of research dealing with the nature of self-esteem in American Blacks. Unfortunately, comparisons between

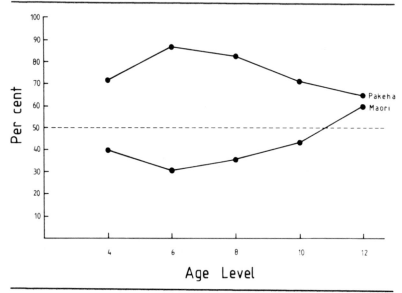

Figure 3.4: Percentage of Pakeha and Maori own-group preference as a function of age.

studies are also confounded by varying methodologies (Adam, 1978; Cross, this volume; Pettigrew, 1978; Powell, 1983; Simmons, 1978). The heuristic value of the social psychological model outlined here is increased to the extent that one also can account for the problems of test and construct validity.

Two final points should be made about input from an existing social structure. The first is the difficulty that a minority group child may experience in relating self to externally provided categories. My studies included a breakdown of Maori results in terms of skin color and of parental race. (These factors were found to be correlated: Those with lighter skin more often also had one parent who was Pakeha.) It was found that young, lighter-skinned Maoris (and/or those with one Pakeha parent) more often identified with and preferred Pakeha figures. (Similar effects have been reported for American Black children; Clark & Clark, 1947; Koch, 1946.) However, after the age of 10 years, nearly all Maoris identified with own-race figures, and tended also to prefer them. An external world dictates that a perceptible racial cue places the child in a Polynesian category.

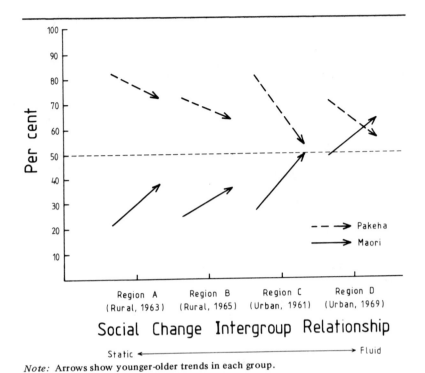

Figure 3.5: Percentage of Pakeha and Maori own-group preference function of social change.

An unresolved research question in multiracial society is whether or not it is possible for a child to develop a truly interracial identity. Yamamota and Kubota (1983) do not distinguish between mixed-race and unmixed-race Japanese Americans: Both groups draw on their cultural (Japanese) heritage in participating in a multicultural society. According to Hitch (1983), there is only a vague category for the half-colored (Black-White) child, and none for the half-Asian, in British society. Yet a colored (Black-White) interracial group is recognized in South Africa. Jacobs (1978) suggests that a child may attain an interracial identity only when society formally recognizes the interracial group involved. Therefore, the question of a group's existence is as dependent on recognition from without (by others) as from within (by its members). Once again, control is exerted by the social structure.

The second point is that the child's manner of relating to that structure can be subtle and may even lead to seeming conflict between studies. An illustration is my finding that the race of the interviewer had an effect on test responses in older Maori children (but not Pakeha or younger Maoris; Vaughan, 1963b). These Maori subjects tended to accommodate to the race of the interviewer. This goes beyond a design issue, and reflects the children's view of an intergroup structure in which Pakehas were perceived as a privileged majority.

Another illustration comes from the minimal intergroup paradigm. Wetherell (1982) demonstrated that the maximum difference strategy is not universally used. She found that immigrant Polynesians (for example, Cook Islanders, Samoans) in New Zealand preferred to use a joint-profit strategy (giving to both ingroup and outgroup), mixed with an absolute gain strategy for the ingroup. The overall effect—to favor one's ingroup, but not at the expense of an outgroup—is consistent with a view that Polynesians traditionally show a high level of generosity to others. We must conclude that predictions here also depend on the social structure, that this structure contains a cultural-values component, and that in this case the component is non-Western.

Summary and Conclusions

This chapter has dealt with two models of ethnic identity development. The first is an individual psychological model formulated to characterize the treatments given by a variety of researchers in the area. It involves cognitive and affective processes that are required to account reasonably for the data. However, some conflict in the data still typifies a restriction in inference that can be drawn from the individual psychological model and that cannot be entirely explained in terms of methodological inadequacies.

The second model is a social psychological one. It incorporates the individual psychological model and emphasizes the role played by social categorization, that is, the tendency in children to group people into categories on the basis of attributes perceived in common. This model goes further to stress that society imposes some of these categories, that is, the child is born into an existing social structure. Furthermore, no society is static, so that a social structure can show change over time. Consequently, contradictory data generated by samples from different regions or time periods may be reconcilable. What appears to be random variation when samples are compared may actually be behavior that is consistent with a process of social change. Research in New Zealand among Maori and Pakeha children has mapped change in intergroup preferences as a function of urbanism and of time. Changes within the interethnic community at large, highlighted by the rise of a Brown power movement, seem to have percolated down to young children. Young Maoris who once showed a preference for white figures now tend to choose brown. A model of ethnic identity development must be sensitive to evolution in the structure of intergroup relationships to account for data like these.

4

Developmental and Social Processes in Ethnic Attitudes and Self-Identification

PHYLLIS A. KATZ

The three previous chapters in this section all deal with various aspects of how children develop ethnic identity and attitudes. Each of the authors has published widely in this area, and their current articles represent in all three instances an insightful and knowledgeable synthesis of a number of factors that are significant in explaining the complex developmental processes involved.

The underlying questions addressed in these works are threefold: (1) How does an infant who is not cognizant of existing social groups come to identify with one of these groups and develop attitudes toward members of other groups? (2) How does a young child's thinking about social groups differ from an adult's (and, as a corollary, how adequate are our measures of children's thought processes in this area)? (3) How does the particular social structure a child is reared in affect his or her ethnic attitudes and identity? Although each of the three chapters touches upon these three basic questions, some focus more on certain areas than others.

Aboud's chapter is concerned primarily with the first question, and the general thrust of her work is to outline a very useful developmental sequence of self-identity that is nicely related to methodological components as well. She argues (based upon both her own work and that of others) that self-recognition is the first clear phase in this process and that this generally occurs at 3 or 4 years of age. Following this, the child demonstrates increasing competence in (a) perceiving similarity of the self to one's own group, (b) categorizing various groups based upon perceptual cues, (c) labeling groups appropriately (that is, in a manner consistent with adult patterns), and (d) recognizing that ethnicity is generally unchangeable. The various steps as outlined take about 4 years to develop, and the constancy aspect generally is not acquired until 7 or 8 years of age.

In contrast to this rather neat paradigm, her discussion about attitudes does not include this sequential treatment. She notes that expressions of ethnic attitudes have been noted in 4-year-olds, most particularly in White children's attitudes toward Blacks. Both Aboud and Ramsey in Chapter 2, however, point out that such statements may have different meanings when young children state them than when adults utter them. The expression of prejudice in young children may reflect the child's perceptual and cognitive limitations more than any stable, organized predisposition to act in a certain way. Some evidence for this viewpoint can be found in the inconsistency between verbal and nonverbal behavior noted by Ramsey. Another interpretation of children's attitudinal statements is that they may be in part an artifact of the particular methodology employed. Aboud argues persuasively that the frequently used forced-choice techniques may, in fact, inflate the actual negativity of such attitudes. Yet a third interpretation of the findings, however, is that attitudes may developmentally precede cognitions about ethnicity (Zajonc, 1976) or may occur at the same time (Katz, 1983). Clearly, no unanimity exists as to the meaning of young children's expressed attitudes, and Aboud makes the very interesting methodological point that the relation between attitudes and cognitive aspects of ethnic socialization may differ at different developmental stages, a proposition that can be assessed only if they are measured separately.

In an attempt to integrate the cognitive and attitudinal data now available, she suggests two possible lines of parallel development. The first begins with affective components, then focuses on perceptual cues, and finally concerns itself with cognitive dimensions. She notes that a second sequence of development begins with attention to self, then to groups, and finally to individuals.

It should be noted that although the interpretation of children's attitudinal responses varies, the findings are more consistent. White children exhibit definite own-group preference by age 4, often express negative comments toward other groups, and never state a desire to be anything else but White. Minority group children, on the other hand, express less own-group preference at early ages (although the extent of other-group preference does seem to be diminishing) and appear to be less prejudiced toward Whites. As Vaughan notes in Chapter 3, it is difficult to make sense of these data without taking into account the effect of the child's social structure. Although Aboud's work is very comprehensive from the point of view of the individual child's development, she does not specifically focus upon the child's social environment in this process.

Vaughan's model, in contrast, maintains that a look at the child's individual development is inadequate to explain ethnic socialization without an accompanying analysis of how the social structure interacts with the child. I am in agreement with Vaughan on this point, for a strictly cognitive, nonsocial learning model cannot account for the apparent discrepancies in majority and minority group children's development. Given the very strong tendency to prefer one's own group, however arbitrarily this is defined (Tajfel, 1981), it becomes necessary to postulate some intervening variables to account for the breakdown of this tendency in the case of ethnic groups that are associated with lower status within a particular society. It should be noted that an analogous situation exists with regard to sex-role socialization as well. Girls at certain ages value their own gender group less than boys do. Thus we cannot explain children's social development fully without taking into cognizance the high prevalence of racist and sexist attitudes in the adults around them. Although we do not completely understand how particular "pecking orders" are transmitted to children (and more research in this would be a worthwhile enterprise), it is clear that children are at least partially aware of these at remarkably early ages.

Although considerable individual and developmental variability exists in the salience of ethnic cues, there are undoubtedly systematic societal variations as well that remain to be examined in more detail, both in their own right and in terms of their effects upon children's perceptions. In this regard the study by Wetherell (1982) discussed by Vaughan was of particular interest. Even the apparently universal tendency to favor one's group for rewards does not exist in all cultures, such as certain Polynesian people. It would seem that more cross-cultural evidence is needed to enlarge our perspectives about what is, in fact, a function of children's cognitive development and how much of this is influenced by the surrounding cultural milieu.

The issue of methodology was raised in various ways by all three authors in this section. As noted earlier, Aboud pointed out the potential pitfalls of certain types of tests in biasing the child's response. Graham's own work utilized multiple measures, a technique not frequently employed with children. This permitted him to assess the various linkages at different age levels. Interestingly, he found that intercorrelations between cognitive and affective measures increased with age, suggesting that the various components in the socialization process may have different rates of development. It is also interesting to note that certain types of problems, such as low reliability, may be of substantive, as well as psychometric, import in dealing with children when inconsistency may be the rule rather than the exception.

Ramsey's chapter provides the reader with vivid reminders of the need to take into account the qualitative as well as the quantitative aspects of children's responses in this area. Working with children from two theoretical vantage points (Piaget; Tajfel), she points out the various ways in which children's conceptualizations about race and ethnicity differ from adults'. Children's tendency to overgeneralize, their inability to deal with contradictory information, and their greater receptivity to global and affect-laden statements may make them particularly prone to prejudicial thinking, a point I also made in an earlier paper (Katz, 1976). Presumably, however, many children "outgrow" these types of reasoning problems, whereas others do not. We know surprisingly little about what accounts for whether a child will or will not change these cognitive patterns with regard to ethnic groups, or about the possible developmental relations between seemingly prejudicial attitudes expressed at earlier ages and those held at later maturational stages. Indeed, additional light could be shed on many of the developmental issues raised in this section by longitudinal data.

Each of the three chapters in this section represents a laudable attempt to differentiate constructs and variables that have often been blended in earlier work. Moreover, they all attempt to integrate findings in an often conflicting, voluminous, and atheoretically guided data base. It appears that each of these works represents a considerable advance in the field. Nevertheless, it also seems that our challenge as theoreticians and researchers extends even beyond the basic issues addressed by these chapters.

The first trend I would like to see is a broadening of the developmental range we study. Most of the work has been conducted with preschool children, and there are now also a number of studies with grade school children. I am not in agreement with Vaughan's supposition that ethnic socialization does not begin until 3 or 4. The data show that children already have rudimentary attitudes and cognitions by that age. This suggests that much may be happening in the first 3 years of the child's life as well, even if we do not have the available technology yet to assess this. There is some suggestive evidence, for example (Lewis & Brooks, 1975), that children as young as 10 months of age already may exhibit same-gender preferences. It may well be the case that they attend to a variety of other-person cues as well. Several years ago I traveled to a remote part of China. When I visited a nursery I noticed that many of the infants showed signs of stranger anxiety only to Caucasian and not to Chinese strangers, suggesting that early concepts of what is familiar and what is strange may well include racial cues. Data about how ethnic information actually is transmitted to young children are needed also. It is my view that ethnic socialization may be conceptualized best (in a manner analogous to sex-role socialization) as a continuous process across the life span. If this view is correct, then we clearly need more studies with adolescents and research that attempts to link childhood socialization experiences with adult attitudes.

A second significant issue not dealt with in the earlier three chapters has to do with the salience of ethnic cues. Although there appears to be general agreement that some categories are perceptually more salient at younger ages (for example, racial versus religious groups), the question of how important ethnicity becomes relative to other-person cues has not been addressed. There are thousands of dimensions along which people differ, and any of these potentially could become a basis for a socially significant category. Within our own society, we differentiate individuals according to gender, age, kinship patterns, attractiveness, nationality, race, socioeconomic status, and region, just to mention a few. We also could use height, weight, rapidity of speech, and eye color, all of which are observable to young children, but we don't by and large. Thus to a large extent the social structure the infant is born into already has predetermined which categories are to have significance (Katz, 1983). Even within this melange, however, ethnicity varies in salience, and we have little understanding of what accounts for this variation. Minority status itself may weight the importance of ethnicity significantly for a child, simply because he or she may be perceived by others as being different relative to a majority norm. Is a certain degree of heterogeneity necessary in a neighborhood or school for this to happen, however? Will a child who has experienced negative responses from others be more or less likely to have ethnic identity become a major self-component? How does parental emphasis upon such identity affect a child's development? In the case of the White child, what kinds of experiences might be needed to bolster the importance of ethnic cues relative to other children? These are but a few of the questions to.be researched that come to mind with respect to this issue.

A third and closely related issue has to do with the relations of ethnic identity to other components of identity formation. I have contrasted ethnic-identity with gender-identity development (Katz, 1983). In that paper, one important similarity was the early ages at which both are socialized. By the age of 3, most children can respond correctly in terms of gender and ethnic labeling. A significant difference noted, however, was in the availability of models of the "other" groups. Both genders typically are available fairly continuously to the infant and toddler. This is not the case with ethnicity, however, unless the child comes from a mixed-ethnic family or neighborhood, neither of which is a likely occurrence. Thus knowledge of the "other" is ordinarily less extensive in the case of ethnicity than with gender. A similar case can be made with regard to age groups. Adults are always available to young children, and although they may not be able to differentiate, say, age cues within adults, the concept of grown-up versus child (or baby) is redundantly exemplified. Given the relative absence of other ethnic models, their knowledge about ethnic groups at 3 or 4 years of age is particularly surprising. We know little about relative weightings of these various social categories for young children nor how they interact in identity formation. Available research suggests that gender is a more primary determinant than ethnicity at younger age levels (Katz & Zalk, 1974). Nevertheless, given the limited cognitive abilities of the preschool child (that is, in terms of thinking of more than one category at a time), the question of how these become coordinated (both in terms of self-identity and preference for others) becomes a very interesting one. If a White girl, for example, selects a Black girl to play with rather than a White boy, does this mean that race is not important or perhaps that it is not even noticed at all?

A fourth issue touched upon in the preceding chapters but not dealt with in any detail has to do with how children obtain information about members of groups other than their own. As noted previously, during the preschool years the relative availability of other-ethnic models may be based solely upon happenstance. (Even for the school-age child, the school environment may be quite homogeneous.) Nevertheless, attitudinal type statements are clearly made by 4-year-olds. How are these transmitted? The obvious answer is that such statements are reflective of parental attitudes. The problem with this answer is that there appears to be (surprisingly) little correlation between children and their parents in this area. Even if one assumes that parental training plays a role, the process of transmission really has never been looked at empirically. Other socialization agents that affect the preschool child include peers, siblings, books that are read to them, and television. Although the first three have scarcely been looked at by researchers, the role of television has begun to be examined. For many White children, television offers the only opportunity to observe other-group members, and the way they are portrayed, therefore, is often determinative of their cognitions of these groups. For minority-group children, such portrayals are equally important from the point of view of self-identity. It is clear that the overwhelming majority of television characters are White. The proportion of Blacks has increased substantially over the past two decades to about 10%, but other minority groups are not as well represented (Greenberg, 1972). Some evidence exists that educational television programs such as *Sesame Street* can have a beneficial effect on White children's attitudes (Bogatz & Ball, 1971). Despite this, however, current research suggests that portrayals of minorities still differ substantially from the way Whites are presented (Reid, 1984) and that subtle racist patterns still are broadcast to children (and adults) as normative.

These considerations lead to a final issue not touched upon previously, namely, what are the best techniques to maximize a child's positive ethnic identity and to reduce negative attitudes toward others. What socialization agents, moreover, are most effective in these regards? Although it is of academic interest to study the sequence of a child's development in this area, the social implications of intergroup conflict and frustrated lives demand that we go beyond the study of socialization by itself and consider these very important issues as well.

In 1975, I reviewed the then extant research of modification of children's ethnic attitudes. The research was relatively sparse and was aimed primarily at the grade-school child in school and laboratory settings. Some of the techniques found to be effective included perceptual differentiation (that is, increasing the child's ability to attend to individuating characteristics of other-group members; Katz, 1973b; Katz & Zalk, 1978), reinforcement for choosing the "other" (for example, Williams & Morland, 1976, who reinforced choice of black over white things), and, less consistently, intergroup contact (for example, Amir, 1976).

In an updated review (Katz, 1982), it was apparent that considerably more work has been done in this area, particularly with regard to defining the types of group contact approach that "work." One of the most exciting is the "jigsaw" technique, devised by Aronson and Bridgeman (1979). This procedure involves teaching children in interracial teams in which every child has learned a part of the lesson that contributes to the whole. Thus in order for any individual child to score well on an examination, he or she must interact with others in the group. Other interesting variants of a learning-team approach have been offered also by Slavin (1983), and schools are beginning to adopt some of these techniques.

What the earlier discussion suggests is that in addition to these school approaches, we need to expand the modification research in a variety of ways. First, we need to direct more efforts to preschool children because early socialization seems so important. Although older children's attitudes clearly are not so intractable they cannot be changed, efforts aimed at younger children might be more effective, at least on an individual basis. Because younger groups are hard to reach consistently, perhaps such efforts should be done through television. Additionally, the use of parents as effective teachers should be systematically evaluated and materials developed for such purposes. Although parents generally have been blamed for negative intergroup attitudes in their children, there has been remarkably little attempt to provide parents with methods of raising children with positive attitudes toward themselves and others.

In summary, a number of problems remain to be answered to complete our understanding of the perceptual, affective, and cognitive components of a child's ethnic socialization. We should not, however, ignore the social implications of this process.

PART II

Minority Status and the Child

The first part of this book dealt with the early development of ethnic awareness, self-identification, and attitudes, with a primary focus on individual children and developmental changes. As children get older, their world widens, and broad social and cultural factors play a more important role in ethnic socialization. This is particularly true for minority children, who become increasingly aware of the lower status, power, and economic resources of their own ethnic group in society. The questions addressed in this section of the book include the following: How does minority status affect the development of children? How do they handle discrimination, disadvantages and the disparagement of their own culture by the majority? How do they deal with the joint demands of being simultaneously members of a minority group and of a larger society, the norms of which often prevail over those of their own group?

In examining these questions, we shift our focus from individual children to the ethnic group and the broader culture. The processes that are emphasized are sociological and economic rather than developmental, although it is recognized that the impact of these forces varies across age. The impact of minority status on the group as a whole is examined. Spencer and Cross point out the distinction between children's feelings about themselves and their feelings about their ethnic group. Furthermore, although studies with young children have assumed that self-identification is an objective fact, the study of older minority children must recognize the subjective feelings, including anger and frustration as well as pride, that may accompany awareness of minority status. However, the issues vary dramatically depending on the particular groups studied. Some minority groups, such as European immigrants to the United States or Australia, can eventually become assimilated into the majority group if they wish. Other groups, notably Blacks, have a castelike status based on appearance that means they can never be completely assimilated. This may result in a sense of dual loyalty, to their group and to the society as a whole. The study of these issues is inevitably value laden, and minority researchers raise the question of whether or not majority researchers can truly comprehend the minority experience. Each of the chapters in this section makes a step toward furthering this understanding.

Spencer shows how structural factors, such as an ethnic group's low status and lack of political and economic power, place minority children at risk. Interventions are therefore necessary to help these children recognize and deal with the issues they face in growing up as minorities in a pluralistic society. Cross emphasizes the distinction minority children make between their identity as individuals and their identity as group members. A healthy personal identity in Blacks can be associated with very different worldviews. One individual may be very militant, with a strong orientation toward Black culture, and another may be more assimilated and oriented toward the majority culture. But both are healthy.

The way in which labels reflect one's orientation is suggested by Cross (that is, the differences between the terms Black and Negro). Buriel's chapter discusses in greater depth the way minority children label themselves. There is no clear objective label for the Mexican descent group that he discusses. Their feelings about their minority status are reflected in whether they call themselves, for example, Mexican American, Chicano, or Latino.

5

Black Children's
Ethnic Identity Formation:
Risk and Resilience
of Castelike Minorities

MARGARET BEALE SPENCER

The major goal of this chapter is to examine ethnic identity formation in Black children in order to identify the special risks faced by these children in their development, as well as the sources of the resilience and coping that they manifest. Black children are at risk because of structural factors in the society that place limits on their opportunity for optimal development. The lack of status, political power, and economic opportunity in the Black community results in outcomes for children that frequently are labeled deviant by the majority culture. Young Black children face prejudice and stereotyping both in personal contacts and in the media. As Black children move into the larger society, they face additional risks if they have not been prepared by parents or other socializing agents to understand and take pride in their own culture. In order to understand these risks, as well as the way Black children cope with these risks, this chapter reviews recent research and demographic statistics and demonstrates the need for a developmental perspective to enhance understanding of Black identity formation.

As a first step in this review, the term *minority* needs to be defined as it applies to Blacks. Ogbu (1983) provides a typology of minorities as either autonomous, immigrant, or castelike. According to Ogbu, autonomous minorities in the United States, such as Jews and Mormons, ordinarily do not experience stratification, although the group may experience prejudice. Their separateness is not based primarily on a degraded economic or political status. The group ordinarily has a cultural frame of reference that manifests and reinforces success. In contrast, immigrant minorities initially occupy the lowest status of the occupational system, lack power, and possess low levels of prestige. These group members may not understand the negative definitions that the dominant group attaches to their menial positions; even if they are aware of the negativism, the evaluations are not perceived as valid, because the immigrants are not part of the local status system. The immigrants more often use their homeland as the referent for success or failure.

Ogbu views African Americans as representative of the third group—castelike minorities—a group incorporated into an existing social system involuntarily and permanently. Black Americans have an ascribed status that was not entered into by choice but by legal and extralegal forces. Native Americans are also castelike minorities because they too were incorporated through conquest and forced onto reservations. Similarly, the initial incorporation of Mexican Americans was also involuntary, through the use of hostile and extralegal means.

This review examines research focused on castelike minorities and their children. Cross (this volume) indicates that "the study of Negro, Black, or Afro-American identity has held center stage in substantive discussions of identity development for people of color living in the United States." Mussen, Conger, Kagan, and Huston (1984) note that "virtually all of the research on ethnic identity has been carried out with Black children" (p. 354). However, few qualitative changes in the interpretation of research findings have taken place over the 30 years since the Brown v. Board of Education (1954) decision or the 20 years since the passage of the 1964 Civil Rights Act. The objective of this chapter is to propose an interpretation of research findings that takes into account both developmental changes and environmental constraints.

Problems with Research
on Black Child Identity

The existing research on Black identity has severe limitations. Except for very recent research (for example, Spencer, Brookins, & Allen, 1985), most available research on Black children lacks a developmental thrust. The knowledge and attitudes of minority children and youth are analyzed by researchers in a fashion similar to behavioral analyses of minority-group adults. Much of this research fails to recognize differences in the way that individuals "make meaning" from their experiences as a consequence of their developmental status (Ramsey, this volume; Spencer, 1985). If the research on Black child identity is examined developmentally and the constructs subcategorized multidimensionally (for example, cultural awareness, group identification, racial preferences, racial attitudes, color stereotyping), nontraditional conclusions are generated. Children are viewed then as unique and qualitatively different from adults.

Second, minority-focused research offered from the perspective of minority scholars is seldom cited by academic psychologists. The issue is well illustrated by the recent, 4-volume *Handbook of Child Psychology* (Mussen, 1983). Not only is there no section on the experiences of African American children or minority children generally, but references to Black scholars who are most responsible for promoting alternative, innovative analyses of Black child development and family processes are lacking also. Research by fewer than 10 minority scholars is referenced in a volume that cites thousands.

Third, analysts (for example, Banks, 1976; Brand, Ruiz & Padilla, 1974; Jones, 1983; Means, 1980; Porter & Washington, 1979; Sudarkasa, 1983) suggest a bleak picture of the worsening conditions of Black children. These interpretations are in contrast to the optimism for the future expressed by Slaughter and McWhorter (1985), who view the 1980s as "a period of new possibilities." Similar optimism concerning research and theory on minority children is noted in the chapter by Cross (this volume). However, without assertively applied interventions, the sociocultural problems of African Americans, elaborated below, suggest the likelihood of more negative outcomes.

Fourth, African American children and youth have been studied, for the most part, in a reactive mode. The term *reactive* refers to the research focus of many majority scholars that begins with assumptions of deviance and pathology in minority status persons. Too often, the research of majority scholars is geared toward reaffirming pathological assumptions. Middle-income White children commonly are compared with lower-income African American subjects, thus confounding caste and class. Research strategies of some minority scholars also have been of this reactive mode, because many feel compelled to react against institutionalized assumptions of "traditional research" involving African

Americans. Clearly, the training of both minority and nonminority scholars unavoidably is based on traditional principles and models.

Black Identity Research and Child-Rearing Strategies

The problem of depressed and alienated children and youth is an issue of general concern in the current decade and is not limited to minority children and youth (for example, see Winn, 1984; Wynn, 1978). However, in the case of castelike minorities marginality exacerbates identity concerns. Ogbu (1974) suggests that the unequal empowerment system afforded minority-group parents often results in an at-risk status. This reality makes the parenting role a critical one. Parental values and beliefs are significant factors in identity formation, and specifically in the findings of race dissonance.

Race dissonance refers to the White preference behavior of Black children. The initial race dissonance findings in Black children by Clark and Clark (1939a, 1940) have spawned significant research efforts and critiques (see Banks, 1976; Brand et al., 1974; Porter & Washington, 1979; Williams & Morland, 1976). Nevertheless, 40 years after Clark and Clark's initial findings, research has shown the same pattern of race dissonance in three regions: the Midwest (Spencer & Horowitz, 1973), the North (Spencer, 1982, 1984a), and the South (Spencer, 1983).

The Southern data obtained by Spencer (1983) demonstrate the role of parenting in the acquisition and maintenance of race dissonance in Black children. Black parents in the study reportedly did not teach their children about Black history and civil rights, or emphasize Black heroes, unless children specifically asked questions. Parents generally felt that the post-60s era represented a much improved period that does not require the reinforcing of race consciousness. Their child-rearing did not stress race but, instead, emphasized more generic "human values." The parents generally felt that the 60s had been effective in altering conditions for minorities; that their efforts had not been in vain; and that the civil rights era had been worthwhile. Generally, their concern was with raising "human beings" and not necessarily "Black" children. Humanistic parenting, however, usually leaves young adolescents unprepared to handle institutionalized constraints that result from racial-group membership. Such humanistic practices actually may exacerbate children's experiences of risk.

In 1981, the sample of Southern parents was broadened and the parents were interviewed again at the end of a crisis: the Atlanta child and youth murders (Spencer, 1984b). Parental responses remained virtually unchanged. Although Black children were being systematically killed, parental responses still suggested a "belief in the system" and a lack of sensitivity to institutionalized constraints. Even more interesting, adolescents interviewed during the crisis gave responses that were correlated with parental responses. They reported that the school was the major source of knowledge concerning Black history and Black people. Further, the one area in which they felt that more information was needed was that concerning the reasons for racism and race discrimination. These results imply that the failure of Black parents to reinforce ethnic consciousness and to deal explicitly with ethnic issues and institutionalized racial oppression may be a factor in Black children's White preference behavior.

Socialization and Ethnic-Identity
Formation in Subcultural Groups

Clausen (1968) clarifies the process of identity formation. He notes that agents of socialization are

> primarily concerned with those kinds of social learning that lead the individual to acquire the personal and group loyalties, the knowledge, skills, feelings and desires that are regarded as appropriate to a person of his age, sex, and particular social status, especially as these have relevance for adult role performance. (p. 7)

Implicit in Clausen's definition is the role performed by specific individuals, groups, and social structures in this process. Black liberation theologists, for example, often describe the critical role of the church in one's socialization experiences, and anthropologists such as Ogbu (1983) or educational psychologists such as Slaughter and McWhorter (1985) focus more on the unique experiences of minorities in American schools. Similarly, the legal system also has a significant role in the socialization process.

The critical socialization task of minority-status children is the acquisition and internalization of positive identity elements in a nonminority preferred society. As noted originally by Clark and Clark (1939a, 1940) and by contemporary writers such as Cross (this volume), Black children demonstrate positive self-concepts although they also manifest White preferences and attitudes during the preschool years. These findings suggest that the "natural," or expected, developmental course of identity formation for African American youth (in a White-biased society) is toward identity imbalance (that is, race dissonance) unless an intervention occurs. That is, the course of development from an undifferentiated to a more differentiated view of self as a member of a devalued reference group requires that a cognitive shift from an egocentric to an allocentric view of culture (that is, group or ethnic identity) must occur (Spencer, 1985).

The most clarifying analogy is represented by the process of gender differentiation for the human embryo. Every human organism begins life as a female (Robeck, 1978); only a redirection of development induced by male hormones (that is, only the presence of a Y chromosome) supports the development of a male fetus instead. Similarly, all fish and reptiles, unless differentiated, develop into males.

African American children and youth are socialized in a Europeanized context. An identity associated with this context is expected unless an intervention occurs, that is, unless there is a compensatory cultural emphasis on the strengths of the castelike minority group by significant others. The discussion earlier in the chapter suggests that parents can, to some extent, provide the necessary intervention by making children aware of the uniqueness and strengths of their ethnic group.

However, in addition to the role of parents, the larger society is an important socializing agent. As castelike minorities, African Americans and Native Americans differ from autonomous or immigrant minorities in the impact the majority culture has on them. Black children, by and large, do not perceive America as an open opportunity structure, full of possibilities; rather, as members of a castelike minority they often see the role for self as a locked room. This perception is in fact an accurate reflection of economic factors that affect the opportunities for Blacks, and which in turn influence and often limit the development of a positive ethnic identity. Some of these economic factors are outlined below.

Demographic Statistics and Ethnic Identity

A plethora of statistics abound concerning the specific at-risk status of minority children and families (National Black Coalition, 1984; Children's Defense Fund, 1984; National Urban League, 1986; United

States Department of Commerce, 1981). As noted by the Children's Defense Fund Report, 20 years ago freedom, justice, and equality appeared to be possible. Currently, the view is one of risk, given the growing poverty and the escalating fight for survival of the Black community.

Garbarino (1982) defines *risk* as the impoverishing of the child's world of the basic social and psychological necessities of life. Children who grow up lacking adequate food, caring teachers, good medical care, and values consistent with intellectual process and social competence develop less well than children who have these things; such children are thus at risk for impaired development.

Poverty. African American infants have a 50% chance of being born into poverty, and they have a 75% chance of living in poverty if the family is female headed. In 1982, 47.3% of all Black children lived in families with incomes below the poverty level, as compared with 16.5% of White children.

Family status and family income. The Children's Defense Fund (CDF) Report indicates that not only is a Black baby three times more likely than a White baby to be born to a mother who is poor, but also is five times as likely to be born to a mother who is a teenager.

Black mothers are more likely than White mothers to be employed and to work longer hours for less money. The CDF Report indicates that 52.9% of all Black children under 6 years old have mothers who work; 44.8% of White children of the same age have mothers who work. Black mothers work an average of 37.8% more hours a year than White mothers and still earn less money. Although Black children are more dependent on full-time child care than White children, their parents are less able to pay for it.

Health. Physical health is linked intimately with ego developmental processes. Black babies are three times as likely as White babies to have a mother who dies in childbirth and are twice as likely to be born prematurely and to die in the first year of life. The Black infant mortality rate in Washington, D.C., is comparable to rates for infants in Jamaica and Guyana. Black infants are twice as likely to be born to a mother lacking in prenatal care, and the pattern is increasing. Statistics for 1981 indicated that 62.4% of Black infants lacked early prenatal care. Not unexpectedly, the statistics correlate with those for low birth weight. Of Black infants born in 1980, 12.5% weighed 2500 grams or less (that is, low birth weight, 5.5 pounds). Although these statistics represent a decline from 1970 for both races, there has been no improvement among the very low birth weight infants—2.4% for Blacks and 0.9% for White infants.

Not only do Black children have only two-thirds the number of routine infant and childhood health visits to doctors as White children, but also fewer are immunized, and thus more become ill. In 1982, only 48.4% of all Black children between 1 and 4 years old were immunized with 3 doses of DPT (that is, diphtheria, pertusis, and tetanus). Only 39.1% were fully immunized against polio.

Overall in 1980, Black children between 1 and 4 years of age were 68.6% more likely than White children to die; between 5 and 9 years of age, the percentage was 46.8%. Between 10 and 14 years the percentage was 22.8%. Only between 15 and 19 years of age were White children slightly more likely to die than Black children, because of auto accidents and suicides. However, Black adolescents are four times more likely to be murdered than their White peers.

Ethnic Identity and the Production Process

Muga (1984) makes the point that ethnicity is more than a "consciousness of belonging" but also needs to be viewed in terms of production and the consequent patterns of interaction. He posits that the way in which a subcultural group fits into the society's production process determines their treatment, and, accordingly, determines the specific nature of children's experiences. The early exploitation of children in the 19th- and 20th-century "sweat houses" in Europe and America during the early period of industrialization supports Muga's assumptions concerning ethnicity and its links with the economic production process. Children's psychological needs and physical health were considered secondary to the nation's industrialization requirements.

Children's evolving identity formation is affected by the nature of the ecosystem and its treatment and representation of children. The manner in which a cultural group thinks about children or conceptualizes the period of childhood usually determines the way adults interact with them (Newman & Newman, 1978). If the needs of children are considered secondary to a nation's production process, then their future may be impaired. Contemporary theorists concerned with the plights of American children propose that youth generally are at risk under the best or most economically sound conditions (see Mackey & Appleman, 1983; Postman, 1982; Winn, 1984; Wynn, 1978; Zigler, 1982). Thus when a minority group has a marginal link with the production process, as generally is the case with castelike minorities, conditions for their children are exacerbated even further.

The argument made by Muga (1984) suggests that ethnicity and the acquisition of ethnic identity represent an empirical problem that is both situational and linked to the production process. Identity is intimately tied to how an individual is responded to by the socializing agents. Ethnic groups are viewed and come to view themselves as significant or marginal as a consequence of their treatment by state agencies—by welfare workers, by federal office clerks, and by the police and other bureaucratic representatives. For example, insensitive treatment by government representatives is a source of negative identity images for castelike minorities.

Muga reasons that state policies toward castelike minorities change in the face of enhanced struggle or the weakening of resistance by the ethnic group themselves. Shortsighted analyses of demographic statistics (most often represented by theoretical assumptions of subcultural group deviance) take on various forms of the attitude to "blame the victim." The onus of poverty is placed on the poor themselves.

According to Muga, academic subcultural theories, which define ethnic groups in terms of their cultural or ideological habits, reduce ethnicity to cultural gestures or indicators such as myths, kinships, folklore, shared speech, folk art, mannerism, or social rites. As viewed by Muga, ethnicity and the acquisition of ethnic identity constitute rather an objective, economic, and empirical problem. A cultural theory of ethnicity requires that the detailed context of economic sociopolitical, and ideological relationships be considered.

As in Ogbu's (1983) formulations, Muga sees the role of history as critical for understanding ethnicity. He notes the neglect of history in most academic subcultural theories. The essence of Muga's argument is that the concept of ethnicity cannot be considered independent from internal processes of capitalist development.

Although Muga's critique might well be viewed as radical by many, his perspective has important implications for ethnic identity processes and contributes at least three major points. First, as a general fault, ethnicity theories are not only ahistorical but fail to relate a group's daily life experiences to the production process of the entire system (see Baron, 1971). Second, ethnicity theories fail to promote improved interpretations of race dissonance findings. Third, ethnicity should be considered in relationship to the production process and with the view toward substantive changes that address more effectively the conditions of minority children rather than offering mere interpretations.

Race, Stereotyping, and Prejudice in Black Identity Formation

As early as 1941, Frazier noted that all components of the ecosystem were viewed as important to the process by which Black children learn to know themselves in relation to opportunities and limitations of their social world. Race and color, in particular, remain unavoidable issues in identity formation.

The environments of Black children in America are infused with negative images of their ethnic group. Color concepts appear to undergird cultural beliefs and are in place prior to age 3 (Spencer, 1977, 1982). The princesses of fairy tales do not cavort in Black gowns or ride on "dark" stallions. They are "saved" by princes in white shining armor who ride white horses. "Good guys," generally, have always worn white hats. They are threatened by individuals of "dark" character, dressed in black, and riding "dark" horses. Mothers admonish children to enter the house before "it gets dark," not "when the sun goes down." The fear of darkness becomes analogous with a fear of all things dark and unknown, including people. Such early environmental experiences become integrated into the psyche prior to learning objective facts.

In addition, the media support a view that Black children are better cared for by White parents (for example, the television programs *Webster* and *Diff'rent Strokes*). Interesting also is the fact that both of the Black male children in the two series are conspicuously undersized for their respective ages. Is this physical reality also symbolic of actual political, economic, and sociocultural relationships?

Also, although the media have been examined and criticized for instances of violence, explicit sex, and conspicuous commercialism, their exploitation of castelike minorities has been less directly and honestly confronted. Children's exposure to biased, stereotypic cultural attitudes remains generally unchallenged, and such attitudes are absorbed in the psyche prior to cognitive awareness.

Isaacs (1968) describes with insight the role of race in interpersonal relations between groups and its effect on group identity. He notes:

Nothing marks a man's group identity more visibly or more permanently than the color of his skin and his physical characteristics. Men have used these primary symbols of what has been called "race" as a basis for their self-esteem or their lack of it. Skin color has served as the badge for master and subject, of the enslaved and the free, the dominators and dominated. Of all the factors involved in the great rearrangement of human relationships taking place today, skin color is the most glandular. Hence none is more sensitive, more psychologically explosive, or more intimately relevant to each individual's involvement in the process of political change. (p. 75)

Similarly, the oppressive role of color is demonstrated in Bradley's (1982) more contemporary view, which follows upon the poignant "cry of invisibility" uttered by Ellison in his classic novel, *The Invisible Man:*

I am a Black. That description may seem a little colorless; it used to seem that way to me—so much so that I spent a lot of time trying to pump a little technicolor into it. Which is not to say I wanted not to be Black. What I wanted was to be something else besides. For somehow I had gotten the idea that I had within me attributes and talents that could produce many colorful effects, and that the measure of my success as a person would be the extent to which I could bring my internal pigments together, to create a multicolored personality that would be visible to the world outside. . . . the notion was naive, silly and quixotic. I have given it up.

So, for all practical purposes, I accept a belief that I have taken to calling achromism (from the Greek *a,* meaning "not," and *chroma,* meaning "color") which is that within the context of the society to which I belong by right—or misfortune—of birth, nothing I shall ever accomplish or discover or earn or inherit or buy or sell or give away—nothing I can ever do—will outweigh the fact of my race in determining my destiny. (p. 60)

Johnson's (1941) view offers another dimension. He suggests that the White community throws all classes of the Black population together. This assumption of the physical and cultural uniformity of Blacks, interestingly enough, still maintains a certain amount of currency in the social science literature to date and has been carefully critiqued by Muga (1984). Johnson suggested that the assumption of cultural homogeneity retards the progress of aspiring Black youth. The burden of presumed "cultural backwardness" reinforces a penchant for elevating one's own status by criticizing certain qualities of the masses rather than by promoting an enhanced ethnic identity for oneself. A healthy ego counteracts ineffective or failed environmental encounters. Children adapt, indicating their resilience in the face of systemic obstacles.

Adaptation reflects an organism's efforts at survival. As suggested by Pierce (1982), people of color survive under daily, mundane conditions of stress.

Risk, Resilience, and Coping

Risk is defined as the impoverishment of the basic social and psychological necessities of life (Garbarino, 1982). Garbarino further suggests that racism, like sexism, opposes the goals of individual development. His perspective complements that of Muga's (1984). Negative images, the marginal relationship of castelike minorities to the production process, and the deprivation of basic economic necessities leave African American children vulnerable and at risk.

However, in the face of many obstacles, African American children seem to have an amazing capacity to cope and to rise above circumstances. Data remain unavailable that might more clearly delineate how minority group parents at the microsystem level prepare children for external threats perceived to be at the macrosystem level. Specifically, more information is needed on what minority parents teach their children about perceived threat and on the manner in which this information is transmitted. Race pride may be one important source of resilience.

In 1931, Brown implied that race consciousness is a major aspect of group consciousness. He defined it as the tendency toward sentimental and ideological identification with a racial group. Ordinarily, race consciousness becomes loyalty, devotion, and pride. Race pride, then, is one aspect of race consciousness. The construct implies the tendency toward emotional and ideological identification with a racial group. This process appears to underlie the comparable identification process of immigrant minorities with their homeland in the context of Ogbu's (1983) typology. Brown posits that race pride, an aspect of race consciousness, involves a tendency to acclaim one's race, to exalt its virtues, and to take pride in its past, its great people, and its achievements. In sum, it would appear to provide "manna" for peoplehood. Similar to Brown's (1931) perspective, Bond (1928) also suggests that race pride bolsters one's self-respect, exalts one's conception of oneself, and inures the individual against the pain incident to a low status.

A person's active efforts to resolve stress and to create new solutions to the challenges of each developmental stage is described as coping (Erikson, 1959). Racial dissonance in Black children represents a method of coping. There is the recognition, however, that coping strategies may entail risk. In the short run, pregnancy and low school achievement might appear to a teenager to be adaptive strategies for dealing with perceived powerlessness, but in the long run they are maladaptive. Paternal absence in order to ensure support of the family by the state might be adaptive in the short run, but in the long run it undermines family functioning and individual development. Staying away from state-operated prenatal facilities may serve as an ego-saving maneuver in the short run, but the long-term effects (for example, inadequate prenatal and infant care) are detrimental to maternal and child health.

The specific methods of coping obviously vary across contexts or situations and would be expected to change in content over the life course. Coping strategies of earlier stages become dysfunctional at later periods in the life course. Clearly, then, the issues of vulnerability and risk need to be considered within a life-span perspective.

Brim and Kagan's (1980) view of human nature suggests a capacity for change across the entire life span. They question the validity of the traditional notion that early life experiences, which have demonstrated contemporaneous effects, necessarily constrain the characteristics of adolescence and adulthood. Baltes and Willis (1979) and Riley (1979) maintain that aging is a lifelong process that is properly and necessarily studied as an outcome of lifelong experiences.

A life-span perspective is thus essential in developing theories of ethnic identity and race dissonance. Coping strategies and variations can be considered in their broadest adaptive forms when viewed over the life course. The differential processes of development that characterize the life-span perspective underscore the notion that the forms of developmental change are not unitary, but, instead, display much diversity both within and between individuals as well as cohorts (Baltes & Willis, 1979).

Summary

The study of Black children has been impeded by a number of factors. The research of minority scholars, who have unique insights into the problems of minority children, has been largely neglected by mainstream developmental psychology. Much research has failed to deal with the impact of social and economic problems of Black children; behaviors and attributes that stem from social and economic problems frequently have been labeled deviant or pathological by majority researchers. In addition, research with Black children, even more than research on ethnic identity in general, has lacked a developmental thrust that takes account of changes in attributes and experiences across time.

In spite of the problems with research on Black children, the material reviewed in this chapter provides some important insights into Black identity formation. Parents are the first source of a child's "sense of self," and Black parents provide their children with fundamental attitudes about themselves as Blacks. However, because of their minority status, Black children inevitably are socialized in a majority context and may thus show a preference for White culture. Furthermore, from an early age they are faced with the results of economic and political disadvantage, including the risks of poor health, poverty, and unemployment. The risks faced by Black children change with age and therefore need to be studied developmentally.

In view of these risks, race consciousness provides a foundation for the coping strategies needed by Black children. Race pride contributes to resilience and may lead to coping strategies that have positive rather than maladaptive consequences. More study is needed on how parents, schools, and communities can prepare Black children both to cope with the risks associated with minority status and to take pride in their ethnicity. In addition, the majority culture needs to recognize the special problems resulting from oppressive conditions related to minority status and take steps to alter conditions harmful to the development of Black children.

6

A Two-Factor Theory
of Black Identity:
Implications for the
Study of Identity Development
in Minority Children

WILLIAM E. CROSS, Jr.

For years the study of Negro, Black, or Afro-American identity has held center stage in substantive discussions of identity development for people of color living in the United States. This will change, of course, as research on Chicano, American Indian, and Asian American identity becomes more prominent. Nevertheless, the analysis of Black identity will continue to be extremely important for some time to come. With this in mind, the focus of the following presentation is a theoretical advancement in the study of Black identity, revolving around the distinction between personal and group identity. This "two-factor" theory first grew out of attempts to explain the effects of identity change in Black adults that took place during the late 1960s (Cross, 1971; Jackson, 1976; Milliones, 1974; Thomas, 1971). Thus the chapter begins with the evolution of the two-factor theory in studies that had as their primary focus Black adults, and then shifts to the applicability of the theory to the ontology of Black identity in children. Finally, it is suggested that the distinctions to be made between personal identity and reference group orientation are probably generic to the analysis of identity development in most minority groups.

Black Militancy in Adults:
Black Identity as an Archetype

The contemporary Black social movement, which lasted from about 1954 through about 1975, had two phases, a "civil rights" phase and a "Black power" phase. The civil rights phase commenced with the 1954 Supreme Court desegregation decision, peaked in 1963 with the March on Washington, and declined from 1966 to 1968. The Black power phase (also called the "Black revolution," the "Black consciousness movement," "Black militancy," and the like) was initiated with the 1965 Watts riot, surged with the introduction of the term "Black power" by Stokeley Carmichael during the 1966 march through Mississippi, peaked from 1968 to 1969 in the aftermath of the assassination of Martin Luther King, Jr., and lost its "mass movement" dynamic by 1974 or 1975. Although today we sometimes take for granted the concept of "Black identity," in point of fact Black identity is a contemporary term given credence by the activities, dynamics, discussions, ideologies, organizational thrusts, and empirical studies of (Black) identity development associated with the Black power phase. During this second period, and especially from 1966 to 1970, Black militancy was linked with Black identity, and for many White as well as Black American observers, they were one and the same. More often than not, the earliest research literature on the (new) Black identity sought to develop political, sociological, and psychological profiles descriptive of an archetypical Black militant (Caplan, 1970).

The analysis of Black identity through profile studies of Black militancy was eventually criticized by a number of scholars (Clark, 1971; Cross, 1971; Hall, Cross, & Freedle, 1972; Thomas, 1971; Turner, 1971). Their criticisms can be summarized in four points: (1) Research that sought to construct profiles of typical Black militants tended to obscure the importance of processes that produced the new Black person; (2) such studies unintentionally promoted an either/or conceptualization of Black identity or militancy that obviates dimensions of identity in transition; (3) most militants were former conservatives who had been transformed into new Black people; and (4) the transformation of Negroes into Afro-Americans seemed to involve a multistage process of which militancy was an important but nonetheless transitory phase. These criticisms generally were forged by process writers such as Hall et al. (1972), who noted that militancy was less an identity and more a trait of identity during metamorphosis.

Process Conceptualizations:
Models of Psychological Nigrescence

The ideal goal of the profile studies was articulation of the similarities and differences between the old and new Black identities; the process studies sought to isolate the developmental stages a person traversed in moving from the old to the new identity. *Nigrescence* means "to become Black" and the process models of Black identity change have been called "models of psychological nigrescence"(Cross, 1978), that is, the psychology of Black identity change. Nigrescence models have generally consisted of four stages: (1) The first stage established the nature of the person's identity before change commenced, that is, the essential dimensions of the old self in the context of the old social order; (2) the second stage made reference to personal encounters or social events that marked the origin of change; (3) the third stage represented the phase of activism, extreme militancy, and identity in transition; and (4) the fourth stage depicted the behavior of an individual who had successfully internalized the new identity. Examples of such models can be found in the works of Crawford and Naditch (1970), Gerlach and Hine (1970), Jackson (1976), Kelman (1970), Napper (1973), Pinderhughes (1968), Sherif and Sherif (1970), and Toldson and Pasteur (1975). The models by Cross (1971) and Thomas (1971) are of particular significance as each has been the object of considerable research (see literature review by Cross, 1978, and the recent study by Parkham & Helms, 1981). Interest in process models of Black identity development in particular and minority identity development in general remains very much in evidence, especially in the field of counseling psychology (Atkinson, Morten, & Sue, 1982). Although details of the various models have been neither confirmed nor contested, the accumulated evidence shows that the identity change experienced by Black adults in the late 1960s reflects the process depicted by the various nigrescence models.

The Effects of Nigrescence:
A Problem of Continuity and Change

Initially, the observers of Black identity change assumed that nigrescence involved comprehensive personality and identity change. This expectation could be explained in part by the romanticism associated with Black nationalism, as with any form of nationalism, in which elements of the accommodationist identity are cast in pejorative terms and things new in overwhelmingly positive phrases. Nevertheless, the trends evident in the research on Black identity seemed to point in that direction (Butler, 1976; Silverstein & Krate, 1975). In depicting both the general personality and group identity in negative if not pathogenic terms, the empirical literature on Black psychological functioning conducted between 1939 and the onset of nigrescence in 1968 made it appear that sweeping changes in the Black psyche were in order (Gordon, 1980).

Upon reflection, however, it did not seem logical that pathology was typical of "Negro" identity and mental health was the province of "Blackness." Given the possibility that the dimensions of the Negro identity were more often normal than pathological, apparently not everything about the Negro identity required change. Clearly something, but not everything, about the person with the (traditional) Negro identity was different from something, but not everything, about the person with a (new) Black identity. Of course, studies of nigrescence demonstrated that we are not talking about two different groups of people, but one group whose traditional identity has been transformed.

In other words, we have a problem involving change and continuity. Understanding what is new may not require the negation of all that was old, for, in the final analysis, any identity change involves (1) carrying over, in an intact state, certain traits or components linked to the old self, (2) transforming old elements into new elements, and, finally, (3) incorporating new dimensions of self that are not traceable to either old or transformed traits associated with the old self. A *new* theory of Black identity had to account for change and continuity and thereby be applicable to an analysis of previous as well as more recent research findings.

Rediscovering the Distinction Between Personal Identity and Reference Group Orientation

The debate over and search for a more plausible explanation of the dynamics of Black identity commenced in the early 1970s with the appearance of a number of key studies (McAdoo, 1977; Porter, 1971; Rosenberg & Simmons, 1970) and literature reviews (Baldwin, 1979; Banks, 1976; Butler, 1976; Gordon, 1980; Nobles, 1973). As is evident from the chapters in this volume, the debate continues very much in earnest. The theoretical perspective that centers on the constructs "personal identity" (PI) and "reference group orientation" (RGO) is particularly compelling in that it leads to a more accurate and balanced characterization of both the Negro and (new) Black identities and depicts nigrescence as a process of continuity and change. In an important book on Black identity, Porter (1971) cautiously notes that, contrary to traditional theory on Negro/Black identity, PI and RGO may not be predictive of each other. Although Porter is usually credited with having first observed this tendency, two other scholars, working independently, reported the same finding in their unpublished doctoral dissertations (McAdoo, 1970; Spencer, 1977). These studies reflect a fundamental problem, in that Porter focused on the constructs personal identity and group identity, and McAdoo and Spencer measured self-concept and racial attitudes. The study of Negro or Black identity had produced myriad terms, constructs, and measures that seemed beyond the pale of a comprehensive theory (Gordon, 1980).

In a recent series of articles, I suggested a solution to the problem (Cross, 1980, 1981). In an exhaustive literature review on Negro/Black identity, I pointed out that in most instances researchers have operated from the perspective that "self-concept" has two superordinate domains: the personal identity sector (PI) and the group identity, or reference group orientation (RGO), sector (Cross, 1980). Each superordinate domain incorporates various subordinate constructs. For example, PI includes such subordinate factors as self-esteem, self-worth, and general personality traits; subdomains under RGO are racial attitudes, group identity, race awareness, and so on. This frame of reference can be depicted schematically as shown in Figure 6.1.

Personal identity research. PI studies focus on variables, traits, or dynamics that are in evidence, to one degree or another, in all human beings, regardless of social class, gender, race, or culture; thus in a sense PI studies examine the so-called universal components of behavior. Everyone is thought to fit on a continuum of high or low anxiety, self-esteem, introversion-extroversion, depression-happiness, concern for others, and so on. In other words, PI variables are the building blocks for all personalities, with culture, class, race, ethnicity, and gender mediating, in many instances, how much of the variable is present across cultures or different groups of people.

Because the researcher believes that PI variables are present in all humans, the same assessment techniques or tests are used with different groups. PI-related research does not require the design of a special test

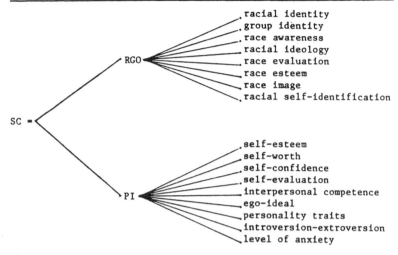

Note: Self-concept (SC) = personal identity (PI) + reference group orientation (RGO)

Figure 6.1: Schematic of two-factor theory of Black identity.

for application with different groups of people, with the exception of language translations. For example, in studying self-esteem in men or women, Blacks or Whites, Asians or Chicanos, researchers have typically used the same questionnaires or tests. Consequently, there is no such thing as the "Black version" of the Thomas Self-Concept Test nor are there such versions designed for use with women or men. In this sense, there is no such thing as Black self-esteem or female self-esteem; rather, research has studied the level of self-esteem in Blacks, Whites, men, women, and the like.

How then does race enter into the equation of PI research on Black people? The answer is that race is treated as an independent or subject variable in PI research. The researcher locates some personality scale, inventory, or questionnaire (MMPI, self-concept scale, Rorschach Test, locus of control scale, anxiety scale, and so on) that purports to tap "universal elements" of personality and that contains no reference to race, nationality, gender, or religion. The device is then administered to Black and White subjects (in the case of scales standardized on Whites, comparisons may be made on the basis of normative data). The researcher then determines whether or not race, as an independent variable, is statistically significant. That is to say, do the results differ according to the race of the subject?

A key point is that, implicitly or explicitly, PI research is trying to establish whether or not a person or group is characterized by adequate psychological well-being. Thus PI research is viewed as a direct measure of psychological functioning and only an indirect measure of one's cultural or sex-role identity. In other words, given that one is told that subjects A and B have high self-esteem and highly effective interpersonal skills, one could not predict whether the subjects were Black or White, men or women. What one could say is that whatever the sex or racial differences between subjects A and B, both appear, within the context of American culture, to have elements suggestive of adequate mental health.

Reference group orientation research. Although PI studies can reveal psychological functioning and the universals of one's self-concept, there still remains the examination of those aspects of "self" that are culture, class, and gender specific. Although PI research seeks to control for social class, ethnicity, and gender, RGO research seeks to discover group differences in values, perspective taking, group identity, lifestyles, and worldviews. In a sense, RGO represents the ethnographic dimension of the self-concept. PI research examines the dynamics and structure of the self, and RGO studies establish the content, context, symbols, values, and reference groups for the self. Though everyone eats food, what a person eats, how it is prepared, and the utensils involved are not the same across cultures. Likewise, every human being tends to rely on groups as a point of reference, but the specific groups one relies on reveal the nature of one's group identity or reference group orientation.

Because the RGO researcher is concerned not with how a person feels in general, but how one feels regarding specific values, preferences, or symbols, these values, preference options, and symbols generally are made an explicit dimension of the dependent variable. Race or color is usually an explicit property of the stimulus condition and it is always a factor in the scoring technique. In some projective devices or open-ended interviews, the researcher may not present race or color as a stimulus, but will search the protocols for race-explicit attitudes, feelings, and so on, that are spontaneously elicited by the nondirective stimulus. Generally speaking the subject must show a particular type of preference or particular attitudes toward his or her socially ascribed group in order to achieve a "highgroup score," the obverse resulting in an "outgroup" or "self-hatred" score. (Note that last term, self-hatred, is clearly inappropriate, for it refers to a PI variable; nevertheless, in studies that have produced only RGO data, it is not uncommon for the results to be discussed as if both PI and RGO information had been generated.) Race- or color-explicit stimulus-scoring techniques are considered direct measures of one's group identity (Lewin, 1948; Porter, 1971), racial attitudes (McAdoo, 1977), racial orientation (Goodman, 1964), or reference group orientation (Cross, 1978, 1980). The latter term is preferred, for in addition to binding these studies to the sociological literature on reference group theory (Hyman and Singer, 1968), it indicates concern with measures that reliably demonstrate how children or adults orient themselves toward their socially ascribed group. In this light, studies of racial attitudes, racial identity, racial self-esteem, racial evaluation, racial preference, or racial self-identification are subcategories of the domain, reference group orientation (RGO).

In summary, PI studies treat race as a subject or independent variable, and make certain that race or color is excluded from the stimulus conditions and the dependent measures. In PI studies, the dependent measure operationalizes some universal personality element; therefore, they generally preclude the possibility of race or color being even unintentionally injected into the scoring procedure. In most RGO studies, on the other hand, the graphic presentation of color or some other explicit race-related symbol constitutes a salient dimension of the stimulus and race-related information is an important, and usually the paramount, element of the dependent measure.

Researchers do not approach either the PI or RGO sector of the self-concept in a monadic fashion. The PI domain is envisioned as one cluster of interrelated variables and the RGO domain consists of another such cluster. For our purposes, however, it really is not necessary to specify subordinate variables, for the debate about Black identity has centered on the relationship between PI and RGO in general, and not the dynamics of lower-level constructs. For Negro or Black subjects, evidence of adequate mental health or the absence of psychopathology as measured by various PI devices has been presumed to be linked to an ingroup orientation, assessed by various RGO measures such as Black doll preferences, in the case of young subjects, or a high score on a Black consciousness scale in the case of older subjects. Conversely, low PI scores (suggesting poor mental health) were presumed to be traceable to an outgroup orientation.

In a comprehensive literature review of studies of Black/Negro identity conducted from 1939 through 1977, Cross (1980) showed that for the period 1939-1968, when the traditional or Negro identity was normative, RGO studies characterized Negroes as having an outgroup perspective; following the period of nigrescence, RGO studies showed Blacks becoming increasingly ingroup oriented. Thus a change was suggested across the time periods. When PI studies were examined, the PI patterns for the Negro period and the (new) Black identity period were identical; a healthy PI profile was evident for both. For example, PI studies showed Blacks with average to above average levels of self-esteem, whether the study was conducted before or after the period of nigrescence. Although few PI studies were conducted on Blacks between 1939 and 1968, the few that were conducted showed a healthy pattern, that is, they showed continuity.

It would be more plausible to make generalizations about PI continuity if it could be confirmed that PI and RGO were not correlated. The last section of the review examined PI/RGO correlational studies, and indicated that PI and RGO are not predictive of each other. Little (1983) reviewed an even larger cluster of PI/RGO correlational studies and came to the same conclusion.

Reconstructing Black Identity Theory

In the traditional pejorative theory, PI and RGO were thought to be the primary components of the Negro identity, but over time this distinction was blurred because the traditionalists believed PI and RGO were highly predictive of each other. Consequently, until recent times, the majority of Negro/Black identity studies were univariate investigations in which data would be collected on only one dimension (either PI or RGO) but the results would be discussed as if data had actually been collected on both sectors. The entire foundation of the self-hatred hypothesis derives from a series of RGO studies that were analyzed and interpreted as if RGO and PI data had been evaluated. Had a significant cluster of univariate PI studies been conducted between 1939 and 1960, the rush to a self-hatred model might have been blunted. (On the other hand, high self-esteem in Negroes might have been analyzed as a reaction formation in the face of self-hatred as shown by group rejection patterns on RGO measures!)

The new theory postulates that PI and RGO need not be predictive of each other. Thus two people may have very similar personality types, but extremely different worldviews. A feminist and nonfeminist may show contrary group identities but indistinguishable levels of self-esteem. Likewise, Black people with a traditional perspective (that is, Negro identity) on life may differ radically from Blacks with the new (that is, Black identity) perspective with regard to cultural values, artistic preferences, political propensities, social preferences, and world-view, but not differ on such measures as level of self-esteem, anxiety, sense of personal worth, motivation, militancy, or activism. The significance of ideology, group identity, nationalism, or reference group stems not from the capacity to create the same personality in people, but rather from the capacity to bring about consensus, unity, or a sense of peoplehood among a group of people who, individually speaking, represent a broad range of personalities.

Black people have achieved personal happiness through a variety of differing group identities; thus Black identity is not predictive of personal happiness, but it is predictive of a particular cultural-political propensity or worldview. PI, though not predictive of a person's RGO, is predictive of ego strength, mental health, and interpersonal competence. PI tells us something about the mental health of a person, independent of his or her group identity. RGO data tell us a great deal about the person's worldview, independent of personality. Thus each sector is capable of predicting extremely important factors, but each is a very poor predictor of the other.

Personal Versus Ascriptive RGO

My associates in clinical psychology noted one implication of the PI/RGO distinction that seemed to contradict their experiences with normal, as well as troubled, clients. On the one hand they agreed that having a particular RGO was not associated with high or low levels of mental health. On the other hand, no matter what the person's level of self-esteem (as a case in point), his or her sense of being and meaning in life seemed to be intimately anchored with a particular group or groups. The clinicians were perplexed by the implication of the PI/RGO studies that seemed to suggest that social anchorage and a sense of connectedness was not a common dynamic of Black people and, by inference, an unnecessary element in the general human condition. Clinicians and empiricists differ in the way they operationalize the term *group identity* (RGO). In clinical settings, the subject's RGO is the object of discovery; like an anthropologist, the clinician can only come to know a specific person's RGO through an analysis of that person's phenomenological worldview. We can refer to a person's self-defined RGO as the personal RGO. In the experimental setting, RGO becomes an imposed rather than self-defined entity, ascribed by the experimenter (ascriptive RGO). Although race may be salient as an ascriptive RGO, it need not be the most salient dimension of a Black person's personal RGO. Some Blacks make religion, sexual preference, class or economic social status, or being American more salient than race. Thus it is not the case that they have a low or negative identity when they attribute little salience to Blackness; they simply downplay (note, not hate, but downplay) their dominant ascriptive identity. In effect, it may be the case that everyone does need a group or groups to relate to in order to experience meaningful existence, but such a group need not be that to which one would usually be ascribed. In a multiracial, polyethnic, multireligious, class-based materialistic society such as the United States, even oppressed groups will find alternatives to making their ascriptive group more salient to their RGO, including the affirmation, "I am simply an American and a human being, not a Negro."

However, an outgroup perspective (RGO) may measure the extent to which the worldview of the mainstream group has been internalized by a member of a minority group. Because many problems faced by Blacks require sustained collective action, the Black community depends on the probability that Black people will make their racial-cultural heritage (ascriptive racial identity) highly salient to their personal RGO, in which case personal RGO and ascriptive RGO are fused. Although the individual Black person could find meaning in life through activities with other than Black people, the political and cultural needs and problems of the Black community require that a critical mass of Black people strongly identify with Black people and Black culture. Thus ascriptive RGO does not predict personal happiness or PI, but it does predict the extent to which a person, neurotic or otherwise, will join in collective struggle.

Identity in Black Adults
and the Effects of Nigrescence

The positive and relatively stable nature of the PI sector of the Negro self-concept helps us better to understand, psychologically speaking, the multitude of accomplishments and heroics that dot the Black experience throughout Black history, a task never seriously approached by the traditional-pejorative theorists. At the group identity level, however, the storyline has been different. The sense of heritage and race consciousness that embraced the Black community during the Garvey Movement and the Harlem Renaissance began to fade through the Depression, was suppressed during McCarthyism, and was considered antithetical to the assimilationist and integration themes of the civil rights movement. Thus the "Negro" was seen as a deracinated person concerned with the stigma, not the heritage, associated with his ascriptive identity and was preoccupied with the development of a reference-group orientation and worldview that would make him or her acceptable to Whites on terms dictated by Whites. Such a person was probably not in need of change at the level of general personality, but under the circumstances of the nigrescence thrust, may have felt compelled to make his or her group identity more nationalistic. Neither the "Negro" nor (new) "Black" identity should be viewed in either/or terms, for both perspectives reflect a decidedly dual reference-group orientation. Each identity involves a different approach to bicultural competence (a point to be taken up more fully in the next section), for both are ways to navigate existence in a world that is Black and White. The "Negro" was often perplexed, if not shamed, by ethnicity and enchanted with the White world. On the other hand, a person with a Black identity sought to negotiate a concept of success that, where appropriate, allowed for the affirmation of ethnicity rather than its denigration, repression, or denial. As we look down the road, we can predict that many of the future generations of Blacks will find greater opportunities accompanied by a muted concern for ethnicity. By opportunity is meant, in part, that one's ascriptive identity will not inhibit the recognition and reward of merit. However, success for a minority group member through merit generally sets the stage for diminished ethnicity. Ironically, the Negro will come again, and he or she will be a spokesperson for the political right. But that's another story.

Finally, any plausible theory on minority-identity development should be capable of distinguishing between the psychological consequences of oppression and the psychological triumphs of an oppressed group. The exploitation of a minority group does not presuppose the dehumanization of that group. If an oppressor can control the reference group orientation of a minority, it does not matter that the exploited group has members who, individually speaking, present healthy profiles on various measures of personal identity (PI). In the early 1950s the

Negro community turned its back on Paul Robeson and W. E. B. DuBois, not out of a sense of personal self-hatred, but rather because their White-oriented worldview dictated that certain kinds of Negroes should be condemned and others, like Booker T. Washington, deified. That today such figures as DuBois, Robeson, Garvey, and Malcolm X, as well as Washington, are held in considerable esteem is hardly a symptom of personality change, but it most certainly reflects a dramatic reorganization of the reference groups to which the worldview of many Blacks is anchored.

PI and RGO: Implications for Studies with Children

The distinctions being made here about the structure and dynamics of Black identity in adults appear to be applicable to children as well. PI studies with children conducted before nigrescence (see Taylor, 1976) and after nigrescence (Cross, 1980; Gordon, 1980) show Black children with normal and healthy PI characteristics, and for the same time period, RGO studies show children shifting from an outgroup to ingroup orientation (Gordon, 1980), even when Banks's (1976) conservative method for analyzing racial preferences is incorporated (Cross, 1980). Furthermore, the handful of PI/RGO correlational studies involving children provide little support, with one exception (Ward & Braun, 1972), that PI and RGO are correlated in a positive linear fashion (McAdoo, 1977; Porter, 1971; Spencer, 1977; Storm, 1971).

PI Studies with Black Children

The tendency of Black children and adults to score within the normal range in studies employing various PI devices might suggest, at first glance, that minority status has little if any effect on the PI domain of Black self-concept. This issue was recently addressed by a panel of experts on child development that was called together by national officials for Head Start.

The panel, which included experts on Black, Asian, Mexican, and American Indian family life, found that minority status does not result in automatic inferiorization; on the contrary, it appears that young minority children enter school with a strong and positive global self-concept (Median, 1980). However, the stigma of racism, ethnocentrism, and poverty may negatively effect the ability of underclass minority children to refine their global self-concept through incorporation of a "self-as-student" or "self-as-learner" component that facilitates successful performance in traditional middle-class academic contexts. In this light, minority performance on global PI measures may not predict role-specific performance, and likewise, minority performance on context specific PI measures may give limited insight into global functioning. Perhaps, a well-planned research program that combines general global PI measures with context specific PI measures will produce results that do not support a pejorative or romantic view of Black children, but rather yield a highly differentiated, complex, and realistic picture that juxtaposes strengths and vulnerabilities.

RGO Studies with Black Children

RGO measures are another matter. First, in studies of children's racial identity, we are not attempting to determine what is the child's personally defined RGO; we are instead assessing the orientation the children hold toward one of their ascriptive characteristics. We are not asking, "Do the children like themselves?" Rather, we are asking, "How salient are children's racial ascriptive identities to their worldview?" In very young children we are measuring the ontogeny of ascriptive RGO, and with older subjects, the function and structure of a fully developed ascriptive RGO.

Interpretation of ascriptive RGO patterns in children should be approached with caution (Alejandro-Wright, 1980; Semaj, 1979). When Black children show preference for White, it does not follow that they "hate" Black or that they want to be "White," unless being White is taken in the following way. In young (normal) children the liquidity of their ego allows for some very interesting transformational fantasies which, if found operative in adults, might define psychosis. When children like something, they often play at being it. Thus in their own minds they can "become" a lion, a tiger, or an airplane. Why should we become alarmed when a Black child expresses an attraction to the White world by playing White? (In the days before nigrescence, little Black girls would sometimes attach a scarf to their hair so that the scarf would "flow in the wind" as they walked or ran to mimic the "flowing hair" of a White girl; down the street, of course, a White child of the same age might be playing "Superman" by wearing a cape around his neck.) As the Black child gets older, the preferences are expressed more and more as malleable traits (style of dress, manner of speech, hobbies, and so on) and less and less as a physical transformation fantasy (dreaming of actually turning into a White person). At adulthood, the preference for White is essentially a perspective on life that may be demonstrated by various traits, manners, and attitudes (Shibutani, 1955).

But before placing too much emphasis on ways to interpret White preferences held by Blacks, we should be reminded that monadic Black or White racial preference trends have not been a consistent finding with Black children (Banks, 1976). In point of fact, a monadic trend should probably have never been predicted as an outcome for Black children. In a recent study (Cross, 1983) involving the content analysis of common-place parent-child activities conducted in the homes of Black and White families with young children, a White-oriented monocultural frame was found in most White homes; however, in Black homes a dual cultural (that is, Black and White) perspective was recorded. Implicitly or explicitly, the Black families seemed to be stressing the development of bicultural competence in their children. At the conclusion of the study, Cross noted,

> If we were to use the information generated by this study to predict racial preference patterns in Black and White children, it would be reasonable to assume that the two groups of children would "play back" reality in a manner similar to the way reality has been presented to them. A categorical same-race preference would be predicted for Whites as a group, and a "split" or dualistic pattern for Blacks as a group. Such patterns would probably have little to say about the level of "self-esteem" characteristic of either group, but a great deal to say about the ontogeny of a White-oriented mono-racial reference group orientation in Whites, and a bi-racial reference group orientation or bicultural competence in Blacks.

When measuring ascriptive RGO in Black children, the dependent measure should make it easy to uncover either a monadic or dualistic tendency, a point emphasized in a recent exploratory study by Johnson (1983). Employing a very popular racial preference measure, Johnson found that comparing the aggregate scores of Black and White children was misleading. More revealing was the ratio of Black to White preferences made to positively worded forced-choice items. The White children in her sample tended to select White, resulting in a monadic White preference set. Black children, on the other hand, tended to show a split pattern, indicating a preference for both Black and White. Thus in scoring only for the "same race" pattern, the device was stacked against the Black child who tended to be bicultural. The Black child's lower aggregate score was not a function of same race rejection; rather it resulted from an attraction to both choices. The problem in such experiments is to stop requiring a monadic pattern in minority children when we know their parents are raising them to be appreciative of and sensitive to the majority as well as the minority worlds.

Assessing the Effects of Interventions with Black Children

The confusion over PI and RGO as explicated in this chapter suggests the need for a better match between what is manipulated and what is measured. Researchers manipulate RGO factors such as the amount of exposure to Black heritage information, in order to assess the consequences of various interventions. They are surprised when their measure of self-esteem (a PI variable) fails to differentiate control subjects from experimental subjects. In other interventions, the RGO manipulation is correctly assessed with an RGO outcome measure but the researcher discusses the results "as if" both the PI and RGO sectors had been the subject of inquiry. The points being made here were amplified in the results of a recent dissertation (Carter, 1974). The control and experimental groups (all Blacks) were exposed to various small group discussions, one of which had an explicit Black heritage focus and the other presented race-neutral information. Subjects kept a diary over the period of the small group discussions; after the interventions, the diaries were analyzed for certain types of entries. The two groups could not be differentiated by the overall number of positive references to self that were not related to being Black; however, students exposed to the Black sessions made more entries in their diaries that were "positive self-references about being Black" than did controls. In other words, both had high levels of personal self-esteem but the experimental group ended the sessions with an enhanced ascriptive identity. Had the experimenter measured only one variable, the results might have gone unmeasured or been misinterpreted.

The same issues arise in studies of Black children who have been adopted by White parents. Recent investigations generally have reported few differences on personality outcomes between such children and cohorts raised in Black homes (McRoy, 1981; Shireman & Johnson,

1980). Once the differences between PI and RGO are really understood, why should one predict that the self-esteem or general personality of Black children raised in White homes will be less positive or psychologically healthy than cohorts raised in Black homes? A more plausible prediction is that the value system, salience of race, and worldview of the two groups of children will differ, with greater differentiation likely with increasing age of the child. Black children raised by White parents are no more or less likely to be psychologically healthy than children raised by Blacks, but the evolving frame of reference of the two groups of children may well differ. In a similar fashion, no one should really be surprised that White Americans can adopt and raise healthy children from Vietnam who differ in worldview from healthy Vietnamese children raised in America by Vietnamese parents.

The price of assimilation for members of a given group is not necessarily "poor mental health," but rather the development of a worldview that can frequently inhibit one's knowledge about, and one's capacity to advocate, political and cultural interests that flow from the frame of reference of the non-assimilated members of that group. With the rising influence of minority group members who are assimilated and right-wing oriented but otherwise "normal" in their behavior, it is important that we make ourselves keenly aware of the PI and RGO distinctions. One of the ultimate values of differentiating PI from RGO is that change in RGO, whether toward assimilation or increased ethnicity, can be comprehended without resorting to either pejorative psychological models that inevitably fail to predict the healthy behavior of the assimilated or romantic "ethnicity" models that imply that through an increase in one's ethnic awareness all of one's problems can be solved.

7

Ethnic Labeling and Identity
Among Mexican Americans

RAYMOND BURIEL

For more than a century the Mexican-descent population in the United States has defied categorization by a single convenient ethnic label. Currently, members of this group express their ethnic identity using one or more of several labels, such as Mexican, Mexicano, Mexican American, and Chicano, just to name a few. To uninformed outgroup members this seeming plethora of ethnic labels may suggest intragroup confusion and uncertainty over an appropriate ethnic identity or even self-identity. Indeed, the term *identity crisis* is frequently used by social scientists to describe the psychodynamics of Mexican-descent persons living in this country (for example, see Derbyshire, 1968). However, to ingroup members, the multitude of labels represent situation-specific identities that permit them to maintain ethnic pride and personal self-worth in the face of varying degrees of Euro-American prejudice.

Ethnicity refers to an individual's membership in a group sharing a common ancestral heritage. This ancestral heritage is multidimensional in nature and involves the biological, cultural, social, and psychological domains of life (Barth, 1969). The psychological dimension of ethnicity is perhaps the most important because, regardless of variations in the biological, cultural, and social domains, if a person self-identifies as a member of a particular ethnic group, then he or she is willing to be perceived and treated as a member of that group. Self-ascribed and other-ascribed ethnic labels are the overt manifestation of individuals' identification with a particular ethnic group.

The Mexican-descent population represents a distinct ethnic group. Biologically, they are predominantly *Mestizo*, which means they are a genetic mixture of European Spanish and New World Indian. This genetic mestizoization (Ramirez, 1983) expresses itself phenotypically in a variety of ways (skin color, facial structure, hair, and so on), which serves to make most members of the Mexican-descent population physically distinguishable from other ethnic groups. As a culture-bearing unit, the Mexican-descent ethnic group is characterized by a fundamental set of values that include a strong sense of familism, personalismo, hierarchical family roles, and adherence to Mexican Catholic ideology (Ramirez & Castaneda, 1974). The common ancestral background and values of the Mexican-descent population imply that many members of this ethnic group share similar behavioral expectations. These shared expectations encourage communication and interaction with fellow members who are "playing the same game." The use of Spanish further sharpens the social boundary that defines this ethnic group.

Historical Antecedents

The Mexican-descent population is spread across two nations, Mexico and the United States. Within the geographical boundaries of contemporary Mexico, the word *Mexicano* defines the preferred ethnic identity of the overwhelming majority of the Mestizo people of that nation. Within the United States, however, there exists a wide variety of kindred labels that describe the ethnic identity of the Mexican-descent population of this country. The glaring disparity between a single ethnic label in Mexico and a multitude of labels in the United States is the result of historical circumstances having to do with Euro-American prejudice and discrimination against Native American and Mestizo peoples.

The Spanish and English New World colonists both subscribed to the racist doctrine of "White superiority" that they used to justify the conquest and exploitation of Native American peoples (Stoddard, 1973). In Mexico, Spanish conquistadores overthrew the Aztec empire and subjugated the indigenous peoples by imposing a stratified society based on racial purity. At the top of this Society of Castes (Morner, 1967) were the Spanish born in Spain (peninsular) and the Spanish born in the New World (creole). Below them were an assortment of racially mixed groups. During the period of conquest and colonization, Spanish males routinely kept Indian concubines, which resulted eventually in a large Mestizo population. By the year 1800, Mestizos outnumbered the Spanish and by the turn of the 20th century they were the numerically dominant group in Mexico. The ascension of Mestizos into sociopolitical prominence in Mexico began with the War of Independence in 1810 and was completed with the Mexican Revolution in 1910. As the dominant ethnic group in Mexico, Mestizos claimed neither an exclusively Spanish nor Indian identity, but instead chose a unique *Mexicano* identity.

In North America, European colonists and their descendents maintained their racial purity by excluding Native American Indians altogether from their racial system. They accomplished this through a systematic process of annihilation and forced relocation of Native American Indian tribes. In time, the Indian population was greatly diminished and the Euro-American population increased dramatically.

The westward expansion of the Euro-American population in the early nineteenth century led to conflict with the Spanish and Mexican settlements in Texas, California, and New Mexico. Initially, the Mexican inhabitants of Texas admitted Euro-American settlers, who were mostly southerners, on the condition that they convert to Catholicism and give up slavery. However, by 1834 Mexicans were greatly outnumbered by Euro-Americans (McWilliams, 1968). In the aftermath of the Mexican American War, Mexico lost most of the territories that are today the southwestern United States, and the Mexican residents of these annexed territories became United States citizens by default. Unfortunately, the hostilities of the previous years continued to poison relations between Euro-Americans and the new United States citizens of Mexican descent. In Texas, local ordinances were passed declaring that the "continuance of the greaser or peon Mexican as citizens among us [Euro-Americans] is an intolerable nuisance and a grievance which calls loudly for redress" (cited in McWilliams, 1968, p. 106). The Texas Rangers and other vigilante groups also terrorized the Mexican-descent population with impunity. In Texas, therefore, the word *Mexican* took on the connotation of a racial slur paralleling the use of the word *nigger* in the South.

The dark historical legacy associated with the word *Mexican* in Texas encouraged the adoption of more prejudicially immune labels to express one's Mexican ethnic identity. These labels recognized the Mestizo origins of the group and avoided any direct mention of the word

Mexican. Among the most popular of these terms to evolve from Texas are the labels *Latin* and *Latin American.*

After the Mexican American War, the Spanish and Mexican residents of California and New Mexico became victims of a fraudulent Euro-American legal system that stripped them of their lands and possessions. The takeover of lands was aided frequently by intermarriages between Euro-American males and the daughters of Spanish land barons. Such marriages were permissible within the norms of the Spanish colonial social system because both parties were of "pure" European extraction. In reality, though, most "Spanish" families in California and New Mexico were extensively mixed with either Mexicans or the indigenous Indian populations of the region. The physical features of many so-called Spanish thus revealed a distinctively Mestizo origin. This made it possible for some Mestizos to "pass" as Spanish and enraged those of pure Spanish descent to the point that they stressed their Spanish ancestry even more in order to differentiate themselves from Mexicans in the eyes of the race-conscious Euro-Americans. As a result, ethnic labels that made reference to an exclusive Spanish ancestry became popular in California and New Mexico. Such labels include *Spanish* and *Spanish American.*

Today, the Mexican-descent population in the Southwest numbers over 8 million people. Of these, only a handful are descendents of the original Spanish and Mexican colonists. The overwhelming majority are descendents of twentieth-century Mexican immigrants who began pouring into this country after 1910, the year of the Mexican Revolution. These waves of Mexican immigrants (estimated at nearly 1 million between 1910 and 1930) numerically overshadowed the indigenous Spanish and Mexican groups and infused the Southwest with their distinctively Mexican way of life.

Mexican immigration took place primarily in the states of California and Texas. The desire to return to Mexico, which was pervasive among these immigrants, helped keep alive a Mexican identity and encouraged its inculcation in the second generation. The second generation, however, expressed a cultural identity that revealed a greater psychological loyalty to the United States. In Texas, the second generation tended to adopt the ethnic identity of the indigenous Mexican-descent population. Thus the children of "Mexicano" parents tended to call themselves Latin or Latin American in order to help blunt the sharp sting of anti-Mexican prejudice in that state. In California, where prejudice against Mexicans is less intense, the second generation adopted either a Mexican or Mexican American ethnic identity. Because Mexican immigration generally bypassed New Mexico, the Mexican-descent population of that state continued to call itself Spanish or Spanish American.

One may wonder why the Mexican-descent population did not just drop any reference to its Mexican ancestry and call itself "American" like the rest of the Euro-American population. The reality was, and still is, that it could not. Unlike most immigrant groups from European countries who could blend in physically with the prevailing Euro-American population in the United States, the Mestizo features of the Mexican-descent population marked it as a highly visible outgroup. To Euro-Americans, members of this Mestizo outgroup were all the same—"Mexican."

World War II was a turning point in the development of the ethnic consciousness of the Mexican-descent population. After serving in the armed forces and suffering a disproportionately high number of casualties, the Mexican-descent population claimed a greater psychological stake in United States society. They had proven to Euro-Americans (and themselves) that they were loyal Americans. (A similar situation occurred with the Japanese Nisei.) Out of this paradox grew a generalized pride in being both Mexican and American. Not surprisingly therefore the term *Mexican American* became an increasingly popular ethnic label among members of the second and third generation throughout the Southwest.

After World War II the Mexican-descent population seemed to follow a pattern of cultural accommodation to United States society, as the postwar economic boom raised the standard of living of all groups in society. By the mid 1960s, however, there was a growing realization that the group's economic gains were only relative; persons of Mexican descent were still at the bottom of the socioeconomic ladder. Also, acculturation had not removed the barriers of residential, educational, and occupational segregation, nor had it opened the avenues to fair political representation. These frustrations exploded in loud social protest in the form of the *Chicano movement* which was a part of the larger civil rights movement of the late 1960s and early 1970s.

The word *Chicano* has always been part of the slang vocabulary of the Spanish-speaking peoples of Mexico and the Southwestern United States. Although the word's origin is unclear, it was generally used by persons of Mexican descent as a somewhat disparaging nickname for persons of their own group, especially someone occupying a socially subordinate status. The civil rights movement in general, and the Black movement in particular, made several persons of Mexican descent aware of myriad social injustices that beset their group and of the need to resolve them. These persons called themselves Chicanos in order to draw attention to their group's plight. By so doing they seemed to be telling the rest of the Mexican-descent population that *we are all Chicanos,* that is, members of a socially subordinate class of United States citizens. Conservatives within the community who were reluctant to admit to their group's oppressed condition eagerly made a distinction between themselves (Mexican Americans, Spanish Americans, and so on) and Chicanos. This distinction only served to heighten the public's awareness of the word *Chicano* and of the ideals it represented. As the civil rights movement gained momentum and began to effect social change, the legitimacy of the Chicano movement seemed substantiated. According to at least one source (Meier & Rivera, 1981), the word *Chicano* "signifies a proud, militant ethnicity with connotations of self-determination, rejecting accommodation and assimilation, and favoring confrontation strategies" (p. 84).

In the wake of the Chicano movement many persons of Mexican descent, especially those under 30, began using *Chicano* as their preferred ethnic label. However, it never surpassed the term *Mexican American* in popularity. In recent years the word *Chicano* has taken on some of its original dark meaning. Thus unless it is used to refer to community activists or university students and professors active in Chicano studies programs, the word generally carries a disparaging connotation for both persons of Mexican descent and Euro-Americans (Fairchild & Cozens, 1981). Among these who do prefer to call themselves *Chicano,* the term is used more often as a political label rather than as a purely ethnic label (Sanchez, 1984). It represents a frame of mind that persons operate from whenever they are aware of the oppression faced by persons of Mexican descent.

In 1960 the United States Census Bureau estimated that there were 3.1 million persons of Mestizo origin (from Mexico, South and Central America) in the United States. By 1970 the figure nearly tripled to 9.1 million persons, despite an acknowledged undercount of persons in this group. In 1980 the number had grown to 14.6 million persons (Bureau of the Census, 1981). As the size of the Mestizo population began to receive national attention in the mid 1970s, it became necessary for demographers and government bureaucrats to find a convenient catchall label to describe this ethnically diverse group. After months of meetings in Washington, D.C., the federal government officially designated this group as *Hispanic.* Estrada, a demographer who took part in some of these meetings, described the process as follows:

I think that every term was brought forth for discussion and was basically rejected. . . . The one term that survived and was adopted was *Hispanic.* [This represents] one of the few times when the government has sat down and debated on what to call somebody and imposed that word on them. If at that time, you had gone to any Chicano gathering and said, "Will all the Hispanics stand up," there would have been confusion and questions of "Who [sic] do you mean?" (Sotomayor, 1983, p. 28)

The word *Hispanic* now appears on all goverment publications that make reference to the Mestizo population in the United States, and also has been popularized by the media and political parties and candidates seeking the "Hispanic vote." But despite its use by government agencies and several institutions in society. *Hispanic* is still less popular with the Euro-American public as an ethnic label for Mestizos than words like *Mexicano, Mexican American,* or *Spanish* (Sotomayor, 1983).

Among Mestizos, the word *Latino* is preferred over Hispanic. The word is Spanish in origin; *Hispanic* is of English origin. The word *Latino* parallels the objective meaning of the word *La Raza.* The term *La Raza,* which means new race, is a very emotionally charged word that recalls the painful process of Spanish-Indian Mestizoization surrounding the birth of the Mestizo peoples of the Americas. The strong feelings of racial pride associated with this word encourage its use more often in connection with nationalistic celebrations (for example, El Dia de la Raza or Columbus Day) rather than as a conventional ethnic label denoting the common ancestry of Mestizo peoples. A Mexicano ethnic identity therefore includes a universalistic dimension that is represented by the concept of La Raza and membership in a Latino community.

Empirical Studies of
Ethnic Labeling in Adults

The discussion of the origins of Mestizo identity provides a useful context for understanding the results of empirical studies dealing with ethnic identity and ethnic labeling. The importance of ethnic identity in relation to the total self-identity is perhaps best measured with procedures such as the Twenty Statements Test (TST; Kuhn & McPartland, 1954.) TST asks respondents to write down twenty answers to the question "Who am I?" The responses are then sorted into different conceptual categories about the self, such as gender, ethnicity, social status, and physical self. This procedure permits respondents spontaneously to generate and put into rank order those traits that are most meaningful to them. Using this procedure in a study with Blacks and persons of Mexican descent, Loomis and his associates (1966; Loomis, 1974) noted that not a single Mexican-descent respondent made any tangible reference to his or her ethnicity. By contrast, approximately 13% of the Blacks made reference to their race in one way or another.

In 1973, Gecas used a slightly modified version of the TST to study the self-identities of 335 parents and children of migrant and settled Mexican-descent families in the Yakima Valley of Washington. Gecas found that on the average, 37% of the migrants and 32.5% of the settled respondents used ethnic labels to describe themselves. The most frequent ethnic label used by both parents and children of the two residence groups was "Mexican"; the second most frequent was "Mexican-American." Together, these two ethnic labels accounted for over 80% of all the ethnic designations used by either parents or children. The only other label to appear with any appreciable frequency was "Chicano," which was mentioned by 10% of the boys.

Changes in the environment may increase the saliency of ethnicity in relation to the total self-identity and explain the discrepancy between Loomis et al.'s (1966) and Gecas's (1973) findings. In 1973, when Gecas did his research, the civil rights movement and the Chicano movement were in full swing. The emphasis on ethnic minorities reflected in both these movements probably enhanced the saliency of ethnicity in the self-identities of many persons of Mexican descent and explains the more frequent use of ethnic labeling in Gecas's study.

Correlates of Ethnic Labels
in Adult Populations

Research with adult populations indicates that socioeconomic status and geographic area of residence are the best predictors of ethnic self-designations used by persons of Mexican descent. In the Mexican-American Study Project (Grebler, Moore, & Guzman, 1970), Mexican-descent respondents from Los Angeles, California, and San Antonio, Texas, were interviewed about a variety of topics, including their preferred ethnic self-designations in both English and Spanish.

In California, respondents of all income levels preferred English-language self-designations that expressed their Mexican ancestry. Thus "Mexican" was the most popular ethnic label, followed by "Mexican American." Moreover, there was a negative relationship between preference for "Mexican" and income level, and a positive relationship between preference for "Mexican American" and income level. Texas respondents, in contrast to California respondents of both income levels, overwhelmingly chose "Latin American" as their preferred English-language designation, and "Mexican" as a distant second choice. As in California, preference for "Mexican" and income were inversely related.

Preferred Spanish-language self-designations in California closely approximated the results for preferred English self-designations. However, in Texas there was greater variability between Spanish and English responses. In particular, preference for Mexican-origin labels (Mexicano and Mexico Americano) increased in Spanish, and preference for Latin-origin terminology (Latino) decreased. The legacy of discrimination against persons of Mexican descent in Texas has created an ambivalence in some individuals about their Mexican ancestry. Thus in the public language of English, many persons of Mexican descent call themselves Latin Americans. But in the private language of Spanish, a substantial number of these same individuals boldly express their Mexican ancestry.

Garcia (1981) used the Survey of Income and Education (SIE) to study the background correlates of ethnic self-designations used by persons of Mexican descent living in the Southwest. From interviews of 150,000 households in Arizona, California, Colorado, New Mexico, and Texas, all Mexican origin persons age 14 and older were extracted for analysis, yielding a total of 5,404 respondents. The Mexican origin respondents were asked to select one of five possible labels with which they identified. The five ethnic labels and their rates of selection are as follows: Mexican-American (50.7%), Other Spanish (20.7%), Mexican (20.1%), Mexicano (4.4%), and Chicano (4.0%). It should be noted in interpreting the results that the labels "Latino" and "Latin American" were not included.

These ethnic labels were then broken down by eight sociodemographic variables: (1) metropolitan versus nonmetropolitan residence; (2) age; (3) state of residence; (4) United States born versus Mexican born; (5) sex; (6) income; (7) education; and (8) language usage. Among the more salient findings were that "Chicano" was preferred by younger respondents, and older respondents preferred "Other Spanish" and "Mexicano." "Chicano" was the most popular ethnic self-designation among respondents with a college education. Nonmetropolitan residents most often identified as "Mexicano" and "Other Spanish," whereas metropolitan residents most often preferred "Mexican." State of

residence showed a strong relationship to preferred ethnic self-designation: "Other Spanish" were predominantly from New Mexico; "Mexican"
was most prevalent in California; Texas had the highest proportion of
"Mexicanos"; and "Mexican American" was most popular in Arizona
and Texas.

Respondents with the highest incomes were those who identified as
either "Mexican American" or "Other Spanish"; the lowest income
respondents were predominantly "Mexicano." Spanish monolinguals
were predominantly "Mexicano" and "Mexican"; and bilinguals were
most often "Chicano" and "Mexican American." The most clear-cut
relationship occurred with respect to country of birth. Over 90% of
those identifying themselves as either "Mexican American," "Chicano,"
or "Other Spanish" were born in the United States. Those who self-
identified as either "Mexican" or "Mexicano" were most often born in
Mexico.

In order to control for covariation among the eight sociodemographic variables and determine their independent contribution to the
selection of ethnic labels, Garcia carried out a discriminant analysis on
the SIE data. Country of birth had the greatest discriminating power,
followed by metropolitan versus nonmetropolitan residence, state of
residence, and a combination of age and language usage.

Garcia's study indicates that geographic variables are the most potent
determinants of ethnic label preference, suggesting that, by and large,
people tend to adopt the most popular ethnic label in use in their region
of the country. The region-specific popularity of these labels is, of
course, related to the sociohistorical circumstances discussed in the first
section of this chapter.

Correlates of Ethnic Labels in Adolescents

Studies of ethnic labeling with adolescents are important because
these individuals are in the process of solidifying their self-identities,
including their ethnic self-awareness.

In 1970, Crystal City, Texas (population 10,000), was the center of
attention in the Chicano movement. In that year, a militant third-party
movement called La Raza Unida had successfully elected a slate of
candidates and gained control of a previously Euro-American dominated City Council and Board of Education. Two researchers from the
University of Texas at Austin took advantage of this situation to study
how the tumultuous changes had affected the political awareness and
ethnic identities of the Mexican-descent adolescents living in this

community. Their study (Gutierrez & Hirsch, 1973) is interesting and important despite the very limited generalizations of their findings due to the unique circumstances surrounding Crystal City and its residents.

All Mexican-descent students (n = 786) in grades 7 through 12 were administered a questionnaire measuring their perceptions of (1) opportunities for success; (2) equality before the law; and (3) the efficacy of collective action. Almost all of the students identified as either "Chicano" or "Mexican American" (49% and 47%, respectively). Analysis took the form of comparing the responses of "Chicanos" and "Mexican Americans." "Chicanos" were significantly more likely to doubt the principle of equality before the law. "Chicanos" were also more in favor of collective action, as represented by the statement "The best way to handle problems is to band together with people like yourself to help each other out."

Students also were given a triad of short story completion tasks designed to measure their perceptions of prejudice. The three stories described the same encounter in which a citizen is stopped for speeding by a policeman, except that the name of the citizen changed from story to story. The three names substituted for each other in the stories were Juan Gonzalez, John Grant, and Beulah Johnson.

When the subject in the story was Juan Gonzalez, "Chicanos" were more likely to perceive the encounter with the policeman as a case of racial discrimination. On the other hand, "Mexican Americans" were more likely to say that the policeman was only doing his job. Both "Mexican Americans" and "Chicanos" agreed that Juan Gonzalez would probably be ticketed (74% and 83%, respectively). However, when the subject was John Grant, more "Chicanos" perceived that he would get off without a ticket. Also, more "Chicanos" than "Mexican Americans" felt that the fine for a ticket would be greater for Juan Gonzalez than for John Grant. The results for Beulah Johnson were uninterpretable, because most respondents were uncertain about this person's racial background.

Gutierrez and Hirsch's (1973) findings indicate that, at least for these Crystal City youths, a "Chicano" identity is associated with a more militant and questioning attitude toward the United States system of justice, and also a greater readiness to engage in collective action for the betterment of the group. The assumption, of course, is that the Chicano movement created a favorable climate for the adoption of a "Chicano" ethnic identity. However, as the Chicano movement waned, so has the tendency for adolescents to select "Chicano" as their preferred ethnic self-referent.

In the spring of 1973, Miller (1976) studied the ethnic labeling preferences and background traits of Mexican-descent youth living in the border region of south Texas. High school sophomores from five towns (Asherton, Rio Grande City, Roma, San Isidro, and Zapata) were surveyed about their *most* preferred and *least* preferred ethnic self-referents, as well as their language usage and family's socioeconomic status. In all, 379 students were surveyed. Respondents gave "Mexican American" as their most preferred ethnic self-referent twice as often as the label "Chicano" (50% versus 25%, respectively). Interestingly, the only other labels to appear with any appreciable frequency were those that implied a denial of identification with Mexican ethnicity. Thus 13% of the respondents answered either "American" or "White" in response to the most preferred name for their ethnic group.

Overall, "Chicano" was the *least* preferred ethnic self-designation, with 43% of the respondents expressing a nonacceptance of this term. "Chicano" was disliked by over 70% of the "Mexican American" self-identifiers. However, only 15% of the "Chicano" self-identifiers rejected the label "Mexican American." Thus it seems that most "Mexican Americans" dislike "Chicano," but most "Chicanos" do not dislike "Mexican American." This is consistent with Garcia's (1981) conclusion that "Mexican American" is the most neutral ethnic label, and therefore the one that is *acceptable* to persons of Mexican descent.

Although members of both sexes preferred "Mexican American," males chose "Chicano" more often than females. In addition, females were more likely to prefer terms that denied identification with Mexican ethnicity. Ethnic denial was particularly pronounced among females in the two towns closest to the border. The proximity of the border may have made some of these young women sensitive to the possibility of being stereotypically compared to women in Mexico.

The effects of socioeconomic status and language usage on labeling preferences were examined separately for each sex. The results for SES showed a relationship only for males. Among low SES males, preference for "Chicano" was about twice as great as it was for high SES males. In addition, ethnic denial labels were popular among high SES males. In these very traditional border towns, where sex roles are often very clearly defined (Ramirez & Castaneda, 1974), males may be more sensitive to the effects of SES on labeling because the expectation is that they will be the primary wage earners who will determine the income status of the family. In general, language usage failed to predict reliably ethnic labeling preferences.

A wide-ranging study by Lampe (1975, 1977, 1978) examined the relationship of demographic and social psychological variables to the selection of ethnic self-designations. Lampe surveyed 699 Mexican-descent eighth graders attending 19 public and parochial schools in San Antonio, Texas. Respondents answered questions dealing with their family SES, their positive and negative prejudice toward several groups, including their own, their degree of Anglo conformity assimilation, and their preferred ethnic designation from among "American," "Mexican American," "Spanish American," "Chicano," and "Latin American."

Students in both school systems selected "Mexican American" (59% overall) as their most preferred self-referent; "American" (22% overall) and "Chicano" (13% overall) were the second and third most popular choices, respectively. All other self-designations were chosen less than 5% of the time by students in either public or parochial school (Lampe, 1977). Despite the similar rank ordering of labels in both school systems, a significantly greater proportion of public school students preferred calling themselves "Chicano" than students in parochial schools. Also, males overall were more likely to select "Chicano," and females were more inclined to select "Mexican American." In contrast to previous research, SES was not significantly related to ethnic labeling. This was due in part to the fact that a preponderance of students of both school systems came from working-class backgrounds, but only a minority were of middle-class standing.

In order to measure positive prejudice, students were instructed to rank in order of preference the following ethnic groups: Anglo, Mexican American, Jew, Negro and Oriental. Results showed that all Mexican American students, regardless of what they called themselves, preferred their own ethnic group over all others. With the exception of working-class students calling themselves "Chicano," all other respondents chose "Anglo" as their second most preferred choice, followed by "Negro." Working-class "Chicanos," on the other hand, favored "Negro" over "Anglo," and thus, according to Lampe (1975), expressed the greatest anti-Anglo prejudice of any category of respondents. All categories of respondents preferred Orientals and Jews less than Anglos. However, we cannot conclude from these findings that the pattern of prejudice exhibited by students of Mexican descent is unique to them, because the prejudices of other ethnic groups were not measured in this study.

Lampe (1978) used Milton Gordon's (1964) 7-point model of assimilation to measure differences in assimilation among respondents who self-identified as either "Mexican American," "American," or "Chicano." Results showed that "American" respondents were more assimilated than "Mexican American" respondents on 6 of the 7 comparisons; the two groups were similar only in terms of their perceived discrimination. Respondents who self-identified as "Chicanos," as compared to Mexican American respondents, were less identified with America and Americans, perceived greater discrimination, and had fewer friendships and acquaintances outside their ethnic group. From these findings, Lampe (1978) concluded that "Chicanos" were the least assimilated of the 3 groups of respondents. However, Lampe also stated that Gordon's model of assimilation is based primarily on the notion of "Anglo conformity," which means that an Anglo-American lifestyle is used as the conceptual yardstick for measuring the degree of assimilation. He noted that if the model of assimilation would change to one of "cultural pluralism," "Chicanos" and "Mexican Americans" might be more "assimilated" than their "American" counterparts.

In summary, Lampe's research (1975, 1977, 1978) indicates that, at least among adolescents living in San Antonio, Texas, the label "Chicano" is (1) less popular than either "Mexican American" or "American"; (2) more often used by public school students than parochial school students; (3) used more by persons who perceive greater discrimination against themselves and their ethnic group; and (4) used by persons who are less assimilated, according to an Anglo Conformity model of assimilation.

Generational Status, Labeling, and Acculturation in Children

Acculturation refers to "changes in cultural patterns to those of the host society" (Gordon, 1978, p. 169), and is often spoken of in terms of cultural identity. An assumption among many researchers is that identity with Mexican American culture decreases in Mexican-descent immigrants from one generation to the next. It is likewise assumed that a decrease in Mexican American cultural identity is synonymous with increasing acculturation to Anglo-American culture. Thus generational status is likely to be an important variable both in acculturation and in self-labeling. A number of studies have addressed these issues.

In 1982, Lamare examined the ethnic self-reference of Texas children in relation to their generational status. He surveyed 550 Mexican-descent children, ages 9 to 14, living in El Paso, Texas. Family background data were used to classify respondents into 1 of 5 generational groups: (1) newcomers: children, parents, and grandparents born in Mexico; (2) first generation: children born in the United States, parents and grandparents born in Mexico; (3) mixed generation: children and one parent born in the United States, other parent and grandparents born in Mexico; (4) second generation: children and both parents born in the United States, grandparents born in Mexico; and (5) third generation: children, parents and grandparents born in the United States.

In addition, all respondents were asked to label themselves as either "Mexican," "Mexican American," "Chicano," or "American." Results show that "Mexican" is the most popular label only among members of the newcomer generation, and that after the first generation, it is the least preferred ethnic self-designation. Between the newcomer and mixed generation, there is an increase in preference for "Mexican American." Preference for this label remains about the same into the second generation, but thereafter declines in the third generation. Selection of "American" follows a somewhat similar pattern as "Mexican American." Thus its popularity increases steadily up to the second generation, but thereafter declines in the third generation. The label "Chicano" shows the most unusual pattern of selection. Initially, "Chicano" is the second most preferred label in the newcomer generation, and the overall most popular label in the first generation. Thereafter, it declines in popularity across the mixed and second generations, but then increases again in the third generation, when it is about as equally popular as the label "American."

In the second generation where parentage is exclusively United States born, popularity for American referent labels—"American" and "Mexican American"—is greater than preference for either "Chicano" or "Mexican." The increase in the popularity of "Chicano" in the third generation may represent the effects of *deculturation* (Berry, 1980; Buriel, 1984). Respondents in the third generation whose families have not been upwardly mobile may feel disillusioned with the American system, and therefore reject an American referent identity.

Unreported data from two published studies (Buriel, Calzada, & Vasquez, 1982; Buriel & Vasquez, 1982), as well as from one unpublished study (Buriel & Vasquez, 1983), reveal a strong association between generational status and the preferred ethnic labels of Mexican-descent youth in California. Respondents in all three studies were high school students drawn from mandatory English classes in the greater Los Angeles area of Southern California.

The first study was concerned primarily with examining the stereotypes of three generations of Mexican-descent adolescents toward members of their own ethnic group (Buriel & Vasquez, 1982). Respondents were 90 Mexican-origin youths drawn equally from 3 subpopulations: first generation (respondent and both parents born in Mexico); second generation (respondent born in the United States, but one or both parents born in Mexico); and third generation (respondent and both parents born in the United States). There were equal numbers of males and females in each generation group.

In addition to measuring respondents' attitudes toward members of their own ethnic group, they were asked to select their preferred self-referent. With the exception of two males who called themselves "Mexican-American," members of the first generation unanimously preferred the label "Mexican." Preference for "Mexican" in the first generation is consistent with Lamare's (1982) findings in Texas.

An abrupt change in ethnic labeling takes place after the first generation. Preference for the "Mexican" label fades almost completely in the second generation and is altogether absent as a preferred self-referent in the third generation. "Mexican American" is the preferred self-referent for both the second and third generations. Also, preference for "Chicano" appears initially in the second generation and by the third generation represents the preferred self-referent of nearly one quarter of this subsample. Preference for the label "Spanish American" is virtually nonexistent.

Unlike Lamare's (1982) study in Texas, the present investigation did not use "American" in the list of preferred self-referents. It is therefore possible that some respondents who chose "Mexican American" would have selected "American" if given the opportunity. It must be noted, though, that the label "Anglo-American" was included in the list primarily for the benefit of Euro-American students, and that none of the Mexican descent respondents chose this self-referent.

An unpublished study by Buriel and Vasquez (1983) obtained similar results. Respondents in this study were 96 adolescents, ages 15 to 17, who were drawn equally from four populations: first-, second-, and third-generation Mexican descent, and Euro-Americans, divided equally by sex. Pictorial stimuli were used to elicit and measure respondents' ethnic group preferences. Respondents also were asked to self-identify with one of the following labels: "Mexican," "Mexican American," "Chicano," "Latino," "Spanish American," and "Anglo-American." Consistent with Buriel and Vasquez's (1982) previous findings, all Euro-American students chose the label "Anglo-American," and all Mexican-descent students self-identified with one of the remaining self-referents.

The results show an overwhelming preference for "Mexican" in the first generation, followed by a virtual disappearance of this label in the second and third generations, where "Mexican American" is now the preferred self-referent. The label "Chicano" is a distant second choice for members of the second or third generation, while preference for either "Latino" or "Spanish American" is practically absent. In addition, there are no sex differences. A third study by Buriel and his associates (1982) also found a similarly strong relationship between labeling and generational status.

As part of the previously mentioned study on ethnic stereotypes, Buriel and Vasquez (1982) measured the Spanish language proficiency of all Mexican-descent students, because Spanish proficiency generally is considered to be an indication of involvement with Mexican culture. First-generation respondents had the highest Spanish proficiency scores, followed by second- and third-generation respondents, in that order. Only the difference between first- and second-generation respondents failed to reach statistical significance. Relating these results to the findings for labeling showed that the choice of an ethnic self-referent was not affected by Spanish proficiency. Thus even though first-generation respondents call themselves "Mexican," they were not significantly more Spanish proficient than their second-generation counterparts who prefer the label "Mexican American." Also, third-generation respondents are significantly less Spanish proficient than second-generation respondents, yet both groups prefer calling themselves "Mexican American." Similar results were obtained in the previously mentioned study by Buriel et al. (1982). Third-generation respondents continued to express a "Mexican American" identity despite their relatively poor Spanish language proficiency.

If Spanish proficiency is a valid index of involvement with Mexican American culture, then these results indicate that individuals may continue to express a Mexican origin ethnic identity despite a lack of integration with their group's ancestral culture. This implies that culture and ethnic identity should be treated as separate conceptual categories. This line of reasoning is consistent with the position of Barth (1969), who noted that if a person self-identifies as a member of a particular ethnic group, then he or she is willing to be perceived and treated as a member of that group. That the person may be ignorant of the prominent cultural and social manifestations of the group is irrelevant. Even at the biological level, a similar situation can occur, for example when Euro-Americans growing up in a predominantly Mexican-descent peer group take on the ethnic identity of that group. This was exemplified in the play *Zoot Suit*, when Tommy Roberts, a Euro-

American who grew up with the pachucos in East Los Angeles, asserted that *he* was "Chicano."

The relationship between generational status and acculturation was further explored in another unpublished study by Buriel. The subjects were 80 second- and third-graders between 7 and 9 years old. Subjects were drawn from four populations: first-, second-, and third-generation Mexican Americans, and Anglo-Americans. All subjects were enrolled at the same suburban elementary school in Southern California and were participants in the school's bilingual/bicultural Follow Through Program. The proportion of Anglo-American and Mexican American students in each classroom was approximately 25% and 75%, respectively. Instruction in the Follow Through Program is in both English and Spanish for all children. In addition, children are provided with a variety of bicultural learning experiences that encourage sensitivity to both Anglo-American and Mexican American cultures. All teachers in the program are fluent bilinguals.

Generational status was defined as in the previous study. Measures of children's acculturation were obtained from teacher ratings using the Bicultural Identity/Respect for Cultural Differences Scale (Ramirez & Castaneda, 1974). The first section of the scale measures four areas of behavior and language usage characteristics of identity with Mexican American culture; the second section of the scale measures three areas of behavior and language characteristics of identity with Anglo-American culture.

Results show first generation subjects to be more closely identified with Mexican American culture than all three remaining groups. There are no significant differences between second- and third-generation subjects, nor between Anglo-American and third-generation children in their identification with Mexican American culture. In terms of identity with Anglo-American culture, first-generation subjects scored significantly lower than all three remaining groups. There is no significant difference between second- and third-generation subjects, nor between either of these two groups and Anglo-American children. Thus although identity with Mexican American culture decreases significantly between the first and second generations, both groups express a stronger identity with their ancestral culture than Anglo-American children. Only third-generation children do not differ from Anglo-American children in their identity with Mexican American culture.

However, there was no support for the assumption that Mexican Americans discard their ancestral culture when acculturating to Anglo-

American society. Support for this assumption depends on a negative correlation between the subjects' Mexican American and Anglo-American identity ratings. But, with the exception of the third generation, all correlations were positive. Thus among members of the first and second generations (and Anglo-Americans as well), individuals who were most identified with Mexican American culture were also most identified with Anglo-American culture. Moreover, although third-generation children as a *group* were least identified with Mexican American culture, and most identified with Anglo-American culture, as *individuals* they did not exhibit an inverse relationship between the two cultures. Instead, there was a near zero correlation for members of this group.

In summary, results of the studies cited suggest that generational status of Mexican-descent children and adolescents is an important factor both in self-labeling and in acculturation. However, in spite of the increasing use of the label "Mexican American" and the increasing identification with Anglo-American culture, these individuals do not lose their identity as a distinctive ethnic group in the United States.

Conclusion

Persons of Mexican descent in the United States have historically been treated as a less privileged minority. Their treatment as a minority group, combined with feelings of pride for their culture of origin, has led to mixed feelings about what they prefer to be called and the culture with which they prefer to identify. Although Euro-American immigrants (for example, Irish Americans, Polish Americans) drop their dual ethnicity label by the second or third generation and call themselves simply Americans, this does not happen as readily with persons of Mexican descent. As a group, they have a distinctive appearance based on their Mestizo origin that calls attention to their non-Euro-American background. They must therefore make a conscious choice about their label and identity. Recent social movements have increased awareness of and pride in Mexican American culture. Furthermore, in geographic areas with a large Mexican American population, children from other backgrounds are adopting some aspects of this culture, such as eating the food and learning the language. It is to be hoped that with the increasing mix of ethnic groups in the population, this acceptance of both one's own as well as others' ethnic groups will continue to grow.

PART III

Later Childhood and Adolescence: Ethnic Identity and Ethnic Group Patterns

The first two sections of this book looked at ethnicity in early and middle childhood, as children learn the labels and attributes of ethnic groups, develop attitudes about them, and begin to come to terms with their own ethnic status. This third section broadens the focus to examine ethnic patterns and the meaning ethnicity acquires in older children and adolescents. The level of analysis is less often the individual child and more typically the community. The individual's relation to the group now becomes an important issue. No longer can individuals be assigned to a group on the basis of external criteria (ascribed identity); their own subjective sense of closeness to a group, and their choices of how they see themselves and how they act, are also important in determining their ethnic identity (achieved identity).

Developmental changes influence the process of defining one's own identity; adolescence brings physical, cognitive, and experiential changes that lead to exploration and decision making in many areas, among them that of ethnicity. However, choices are made within the constraints of the society, that is, the degree of support provided for ethnic activities, such as the opportunities to speak the language or read an ethnic periodical.

A number of different methodologies are represented in this section, including quantitative psychometric and self-report methods, projective videotape measures, and ethnographic methods. Each of these methods gives a somewhat different perspective on the meaning of ethnicity, including choice of activities (language, food, and so on), adoption of implicit behavior patterns or characteristic conversational styles (for example, rapping), and cultural coping styles. The groups studied are also broader in this section, including Mexican children, immigrant groups in Australia, bilingual children in Canada, and Black and Mexican American children in the United States.

The section begins with Rosenthal's examination of ethnic identity in adolescence. Rosenthal stresses the dynamic nature of ethnic identity during adolescence, as it is influenced by the development of the individual, the supports provided by the ethnic group, and the contact with other groups. A central issue at this age is the extent to which minority group adolescents experience problems as a result of conflict between their own and a dominant culture. After reviewing research on this issue, including studies of the immigrant experience in Australia, she concludes that a variety of strategies are used in dealing with living in two cultures, and that most adolescents do not suffer serious distress because of conflicting cultural norms.

An alternative method of dealing with two cultures is examined by Heller. As a sociolinguist, she focuses on the role of language in the development of ethnic identity. Language is seen as a social construct, grounded in social interaction. Only with a common language can children develop common understandings and behaviors. The focus of her chapter is an ethnographic study of native French- and English-speaking children who attend a school in which French is the official classroom language, but English is used in most peer-group activities outside of class. From observations and tape recordings of spontaneous speech at school, she presents examples of situations in which students negotiate and define their identity through their use of language. Given the tensions associated with the two contrasting languages (and identities), students who are competent in both languages use bilingual joking and code-switching (from one language to another) to maintain an equilibrium and establish a new identity that bridges the gap between two competing cultures. Through bilingual language usage such as punning two individuals who would otherwise have contrasting identities can establish a common bond.

The variations among ethnic groups in norms and behavior patterns are suggested in the chapters by Rosenthal and Heller. These differences are the explicit topic of the chapter by Rotheram and Phinney. They review existing research with children from a wide variety of cultures and suggest four dimensions on which ethnic groups have been found to differ: individual versus group oriented, active versus passive, authoritarian versus egalitarian, and expressive versus restrained. Reporting on their own work with Black and Mexican American children, they demonstrate differences in behavioral norms in a variety of everyday school situations, and show that these differences become clearer as children get older. Identification of these behavior patterns permits examination of the extent to which individual children match the norms of their own group, thus providing a measure of ethnic identity in behavioral terms.

The behavior patterns typical of a particular ethnic group are the subject of Kochman's chapter. He discusses the salient features of Black language and culture that give Blacks their identity as a distinct group; his focus is on interactional style, including behaviors such as boasting, ritual insults, and verbal dueling. He shows how Black adolescents are socialized to handle the verbal confrontations characteristic of Black speech without becoming overwhelmed by them.

In the final chapter in this section, Mexican psychologist Diaz-Guerrero shows how cultural behavior patterns are influenced by the underlying assumptions about social interactions held by members of a culture. He points out that these assumptions are influenced by economic factors and illustrates his position with research on differences between Mexican and American children. Together these chapters show the increasing impact of ethnicity on children as they mature socially and cognitively and have increasing contact with the world beyond their family and neighborhood.

8

Ethnic Identity Development in Adolescents

DOREEN A. ROSENTHAL

Achieving a sense of identity is one of the most important psychological tasks for the adolescent. The ability to know and understand oneself as an individual, as well as recognizing one's particular place in society, stems from a number of sources. These include the many social contexts that give rise to a variety of specific social identities based on, for example, gender, class, or ethnic group membership. It is the last of these that is the focus of this chapter. Although gender and class identity have important psychological and behavioral consequences for adolescent development, the impact of ethnic identity is especially relevant in societies that are heterogeneous in nature, where one or more minority groups exist alongside a dominant social group.

We shall be concerned with the nature of ethnic identity, its component elements, and with the factors influencing the salience of ethnic identity and its contribution to adolescent development. The last part of the chapter draws substantially on Australian data and deals with the link between minority group membership and adjustment or psychological well-being. Although this section focuses on the experience of immigrants, the issues raised are germane to any situation in which minority groups coexist with a dominant social group.

The Concept of Identity in Adolescence

The importance of adolescence in the human life cycle has been attested to by a burgeoning literature, academic and popular, claiming to elucidate the developmental processes and social meanings of this period. Because adolescence is a time of considerable cognitive and physical development, as well as a time when social expectations change dramatically, this particular life stage may be especially problematic, fraught with chaos and confusion. During adolescence, the ability to think beyond concrete reality to hypothetical situations evolves. Concerns with other-directed morality, with ideals and social issues, and ultimately with one's place in the world, become paramount. Coupled with these cognitive changes are physical changes, which alter the adolescent's sense of his or her own body. At the same time, the demands placed by society on these emerging adults become complex and conflicting. Expected to take adultlike responsibility for some aspects of their lives, but treated as children in other areas, it is a matter for wonder that so many adolescents appear to make the transition to adulthood without evidence of psychological dysfunction (see, for example, Coleman, 1974; Douvan & Adelson, 1966; Offer, 1969; Offer, Ostrov, & Howard, 1981).

Although various theories of adolescence deal separately with intrapsychic, cognitive, and cultural factors that influence development, Erikson has come closest to focusing simultaneously on the internal and external worlds of the adolescent. Adolescence, Erikson (1959) argues,

> can be viewed as a psychosocial moratorium during which the individual through free role experimentation may find a niche in some section of his society which is firmly defined and yet seems to be uniquely made for him. In finding it the young adult gains an assured sense of inner continuity and social sameness which will bridge what he was as a child and what he is about to become, and will reconcile his conception of himself and his community's recognition of him. (p. 111)

Erikson called this process *identity formation*. Identity is a construct that denotes "a conscious sense of individual uniqueness . . . an unconscious striving for continuity . . . [and] a solidarity with a group's ideals" (1968, p. 208). Although the development of a sense of one's identity is a never-ending process, Erikson regarded adolescence as the crucial period for identity formation, when the developmental task is to reintegrate childhood identifications with basic drives, native endowment, and opportunities offered in social roles.

Notwithstanding problems of definition and operationalization (details of which are beyond the scope of this chapter, but see, for example, Bourne, 1978a, 1978b; Harris, 1980; Marcia, 1966; Rosenthal, Gurney, & Moore, 1981), the construct of identity has great heuristic value and an intuitive "ring of truth." Part of its attraction and its difficulty is that identity formation is embedded in the context of the continuing psychosocial development of the individual. Erikson conceived of the life cycle as comprising eight separate "epigenetic" stages. The psychosocial crisis of each stage must be at least partially resolved before the individual can pass on to the next level. Once a stage has been resolved successfully, that area is integrated into the person's identity. As each of the stages is systematically related to all other stages, the way in which each is resolved is influenced by the means and effectiveness of all previous resolutions.

According to Erikson's model, throughout the life span, but particularly at adolescence, small and apparently trivial decisions or behaviors contribute to the process of identity formation, yielding a consistent core. As Bourne (1978a) notes, identity is not simply a "structural and/or experiential entity but also a type of relationship" (p. 227). In this way we are provided with external definitions of the self in terms of our relationship to and membership in certain groups in society. As a result of participation in a variety of social situations, we are provided with means of self-definition in the social context, producing a series of social identities (Tajfel, 1981). One's sense of identity, then, is synthesized from a number of social identities, such as female, sibling, parent, and student.

Evidence for the salience of particular social identities in identity formation comes primarily from the investigation of the influence of gender on identity (Douvan & Adelson, 1966; Hodgson & Fischer, 1979; Schenkel & Marcia, 1972; Waterman & Nevid, 1977). In contrast to the relative interest in the impact of gender, there is a marked dearth of studies exploring the influence of cultural background and the relationship between minority-group membership and identity formation. Erikson has dealt with this issue in general terms, most clearly in tracing patterns of child-rearing of the Sioux and Yurok (Erikson, 1963). In two studies of the psychosocial development of adolescents of different cultural backgrounds who share a common environment (Chapman & Nicholls, 1976; Tzuriel & Klein, 1977), results support the hypothesis that identity achievement is facilitated by being a member of the dominant group in a pluralist society. This hypothesis is based on the assumption that adolescents may find it difficult to integrate the different expectations held by the dominant and subgroup cultures, particularly when competing claims from family and from society present conflicting or unclear messages about appropriate behavior, values, and attitudes.

However, in a study of Anglo-Australians, Greek Australians, and Italian Australians, Rosenthal, Moore, and Taylor (1983) found that Anglo-Australian adolescents (members of the dominant societal group) showed no better resolution of the identity crisis than two groups of adolescents who were themselves or whose parents were born in Greece or Italy. One possible explanation of these different findings is that in the first two studies comparisons were made between racially distinct groups (Pakehas and Maoris, Western and Oriental Israelis). In the third study different ethnic groups, all of the same racial group, were compared. It may well be that differences between same-race ethnic groups are too subtle to emerge in measures such as global identity achievement.

The impact of cultural forces on identity development, then, appears to be complex and uncertain. Although it seems that for some, membership in particular cultural groups in society may have a deleterious effect, for others their cultural background plays a minor role. To unravel the contribution of culture to adolescent development, it may be more useful to explore the meaning of adolescents' cultural background as they strive to achieve a strong and stable sense of self.

The Origins of Ethnic Identity

One of the social categories by which individuals are defined is the ethnic group of which they are members. Ethnic group membership can be defined objectively in terms of ascribed characteristics, such as national or geographic birthplaces of individuals or their ancestors, language, religion, race or physical characteristics, history or customs. However, although people may be identified by society as members of particular groups, such external ascriptions are not necessarily consistent with the individual's subjective affiliation. For example, Doczy (1966) has demonstrated that the degree of involvement that adolescent boys feel with their ethnic group, their willingness to identify with the group or to recognize themselves as members of that group, is independent of an external measure elicited from the boys' teachers.

It is the subjective identification with an ethnic group, assimilating into one's self-concept ethnic characteristics and feelings of belonging, that leads to the development of a social identity based on ethnic group membership. Identification is implicit in Gordon's (1964) definition of the ethnic group as having a shared feeling of peoplehood, or, for Keyes (1976), a sense of shared descent. Such ingroup "communion," an unspoken but shared understanding that excludes nongroup members, is regarded by Lyman and Douglass (1973) as a defining feature of ethnicity. The invisible bonds resulting from individuals' unique experiences as members of an ethnic group unite them and separate them from others.

Consciousness of membership in an ethnic group functions to ensure cohesion by establishing a boundary around the group, separating its members from nonmembers (Ballard, 1976). For the individual, clear boundaries are necessary for an articulated sense of ethnic identity to develop (Giles & Johnson, 1981). Furthermore, as Giles and Johnson note, the nature of ethnic identity with its component myths and values is dynamic and responsive to changing conditions.

Ethnic identity involves past cultural traditions, present sociological factors (including economic conditions and social and political realities), and a psychological dimension related to early socialization (DeVos, 1980). That is, ethnic identity arises in interaction and is a function not only of the individual and his or her relation to the ethnic group but of that group's place in the wider social setting.

The strength of ethnic identity will depend on the nature of the boundaries established. Giles and Johnson (1981) describe three characteristics that contribute to the clarity of group boundaries: distinctiveness, strength, and value. Boundaries are *distinct* when members and nonmembers can be clearly identified, for example on the basis of language or physical features. Boundary *strength* reflects the pervasiveness of the group's relevance across a wide range of activities. Finally, attitudes of the group such as language or social customs may be given a positive or negative *value* by group members. Giles and Johnson conclude that when individuals can differentiate clearly between their own and other groups, a firmer and better developed sense of ethnic identity will result.

Isajiw (1974) distinguishes between internal and external boundaries. For any group there is imposed

> a double boundary, a boundary from within, maintained by the socialization process, and a boundary from without established by the process of intergroup relations. (p. 122)

The "boundary from within" arises from the primary identifications with significant others. Parents, siblings, and other family members provide a cultural context that becomes for the child a lens through which to view the world. The "correctness" of these values, their representations of objective reality, are unquestioned and become integral aspects of the child's life.

Notwithstanding the primacy of family members, the ethnic community may itself contribute directly by providing a subculture in which cultural values are legitimated. To the extent that an ethnic group can establish institutions that are central to the individual, such as school, religion, or clubs, then the social interactions of group members will take place largely within the group. Such institutional completeness (Breton, 1964) leads to a maintenance of group boundaries by enhancing the distinctiveness of the group in relation to others. The ethnic consciousness that arises from socialization experiences not only within the family but also as a member of a distinctive and strong community (the boundary from within) will be translated into an integral part of one's self-definition.

Just as the boundary from within reflects an individual's associations with his or her own ethnic group, the "boundary from without" results from interactions with members of other groups and, in particular, the dominant societal group. The opportunities afforded and constraints imposed by the majority society; the power, status, and prestige accorded an ethnic minority group; the subjective evaluation of the ethnic group by nongroup members; and the ensuing degree of social acceptance are all important in influencing one's sense of ethnic identity. Isajiw (1974) suggests that external boundaries would be reflected, for example, in the rationale underlying specific immigration policies or policies regarding cultural minorities.

Thus it is clear that ethnic groups will vary in terms of their internal and external boundaries and that the relative strengths of these may be independent of each other. Dreidger (1976), in a Canadian study, describes three ethnic types resulting from an analysis of such sociostructural features as institutional completeness (internal) and group status (external). *Majority assimilators* (in Dreidger's sample, British and Scandinavians) have no need for separate ethnic institutional completeness because they accept (in the case of the British, provide the basis for) Canadian majority structures and have high status and power. This group neither strongly affirms nor denies its ethnic identity. *Ethnic identifiers* (French and Jews) have a high degree of ethnic institutional completeness, with moderately high status within Canadian society, giving a strong sense of ethnic identity. In contrast, in *cultural marginals* (Germans, Ukraines, Poles), a low to moderate level of institutional completeness is combined with relatively low status within the broader society, resulting in a level of ethnic affirmation consistent with the majority assimilators and significantly lower than the ethnic identifiers, but with a higher level of ethnic denial than either group. Thus to determine the extent to which ethnicity is essential to an individual's identity it is necessary to chart not only the nature of the internal boundaries, but also the perceived external boundaries; that is, the individual's perceptions of his or her group's place within the broader society.

The Nature of
Ethnic Identity in Adolescence

The study of ethnic identity in the past has been primarily concerned with young children's understanding of their membership in an ethnic minority group and their identification with this group. As Aboud notes (this volume), many techniques have been used that are designed to explore children's ability to describe themselves in terms of at least one critical attribute of their ethnic group, to distinguish themselves from members of other groups, or to perceive the stability of ethnic identity. Research on adolescents' ethnic identity has in many respects paralleled this research, but in more sophisticated language and with measures more appropriate to an older population.

Most studies have focused on aspects of the internal boundaries. In some of these, ethnic identity is treated as a global concept and a direct question is asked of the adolescent: "How X do you feel?" The concern of these researchers is usually with broader issues, such as the adjustment and adaptation of members of ethnic minority groups. There is no concern with the components of ethnic identity nor how or why identification with an ethnic group develops. Although responses to such a question may indeed reflect respondents' feelings of ethnic identification, they tell us little about the nature of ethnic identity and in fact neglect the possibility that the salience of ethnic identity varies at least as a function of situation. It has been shown (for example, Bond, 1983) that the ethnic background of interviewers and the language used in the interview can influence responses to questions about ethnic identity. Moreover, Rosenthal and Hrynevich (1985) found that adolescents reported in some situations (for example, with family, with immigrant friends, when speaking their second language) that they felt strongly Greek or Italian. In other contexts (in school, during recreation, with Australian friends) they felt really Australian. Callan and Gallois (1982, 1983) confirm that Greek Australian adolescents can alternate between Greek and Australian roles according to situational requirements.

A more cognitive approach that recognizes the complexity of the concept has been to elicit from respondents the dimensions that form the basis of ethnic identity. The focus here is to map those features of the reference group that contribute to an individual's sense of ethnic identity. Adolescents are required to describe themselves in terms of those dimensions that may be regarded as critical attributes of the ethnic group. This work has suggested that some factors are more salient for certain cultural groups than others, and confirmed that one's reference group is a source of a number of features contributing to ethnic identity.

Language and Ethnic Identity

The importance of language has been well documented in a series of studies conducted primarily with Canadian and Welsh respondents (for example, Giles, Taylor, & Bourhis, 1977; Giles, Taylor, Lambert, & Albert, 1976; Taylor, Simard, & Aboud, 1972; Taylor, Bassili, & Aboud, 1973). In an investigation of Anglo- and Franco-American high school students, Giles et al. (1976) explored the roles played by language, cultural background, and geographic region in the formation of ethnic identity. Language emerged as an important dimension for Franco-Americans who spoke French and also for Anglo-American respondents. For Franco-Americans who were not fluent in the French language, cultural background was the most salient feature.

In a more recent study (Giles, Llado, McKirnan, & Taylor, 1979), Puerto Rican schoolchildren sorted a number of stimulus cards that included features such as language, religion, skin color, and a key anchor item, "myself." Respondents were presented with pairs of stimuli and asked to judge the degree of similarity between them. Using multidimensional scaling analysis (based on these similarity judgments) the dimensions underlying ethnic identity as well as their relative salience were identified. These Puerto Rican children identified strongly with their parents, skin color, and religion, rather than language. The importance of physical appearance confirms Kozhanov's (1976) conclusion that distinctive physical characteristics are crucial means of categorizing individuals.

The relative importance of language appears to be dependent on the societal context. Language functions not only as a mode of expression but as a means of structuring and interpreting the environment. Sotomayor (1977) claims that establishing a sense of ethnic identity is closely linked to linguistic symbolic structures. The actual vocabulary that exists is indicative of that which is essential to the culture, therefore language reflects the culture. Plainly, language must be regarded as contributing to ethnic identity, especially for those cultures that are language centered (Smolicz, 1976; Smolicz & Seacombe, 1979). To the extent that ethnic minority groups, such as the Welsh in Great Britain and the French in Canada, rely on language as a key factor in differentiating their group from others, then their language will be an integral part of their self-definition.

Group Differences, Structural Features, and Ethnic Identity

It seems clear that different ethnic groups, as a result of their cultural history or place in the broader society, may emphasize different aspects of the culture. Driedger (1975) has noted in studies of Jewish identity the importance of religion, solidarity with the ethnic community, and endogamy. Taft (1973), in a study of Jewish adolescents in Australia, investigated a number of dimensions of ethnic identification, including community involvement, religion, language, social relations, positive emotional involvement, and identification with Israel. Taft found that individuals exhibited different patterns of identification (high on some dimensions, low on others). In addition, the degree and type of identification varied as a function of national background (for example, whether they were born in Poland, Britain, or America). Further evidence for the complexity of ethnic identity comes from a study conducted by Steinkalk (1983), who used a semantic differential technique with a sample of Jewish Soviet immigrant adolescents and their parents. She found that respondents rated "myself" as more like "Australians" than like "Jews" or "Russians" on an evaluative dimension, but more similar to "Jews" or "Russians" than "Australians" on potency and activity dimensions.

Although differences between ethnic groups in their cultural beliefs and behaviors lead to different emphases, structural features of the groups also may have an impact on ethnic identity. In a study of Australian adolescents, Rosenthal and Hrynevich (1985) explored the influence of institutional completeness on ethnic identity.

In Australia, two groups that enjoy differing degrees of institutional completeness are immigrants of Greek and Italian origin. Not only do these groups constitute the two largest ethnic minorities in Australia, they also have similar histories of immigration and are similarly regarded by the dominant social group (which is of Anglo-Celtic origin). The Greek community, however, is highly organized with considerable institutional supports. In particular, their church and language schools provide a focus for community members (Bottomley, 1979; Tsounis, 1975). The Italian community is more fragmented and diffuse, with a relatively high level of assimilation into the Anglo-Celtic society (Ware, 1981). It was anticipated that the structural and cultural differences between the two groups would affect the relative salience of elements underlying ethnic identity (McGuire & Padawer-Singer, 1976; McGuire, McGuire, Child, & Fujioka, 1978).

Accordingly, Rosenthal and Hrynevich used both an interview and a self-report questionnaire with 14- and 16-year-old Greek Australian and Italian Australian adolescents, to explore feelings and attitudes toward their own and other ethnic groups and behavior with respect to ethnic institutions. Through factor analytic techniques, Rosenthal and Hrynevich confirmed both the multidimensional nature of ethnic identity and the importance of distinctive group characteristics underlying ethnic identity. These characteristics included language, religion, social activities, maintenance of cultural traditions, family life, and physical characteristics. The importance given to language was consistent with earlier research in cultural contexts in which language differences form a basis for social categorization (for example, Christian, Gadfield, Giles, & Taylor, 1976; Giles et al., 1976; Taylor et al., 1973). For these adolescents, all of whom spoke Greek or Italian at home, language may assume increased salience because it highlights differences in a society in which English is the official language. The relative unimportance of physical appearance in defining ethnic identity may be a function of the lack of distinctiveness in this respect, because most Australians are of European descent. It is likely that for Asians or Aborigines, physical appearance would be more salient. The relatively greater emphasis by Greek Australians on religion may also arise from the unique nature and thus enhanced salience of the Greek Orthodox religion.

The construction placed on membership in their ethnic group differed for the two minorities. Each group perceived itself as culturally different from the others; there was a high degree of recognition of group membership and an awareness of boundaries between their ingroups and outgroups. For Greek Australians, a factor labeled "pride in cultural background," reflecting a positive valuing of ethnic origins, discriminated between adolescents. This was not the case for Italian Australians. Rather, a factor indicating a positive attitude to assimilation emerged. Thus differences were found in the nature of the attachment subjects felt for their respective ethnic groups.

Where membership of an ethnic minority group provides a negative identity it is assumed that group members will enhance their self-image by means of certain strategies (Tajfel, 1981). Although Italian Australian perceptions of ethnic identity did not show direct evidence of a negative self-image, their stress on assimilation and their negative attitudes to members of another ethnic minority, the Greeks, suggest that their ethnic group membership may not be satisfying. Italian Australians appear to be using two strategies to improve their self-image: attempting to move into the dominant social group and comparing themselves favorably with another ethnic minority. Greek Australians, on the other hand, evaluate their Greekness favorably, possibly as a result of their membership in a cohesive and structured community.

Although this study revealed subtle differences in the perceptions of two ethnic minorities within a particular multiethnic society, a further study of Italian Australian adolescents in the same society (Cichello, 1984) did not yield evidence of positive attitudes toward assimilation. This discrepancy serves to highlight the dynamic nature of ethnic identity. Cichello argues that the recent emphasis in the Italian community on promoting a new ethnic awareness through social action may have led to a devaluing of assimilation and revaluing of Italian identity.

Ethnic Identity as a Dynamic Concept

For the most part, ethnic identity has been treated as a static concept with little concern for the processes underlying development and change. Of the few studies that have incorporated a dynamic process-oriented view, several have addressed the issue through observing differences between younger and older adolescents (for example, Giles et al., 1979; Rosenthal & Hrynevich, 1985). Others have been concerned with the degree to which an individual's sense of ethnic identity is influenced by the broader social context, charting in part the nature of constraints imposed by external boundaries (for example, Christian et al., 1976; Cichello, 1984; Driedger, 1976; Hofman & Rouhana, 1976; Vaughan, this volume).

Given that identity formation is consolidated throughout the period of adolescence, the meaning of ethnic group membership may well undergo developmental changes in this period. Moreover, the psychosocial tasks of adolescence assume different emphases during this developmental transition. The onset of puberty leads to a concern with body image and sexuality that is transformed in late adolescence to choices about intimate relationships. An absorption with creating an image for an "imaginary audience" (Elkind, 1974; Elkind & Bowen, 1979) reflects a self-consciousness about appearance and behavior that is highlighted later rather than earlier in adolescence. In addition, vocational choice becomes an important issue. In all of these developments, adolescents of minority group status are likely to be confronted by differences as well as similarities between their ethnic group and others in the society. It could be predicted that when ethnic identity provides a sense of positive rather than negative social identity, development through adolescence will see a consolidation of ethnic identity as a source of positive evaluation and self-definition.

Unfortunately, the data exploring developmental changes through adolescence are sparse and cross-sectional (thus subject to cohort differences, a problem highlighted by Cichello's study). Of these, Giles et al. (1979) found little evidence for developmental changes in the dimensions underlying ethnic identity, a finding confirmed by Rosenthal and Hrynevich (1985). One difference that did emerge in the latter study was that younger adolescents were less likely than older adolescents to perceive their own group as a culturally cohesive entity. For 16-year-olds, issues such as the retention of cultural traditions, endogamy, maintenance of ties with other members of their cultural group, and rejection of assimilation were all associated with membership in their ethnic group. This suggests that even for adolescents over a narrow age range the meaning carried by their ethnic group may change subtly. Whether the perception of relatively strong boundaries between their own and other ethnic groups is advantageous or not is unclear. It is, however, significant that a heightened awareness of these boundaries occurs at a period when interpersonal issues and the adolescent's position in the wider social context become increasingly important.

Intergroup Dynamics and Ethnic Identity

Very few studies have sought to explore the meaning of ethnic identity at adolescence as a function of between-group factors, that is, aspects of groups' external boundaries. In two such studies, conflict between groups led to enhancement of ethnic identity. Christian et al. (1976), by experimentally manipulating the salience of between-group conflict for a sample of Welsh adolescents, found that heightened awareness of conflict between Welsh and English led to a strengthening of Welsh identity and sharper differentiation of Welsh and English identity. Hofman and Rouhana (1976) found that, for young Israeli-born Arabs, identity as Arabs assumed greater importance and attraction than their identity as Israelis. It seems, therefore, that when one social identity, that is, membership in an ethnic group, is seen as incompatible with another social identity, individuals will deny or reject the less favored identity. Interestingly, Hofman found in a later study (Hofman, 1982) that a strong Arab identity interfered with a readiness for social relations with Jews, whereas a strong identity as Israeli citizens positively mediated Arab-Jewish social relationships.

In a further example of the impact of intergroup dynamics on ethnic identity, Driedger (1976) found that high status within the community, coupled with high institutional completeness, led to strong affirmation and low denial of ethnic identity and vice versa in his sample of college students. Unfortunately, the separate effects of these two variables were not studied. Nevertheless, Driedger's study confirms Rosenthal and Hrynevich's claim that structural features of the ethnic group influence ethnic identity.

In a study exploring relationships between second-generation immigrants and members of the majority community, Novakovic (1977) found that Yugoslav Australian adolescents whose peer group comprised only members of their ethnic group reported less rejection of Yugoslav customs and traditions than those whose peer groups were mixed or wholly Anglo-Australian. Thus the degree to which these adolescents crossed the ethnic group boundary in their relationships with peers influenced their degree of identification with that ethnic group. Cichello (1984) included a measure of the degree to which Italian Australian adolescents perceived that there were barriers to assimilation imposed by the dominant society. Surprisingly, perceived barriers to assimilation did not predict adolescents' ethnic identity. Degree of identification with their ethnic group was predicted only by parental embeddedness in the Italian community. When parents maintained links with the community, for example, speaking Italian and reading community newspapers, their children felt strongly Italian; when parents turned to the dominant Anglo community for social support, adolescents felt less Italian, confirming Novakovic's findings. Not unexpectedly, then, parental influence appears to be a potent force in determining adolescents' affirmation of ethnic identity.

Conclusion

The difficulty in interpreting findings such as these points to the complexity of the phenomenon. If the elements constituting ethnic identity are likely to be different for each group studied, so too are the relative weightings given to these elements. Moreover, in attempting to capture the dynamic nature of ethnic identity, we should consider not only objective differences in context but also the subjective meaning of that context. Although it is apparent that an ethnic minority group may assume psychological significance in terms of adolescent self-identity, the conditions under which this is the case are by no means clearly spelled out. That ethnic identity is a dynamic phenomenon is evident, as attested to by fluctuations in intensity, importance, and evaluation, depending on context. Rather than attempt clarification of the processes influencing the nature and salience of ethnic identity, many researchers have chosen instead to take the individual's psychological functioning within the societal context as their main focus. Using this strategy, the relationships among ethnic group membership, ethnic identity, and adaptation in a multiethnic society have been identified and the implications for the psychological well-being of minority group members explored.

Ethnic Identity, Minority Group Membership, and Psychological Well-Being

**Culture Conflict and
Minority Group Membership**

Early interpretations of the immigrant experience, as of the minority experience, assumed that living in two cultural worlds would result in intense conflict and confusion because of discrepancies between two competing cultural systems. Initially, the adjustment of immigrants was conceptualized as a function of assimilation of new and rejection of old cultural values. Adoption of the behaviors and values appropriate to the host society and identification with that society were seen as adaptive and were regarded as incompatible with retention of the old culture. Assimilation of host group values was assumed to result in alienation from the ethnic minority group. More recently, it has been recognized that alternative outcomes are possible (Bochner, 1982; Putnins, 1981; Smolicz & Seacombe, 1979). For some individuals, the choice is to remain "ethnic"; the new culture is rejected and the old retained (Cichello, 1984; Rosenthal & Hrynevich, 1985).

Another possible resolution results in a sense of marginality. Taft (1974) outlines four types of marginality, characterized by a feeling of belonging to neither group, or by oscillating between groups, leading to uncertainty about appropriate behaviors and/or attitudes. The latter represents the *culture conflict* model, the assumption being that identification with two cultures will necessarily result in conflict and may lead to problems in adjustment for the individual, especially when there is little common ground between the cultures. This neglects a further possibility; for some, a bicultural resolution may occur, whereby two cultures are synthesized. These "mediating" individuals (Bochner, 1982) can select appropriate features of their two worlds, resulting in a degree of psychological flexibility that enables them to adapt their behavior to the demands of different situations and therefore avoid conflict. In Australia, evidence for the capacity to live harmoniously within two cultures comes from Bottomley's study of Greeks (Bottomley, 1976, 1979), Putnins's (1981) study of Latvians, and Taft's (1973) study of Jews, as well as Rosenthal and Hrynevich (1985).

To understand better the processes of adaptation, it is important to recognize some of the influences on the coping strategies chosen by ethnic minority group members. The first of these relates to the migration process itself, including the discrepancy between the immigrant's former and current life, between the type of occupation in each country, and between the old and new cultural values and behaviors. The reasons for migration and the commitment to the new country also can influence the nature of the adaptive process. In the host society, attitudes to ethnic minority groups are important. Taft (1965) has identified prejudice and discrimination as important in the nonassimilation of migrants.

Another important dimension reflects within-group characteristics. The ability of the ethnic group to cater to the needs of its members is of special relevance. When few of the group members' activities take place outside the group, the opportunities for learning about the new culture are reduced. The work of Giles and his colleagues on subjective ethnolinguistic vitality (Bourhis, Giles, & Rosenthal, 1981; Giles, Bourhis, & Taylor, 1977) has shown that certain sociostructural characteristics, such as status variables, are potent factors in minority group members' perception of their group's vitality. Moreover, it has been demonstrated that adolescents in one such group overestimate their group's status relative to the dominant social group, presumably to enhance their own group membership (Giles, Rosenthal, & Young, 1985). In addition to external factors relating to minority group membership, characteristics of the individuals themselves are important. For example, the desire for assimilation is likely to be less when immigration occurs later in life after cultural norms have become entrenched. Women, through more limited access to the new norms, may have less desire and less need than men to assimilate the mainstream culture.

Given that these factors are but a few of the many that influence the adaptation to two cultural systems, how, then, do adolescents deal with a minority group identity in the context of their broader social environment?

Most research on this issue is predicated on the culture conflict model. There is abundant anecdotal material supporting the belief in a high level of conflict both within the individual and between adolescents and others within their environment, notably their parents. Their stories often illustrate poignantly the dilemmas they face in attempting to find an acceptable place in their world:

> I am trying to decide how much of one's culture is internalized. . . . A re-evaluation has become necessary because often I find myself in situations where people take it for granted that I will react in a particular culturally accepted manner but I react quite differently. At times, I am not aware that my behavior is inconsistent. Occasionally, not even I can explain why I react in a certain way. (Starc, 1980, p. 91)

Conflict with parents is frequently described in emotional language that reflects the writer's personal experiences:

> Frustration caused by cumbersome communication facilitates the breakdown and alienation sets in. . . . Thus an immediate conflict ensues between the Greek youth and the older generation. (Giannopolous, 1978, p. 39)

Presumably the consequences of such conflict would be revealed in relatively poor psychological well-being, such as poor self-concept, problems with psychosocial development, and maladjustment.

Self-Concept and Ethnic Identity

The adverse effects of minority group membership on self-concept and self-esteem is an old theme. The underlying assumption is that feelings of inferiority would stem from such factors as relatively lower status, poverty, and perceptions of prejudice and discrimination. Kourakis (1983), however, claims that the evidence linking racial and ethnic group membership to inferior self-concept and low self-esteem is tenuous. Burns's (1979) review suggests that the self-concepts of Black children in the United States are not significantly different from those of the dominant group. Akoodie (1980) found no differences in the self-concepts of West Indian, East Indian, and Canadian high school students. Montijo (1975) showed that Puerto Rican identity was positively correlated with self-esteem in a sample of adolescents in Puerto Rico. Identification with their primary group had adaptive qualities for these adolescents and identification with a second group (in this case American) did not seem to have a negative effect on self-esteem. In a study by Soares and Soares (1969), it was shown that Negro and Puerto Rican children in "disadvantaged" schools held more positive self-perceptions than White middle-class children in "advantaged" schools. Apparently children in the former group were using other disadvantaged children as their referent group, hence their enhanced levels of self-perception.

Kourakis points to methodological problems with much of the research on self-concept and ethnic identity. These include using culture specific measures of self-concept or poor experimental design (such as failures to use a control group drawn from the dominant social group), or to equate subjects for factors such as socioeconomic status, intelligence, age, and sex. The measures of ethnic identity used also may be problematic. Rovner (1983) reported that in scales that included both ethnic centrality and ethnic satisfaction items, the former were likely to mask or suppress the relationship between the latter and self-esteem.

Several studies of minority group adolescents' self-concept and psychological development have been conducted in Australia. Kourakis (1983) found no evidence for an association between Greek Australian biculturalism and low self-esteem. Similarly, Rosenthal et al. (1983) found that the self-image of Greek Australian adolescents was not significantly different from that of Anglo-Australians. They found, however, that Italian Australians had a poorer self-image than both their Greek Australian and Anglo-Australian counterparts.

Rosenthal et al. extended the exploration of self-concept by using a measure of psychosocial development based on the first six stages of Erikson's model: Trust versus Mistrust, Autonomy versus Shame and Doubt, Initiative versus Guilt, Industry versus Inferiority, Identity versus Identity Confusion, and Intimacy versus Isolation. No differences were found in resolution of these psychosocial crises among the three groups except for Trust, when Anglo-Australians scored higher than Italian Australians but not Greek Australians. Rosenthal et al. interpreted these findings in terms of differences between the two minority communities. For the Greek Australians, with a high degree of institutional completeness, a strong and stable sense of ethnic identity may contribute to the developing sense of self-image. For Italian Australians, the emphasis on assimilation into the Australian culture may, in the short term, at least, lead to greater feelings of conflict for adolescents. The adolescent must cope not only with the changes associated with age but also with conflicts between the values of the family and the wider community. Some areas of self-concept appeared to be less sensitive to the impact of ethnicity. These related mainly to work and vocational goals, morality, and relationships with others, domains that are strongly and positively valued by all three groups. Differences between groups related most strongly to the affective dimensions of self-concept and to feelings of being able to cope.

Different patterns of self-concept development between Italian Australian and Anglo-Australian adolescents were confirmed by Cichello (1984). Interestingly, he found that positive self-image and resolution of Erikson's stages were predicted better by parental embeddedness in the Italian culture and perceived lack of problems in being Italian (for example, in relation to obtaining jobs or experience of prejudice) than by ethnic identity. Cichello's findings confirm those of Grossman (1982), who concluded that her study of high school students provided no basis for assuming a direct relationship between ethnic identity and self-esteem. Vasta (1975), however, argued that parental assimilation did affect the self-concept of second generation Italian children; better self-concept was correlated with greater parental assimilation. In Kourakis's (1983) study, the degree of paternal assimilation of host group cultural norms did not significantly affect self-esteem in her Greek Australian sample. The discrepancy between Cichello's and

Vasta's findings might be explained in the recent positive reevaluation of Italian postulated by Cichello.

In both the Kourakis and the Rosenthal et al. studies there was some evidence for the greater vulnerability of females in terms of self-concept. There is ample evidence that the traditional sex roles of Greeks and Italians differ from those of Anglo-Celtic origin. For example, Vasta (1980) and Eppink (1979) report closer supervision by Greek and Italian parents of their adolescent girls than would generally be the case in Anglo-Australian families. Further, Greek and Italian family structures have been described as patriarchal, with a more rigid difinition of sex roles than among families of Anglo-Celtic origin (Lambert, Hamers, & Frasure-Smith, 1979). Bottomley (1975) and Callan and Gallois (in press) note that among second-generation Greeks, attitudes to marriage and to sex roles reflect traditional values. This commitment to old cultural values may be reflected in the finding that Greek Australian adolescents show different patterns of gender typing from those of Italian Australians and Anglo-Australians (Moore & Rosenthal, 1984). It is suggested from this research that immigrant girls in Australia are more likely to be at risk when they come from cultures where sex roles are sharply differentiated and where the male role is accorded high prestige than in cultures where there is less sex role differentiation.

From the research presented here, the evidence for a link between ethnic minority group membership and problems with self-concept seems to be a function of the measures used, the experimental design chosen, and the groups studied. It should be stressed that even when a link is shown, the self-concept of these minority group members is still relatively positive. There is little evidence for pathologically low levels of self-concept as might be predicted by a culture conflict model.

Psychological Well-Being and Ethnic Identity

When we turn to other aspects of psychological well-being, the links among biculturalism, culture conflict, and maladjustment are no clearer. There is evidence that the degree of biculturalism is unrelated to poor adjustment (Johnston, 1972; Kourakis, 1983; Taft, 1977). Hills (1973), for example, found that second-generation immigrants expressed no greater alienation from society than comparable Anglo-Australian adolescents. Taft (1973) found no indication of "ethnic self-hate" in his study of Jewish adolescents. Aellen and Lambert (1969) found no evidence for personality disturbance, social alienation, and anxiety among a group of Canadian adolescent males of mixed English and French descent, and Bhatnager (1980) showed that a sample of bilingual-bicultural Italian immigrant children in Canada had better levels of adjustment than similar groups of French or English monolinguals. Nevertheless, in Australia some studies report that the dual cultural experience results in, for example, mental health problems (Giggs, 1977), low academic achievement (Wiseman, 1971), and a confused sense of personal identity (Greco, Vasta, & Smith, 1977). The reasons for these disparate findings may be based on factors such as the environment in which the immigrant lives and works or is schooled, the particular cultural groups or subgroups studied, the solidarity of the ethnic community, and its status within the receiving society.

As with the research on self-concept, the weight of evidence implies that maladjustment in minority adolescents is not clearly related to degree of biculturalism or to perception of discrepancies between the two cultural systems.

Bicultural Conflict in Families

It is more plausible to expect that culture conflict will be manifested in tension within families. Immigrant parents may feel threatened by their lack of knowledge of the majority culture, and insecure and confused about roles. They may thus become increasingly authoritarian in the family, which is the only system over which they now feel that they have control. Increasing demands for obedience are likely to result in frustration and resentment from an adolescent seeking to test his or her ideas in a newfound world. The pressure on immigrant children and adolescents to achieve academic excellence and thus a "better life" than their parents has been documented and may well be a source of conflict as the younger generation attempts to meet aspirations that are frequently unrealistic. Given that adolescents may have only a limited command of their parents' language and that parents may have an equally limited facility with the new language, communication about the complex and abstract issues confronting both parents and their children may be inadequate, resulting in frustration or misunderstanding. Perhaps most important, in those immigrant families in which parents cling to the old culture and resist the new, problems are likely to arise if the younger generation seeks to be assimilated to the majority culture. Many second-generation adolescents (and girls in particular) complain about conflict with their parents. However, if biculturalism is to be used as an explanation of intergenerational conflict for immigrant families, it is necessary to demonstrate that these families experience more conflict than those from the majority group.

Although relatively few studies have addressed the issue of intergenerational conflict in Australia the weight of evidence suggests that there is not heightened conflict between adolescents who are part of two cultural worlds and their parents. Certainly tension and disagreement are expressed in the responses of non-Anglo-Australian adolescents. In a small study of Greek families (Salagaros, Humphris, & Harris, 1974), highest levels of tension were associated with boy-girl relationships, friends' cultural origins, and ethnic group identification. There was considerable compliance with parental demands, especially for girls, but, most important, the overall incidence of tension was low. Hostility toward parents and increased antisocial behavior and truancy were reported in another study of young Greek girls (Koutsounadis, 1979). In neither of these studies was there a control group to establish levels of tension in Anglo-Australian parent-adolescent relationships. Johnston (1972) found that tension was at its peak in adolescents of Polish, German, and British descent where parents opposed assimilation and that the causes of tension varied among cultural groups. Nevertheless, levels of tension were not so intense as to produce significant problems. Other studies of Greeks (Kourakis, 1983), Poles (Taft & Johnston, 1967), Jews (Taft, 1973), and Southern Europeans (Doczy, 1968) report similar findings: relatively low levels and varying sources of tension depending on the group studied.

Of those studies in which an Anglo-Australian control group was used, one (Connell, Stroobant, Sinclair, Connell, & Rogers, 1975) found that second-generation immigrants were more alienated from their parents than the controls. This conclusion must be viewed with caution as social class was confounded; the majority of controls were upper middle class but the majority of immigrants were working class. In contrast to this finding, it has been shown (Hills, 1973) that Anglo-Australians report more conflict with parental authority in matters of general social concern than adolescents of Dutch, German, Italian, and Greek descent. In issues relating to the adolescents themselves (for example drinking, driving) all adolescents reported disagreements with parents.

In Rosenthal's (1984) study, Anglo-Australian adolescents and their parents reported less conflict than their Greek Australian and Italian

Australian peers, with Italian Australian girls (relative to their male counterparts) perceiving the greatest conflict. Issues that discriminated most between the Anglo-Australian and immigrant groups were going out with the opposite sex, use of spare time outside the home, and drinking and/or smoking. The degree of identification with either their original culture or the dominant culture had little impact on the amount of familial conflict for either immigrant group. There was, however, a trend for the more assimilated adolescents to be associated with higher levels of conflict. For these adolescents, conflict arises not because they have adopted two different normative systems of behavior but because they have taken on the attitudes and behaviors of their Anglo-Australian peers and their parents retain their traditional culture.

One may conclude from these studies that familial conflict is not restricted to bicultural families, that the level of reported conflict between generations is not especially high and that, when conflict exists, it is related to issues that are important in particular cultures. To refer to bicultural conflict within families without taking into account the diversity of ethnic groups and their cultural traditions is to oversimplify the matter. Moreover, it is important to understand the origins and nature of conflict when it is expressed. In interpreting a finding of greater conflict within immigrant families, differences in family systems should be considered. In Anglo families, more individuality is tolerated, with greater stress on personal freedom. In some non-Anglo cultures, notably Greek and Italian, adolescents are subjected to more authoritarian, parent-centered control, with greater expectations that they will conform to family demands. Evidence (Lambert et al., 1979) that Greek and Italian parents, in contrast to Anglo parents, do not favor autonomous behavior in their children suggests that attempts by adolescents to behave in nonacceptable ways would lead to disagreement or conflict. Thus tension may arise because of child-rearing practices rather than as a result of a clash of cultures.

Finally, we need to explore more carefully the meaning of conflict. Given the relatively good levels of adjustment of these second-generation immigrants, it would seem that higher levels of family conflict are not necessarily associated with problems in psychosocial development. Indeed, it has been argued by psychoanalytic theorists, at least, that some degree of conflict is necessary for psychological growth. Unquestioning acceptance of parental and societal attitudes and values may in fact lead to difficulties in resolving the identity crisis at adolescence (Erikson, 1968).

Summary and Conclusions

In an ethnically diverse society like Australia where approximately 25% of the population is of non-Anglo-Celtic descent and where some schools take up to 90% of their students from these minority groups, issues relating to biculturalism are of considerable relevance. In summarizing the evidence available, it seems that second-generation immigrant adolescents adopt a variety of strategies in dealing with their dual cultural environment. For some, the primary ethnic group serves as the most potent identification. Others adopt a more assimilatory position or view themselves as members of two cultural worlds, switching identifications according to the situation. Whatever the strategy, the old assertion that biculturalism inevitably leads to conflict and maladjustment needs to be questioned. Research increasingly shows that adolescent children from minority groups are not fated to suffer intense psychological distress because of conflicting cultural norms.

Interestingly, difficulties seem to arise when adolescents perceive that membership in a particular ethnic group results in problems for their functioning in the broader society. This suggests that any study of the link between ethnicity and adjustment needs to take into consideration not only the internal boundaries imposed by the ethnic group, but also group members' perceptions of their group's status and function in the majority culture. It is reasonable to hypothesize that when their ethnic group is held in low esteem by the dominant group, individuals may adopt a less positive attitude to their groups and hence their identification with that group could be attenuated.

Kourakis's (1983) work provides a reminder of the importance of providing an external frame of reference in examining questions of bicultural conflict. By using a group of adolescents from the home country, Kourakis was able to demonstrate that the poorer adjustment in some areas of her Greek Australian adolescents was not a function of culture conflict. Rather, she concluded that adolescence appears to be a more problematic period for Greeks than for Anglo-Australians.

Another issue is whether or not the conclusions of relatively low levels of conflict for these adolescents can be generalized beyond Australia. There is in Australia an overt tolerance of ethnic minorities and there have been a number of positive measures, such as the teaching of community languages in schools and provision of ethnic radio and television programs, that enhance the status of ethnic minorities. Given that the weakening of community ties may be related to somewhat poorer self-image in second-generation immigrant adolescents, a policy that supports the maintenance of strong communal links might be psychologically beneficial. Such a policy should result in a resurgence of ethnic identity comparable with that of third-generation immigrants in the United States recently (see, for example, Scourby, 1980), together with more positive attitudes and greater acceptance on the part of the majority social group. On the other hand, maintenance of old cultural traditions and heightened ethnicity may lead to greater conflict if external boundaries become more rigid and less permeable.

Part of the difficulty in providing a coherent overview of this research rests in its atheoretical nature. Studies have provided pointers to the determinants of ethnic identity and the factors that moderate its strength. The work of the McGuires suggests that the distinctiveness of a characteristic will render it salient. The work on intergroup conflict and assimilation points to predictors of the strength and salience of ethnic identity. The group's vitality may provide a further measure of satisfaction with, and commitment to, the ethnic group. Clearly, to explore the meaning and functions of ethnic identity in adolescence, we need to employ a more process-oriented approach, accounting for the dynamic nature of the concept. The adolescent who can wholly ignore his or her ethnic background is a rare creature. Happily, the evidence seems to suggest that the integration of two cultural worlds can be an enriching experience yielding flexible individuals with skills that enable them to function adaptively in a variety of contexts. For some, however, their ethnic background provides a source of conflict. To determine why this is so is a task still largely ahead of us.

9

The Role of Language
in the Formation
of Ethnic Identity

MONICA HELLER

The goal of this chapter is to examine the role of language in the formation of ethnic identity. The view taken here is that ethnicity is a social construct, and that in order to examine the process of the construction of ethnicity it is necessary to examine the processes of social interaction on which that construction is based. Social interaction is, of course, a communicative process, including both nonverbal and verbal communication. Although nonverbal communication will be dealt with briefly below, the emphasis in this chapter is on verbal communication.

I argue that the basis of ethnicity can be found in the social networks within which individuals form relationships and carry out the activities of their daily lives. Ethnic networks may crosscut or coincide with networks based on other sources of social differentiation (class, sex, age, and so on). Where there are gaps in the network, one finds social

AUTHOR'S NOTE: The research on which this article is based was supported by a postdoctoral fellowship through the Development of Bilingual Proficiency Project of the Modern Language Centre, the Ontario Institute for Studies in Education, and was funded by the Social Sciences and Humanities Research Council of Canada. I would like to thank the principal investigators of that project, Patrick Allen, James Cummins, Raymond Mougeon, and Merrill Swain, for their support. I would also like to thank Timothy Kaiser for his comments and criticisms. I am particularly grateful to the administration, staff, parents, and students of St. Michel for generously sharing so much of their time.

boundaries. Thus the first principle of ethnic identity formation is participation in ethnic social networks, and therefore in activities controlled by ethnic group members. Language is important here as a means by which access to networks is regulated: If you do not speak the right language, you do not have access to forming relationships with certain people, or to participating in certain activities. Beyond this basic principle, there is the consequence of continuous interaction over time within social networks: shared experience, shared knowledge, shared ways of looking at the world, and shared ways of talking. Shared language is basic to shared identity, but more than that, identity rests on shared ways of using language that reflect common patterns of thinking and behaving, or shared culture.

In the sections that follow, I will discuss the theoretical background of this view and some of the research questions and methodological issues that emerge from that background. This chapter focuses on short-term social processes; in order to relate them to the construction of ethnic identity they need to be understood as processes that develop both over time and across social space. Over time, these incipient processes may develop, transform, or stabilize, as individuals' experiences of social life are influenced both by underlying social changes that may be occurring in the community, and by the sorts of changes that are brought about by age-related passage from one status to another. Across social space, the kinds of experiences that children have of language use and of access to social networks in school may resemble or differ from their experiences of these phenomena outside school. Further, the experiences of this small group of children may or may not be shared by large segments of the population.

In order to be truly identified as ethnic processes, the incipient ethnic processes described here must be reinforced and not confounded by the experiences of relatively significant numbers of people over time and across the various domains of social activity they encounter. It is not my purpose here to examine in depth the extent to which the processes discussed are indeed reinforced or confounded; I see this as a direction for future research, although some reference will be made to those contexts here. However, from both a theoretical and a methodological point of view, it will be useful to keep in mind that this study concerns one part of a larger set of social experiences that individuals encounter as they grow older and participate in ever-widening circles of social life. Nonetheless, as I hope will become clear below, I consider this case study to be an example of the kinds of factors that enter into the development of ethnic identity under any circumstances, whether or not the actual social networks and identity constructs developed by the children described here turn out to be stable over time and across social space.

This chapter, then, reports on an ethnographic, sociolinguistic study of the role of French and English in the formation of ethnic identity among students in a French-language minority school in Toronto, Ontario. This is a case study of language contact, and examines what happens when children of diverse backgrounds experience situations associated with different languages and different social groups. The strategies that these children develop for managing the competing demands of various arenas lay the groundwork for their eventual long-term construction of or participation in social networks or social situations that may be associated with ethnic identity. This case study will serve to illustrate some of the theoretical and methodological issues raised in the first part of the chapter, and will provide evidence that (1) ethnicity is grounded in social relationships that are formed through interaction, but that are constrained also by contextual factors; and (2) language choice and language use play central roles in the formation of those social relationships.

Theoretical Background

Ethnicity, culture, and knowledge. The theoretical background of the view of ethnicity taken here is based on ecological and situational analyses of ethnicity and on interactionist approaches to the role of language in the social construction of reality.

Ecological analyses of ethnicity (see Barth, 1966, 1969; Despres, 1975; Hechter, 1975) ground the concept of ethnicity in larger models of social organization and of the relationship of social organization to the ways in which members of groups go about making a living. These analyses view ethnicity as a product of social networks and of the shared experiences of members of those networks; networks, in turn, are subject to the external constraints of the social and physical ecology of their environment.

Ethnicity is based on boundaries; it does not acquire meaning except as a function of opposition to that which lies on the other side of the gap in social ties that differentiates one ethnic group from another. To be a member of an ethnic group is to participate in certain social networks, and therefore to have access to certain social roles and to the resources controlled by members of the ethnic group. To give a (somewhat oversimplified) example: The French in Canada in the 1950s worked in primary resource occupations (agriculture, forestry, mining, fishing), in the professions (medicine, law), or in the Catholic Church. They married within the group, indeed, had almost all social ties within the group. Their choice of religion, schools, and even leisure activities were constrained by group membership, as were residence, finance, and just about every other activity of daily life. The French did not have access to management positions in private enterprise, which was an anglophone preserve; French and English institutions were separate, and contact was restricted to two domains, the workplace (where francophone workers encountered anglophone management) and service encounters. Passing did occur, but that only reinforced the separation of the two groups: In order to participate in French or English activities, one had to begin to see oneself as French or English.

The issue of who is French and who is English, that is, of the criteria used to define group membership, is clearly important here. Historically, as described, ethnic identity in Canada was relatively unproblematic: self-identification, identification by others, language, religion, kinship and friendship networks, occupation, residence, and so on, were all congruent. However, social change has undermined the ecological bases of French ethnic group boundaries, and so criteria of inclusion are no longer so clear. Some people consider that all those who speak French (francophones), whether or not they also speak other languages, have French identity, and others feel that a single criterion is not enough.

Here, the term *francophone* will be reserved for all those who speak French better than they speak any other language, whether or not they consider themselves or are considered to have French identity. However, it should be pointed out that currently some people do use the term *francophone* as an index of identity, although others use such terms as *Français, Canadien français, Québecois,* or *Franco-Ontarian.* Sometimes these terms reflect criteria based on territorial coresidence (Lee & Lapointe, 1979), language, something referred to as "culture," or some combination thereof. Sometimes different people will use different terms to mean the same thing, or mean different things by the same term. What this reveals is that the definition of identity is negotiable and subject to change.

Further, as situational analyses of ethnicity have revealed (see Briggs, 1971; Nagata, 1974, 1979), the way in which ethnicity is defined is subject to change not only over time, but also across social situations. Most important, it is precisely in situations of contact (or where contact is part of the context) that ethnicity becomes important. In isolation, it means nothing to be French or to be English; it is for this reason that, as has been so often cited in the anthropological literature (see Moerman, 1965) isolated groups tend only to refer to themselves as "the people." Ethnic identity is, then, a function of opposition (see Barth, 1969). Further, it is not necessarily an important part of all aspects of everyday life: Rather, there will be certain activities in which ethnicity is more meaningful or central than others. Finally, ethnicity is related to the control of access to participation in the social networks and activities of each group; differences in the actual content of ways of life, of beliefs and values, and of ways of behaving are seen as a *product* of the social separation of groups rather than as its cause.

Gumperz (1972, 1982a, 1982b) has shown that social organization (dividing people into groups) constrains individuals' opportunities for social interaction. Comembers of a group, obviously, interact more with each other than they do with anyone else, and as a result they share experiences. Their shared experience forms the basis of a shared way of looking at the world; through interaction they jointly construct ways of making sense of experience. These ways of making sense of experience, these beliefs, assumptions, and expectations about the world and how it works underlie what we think of as culture. However culture is not only a set of beliefs and values that constitute our normal, everyday view of the world; it also includes our normal, everyday ways of behaving.

When our ecology is stable we can take for granted a good deal about how the world works and how to behave in it; if we could not take things for granted then in each and every interaction we would have to start again from scratch to establish what we need to know in order, for example, to conduct a conversation. When activities occur in ways that we are accustomed to, then we can draw on a wealth of experience that enables us to interpret what is happening and to participate appropriately. Our ways of thinking become conventional, normal, and function as signals or signs that call into play the taken-for-granted frames of reference that are pertinent to our activities. New experiences are made sense out of in terms of old frames of reference. To the extent that they fit, the frame of reference is reaffirmed; to the extent that they do not fit, the experience is either assigned to the realm of the unexplainable, or changes are made to the frame of reference (Cicourel, 1975, 1978; Heller, 1982a; Tannen, 1982).

The things that people do in interaction contribute directly, then, to the maintenance of or change in their background knowledge and to their conventions of behavior. To belong to an ethnic group means to share with other members of one's group ways of looking at the world and ways of behaving: ways of making sense of the experiences of daily life.

Communication conventions and identity. A great deal of work has been done documenting cultural conventions of both nonverbal and verbal behavior, and the culturally conventionalized inferences group members make on the basis of behavior in social interaction. Studies by Erickson (1976) and Erickson and Schultz (1982) represent an excellent example of work in the area of nonverbal behavior. Their work in the area of cross-cultural job counseling interviews demonstrated that eye gaze, for example, is a conventional signal of speaking and listening behavior: White speakers conventionally let their gaze wander, but Black speakers look directly at the listener, and White listeners look directly at the speaker, but Black listeners direct their gaze downward. Unfortunately, in Black-White interactions, each participant is met with unexpected behavior: White speakers feel that their Black listeners, with downward gaze, are not paying attention; Black listeners feel that White speakers, with their wandering gaze, are not really wholeheartedly involved in the conversation; when Blacks speak, eyes lock, and each participant feels the other is being aggressive. Each group makes inferences on the basis of what is considered normal within their group.

In the realm of verbal behavior, ethnomethodologists have demonstrated the conventionality and systematicity of conversational routines, notably turn-taking (Sacks, Schegloff, & Jefferson, 1974), openings (Schegloff, 1972), and closings (Sacks & Schegloff, 1973). For example, in his discussion of conversational openings, Schegloff (1972) demonstrates that if, for some reason, the greeting routine goes wrong (say both participants speak at once instead of in turn), interlocutors recycle to the beginning in order to accomplish the routine properly before they feel free to get to the heart of the matter. My study of service encounters in Montreal (Heller, 1982a) showed that until conventions of language choice (English/French) could be established, interlocutors could not proceed to the issue at hand (for example, making an appointment with a doctor, placing an order in a restaurant), even when all participants were obviously fluently bilingual. Systematicity allows speakers to know how to repair or renegotiate; conventionality anchors conversation in a known frame of reference, so that speakers can be prepared for what is to come next.

Ethnographers of speaking and sociolinguists (see Bauman & Sherzer, 1974; Gumperz & Hymes, 1972; Sanches & Blount, 1975) also have demonstrated the pervasiveness of cultural conventionality of ways of speaking for all groups, across all speech situations, and in all areas of language: linguistic (Gumperz, 1982a; Labov, 1972b; Poplack, 1980; and Sankoff, 1980) and paralinguistic (Gumperz, 1982a; Irvine, 1974), at the utterance level as well as at the level of discourse (Gumperz, 1982a; Keenan, 1974; Schieffelin, 1979; Scotton, 1976; Tannen, 1982). They have demonstrated the importance to social interaction of knowing how to use language appropriately, and they have shown that ways of speaking are grounded in the social organization of everyday life.

Recent work also has examined more closely the use people make of culturally conventionalized ways of speaking in order to accomplish conversational tasks (Cazden, in press; Cicourel, 1975, 1978, 1980; Gumperz, 1982a, 1982b; Heller & Freeman, in press; Mehan, 1979, 1983; Michaels, 1982). Attention also has been paid to the way language can be used not only to reaffirm background knowledge, but to create it, and on the basis of new background knowldege, to define new conventions of behavior (Heller, 1982a, 1984; Maltz & Borker, 1982; Wolfson & Manes, 1979). When the ecological basis of social relations changes (recently we have felt this most in interethnic and in male-female relations), old ways of speaking are no longer appropriate. However, it is far from clear what *is* appropriate, because the new order has yet to emerge. In such circumstances, conversation becomes a resource for defining the new order. For example, social change in Quebec radically altered the bases of French-English relations (Clift & Arnopoulos, 1979; Heller, 1982b), thereby causing a breakdown in conventions of behavior. Especially in specific arenas at the frontier of change (for example, the workplace and service encounters), interlocutors passed through a period of stress in which every conversational act was problematic, and frames of reference had to be explicitly defined, otherwise conversation broke down entirely. Finally, a new routine developed, based on code-switching, that enabled interlocutors to define a new, neutral frame of reference.

Work in the area of children's acquisition of bilingualism has shown that children do associate languages with the people who commonly speak them and the situations in which they are commonly used (Genishi, 1981; McClure, 1981). Similarly, children learn to code-switch where that is a conventional speech mode in social situations in their community (Zentella, 1981), although they also may switch languages as part of their strategy for learning the language use conventions of their community and for learning to differentiate language varieties in the community repertoire (Huerta, 1980). Through their own social experience they learn the social significance of language use, and are able to use languages to accomplish primarily social or discourse ends (for example, indirectly telling on a classmate to the teacher, emphasizing, shutting others out of conversations).

What this work shows is that shared ways of speaking are basic to the formation of social relationships, and so to individual access to social networks and to participation in social activities. Shared ways of speaking become symbolic of shared background knowledge, of shared culture. Language becomes one way in which shared culture not only can be established and defined, but also ultimately a symbol of it. To be a member of an ethnic group, then, also means knowing certain things about how the world works and about how to behave (including how to talk) in the various situations encountered in everyday life, as well as about how to make inferences on the basis of others' behavior: This is the basis of ethnic identity. Identity, then, is a social construct, grounded in social interaction in the activities and situations that arise as a product of the relationship of a social group to its social and physical environment. Clearly, shared ways of thinking and behaving influence the definition of identity; at the same time, if one knows the identity of one's interlocutor, one can assume a great deal about what he or she is likely to believe and about how he or she is likely to behave.

Finally, it is clear that in order for comembership to be established, people have to share ways of thinking and talking: Language is a means of establishing the social ties and the participation in social activities that underlie entry to a social network. It is thus central to any understanding of the processes of inclusion and exclusion that constitute the maintenance or change of the boundaries on which ethnicity is based.

Research Questions and Research Methods

The view of the role of language in ethnic processes outlined above leads to the formulation of research questions which, in turn, lead to questions regarding appropriate research methods. The research questions can broadly be categorized as follows:

(1) What exactly is it that languages symbolize about the ethnic groups that speak them?

(2) What are the ethnic differences in conventions of language use in any given interethnic contact situation, and what are their consequences for interethnic interaction?

(3) How do people use language in the formation and definition of ethnic group boundaries and ethnic identity?

The first research question, concerning the symbolic value of languages, has been addressed largely within the framework of social psychology (see Gardner, 1973; Genesee, 1978; Giles & St. Clair, 1979; Giles, Taylor, & Bourhis, 1973; Lambert, 1972; Ryan & Giles, 1982). The matched-guise technique is the preferred research tool. Subjects are asked to provide evaluative reactions to tape-recorded messages in each of several languages or language varieties (Lambert, 1967). Because everything but language (context, speaker, message) is held constant, it is assumed that speakers are reacting to something symbolized by the language variety. In this tradition, language is treated as a symbol, and is examined outside its role in the social process of interaction. Because work in this tradition is largely outside the purview of the approach taken here, I will not discuss it further.

The first part of the second research question, regarding conventions of language use, has been addressed primarily through ethnographic work; the second half builds on this ethnographic work and goes on to examine in detail the impact of conventions of language use in interaction. In this approach (see Collins, 1982; Erickson & Schultz, 1982; Gumperz, 1982a, b; Gumperz & Roberts, 1980; Jupp, Roberts, & Cook-Gumperz, 1982; Michaels, 1981) "Key situations" are identified, and conversation within those situations closely analyzed. "Key situations" are, loosely defined, situations in which the outcome of a conversation is going to make a difference to participants' lives, for example, job interviews, counseling, medical diagnostic interviews, and school evaluation. The purpose of fine-grained analysis here is to identify recurring patterns of speech, and to match them with both internal evidence of conversational cooperation or conversational trouble (found in the rhythm and flow of speech: turn-taking, back-channel responses, coordinated body movements, and so on), and the outcome of the conversation (in terms of tasks accomplished, decisions made). Analyses can be verified by role play, that is, by having subjects act out the roles of, say, interviewer and interviewee. To the extent that they reproduce the same behavior patterns under the same conditions as found in naturally occurring encounters, the analysis is confirmed. It is further strengthened by involving participants in the identification of cooperative and uncooperative conversation, and by describing their intentions and reactions. In this type of research specific instances of language use must be contextualized. In order to understand what is happening in interaction it is necessary to have some idea of the background knowledge that participants bring to the interaction. This allows the analyst to have clues as to the extent to which participants are likely to be able to establish shared knowledge.

This work has been especially important in that it has provided a method of identifying exactly what it is about the way different people talk that leads to the establishment of inferences and so to interlocutors' ability to make (joint) sense out of what is happening and to establish conversational cooperation, which underlie the formation of social relationships and potential for access to participation in social networks and activities.

The same is true of work addressing the third research question regarding the role of language in the formation of ethnic group boundaries and identity. To my knowledge there has in fact been very little work done in this area, with the exception perhaps of Scotton's work in Africa (1976, 1983) and my own work in Quebec and Ontario (Heller, 1982a, 1982b, 1984; Heller, Bartholomot, Levy, & Ostiguy, 1982; see below). Work in this area draws heavily on the type of studies outlined above, although in this case the focus is on situations in which ethnicity is reaffirmed, defined, and/or formed. These tend to be situations of interethnic encounter, although they also include intra-group interaction where the "other" group matters at a higher level of contextualization. Interaction in these situations is analyzed primarily in terms of the establishment of the ties basic to ethnic group membership and in terms of the conventions of language use characteristic of (I would claim constitutive of) comembership. The case study to be presented below falls within this last theoretical and methodological category.

An Ethnographic Case Study: Language and the Formation of Ethnic Identity among Students in French-Language Schools in Toronto

The case study to be presented here focuses on the formation of French ethnic identity among an ethnolinguistically heterogeneous population of students enrolled in a French-language minority school in Toronto, Ontario, a school that explicitly considers its mandate to be the preservation of French language, culture, and identity in the English-dominated Toronto community. In order to contextualize the process of ethnic identity information at the level of everyday life at school, I will first present background information regarding Ontario's French-language schools and the particular school chosen as a research site. I will then examine data collected through participant and nonobtrusive observation and through the tape recording of the natural spontaneous speech of a sample of eight target students at the Grade 7/8 level. The data collected in this manner consist of language use in events in everyday life at school in which ethnicity is called into question, and in which through talk (or lack of talk) students negotiate and define their own identity in the context of their own experiences of life inside and outside school.

French-language schools in Ontario. French-language education has long been seen by Ontario's francophones as the central pillar of support for the preservation of their language and their culture (Choquette, 1975; Mougeon & Canale, 1979). Their social identity was intimately linked to their language, and schools became the main way of passing on that language as the importance of other social institutions (such as the Church) declined, as geographic mobility increased, and as assimilation and language shift to English became more and more common (Castonguay, 1977; Churchill, 1976; Joy, 1972; Lachapelle & Henripin, 1980). However, the French language and culture, which it is their explicit goal to preserve, are the language and culture of the relatively homogeneous and tightly knit communitites of northern and eastern Ontario (Arnopoulos, 1982). The clientele of Toronto's French-language schools, on the other hand, is extremely heterogeneous and scattered. Although some students come from majority francophone communities, others come from minority francophone communities, and many do not claim French identity at all. Indeed, Toronto's French-language schools have been supported in part by intellectual, upwardly mobile middle-class anglophones, who, since the 1960s, have become increasingly aware of the social prestige and economic importance of French. The schools also have drawn from non-anglophone immigrants whose second language is French and/or who are equally aware of the importance of French/English bilingualism for success in their new country.

The case study site: St. Michel. The school chosen as a research site, St. Michel, is a Catholic French-language elementary school in the

Toronto metropolitan area. The client population of St. Michel reflects the heterogeneity of the Toronto francophone population. About 40% of the families are of linguistically mixed marriages; in most of them it is the mother who is francophone. Another 30% are French and 11% are English; the rest are composed of families in which the parents' mother tongue is Italian, German, Arabic, Gujurati, Lithuanian, or Armenian. The large numbers of anglophones can be accounted for partially by the fact that several anglophone families were instrumental in getting St. Michel established in the late 1960s and early 1970s. These parents had an ideological commitment not only to bilingualism but to biculturalism, to the mastery of both French and English and to access to both social groups, to support for both languages, and for the social institutions that are the basis for both groups. As a result, they believe in the importance of French-language minority education, and perceive cultural benefits and practical social benefits in sending their children to French-language (as opposed to immersion) schools. There are, in addition, commitments to bilingualism on the part of mixed French/English families, and on the part of Franco-Ontarians from minority communities accustomed to the economic necessity of speaking English.

The population of the school is scattered all over one half of the Toronto area. As a result, St. Michel students go home to nonfrancophone neighborhoods. It is thus difficult for them to maintain friendships established at school. This residential dispersion seems to indicate that francophone families choose where they want to live on bases other than ethnolinguistic affiliation.

The school's policy has changed over time, from de facto bilingualism to explicit French monolingualism. Now the school functions only in French: It communicates with parents only in French and insists on the use of French by students on school grounds. It is an uphill battle, however: teachers spend a great deal of time alternately encouraging students to speak French and admonishing them for not doing so.

Why should this be so? An examination of students' language choice and language use patterns shows that students' backgrounds, experiences, and goals influence the way they use language to make sense of the basic tension between the monolingual French goals and identity of the school (and of some homes), the heterogeneous composition of the school population, and the domains of life outside school, which are dominated by languages other than French.

The following section focuses on the importance of language choice in the establishment of participation in social networks and social activities, and in the formation of social relationships, all of which together consititute basic ethnic boundary maintenance and ethnic boundary definition processes. It also treats conventions of language use that reveal the extent to which students share background knowledge, and so reveal the nature of the meaning of languages for members of different groups as part of their identity.

Language Choice and Language Use as Ethnic Processes

Language choice and the definition of ethnic boundaries. At St. Michel, language choice is central to participation in activities and to the formation of social ties. French is essential for all teacher-centered and curriculum-related activities. In the classroom, French is supposed to be the language of communication. However, most peer group interaction involves activities that are not school-derived (games, television, movies, sports), and most students interact with each other in English. Students generally can function in the classroom in French and in the peer group in English.

What happens to new students if either French or their English is poor? A few English-dominant students are admitted each year in the upper grades, often from French-immersion programs. They have no trouble making friends, because so much peer talk is in English anyway. However, they participate relatively little in classroom activities, and can be (visibly) uncomfortable when called upon to perform in class. One Grade 6 boy, when asked to improvise in the role of a little boy who has come home late, was only able to produce, after much hesitation, "Je jouais au parc" (I was playing in the park). Upon continued pressure from the teacher the utterance was reduced to "je jouais," then to "jouais," and then to silence. Although this is an extreme example of teacher pressure, it illustrates the difficulties English-dominant students encounter in classroom activities.

French-dominant students or monolingual francophone students encounter the reverse problem. Their ability to interact with the teacher and to participate in classroom activities is great, but they have difficulty making friends.

For example, Marc is a Grade 1 student from France. His parents encourage him explicitly not to lose his language. In Grade 1 the school's norm that French be spoken is largely respected, even if that means that some students do not talk very much. Marc talks a lot in class, and makes much of his French identity (for example, the battleships in his drawings fly the French flag). On the other hand, he is extremely hurt when a school friend tells him that he won't be invited to the friend's birthday party because he doesn't speak English. Marc's reaction to this is to withdraw further and make more of his Frenchness, a reaction typical of many other francophones.

Eric is in Grade 3, and arrived recently from Montreal. A charismatic young man, he quickly became a kind of spokesperson to the teacher for a Grade 3 gang of boys. However, outside the classroom he remained, although a participant, on the edge of games, and in interpersonal interaction he often had to rely on the services of a bilingual broker. In one incident, Eric got into an argument with another boy over who was allowed to hang his coat on a particular hook. The argument was getting nowhere when a third boy stepped in and resolved the issue, speaking French to Eric and English to the other boy.

Eric's older brother, Robert, entered Grade 6, a class with a fairly loose peer group network. Robert hung around on the edge of activities, and rapidly picked up some essential routines, such as "Shut up" and "Leave me alone." These routines (despite their content) demonstrated that Robert was part of the action, and that he was playing by the same rules as everyone else. Although Robert's English was significantly worse than almost everyone else's, he was not shy to use it. On the contrary, he seemed to seek out opportunities to do so.

This behavior contrasts significantly with that of Johanne and Christiane, both of whom are francophones recently arrived from Quebec. Both Johanne and Christiane remained fairly isolated all year and resisted speaking English most of the time. They were known to the rest of the class as francophones, and it was generally acknowledged that in order to interact with them it was necessary to speak French. Johanne made friends with one francophone girl recently arrived from Northern Ontario. However, there was very little interaction between the two of them and the others, beyond some teasing involving the boys who shared their table.

These examples demonstrate that francophones who arrive at St. Michel must make a decision about learning English if they want to participate in peer group networks and activities. When faced with this decision, many children view it as a direct threat to their identity as "francophones" (or as "Français" or as "Québecois"). They talk about their dilemma in terms of how their language and their friends affect who they are. This is, of course, supported by the fact that when they reject English they are explicitly singled out and identified by the others as "francophones." By the same token, they differentiate themselves from the others by referring to themselves as "francophones" and the others as "anglophones." English-dominant students, in some respects, suffer less. Although the classroom can be stressful for them, their peers act as a buffer, and it is easier for them to avoid having to deal with any identity-related issues. Identity then is more of an issue for francophones than it is for anglophones, because anglophone ways of behaving are reinforced by most of their experiences outside school, but francophones have fewer contexts in which to be themselves. However, both groups have to manage access to social activities as it relates to language use and identity. Anglophones must legitimate their presence as anglophones in a French-language school: They tend to do this by using English and avoiding French as much as possible and by profiting from their bilingual peers who act as brokers for them. Francophones also may adopt this strategy insofar as they form exclusive peer alliances with the few other francophones available, thereby preserving their identity. Alternatively, francophones and anglophones may begin to adopt the conventions of the majority bilingual peer group, using at least some English with peers and French in classroom contexts, thereby transforming their identity as a result of new experience. It should be noted that although the majority of students consider themselves to be bilingual, most of them tend to speak better English than French. This is most likely due to the extremely limited contexts in which they use French (see Gal, 1984).

It is reasonable to hypothesize that the bilingual group eventually assimilates the francophones and the anglophones, because its distinguishing characteristic is length of residence in an English-dominant milieu coupled with attendance at a French-language school. Yet although it is possible for francophones and anglophones to become bilingual, the reverse never happens: Students who start out bilingual never become francophone or anglophone (that is, French dominant or English dominant).

This group of bilingual students says explicitly that it values bilingualism largely for practical purposes: to get a better job, to be more geographically (and, one suspects, socially) mobile. The additional vague notion that somehow bilingualism is better is perhaps best analyzed in terms of the social prestige accorded to French/English bilingualism as a result of its use for access to certain higher-level jobs. However, for these students, bilingualism does not mean biculturalism, because they do not all participate in each of two distinct societies.

Instead, they all share limited participation in French activities, mainly in the classroom, and a mix of activities outside school, most of which are conducted in English.

Thus, on the one hand, anglophones and francophones inhabit a world in which use of English and French form the major contexts of their social lives. They can, in some sense, afford to use avoidance as a strategy for managing activities that require the use of the other language, because they have little to lose by not participating in those activities, and much to preserve. Bilinguals, on the other hand, whatever their background, have experienced major arenas of their lives in both languages, sometimes simultaneously, over long periods of time. They have invested too much in the French and English domains of their lives to be able to adopt freely an avoidance strategy. Instead, their shared experience forms the basis of a shared understanding of what French and English represent, and permits them to neutralize the tension between French and English. Thus they can manage their identity in a situation in which their position with respect to ethnic boundaries may be less than clear. This shared knowledge is reflected in their patterns of language use, which distinguishes them from their francophone and anglophone classmates.

Language use, shared knowledge, and identity. Two patterns of language use characterize the verbal behavior of the bilingual students. The first is bilingual joking or punning, the second is code-switching. These two patterns are important for three reasons. First, they illustrate how shared experience, through participation in the same or similar social networks and activities, results in shared ways of speaking. Second, these shared ways of speaking reflect a common view of the world. In this case, they show how bilinguals find themselves in a situation in which it is difficult to maintain participation in both French and English activities, but where they nonetheless try to do so (and perhaps have to do so). In fact, it is *through* punning and code-switching that bilingual children maintain an equilibrium between two different, and often competing, spheres of activity. This underlies the third reason for the importance of these patterns, namely, that they are examples of the role language can play in defining shared knowledge and in forming bonds between people who share the same experience. Although it may be inappropriate to say that these children have developed a bilingual "identity," what they are doing differentiates them from "francophones" and "anglophones," and lays the foundation for the development of a stable position on the frontier between French and English. This is supported by the fact that bilingual children do distinguish themselves from others, do talk of themselves as "bilingual," and do refer to their ability to participate in both "worlds," although this is based more on access to various French- and English-language institutions than on immediate access to social groups.

Bilingual joking depends, for its effect, entirely on adequate knowledge of both languages; it is funny because it collapses two languages in a situation where only one is expected, and because through the second language associations the frame of the situation is broken. Only bilingual students make these jokes, and only bilingual students understand them: francophones who are present just do not understand. Even perfectly bilingual teachers may not get these jokes. These teachers, even if they rarely speak French outside school, are "professional francophones" at school; not just teachers, they are engaged in the mission of transmitting French language and culture.

Two examples of these jokes are: (1) Grade 8 prepares a skit for graduation on a significant event in Canadian history: the taking of Quebec by the British General Wolfe. The narrator walks out on stage and asks the audience if they have ever heard the history of "Pierre et le Loup" (Peter and the Wolf). "Non?" she says, "eh bien, regardez!" (No? Well, watch!). What follows is a skit built on the idea of "Peter and the Wolf": French soldiers are playing cards when the lookout arrives, shouting, "Wolfe est là! Wolfé est arrive!" (Wolfe is here! Wolfe has arrived!) The soldiers rush to arms, and the lookout bursts out laughing, saying, in effect, "Gotcha!" (false alarm). The next time the lookout bursts in panickedly announcing Wolfe's arrival no one believes him, although, of course, this time it is true. Here the effect of the whole skit is built on an association of the French word *loup* (*wolf*) with *Wolfe*. (2) A senior kindergarten boy asks his teacher what "je m'en fiche" (I don't care) means. She tells him to go ask his friends. A little while later he returns and proudly announces that he now knows what it means. When she asks him what, he says "Je m'en poissonne" (from *s'en poissonner,* a nonsense verb derived from *poisson = fish*). The teacher doesn't understand, so the boy explains "Fiche, fish!" Here the joke is based on the association *fiche - fish - poisson/s'en ficher - s'en fish - er - s'en poissonner.*

Code-switching among bilingual students occurs primarily in situations in which both the teacher (or something else representative of the school) and classmates are present. It occurs a great deal, for example, in the whispered conversations that students have with each other during class, and it also occurs when individual students address the teacher in front of the rest of the class or when they perform in some formal way (for example, in the presentation of science projects). In these formal presentations it is the side comments and gap fillers that are in English, such as "um, okay," "let me see," "gimme a chance," and so on. Three types of code-switching predominate: switching between emblematic tags and fillers (as above), interlocutor-based switching (that is, bilinguals tend to speak French to people they know to prefer French), and turn-based switching. In this latter type of switching several turns will occur in one language and then a switch will occur at another turn.

The following is part of a talk in the classroom with the teacher regarding notes the teacher is writing up on the blackboard:

A: Monsieur, McDonald est mort en 1932 et est né en 1933?	(Sir, McDonald died in 1932 and was born in 1933?)
B: Yeah, way to go monsieur, sure	
Teacher: ce n'est pas une faute c'est une erreur	(It's not wrong, it's an error)
C: Monsieur, il y a un K à Carmichael	(Sir, there's a K in Carmichael)
D: Sure, why not	

Sometimes code-switching is within an utterance, for example:

A: Je m'excuse de vous déranger monsieur I know I better be mais est-ce que je peux avoir le poids rond et le poids à distance?	(Excuse me for disturbing you sir *I know I better be* but may I have the round weight and the distance weight?)

Code-switching is, however, relatively rare.
On the other hand, bilinguals often use English to fill in lexical and phrase gaps, for example:

Teacher: Treize ans quatorze ans, qu'est-ce qu'il faut faire?	(Thirteen fourteen years old what do you have to do?)
B: décider quel high school c'est that's about it	(to decide which *high school* that's *that's about it*)

They also use English strategically, to resist teacher's authority, for example:

Teacher: Parlez français!   (speak French!)
A: It's not nine o'clock
     yet monsieur
(Class starts officially at nine o'clock).

Another example:

Teacher: Parlez francais!   (speak French! What page
     Vous êtes à quelle page?   are you on?)

André: page forty-three
Teacher: André!
André: page quarante-trois   (page forty-three)

Here, André clearly understood what the teacher meant when she angrily shouted his name. Once he complied by responding in French the lesson could continue.

Their two distinct patterns of language use (bilingual punning and code-switching, including strategic language choice) characterize the group of bilinguals and set them apart from their francophone and anglophone peers. This distinctiveness is interpretable in the context of the bilingual students' experience of French and English in daily life, and analysis of these patterns reveals the role that language plays in the formation of group boundaries and in the definition of these children's ethnic identity.

Conclusion

The contextual factor that distinguishes bilingual students from their francophone and anglophone peers is a relatively long period of residence in Toronto while attending French-language schools. Unlike the others, it has been the case for most of their lives that they experience relatively circumscribed domains of use of French and English. Furthermore, there is pressure from parents and from the school to speak, indeed sometimes to see themselves as French, and pressure from peers, increasingly so as they grow older, to speak English in activities outside school. Finally, they themselves have internalized a desire to participate in both French and English milieus; in some ways, the "identity" of bilingual resolves what they often experience as a conflict between the French and English domains of their lives. Punning and code-switching break down the barrier between the separate frames of reference of French and English, they neutralize the tension between them, and they allow the bilinguals to be both French and English at the same time, and yet neither one alone. Punning accomplishes this by unexpectedly calling into play at the same time the world of English and the world of French in situations where the worlds are supposed to be separate, but where bilinguals have difficulty maintaining the separation. This difficulty creates tension, tension that is dissipated by deliberately violating the separation in unusual ways, at unexpected moments. Code-switching similarly breaks down the barrier simply by, in essence, doing two different things (speaking French *and* English) at the same time. The fact that students deny that they code-switch only reinforces how strong the barrier is for them, and how significant it is that, just the same, they need to break it down.

This is understood by the francophones, who see that in order to remain what they are they must resist English, and yet to do so means giving up chances to make friends and be part of peer activities. Anglophones seem able to maintain their marginal participation in school activities through limited competence in French. The choice for them is less directly focused on their identity, because the available French network and set of activities is so much more limited than those that are carried out in English.

Language use is thus involved in the formation of ethnic identity in two ways. First, it constrains access to participation in activities and to formation of social relationships. Thus at a basic level language use is central to the formation of group boundaries. Second, as children spend more and more time together they share experience, and language is a central means of making sense out of that shared experience. Thus patterns of language use reflect the shared background knowledge and shared ways of establishing that background knowledge that underlie group membership and ethnic identity.

In the case presented here, the incipient processes seem to be leading toward the following alternatives: maintenance of francophone or anglophone identities through restricted participation in outgroup activities, or transformation of identity in order to permit stabilization of a position on the boundary between groups. Language practices, as reflected in access to school networks, reveal the process of formation of social boundaries: Here, the bilinguals *are* the boundary. As a result, although bilinguals do not have *an* ethnic identity along the line of that which flows from the relatively homogeneous worlds of francophones and anglophones, their identity is crucial to ethnic processes in the Toronto French-language school milieu.

Finally, in order to explain how social experiences come to be the way they are, it is necessary to contextualize the situations of everyday life in terms of larger-scale social and historical processes. It is clear that students' experience of life at St. Michel is influenced directly by the historical development of French-language education in Ontario, and by economic processes affecting the migration of francophones to Toronto and their patterns of settlement in Toronto. It is, however, equally clear that social processes are in turn affected by social interaction in daily life. The formation of children's ethnic identity can best be understood by contextualizing their communicative patterns in social interaction, by explaining them with reference to wider socioeconomic processes, and by focusing on language as both a symbol of ethnic identity and a means of defining ethnic boundaries and ethnic identity.

10

Ethnic Behavior Patterns as an Aspect of Identity

MARY JANE ROTHERAM
JEAN S. PHINNEY

The impact of ethnicity on children includes ethnically linked ways of thinking, feeling, and acting that children acquire through socialization (Whiting & Whiting, 1975). Parents pass on to children not only a language, customs, and rituals, but also implicit assumptions regarding the nature of social relationships and the role that the child must fulfill (Forgas, 1979; Harre, 1980; Triandis, 1972). These assumptions are reflected in behavior patterns that vary among cultures. This chapter deals with children's acquisition of these ethnic behavior patterns as an aspect of ethnic identity. Following a review of the literature on cultural variation in children's behavior, we present data from our studies of behavioral differences among children from two ethnic groups and suggest how such differences may be related to children's ethnic identity.

Dimensions that Structure a Child's Behavior

In the introductory chapter we suggested four dimensions along which behavioral differences can be organized. In this section we review evidence for variation among cultures along these dimensions, with emphasis on research with children.

Group versus individual orientation. The dimension defined by an orientation toward the group at one extreme and an individual orientation at the other is one of the most widely discussed in the literature. Some cultures as diverse as Japanese, Hawaiian, and Mexican are seen as emphasizing affiliation, cooperation, and interpersonal relationships; others, such as mainland American and most Western European cultures, are seen as focusing more on individual accomplishment, competition, and independence from the group (Burger, 1973; Dore, 1958; Gallimore, Boggs, & Jordan, 1974; Kerlinger, 1951). These differences also emerge between minority and majority groups within the United States. Although two researchers have found no ethnic differences on this group dimension (Halpin, Glennelle, & Gerald, 1980; Preston, 1972), the majority of the research suggests that Black and Hispanic Americans are more oriented toward the family and group than the more individually focused White American child (Burger, 1973; Dore, 1958; Mock & Tuddenham, 1971). This group orientation is reflected in children's behavior in a number of areas: an emphasis on affiliation and social stimuli rather than objective tasks, cognitive styles, attitudes toward property, and cooperativeness in children.

For example, when the emphasis is on group affiliation, individuals are likely to be more attentive to the feelings and attitudes of other people than to objective aspects of a situation. With Mexican American and Black adults, it has been demonstrated that the nature of the interpersonal relationship must be established before instrumental tasks can be accomplished in therapeutic (Gibbs, 1980) and work settings (Hofstede, 1984). With young kindergarten and second grade children, Knudson (1979) found Mexican American children to be more prosocial than White American children. In another study, 2- to 4-year old Hupa Indian children were observed to show more sociable-intimate behaviors than a matched sample of White American children (Batchold, 1982). In an ethnographic study of Black and White American kindergarten children's strategies for entering and cooperating in reading groups, very different social styles emerged. Unless able to match the social and academic behavior of White students, the Black children's access to the reading groups was limited (Diss, 1979). With slightly older children the social orientation is reflected in a higher need for affiliation among Mexican American children compared to White children (Sanders, Scholz, & Kagan, 1976). A rich description of the misunderstandings between Black and White adolescents that emerge from White adolescents' attention to tasks rather than social rituals is provided by Kochman (1970). Kochman's accounts of classroom interactions show how ethnic differences in social expectations lead to prejudice and conflict.

In general, the family is seen as providing the context and training for the development of an orientation. For example, Gallimore et al. (1974) suggest that interdependence is the major feature of the Hawaiian family, with each member contributing in a spirit of cooperation and helpfulness. Stewart (1972) points out that from an early age, the American child is encouraged to be autonomous and to make decisions for him- or herself, whereas the Chinese family, among many others, encourages dependence on others. From an observational study of European and Polynesian children in New Zealand, Graves and Graves (1976) conclude that Polynesian children's style is inclusive and group oriented in contrast to the exclusive European style. European children are more independent and cliquish, whereas the Polynesian children are more friendly and cooperative. Within the United States, Kagan and Endler (1975) have demonstrated that Mexican American mothers reward children noncontingently, and White American mothers' rewards are more performance based. Gallimore et al. (1974) suggest that classroom environments for Hawaiian children must be structured to reflect the spirit of the intimate home environment where cooperation and helpfulness are the central themes.

A study of early language acquisition gives an indication of how such an orientation may develop. Mexican American children aged 2 to 4 were observed in the home interacting with their families (Eisenberg, 1984). The focus of questions addressed to Mexican children was on interpersonal issues, such as "Who is in the picture?" or "Where is Papa?" rather than on the more impersonal, object-oriented questions addressed to White children (for example, "What is that?").

The group versus individual dimension is related conceptually and empirically to that of cooperation versus competition, which has been studied widely in school-aged children. In group-oriented cultures, children tend to be more cooperative and to function better in classrooms structured to foster less individual competition by having children work in small interdependent groups (MacDonald & Gallimore, 1971). Research with American Indian children and Mexican American children show both groups to be more cooperative than White American children (Batchold, 1984; De La Serna, 1982; Kagan, 1977; Kagan & Knight, 1981; Kagan, Knight, Martinez, & Santa, 1981;

Kagan & Madsen, 1971; Knight & Kagan, 1982; Miller, 1973). In a number of these investigations, the child's cooperativeness appears to be related to other characteristics, such as a lower need for achievement and a higher need for affiliation, an external locus of control, and decreased aggressiveness. But Knight et al. (1982) found competitiveness related to achievement only for Anglo-Americans, not Mexican Americans.

A high group orientation also appears closely related to the cognitive style identified as field dependent. Early studies of cognitive style focused on its relationship to mental activity, but more recent work has examined it in relation to social behavior (Witkin, 1979). Field dependent people, compared to field independent, are more attentive to social cues, more socially outgoing, and prefer to be physically closer in social interactions. They may also be more effective in solving interpersonal disputes (Witkin, 1979). Results of research on cultural differences in cognitive style show that Mexican, Mexican American, and Black children are more field dependent than are American children (Holtzman, Diaz-Guerrero, & Swartz, 1975; Ramirez & Price-Williams, 1974). Mexican American children, aged 5 to 10, stand closer together in natural settings than do White American children (Baxter, 1970). Shade (1982) notes that Black children tend to view the whole rather than the parts, that is, to be more field dependent; and to attend more to people than to nonsocial stimuli. Thus, in their interactions with others, children from these groups are more likely than White American children to be attentive to the feelings and expectations of those around them.

The orientation toward the group may include an attitude toward property. For example, Staples (1976) suggests that Black American culture tends to consider property a collective asset. Thus a Black child may feel free in taking an object that a White child would see as belonging to the child who has been using it. This difference could account in part for the evidence that Blacks engage in more aggressive acts such as grabbing (Finkelstein & Haskins, 1983).

Finally, it is important to remember that descriptions of "Hispanic" Americans mask considerable within-group differences. For example, Puerto Rican Americans are less group oriented and more passive in style than Mexican Americans (Lewis, 1975).

Active versus passive coping style. An active coping style is associated with "doing" and "getting things done," rather than being or becoming; a future time orientation where time moves quickly; and a perception that we control our environment, in contrast to a sense of fatalism

(Burger, 1973; Diaz-Guerrero, 1967, 1979; Stewart, 1972). Mexican Americans are less active in orientation than Black or White Americans (Boney, 1971; Diaz-Guerrero, 1973, 1979; Holtzman et al., 1975; Kagan & Carlson, 1975; Nevius, 1982). Diaz-Guerrero (1967), who originally introduced this concept of active versus passive coping style in cross-cultural investigations, has emphasized how time is slower and more present oriented for Mexican Americans in contrast to Anglo Americans. Black children, according to Shade (1982), also tend to use approximate concepts of time and space, in contrast to the precision and exactness expected in the White culture.

A tendency toward activity is associated with a sense that one is in control and able to change the environment; a passive style reflects a more fatalistic view that one is controlled by external circumstances (Burger, 1973). There is evidence that American preadolescents have a greater sense of internal control than a comparable group of Brazilian children (Biaggio, 1969). At the university level, Japanese students feel more controlled by chance than do American students (Bond & Tornatzky, 1973; Mahler, 1974).

This orientation is reflected in school children in the United States. Mexican American children are less likely to say they would take action when they need materials in a classroom situation and are more likely to wait to be helped (Rotheram & Phinney, 1983). Ethnicity appears to influence the acquisition of assertiveness, with White Americans acquiring assertiveness earlier than Mexican American children. This pattern varies with the sex of a child.

Attitude toward authority. A pervasive dimension identified by many writers as important in structuring social interactions is power. With children, this dimension translates to whether a child regards parents and teachers as clear authority figures whom one respects and obeys without question or rather sees them as more nearly equal figures with whom one may disagree and question. Differences on this dimension are evident in young children in their relationships with both parents and teachers. Young Mexican American and Asian American children are more obedient, respectful, and accepting of authority than are White American children (Diaz-Guerrero, 1967; Kitano, 1982). Hupa Indian children are less authoritarian than White American children (Batchold, 1982, 1984). Although Anglo-American school children may reject a teacher's commands and want to decide for themselves, both Mexican American and Black children expect to be commanded and may perform less well in school if required to make their own choice (Burger,

1973). Because of their desire to please adults, it is difficult for researchers or examiners to get accurate answers in test situations from Mexican American children (Cedillos, Smith, & Rotheram, 1983).

Open, expressive versus restrained, private. Americans, according to Stewart (1972), see themselves as direct and open in social interactions, particularly in contrast to the polite, ritualistic manners typical of the Japanese and other Oriental cultures (Burger, 1973). Asian Americans, similarly, are cautious in expressing feelings and thus appear more socially introverted, in comparison to Whites (Sue & Wagner, 1973). However, for Anglo-Americans, the characteristic openness and expressiveness is limited by several factors: a sense of when one should use expressiveness (for example, not during business discussions or in school), and a limit to how personal an interchange may be, so as not to intrude on another's privacy and personal space. Aiello and Jones (1971) found this reflected in the interpersonal distance of Black, Puerto Rican, and White 6- to 8-year-olds, with White children requiring the greatest interpersonal distance.

In contrast, Blacks are more openly and freely expressive in a wide variety of situations (Kochman, 1981; Cheek, 1976). Kochman (this volume) describes Black culture as a "high intensity" culture in which feelings, both negative and positive, are openly expressed. From an early age Black children gain experience through play in dealing with the intense feelings expressed, and learn to handle situations which to a White child might appear highly threatening. The tendency of Blacks to be more open in expressing anger may contribute to the perception of Black children as more aggressive or more negative than Whites (Finkelstein & Haskins, 1983; Kurakawa, 1971; Sagar & Schofield, 1980). Openness in confronting conflict may also result in seeing less threat in ambiguous situations. Sagar and Schofield (1980) found that Black sixth-grade boys, compared to Whites, tend to read less threat into ambiguous behaviors involving one person acting to obtain materials from another. Black children are less likely to see such acts as negative. Black kindergarteners and first graders rated children who engaged in grabbing and snatching in videotaped episodes as significantly more likable than did White children (Steinberg & Hall, 1981). A tendency toward open expressiveness may account, in part, for evidence that Black children were found to be considerably more friendly toward both same-race and other-race children than Whites (Hallinan & Tuma, 1978) and were more active in interracial interactions in elementary school (Sagar, Schofield, & Snyder, 1983).

Open expressiveness may be related to the tendency of Black children to become more emotionally involved in a discussion and more likely to interrupt than White children (Kochman, 1981; Longstreet, 1978), a difference that may lead to interethnic misunderstanding. Kochman (1981) describes the misunderstandings and conflict that result from interactions in college classrooms when Whites misinterpret the expressiveness of Blacks and vice versa.

Ethnic Profiles

The differences observed in behavioral styles lead to the concept of ethnic profiles. An *ethnic profile* is the description of an ethnic group in terms of its position on each of the four dimensions outlined above. For example, Spiegel (1982) has characterized Italian Americans as being oriented more to the present than the future, less active, more group oriented, and more accepting of authority relations than White Americans. This profile will predict social rules endorsed by Italian Americans as well as their behavior in a variety of settings. When such a profile is based on quantitative analysis, it allows for precise comparisons between two cultures in terms of their similarity in behavior, comparisons which in the past have been based on anecdotal evidence and intuition. Although some groups may share a similar position on one or two of the dimensions described, they are unlikely to be similar on all dimensions; thus some dimensions may be more critical than others in distinguishing between two groups.

In defining ethnic profiles in terms of dimensions, it should be noted that dimensions are interrelated and interactive. For example, evidence suggests that both Black and Mexican American children are generally emotionally expressive; however, Mexican American children are more accepting of authority relationships. Thus in situations with authority figures, their deference to a superior may suppress the tendency to be expressive, whereas the Black child would be equally expressive with superiors and peers.

It is important to emphasize that there are no "good" or "bad" ethnic profiles. Neither end of a dimension is better in an absolute sense, although some behaviors are more adaptive than others depending on the situation. Resistance to the systematic study of ethnic differences could emerge on the grounds that evidence for differences might reinforce negative stereotypes. The description of behavior patterns as positions on continuum permits examination of concrete events and patterns in place of value-laden attributions. For example, evidence that Black adolescents talk more loudly and interrupt more in group discussion (Longstreet, 1978) can be seen objectively as part of their greater expressiveness. Only if one attaches positive value to reserve and restraint is this behavior labeled as "offensive" or "aggressive."

The child's developing identity will be influenced by the way his or her own group profile relates to the profiles of other groups with which he or she comes in contact. The relationship between any two groups within a culture will depend to some extent on the degree of match between their profiles. The identification and description of ethnic profiles allows objective comparisons in place of ethnocentric evaluations of minority groups.

The study of ethnic profiles can also increase awareness of behavioral options in specific situations. Research on sex-role behaviors has made men and women more aware of existing differences between the sexes and of the individual's own patterns relative to these differences. It has also made individual men and women more aware of their options in particular situations; for example, men can choose to be more nurturant with children, or women can be more assertive in their careers. Similarly, an awareness of ethnic differences could help the individual to recognize his or her options either to adopt group patterns or to alter them as appropriate in a particular situation. Madsen (1971) found that Anglo American children are often so highly and inappropriately competitive that they lose the opportunity to win prizes that require even minimal cooperation. The more cooperative behavior of Mexican American children in a similar situation demonstrates alternative ways of behaving in situations of personal confrontation.

In addition, the study of ethnic group profiles can help identify and document changes in behavior patterns over time. Culture is continuously evolving, subject to a wide variety of social forces. As such changes are documented, the stereotypes change; the stereotype of the Asian immigrant has shifted from one of an uneducated laborer in early California history to a high academic achiever today (Sue & Wagner, 1973). The study of differences among groups can also establish the amount of similarity and overlap between groups (LeVine, 1982) and, more important, the amount of variation within groups. Although many individuals show behavior patterns typical of their ethnic group, others do not.

Finally, and most important for the research to be reported, descriptions of group differences in terms of ethnic profiles permit a comparison of the individual's profile with the profile of his or her own ethnic group, as well as the profile of other groups. This comparison provides a behavioral measure of an individual's identification with his or her own group. Profiles of various groups have been studied in a number of ways. Previous researchers studying behavioral differences between groups have been either anthropologists who gather data through observation (a rich data source, but one that makes an analysis of individual differences difficult) or social psychologists who use sophisticated rating scales (Forgas, 1979; Tajfel, 1978, 1981). For example, Forgas (1979) had the subjects (students, housewives) rate a large number of social situations on factors such as similarity; the results were then analyzed by means of multidimensionsal scaling or factor analysis. However, the ratings or discriminations required in such studies are too sophisticated for children; thus there have been no statistical studies of behavioral profiles with children.

Measuring Children's Ethnic
Socialization and Ethnic Identity

The above review suggests the importance of studying the behavioral aspects of ethnicity, particularly as they relate to the development of ethnic identity. We are interested in how an ethnic profile is transferred into specific interpersonal interactions that children encounter at school. The methodology we have developed is aimed at (1) identifying ethnic differences in behavior patterns, (2) gaining an understanding of the developmental acquisition of such patterns, and (3) examining individual differences in the acquisition of these patterns. We present this as one possible methodological approach to studying behavioral aspects of ethnicity.

We developed a videotape measure called Profiled Assessment of Children's Ethnic Socialization (PACES). The measure consists of a series of videotaped social encounters of children in everyday settings, taped separately with Black and Mexican American children. The social encounters are situations in which it is anticipated that Black and Mexican American children will differ regarding the appropriate social behavior. The scenes are also selected to represent broadly the dimensions in which other researchers have found ethnic differences in behavior. Children view the tape and respond by reporting the expected outcome of the situation.

We currently have results of studies using the PACES tapes with three samples: (1) Black and Mexican American third- and sixth-grade boys (Empey, Phinney, & Rotheram, 1984; Rotheram & Phinney, 1983); (2) Black and Mexican American third- and sixth-grade boys and girls (Phinney, Rotheram, & Romero, 1985; Rotheram & Phinney, 1985); and (3) Black, White, Puerto Rican, and Mexican American adolescents (Rotheram, 1985). In this chapter we will discuss the results from the first two studies.

In the first study, 65 Black and Mexican American children, drawn from ethnically balanced third and sixth grades, were shown eight videotaped scenes, each filmed in two versions (once with Black peers and once with Mexican American peers). In the first phase, children viewed tapes of same-ethnic peers and were asked what they themselves would do. Children's responses were coded in response categories; the range of responses to each scene was small (three to five categories per scene).

Rather than describe the pattern of results for all eight scenes, we will describe in detail the results from Scene 5. The scene consists of a tape of two children sitting at desks with crayons placed at the far side of one child so that they are inaccessible to the second child. The teacher is heard saying, "Take your green pencil and finish coloring." Subjects are asked what they would do or feel if they were the child who cannot reach the crayons.

(1) Feel bad: "I would feel bad (sad, or hurt)"
(2) Ask: "I would ask for the crayons (or get the crayons)"
(3) Rule statement: "Friends (children) should share"
(4) Feel or get angry: "I would be angry"

In Figure 10.1, the percentage of Mexican American children (top graph) and Black children (bottom graph) reporting each alternative for the scene with same-ethnic peers is shown by the left-hand bar of each pair. (The right-hand bar shows responses to the scene with cross-ethnic peers and will be discussed later.) Black and Mexican American children's responses for Scene 5 clearly discriminate between the groups. Mexican American children typically report that they will feel bad (45.2%) in this situation, or somewhat less frequently that they will make a rule statement regarding their peer's behavior (30.2%) or request the crayons (24.6%). Mexican American children never report feeling angry. In contrast, Black children report most frequently that they

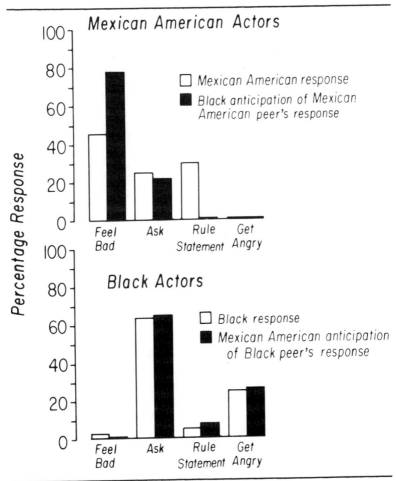

Figure 10.1: Responses of Mexican American and Black children to scene filmed with Mexican American actors (top) and Black actors (bottom).

would make a request (64.9%) or get angry (25.1%). Rule statement (6.7%) and feeling bad (3.3%), the most frequent responses of Mexican American children, are almost never reported.

Table 10.1 lists the videotaped scenes and the children's most frequent responses to these scenes. Examination of the content of the scenes and the differences in response patterns between Mexican American and Black children across the eight scenes allows construction of a descriptive ethnic profile. Mexican American children fall at the

TABLE 10.1
Videotaped Scenes and the Most Frequent Responses
of Mexican American and Black Children

Situation	Mexican American Response	Black Response
A peer comes up to you and says, "Can I borrow 35¢?"	share or ignore request	share or question the request
A teacher approaches you and says in a sad voice, "John/Sylvia, I am very disappointed in you. I saw you on the playground today and you did not share."	change my behavior, feel bad	defend myself, feel angry
You are reading aloud in class. You misread a passage saying, "The *is*-land of Hawaii is beautiful." A peer corrects you and says, "No, that is not right, it is the *i*sland of Hawaii."	feel bad	change the pronunciation, retort
Two children are sitting at a work table. One child has a box of crayons to the side. The teacher's voice is heard, "Children, take your blue crayon and color the water." One child starts coloring.	feel bad	get the crayon
You are eating lunch with a friend. A third child approaches. Your friend says, "Here comes John, you do not like him." John comes up and says, "I forgot my lunch."	ignore, share	feel angry, do not share
Three peers are about to play ball. One child points and says to the peers, "You can play." When he or she comes to you, he or she says, "You cannot play."	do something else, feel bad	get angry, feel bad
A teacher approaches a seated child and says in an irritated voice, "I told you to use the green crayon, not the yellow. You made a mistake again."	change my behavior, feel bad	defend myself, feel angry
Two children are fighting and you are watching.	tell the teacher	stop the fight

passive end of the continuum on several of the scenes. When they need a crayon, they tend to feel bad, but not ask for it; they are likely to ignore a request for a loan of money; and they do not intervene directly to stop a fight. Black children tend in each case to be active. They ask for or obtain the needed crayon in another way, they question why a loan is needed, and they act to stop the fight. In three of the scenes, Mexican American children show attention to social stimuli and an orientation toward the group expressed as concern for sharing. They feel bad when corrected, state that the crayons should be shared (as a secondary response), and are likely to share their lunch with a peer, even one who is not liked. Black children in these situations are less concerned with the interpersonal issues and make the necessary correction, get the crayon, and eat their own lunch without sharing. They show less orientation toward the group.

The tendency of Mexican American children to be deferential to authority figures is seen in two scenes in which the teacher scolds a child. The Mexican American child is most likely to accept the teacher's remarks and to state that the negative behavior will be changed or corrected. The Black children, in contrast, do not defer to the teacher but rather defend themselves. Similarly, when two peers are fighting, the Mexican American children typically resort to authority, that is, tell the teacher, but Black children handle the situation themselves.

In situations that evoke negative feelings (being corrected, criticized, or rejected), Mexican American children tend to direct the negative feelings inward and feel bad; the Black children direct feelings outward and feel anger toward the teacher or peer involved, or perhaps make a retort or defend themselves. Conflict avoidance by Mexican American children is seen in their finding something else to do when rejected, and their tendency not to get involved in a peer quarrel. Black children tend to be more assertive in these situations.

These results were reexamined with a second sample of 128 children drawn the next year from schools with a similar ethnic balance, socioeconomic status, using the same situation, but with videotapes of girls as well as boys. This allowed us to examine sex differences (Rotheram & Phinney, 1985). Overall, the sex differences were far less significant than the ethnic group differences, and are only noteworthy for two scenes. In the scene in which a peer corrects the target child for mispronunciation, Black third-grade girls were much more likely to feel bad, relative to Black third-grade boys and Mexican American third-grade girls. When rejected by a peer group who are about to play ball, girls did not report feeling angry, but rather uncomfortable and hurt.

The ethnic group differences were similar to the first sample in seven of the eight scenes. Taken together, these results suggest group profiles that distinguish Mexican American and Black children. Mexican

American children appear generally more passive, attentive to social stimuli, and deferential to authority. They tend to direct feelings inward and act to avoid conflict. Black children are more active, attentive to their own needs, and assertive. They are more likely to direct their feelings outward and not accept authority without question. However, these differences cannot be assumed to operate in a simple way that will allow clear predictions; rather, they will be related to the specific situation. For example, a Mexican American child may be quiet and polite with an authority figure but very expressive among peers. Currently this methodology is being used with adolescents (Rotheram, 1985). Scenes are being selected to examine how these dimensions are reflected in specific situations and how different dimensions relate to each other across ethnic groups.

Cross-Ethnic Awareness

In general, the relationship between any two groups within a culture will depend to some extent on the degree of match between their profiles. We predict that in areas in which there is similarity between groups there will be compatibility, whereas in areas in which norms or rules differ, there will tend to be cross-ethnic conflict.

However, the degree of cross-ethnic conflict will be modulated by each group's awareness of the social norms of the other group. We assess this when children view scenes videotaped with cross-ethnic peers and are asked what that child will do. These responses are shown by the right-hand bars in each pair in Figure 10.1. Children who report the response given by the majority of cross-ethnic peers to that scene are demonstrating awareness of the behavior of the other group. Cross-ethnic awareness is indicated by the degree of match between one's predictions about another group and that group's own expected behaviors; it can be seen by comparing the solid and dotted lines on the graphs. For example, in the scene with Mexican American actors, Black children are aware that the Mexican Americans are likely to get angry and that they may ask for the crayons. However, they do not expect them to make a rule statement and they overestimate their feeling bad. The results from this scene suggest a higher cross-ethnic awareness among Mexican American children.

When analyzing the pattern of awareness across the eight scenes, we found the cross-ethnic awareness of Mexican American children was in fact somewhat higher than for Black children. The overall results are misleading, however. Mexican American children showed very high accuracy in predicting Black responses to some scenes, but very poor accuracy in others. Each of the scenes for which Mexican American children had high cross-ethnic awareness involved situations in which Black children were more assertive than Mexican American children. The cross-ethnic awareness scores suggest that the PACES procedure may be useful for specifying domains in which children have inappropriate stereotypes or misunderstandings of their cross-ethnic peers.

Developmental Acquisition of Ethnic Identity

The child's ethnic identity is not a static attribute but evolves with personal identity, in response to developmental and cohort changes and new environmental challenges. Erikson (1968) has most thoroughly addressed the issue of identity development throughout the life span. His model assumes the critical importance of a child's social relationships at each stage of development and stresses the cultural context in which identity evolves. Research on the generalizability of Erikson's stages across cultures points to the importance of ethnic group membership in shaping personal identity (Ciaccio, 1978). Research on ethnic identity development has focused on ethnic self-identification in young children (Aboud, this volume), on the subjective sense of group identification in adolescents (Rosenthal, this volume), or on Black adults (Cross, this volume). There has been little research on the developmental acquisition of the attitudes, values, and behaviors that characterize ethnic identity.

One goal of the PACES research has been to examine developmental changes in ethnic behavior patterns. When the data discussed above are examined separately for third and sixth graders, we see clear developmental changes. On five of the eight scenes, the response patterns become clearer and more differentiated with age. Among the older children, the percentage of children reporting modal responses for each ethnic group is higher, and the differences between the typical responses of Mexican American and Black children are clearer. These results suggest that ethnic behavior patterns become more stable and differentiated with age.

Individual Ethnic Identity and Ethnic Profiles

Age changes analyzed at the group level do not give a full picture of individual differences in ethnic identity. Although with age children increasingly manifest the behavior patterns of their group, there are significant individual differences in the acquisition of these patterns. In order to understand an individual child's ethnic identity, we must examine the relationship between individual and group profiles. The degree of consistency among the child's behavior, perceptions, and values and that of his or her group will materially affect the child's identity development.

In one of the few empirical studies assessing the position of children relative to their ethnic group, Lambert and Tucker (1972) had children rate themselves and others on adjectives on a semantic differential scale. If children described themselves as more similar to another ethnic group on half the items, they were labeled bicultural. If their rating matched those of their own group, they were considered monocultural. This study provides the most empirically based definition of monocultural or bicultural identity in the literature.

The PACES data allow us to examine the relationship of the children's behavioral patterns to those of their group. A child's responses, when compared to the responses of the child's same-ethnic peers and the responses of peers from the other group, gives a behavioral index of ethnic identity. To analyze these relationships, children receive weighted scores indicating the degree to which their responses match those of their own group and those of the other group. These scores provide the basis for our operational definitions of types of ethnic identity. A monocultural identity is inferred for children whose responses are clearly more similar to the responses of their own group than to those of the other group. A bicultural identity is indicated when half the responses match the modal responses of their own group and half match the other group's responses. Outgroup identity refers to a response pattern that primarily matches that of the other group.

The data for the Black and Mexican American sixth-grade boys from the first sample are plotted on Figure 10.2. On the horizontal axis is the weighted score for degree of similarity to Mexican American responses; on the vertical, the degree of similarity to Black responses. Each child is shown by a dot indicating his or her scores on each axis. Among these boys, 21 (78%) demonstrated a monocultural identity; these are the clearly distinct groups above and below the diagonal. Three children's responses (11%) fall along the diagonal. A third group of three (11%) revealed a pattern more typical of cross-group peers. Only Mexican American boys showed this pattern, characterized by higher Black than

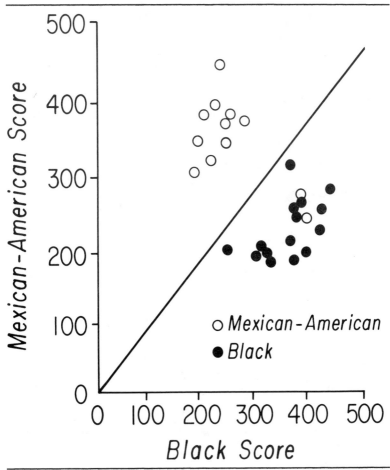

Figure 10.2: Individual plots of Black and Mexican American identity scores for sixth graders.

Mexican American scores. These latter two patterns we label *bicultural*.

The data from the second sample of third and sixth graders were consistent with the first sample. We found 69% of the children to be monocultural, 12% to fall between the two groups, and 19% to be similar to cross-ethnic peers. In the second sample, only female sixth-grade Mexican American girls showed a cross-ethnic pattern.

Also of interest is the correlation between own-group identity scores and self-esteem. Correlations between the Piers-Harris self-esteem measure and own-group score for third graders were .32 for Mexican American children and .27 for Black children. At the sixth grade, the correlations were .57 for Mexican American children and .63 for the Blacks. These results from the first sample are suggestive of an increasing relationship between ethnic identity and self-esteem, but more data are needed. We were unable to obtain measures of self-esteem in the second sample. Specifically, a measure that distinguishes the components of self-esteem (for example, Harter's 1982 scale of cognitive, social, and physical perceived competence) should be used with identity measures. Our clinical impression is that children with a monocultural identity may be well adjusted at home or with same-ethnic peers, but less well adjusted in the classroom.

Summary

This chapter focuses on the importance of ethnic behavior patterns and implicit expectations of behavior as aspects of ethnic identity. Differences in behaviors between groups are not random, but are organized in dimensions. Groups can be described by an ethnic profile based on these dimensions that will predict social rules in a variety of interpersonal situations. The group's characteristics and the group's attributes relative to the dominant culture influence children's social expectations, cross-ethnic awareness, and ethnic identity. The degree to which children demonstrate these characteristics relative to their group norm defines monocultural and bicultural identity. The age at which these norms are acquired, the impact of a group's specific behavioral norms on a child's ethnic identity, and individual differences in a child's identification with a group emerge as important issues to be studied.

This chapter suggests one possible methodology for examining these issues, PACES. This measure provides a way of specifying the impact of ethnicity in children's everyday social encounters. It allows us to examine ethnic group differences in social behavior and analyze how these differences relate to underlying dimensions that distinguish ethnic groups. Age changes in the acquisition of behavioral norms can then be examined. Cross-ethnic awareness and stereotyping can be analyzed as they affect social interaction.

11

The Ethnic Component in Black Language and Culture

THOMAS KOCHMAN

One of the aims of the present volume is to focus on variations in ethnic patterns as they relate to the child's ethnic identity. Another is to obtain some comparative information as to how (and perhaps also when) children from different ethnic groups become aware of their own ethnic patterns.

To begin to answer these questions with regard to Blacks in the United States, it is necessary first to get a fix on which Black group patterns could be regarded as "ethnic" based upon established definitions of what the terms *ethnic* or *ethnicity* mean. This chapter proposes to do this, although this goal is qualified in two important ways. First, the focus of this investigation is limited to patterns that fall within the framework of Black cultural communication, which is to say, patterns of social interaction within the ingroup. Second, these patterns will have been established as existing within the culture by means of ethnographic (that is, anthropological) methodological presuppositions and practices discussed below.

In the first part of this chapter, I propose, on the one hand, to see which aspects of Black communication and culture would qualify as *ethnic,* based upon established definitions of the term; on the other, to see whether or not definitions of *ethnicity* are able to encompass those culturally distinctive Black patterns of social interaction that contribute to giving Black people their special identity as a social group. In that last regard I distinguish between emblematic and nonemblematic ethnic indicators. *Emblematic indicators* are those racial and cultural features that serve an identity function or otherwise mark and maintain social boundaries between Black (ingroup) and White (outgroup) members. *Nonemblematic ethnic indicators* are those distinctive Black cultural patterns that do not serve such a function.

The second part of this chapter considers children's acquisition of characteristically Black cultural patterns of behavior. It addresses the issue of how children acquire the ethnic patterns of their own group, specifically the way that children are socialized through play. This discussion deals with the way play structures organize and develop distinctively Black patterns of social interaction. It presents behavioral patterns as they exist in adolescence, based on research with this age group (though children begin to acquire some of these patterns as early as age three). The understanding of these behavior patterns and how they are used by individuals to express their ethnicity has important implications for ethnic identity: the extent to which ethnicity is ascribed or achieved. This chapter, then, focuses on specific Black behavioral patterns, how these differ from equivalent White patterns, and how these patterns develop in adolescents.

Theoretical Framework

This chapter fits within the disciplinary framework of sociolinguistics, most specifically, within that area known as ethnography of communication or ethnography of speaking (Gumperz & Hymes, 1972). The ethnography of communication focuses upon the interaction between language and social life, especially the various nonidiosyncratic social constraints that act upon and guide language choice.

> Language usage—i.e., what is said on a particular occasion, how it is phrased, and how it is coordinated with non-verbal signs—cannot simply be a matter of free individual choice. It must be affected by subconsciously internalized constraints similar to grammatical constraints. (Gumperz & Hymes, 1972, p. vi)

Ethnography of communication operates with the notion of communicative competence: best understood, perhaps, as what a speaker needs to know to communicate effectively or appropriately in culturally significant settings (Gumperz & Hymes, 1972, p. vii). Frake (1964) talks about ethnography as a descriptive theory: that knowledge that would enable an outsider to a culture to generate and interpret behavior in ways that native members of the culture would regard as authentic (1964, p. 112). Spradley's definition of culture as "the acquired knowledge that people use to interpret experience and generate social behavior" (1979, p. 5) is akin to the notion of communicative competence that sociolinguists use; it is from the plane where the disciplines of linguistics and anthropology intersect that ethnographers of communication draw their methodological presuppositions and practices.

One can also relate the present study to phenomenological studies in psychology and sociology. These deal with a concept of "reality" as being constituted by the "meaning of our experience" and not the "ontological structure of the objects" (Schutz, 1970, p. 125). From such studies emerged a notion of "cognitive style," a way of looking at the world, which could formally be represented by a cognitive map. Such a map would reflect the meanings that members of a group attach to behavior and events that occur in their everyday social experiences (Goffman, 1974, pp. 1-20).

Some linguists looking at discourse explore the relationship between the sociocultural realm and its effect on discourse in a naturalistic setting (see for example Gumperz, 1982b; Kochman, 1981; Tannen, 1982). Within this approach analysts interested in discourse production and comprehension might well concern themselves with what Freedle (1977) calls the strategies that speakers from various cultural backgrounds bring to bear in comprehension. These strategies suggest bases or schemata that one would need to know to determine which presuppositions are likely to be correct in comprehending the covert intentions of a speaker (Freedle, 1977; see also Gumperz, 1982a; Hymes in Shimanoff, 1980). Part of the present chapter deals precisely with the schemata that Blacks bring to verbal dueling which also can be considered an integral and determinative part of Black cognitive (or cultural) style.

What's going on? And from whose point of view? And what are the organizing schemes that give rise to the kinds of productions and understandings that individuals from various sociocultural realms generate in their everyday social interactions? These are the basic questions that ethnographers generally grapple with whether the larger disciplinary frames of reference are in ethnographic and/or cognitive sociology, cognitive anthropology, interactional sociolinguistics, ethnography of communication, or discourse analysis. These are also the questions that have generated the methodological assumptions and practices that are being brought to bear here on questions relating to children's ethnic socialization.

Definition of Terms:
Ethnic, Ethnicity, and Ethnic Identity

Royce (1982) developed the following definition, which serves our purpose well here.

> An ethnic group is a reference group invoked by people who share a common historical style (which may only be assumed), based on overt features and values, and who, through the process of interaction with others, identify themselves as sharing that style. (p. 27)

Elsewhere, Royce defines "style" as

> a complex of symbols, forms, and value orientations that, when applied to ethnic groups, signals both the overt cultural contents and underlying subjective values and standards by which performance is judged. (p. 28)

The advantage of Royce's definition is that, following the earlier work of Barth (1969), it allows for performance criteria as well as ascribed criteria to determine ethnic identity, a phenomenon that Barth found to be required within many systems. As Barth (1969) put it,

> Ascription is not conditional on the control of any specific assets, but rests on criteria of origin and commitment; whereas performance in the status, the adequate acting out of roles required to realize the identity, in many systems does require such assets. (p. 29)

Such a definition is quite useful here because Blacks regularly use performance criteria to make judgments about the degree of a Black person's cultural or community involvement, and, from that, his or her likely group identification and allegiance. This is exemplified, for example, by the Black term *oreo,* which denotes a person who, Blacks claim, is "Black on the outside but White on the inside," an ingroup determination that is made entirely from performance criteria (a matter we shall consider further below).

Royce's definition of ethnic group also identifies a subjective, as well as objective, component to the establishment of an individual's ethnic identity. Thus the basis of the ethnic identity of an individual is not simply what De Vos (1980) has called *emblematic* (attributes "worn or practiced for others to see" or a matter of what others understand qualifies membership status within that ethnic group) but criteria that members themselves establish for ethnic group membership.

Moreover, to make the connection between ascribed and performance criteria and the terms *subjective* and *objective*, Royce (1982) points out that there are often two standards or boundaries in operation here: an outer boundary and an inner one, with the outer boundary generally consisting of "objective" ascribed criteria, but the inner boundary also consisting of "subjectively based" performance criteria.

> If we recognize that there is a greater complexity of shared knowledge within groups than between groups, where interaction is restricted to certain structured situations, then it follows that performance becomes important within the inner boundary. It is there that individuals are judged on the extent of their cultural knowledge. Their claims to membership in the group are judged on their ability to behave adequately in the role rather than identity based on ascription. (p. 30)

However, Royce's definition of *ethnic* and *ethnicity* is not entirely satisfactory. First, Royce defines the terms *ethnic* and *ethnicity* only with regard to criteria that are emblematic of ethnic group identity. This would preclude our considering as ethnic criteria those that do not serve an "identity" or boundary maintaining (we/they) function. Second, Royce has restrictively labeled as *ethnic* only those criteria that ingroup and outgroup members are able to identify as qualifying individuals for membership within a group. This means that distinctive cultural patterns that ingroup members might be aware of as distinctive, but that do not serve an identity or boundary maintaining function, could not be considered "ethnic." Similarly, those culturally distinctive patterns that ingroup or outgroup members are not aware of as being distinctive would not be "ethnic."

In order to consider all culturally distinctive group patterns as "ethnic," which is what I propose, one must permit a broader "objective" basis for the classification of group behavior—one that goes beyond what either ingroup members or outgroup members, at any given moment in time or place, are aware of—and also include as characteristic of ethnic group membership criteria that do not have a clear or explicit identity or boundary maintaining function.

This would allow ethnic classification to be made by language and cultural historians and analysts, who, because they view language and culture patterns of a group from a comparative cross-cultural perspective, are often in a good position to identify what is distinctive of a particular group, even when the average outgroup or ingroup members cannot. Outgroup members are too far removed from the context in which such distinctive ingroup cultural patterns are displayed. Ingroup members, on the other hand, are often too close to their own culture to be able to see it ("One can't see one's culture for wearing it," the saying goes).

Moreover, the lack of awareness of ingroup members as to the distinctiveness of their culture, at any given moment in history, may not be a permanent condition. For it is common for ethnic groups, especially minorities thrust in the maelstrom of social and political upheaval, such as Blacks in the United States in the past two decades, to become aware of their culturally distinct patterns and transform them into ethnically qualifying identity or boundary markers.

Having argued that culturally distinctive patterns that are nonemblematic to the average ingroup or outgroup members should, nonetheless, also be considered ethnic, I do not wish to suggest that the distinction between emblematic and nonemblematic criteria should be obliterated. Quite the contrary; the different function that emblematic criteria serve for ingroup and outgroup members as identity or boundary maintaining markers, would, within the ethnographic methodological framework being used here, automatically give them separate and distinct categorical status.

Consequently, the following section will be divided into two main parts. The first part will deal with emblematic ethnic indicators: those features of race and culture that serve an identity or boundary maintaining function. The second part will deal with nonemblematic ethnic indicators: those distinctive Black attitudes or behavior patterns that do not serve such a function but are nonetheless characteristic of Black cultural style, historically.

Emblematic Ethnic Components
in Black Language and Culture

Individuals need to be aware of criteria at some level if these criteria are to function as identity or boundary maintaining markers, that is, to be considered "emblematic." The methodological problem is often how to go about establishing that such awareness exists. One approach that ethnographers have relied upon has been to do an ethnosemantic analysis of a list of words that can be said to be characteristic of a particular group for the purpose of revealing the conceptual principles underlying their generation and patterns of use (Frake, 1969, p. 29). The anthropological assumption here is that consciousness is registered through a process of naming. In that regard, many names for the same kinds of things by members of a particular group would be understood by ethnographers as an index of its importance for members of that group.

Several years ago I applied this method to an examination of race labels that were used by Blacks and Whites for themselves and each other (Kochman, 1976). From an anthropological standpoint, the number of such terms itself established racial awareness for members of these two groups. I analyzed them further to document more specifically the kinds of cognitive orientations that underlay their proliferation and use. What I learned there has a great bearing on the issues raised here relating to group identity and boundary maintenance: among other things, providing information on ingroup (sociocultural) criteria that Blacks have established for judging the qualifications of other Blacks for ingroup membership.

Racial Identification and
Social Attitudes in Race Labels

White labels for Blacks. All of these were derogatory, focusing almost entirely on Black physical features. Thus a Black person is characterized as "nigger," "burr head," "liver lips," "shine," "spade," "monkey," and so forth (see also Allen, 1983, pp. 45ff.). The only exception to this is the White label "militant," which denotes those Blacks who are aggressively outspoken in their protests against White racism. The last label, unlike the others, can be regarded as an attitudinal label, the social significance of which will be discussed below.

What these labels say is that White perceptions of Blacks have been either limited to race identification, a minimal kind of "categorical" or "status" classification, or grew out of the attention that Whites gave to the degree to which Blacks were aggressive in defense of their "rights." This last White perception is not a new one, of course. Blacks already were characterized along this line in the South as "uppity," "smart-alecky," and such, labels that designated Black individuals who, according to Whites then, "did not know their place." The 60s label "militant" extends the same perspective. And, of course, the extent to which Blacks could be counted upon to be aggressive in defense of those rights created a commensurate amount of risk for Whites.

Thus what has been historically "emblematic" of Blacks for Whites has and continues to be race; beyond that, Whites only took account of attitudes revolving around the willingness of Blacks to accept a submissive and subservient social role. But this distinction grows out of White social self-interest. Thus it can hardly be said to serve as an outgroup perception of those performance criteria that Blacks in the ingroup use to qualify Black ethnic group membership.

White labels for Whites. White labels for Whites clearly go beyond the category of race (Kochman, 1976). Only two racial terms, "nigger-lover" and "redneck," were identified, both attitudinal type classifications and both pejorative, and denote respectively, a White person who does not hate Blacks (from the perspective of Whites who feel they should), and a White person who does hate Blacks (from the perspective of Whites who feel they should not). Other White labels fall clearly into the ethnic, rather than racial, category, such as "spic," "dago," "mick," "kike," "polack," and so on, showing in effect that, for Whites within their own racial group, it is ethnic group membership that is the social category of risk (and therefore focus) for themselves, and that apart from terms designating racial attitudes toward others, Whites have no identification of themselves as a racial group. Consequently, "White" does not function as a self- or group identity classification for White Americans.

Black labels for Whites. Although most of these labels are negative, not all of them are. Thus amidst such negative terms as "cracker," "honky," "ofay," "devil," there are also terms such as "blue-eyed soul brother," "free thinker" (Kantrowitz, 1969), "half-and-half," and "straight." These latter terms denote Whites who are not prejudiced against Blacks and/ or who interact on a level of social equality with Blacks. It is clear that for Blacks the crucial distinction was between those Whites who were racist and those who were not. Consequently, it is exclusively White peoples' racial attitudes toward Blacks that underlie the Black classification of Whites.

In comparing these three different sets of race labels, some interesting findings emerge. One is that Blacks, in their attitudes toward Whites, show their social vulnerability by being reactively dependent upon White attitudes toward Blacks. That is, Blacks hate "honkies" *because* "honkies" hate Blacks. But Whites do not hate Blacks *because* Blacks hate Whites. White racist attitudes toward Blacks are proactive and independent of Black attitudes toward them. Consequently, the White labels for Blacks do not differentiate Black attitudes toward Whites, except in the special case of "militant." This attitudinal difference is a reflection of which side of the power axis a group or an individual is on. As a matter of personal and group survival, socially weaker individuals or groups need to know the attitudes toward them of those who are in a position to hurt them. At the same time, those Whites who reject others as social outcasts regularly reduce Blacks to (simply) categorical status.

Whites, until recently, found no need to differentiate Blacks further according to their racial attitudes. This changed when Whites were socially involved with Blacks, for example, in classes on college campuses. Because it then did matter, college campuses also became the social context that caused Whites to generate and use the Black label "militant."

Blacks, historically, have not differentiated Whites in terms of their ethnic group membership. Thus Blacks have terms for Whites like "paddy" (derived from the common Irish first name, Patrick), and "bohunk," and "hunky" (derived directly from the Bohemian and Hungarian ethnic groups whom Blacks lived next to in the Hough area in Cleveland, Ohio; Johnson, 1972). Yet, these terms do not respectively distinguish among Irish, Bohemian, and Hungarian Americans, but rather denote White Americans generally. As Blacks say in explanation of this view, they did not see any difference among White ethnic groups when it came to their respective racial attitudes toward Blacks.

Black labels for Blacks. Unlike the use of the term "nigger" by Whites, this term covers a range of meanings when used by Blacks, from the soulful (Brown, 1972) to the contemptuous. The terms "blood," "member," "brother," and "sister," denote strong ingroup affiliation and allegiance, thus indicating Black people's strong desire to register and promote community and political solidarity. The "oreo," in this context, is also a person whose allegiance to the group could not be counted upon, at a time, such as in the middle and late 60s, when degree of blackness and militancy were perhaps the core notions underlying the organization of Black political unity.

The term "tom," and others like it, for example, "jeff," "jeff davis" (see Kantrowitz, 1969) again reflect the Black sensitivity to other Blacks who act in a subservient, submissive, or deferential manner toward Whites, especially in contexts in which other Blacks would perceive there to have been options not to behave in that way.

In sum, Black labels for Blacks identify specific performance criteria that Blacks use to authenticate other Blacks' claims to membership within the group. Thus what is essentially a sociopolitical attitude appears to qualify as an inside (ingroup) ethnic boundary marker. As a "value orientation" it falls well within Royce's definition of *style* quoted earlier. And even if that attitude did not originate within the ingroup independent of Black people's experience as a racial minority, it does bring to mind Spicer's (1971) point, also found in Royce (1982), that every ethnic group or identity system is responsive to and reflective of the larger social context in which it finds itself.

Names, like the race labels discussed above, are more indelibly impressed onto the consciousness of a group than are terms or expressions that essentially emerge only as a consequence of events within a particular context or situation. These last terms are equally important in revealing emblematic ingroup performance criteria. The problem from a methodological standpoint, however, is that although names, such as race labels, can be elicited independent of the contexts in which they would ordinarily occur, the ethnographer must actually be part of ongoing ingroup situations to obtain this latter kind of data.

Black Intonation

Black intonation patterns function as an inside (ethnic) boundary marker for Blacks; those who do not manifest the distinctive Black intonation in their speech regularly acknowledge the adverse criticism they receive from other Blacks, the substance of which characterizes them as being "assimilationist-oriented," or "acting White." I have observed often the nonverbal criticism directed at these Blacks by other Blacks who do manifest such intonation patterns (a criticism often also verbalized about them later on, when that person is no longer present).

Those accused often are called upon to demonstrate the extent of their group affiliation in other ways, and may be further tested for their "Blackness," before any final judgment is rendered. Thus because further testing often is conducted, one can argue that the social potency of the absence of Black intonation, by itself, may be considered more suggestive than conclusive as to "where that person is (ultimately) coming from" (that is, whether his or her basic group allegiance is White or Black).

Expressive Intensity

Expressive intensity is another feature that Blacks use as a self- and group identifying ethnic marker. This can be seen again by the criticism leveled at other Blacks whose expressive style tends to be relatively subdued, as was the case with one Black woman who was regularly accused of "acting White" because of her low-keyed self-presentation style, notwithstanding that her response patterns otherwise were culturally quite "Black."

Likewise, a Black teacher from a predominantly White suburban school district complained about being rated "unsatisfactory" each year by the White school principal. The latter considered his teacher presentation style to be "too forthright and expressively intense." However, the Black teacher felt that were he to mute the intensity of his presentations to the level that his principal wanted, he would no longer consider himself Black, but White.

Thus insofar as animation and vitality are simultaneously core components of various Black speech acts and events and (more generally) of expressive intensity, we can see that as Blacks enact one or another of the above speech acts or events, they are also, in effect, qualifying themselves and their presentations as Black, ethnically.

A case in point in this last regard is in the Black speech event argument in its use as a truth creating process (as opposed to argument as quarreling). In argument we see expressive intensity functioning as an essential concomitant feature to presenting a point of view in which you care about what you are saying. Consequently, the absence of expressive intensity that Whites display in discussion (Kochman, 1981) makes their presentation suspect from the Black perspective. Blacks begin to question the sincerity of the speaker. This is partly because White presentation models in discussion resemble the behavior that Blacks engage in when they are "frontin'," which for them is a form of dissembling, and therefore, the antithesis of being "for real." So here again, we see a manifestation of Black recognition of expressive intensity as an ethnic indicator. For, in order for Blacks to realize the state that they call being for real, they have to be in situations in which they can be free to be themselves, that is, a situation in which they feel free to express themselves openly, which is also to say, free to express themselves intensely.

Nonemblematic Ethnic Components
in Black Language and Culture

To restate our earlier definition, nonemblematic ethnic components are those distinctive cultural patterns that do not serve an identity or boundary maintaining function and of which ingroup members may or may not be aware.

Black Boasting

Boasting for Blacks functions as a source of humor, much like a joke (Kochman, 1981). Consequently, the appropriate response to a boast within the Black cultural pattern is laughter. In White (mainstream) cultural etiquette, on the other hand, boasting, like bragging, is negatively valued; thus it is hardly something that Whites feel an audience should encourage through laughter or other appreciative type responses. However, a Black person is unlikely to criticize another Black for "acting White," or "not acting Black," if the latter did not see boasts as something to be laughed at.

Most of the instances in which I have seen this occurring have been when Blacks, before an essentially White audience, start their presentation with a boast, and then react to the audience's noncommittal response. On one recent occasion, a well-educated professional in that situation stopped and wryly informed the audience that he intended his boast to be a joke, by saying, "Can't I at least get a little smile, after that?" In the few instances I observed in which a Black person boasted and did not get a positive response from Blacks, it was because the situation was considered too serious for joking or because the boast wasn't regarded as especially funny. But there was no indication then or later that the speaker saw the audience as not behaving Black because it did not laugh in response to the boast.

Thus boasting can be classified as a nonemblematic, rather than emblematic, Black ethnic indicator insofar as it is an integral part of a distinctive Black cultural pattern and more generally as part of Black cultural and communicative style, but also one that does not serve an identity or boundary maintaining function.

Accusations and Denials in the
Determination of Guilt and Innocence

Additional distinctive Black cultural patterns that are nonemblematic are general accusations of the kind, "White folks are ------," "Men are ------," "Women are ------" (see Kochman, 1981). Such statements generally are taken to be categorical by Whites. Thus everyone who respectively fits one generic criteria of "White folks," "men," "women," and so on, is included (or accused, as the case may be). For Blacks, however, such statements are intended to be general rather than categorical. Thus Blacks do not intend such statements to be all inclusive with regard to the named generic criteria.

Another point of difference here is that Whites see the persons making the general accusations responsible not only for the validity of the accusation but for all targets that are hit. So those who have felt themselves unjustly accused feel that they can approach the person who makes the accusation and ask for a personal dispensation, which the accuser is expected to grant by saying something like, "Oh, I didn't mean you, ------."

But for Blacks, it is not the accuser but the accused who is seen to be responsible for validating the accuracy of the accusation. The Black rule is, "If the shoe fits, wear it." Consequently, from the Black side, if the accusation does not fit, then the individuals themselves are expected to apply the individual exclusion rule "he or she ain't talkin' to me." For Blacks, admitting that they feel themselves accused is tantamount to an admission of guilt. This is because Blacks feel that only the true accusation has the capacity to provoke a strong defensive response.

The justification for considering this distinctive Black cultural pattern nonemblematic then, rests on the surprise that Blacks typically register when I present them with this cultural difference, as this pattern operates unconsciously for them (as it does for Whites, too). That is, it does not serve a Black identity or boundary maintaining function, and Blacks have shown themselves to be unaware of it as being culturally distinctive.

The Socialization of Ethnic Patterns

I have said elsewhere (1981) that Black culture generally is a high stimulus culture. For Black culture to maintain itself as a high stimulus culture, it is important to develop capacities among its members to manage the impulses that potent stimuli produce without becoming overwhelmed by them. Individuals can be more powerful in their assertions if they also know that others can receive them without becoming overwhelmed. Black culture, through the structure of a variety of speech acts and events, develops capacities, strategies, attitudes, and sensibilities that enable Blacks to manifest and manage the expressive intensity that functions for them as an emblematic identity marker. In this section, I will discuss some of the ways in which this is accomplished.

Black Talk

The Black cultural capacity to manage behavior that is expressively intense both in the context of self-presentation and in the social interaction with others is aided by the way Black culture conceptualizes the boundaries among play, nonplay, and ambiguity within the framework of talk, and, within the larger culture, the boundary between "talk" and "fight."

In Black culture, *talk* is conceptually differentiated from *fight,* in that for fight to begin, in addition to the necessary components such as insults, threats, anger, or other forms of intimidation, someone would need to make a provocative move. Such a move is one that is not part of that person's customary way of talking: for example, closing the distance between yourself and another person, or reaching into your pocket, or, as in one instance of an argument in a bar, one Black man warning another "not to raise that glass" (as if to take a drink—in that context, that would have been an ambiguous movement and, therefore, also provocative; see Kochman, 1981, for a more detailed discussion).

By way of contrast, the White cultural conceptualization of fight already begins within the larger framework of talk. A verbal confrontation in which anger is present, insults are traded, and threats are issued, all would be seen by Whites as a fight already having gotten started, with actual violence imminent, even though no one had as yet made any actual physical move. Public expressions of hostility for Whites are on a words-actions continuum, a view that is revealed by White couples saying they "had a fight last night," when it turns out that all they had was an argument.

Blacks, on the other hand, make clear distinctions between the forms of the two activities, that is, talking and physical movement. Consequently, when Black couples say they had a "fight," violence occurred; they weren't just "arguing." And Blacks in other ways, too, indicate the clear conceptual separation between talking and fighting when they say, "So long as I'm talking, you got nothin' to worry about. But when I stop talking, then you might have something to worry about."

Also, Blacks use the term *woofing* to describe verbal confrontations that consist of anger, heat, threats, and insults, as between rival gang members (Keiser, 1969), where the only culturally supported options in that situation are between serious "woofing" and "humbugging" (that is, actual physical fighting). For Blacks, the boundary between talking and fighting is conceptually (and critically) organized around forms of the activity, whereas for Whites the conceptual (and critical) focus is organized more centrally around confrontational intensity.

Interactional Responsibility

In Black culture, within the context of verbally aggressive talk, as in woofing, participants are held to be responsible not only for their actions, but also for their reactions. That is to say, insults, threats, and other forms of verbal aggression are held to be provocative (necessary), but not determinative (sufficient). Recipients of such verbal attacks are still seen as having control over several different options, and consequently must assume responsibility for how they ultimately choose to respond. Moreover, because Black culture clearly separates talking from fighting, with verbally aggressive and intimidating behavior such as woofing still seen as "only talking," for a recipient to respond to woofing with violence is to have responded to "talk" with "fight." Consequently, within Black culture this would place the recipient in the accountable position of having started the fight.

By way of contrast, White mainstream culture sees verbal confrontation, anger, heat, insults, and threats between males, as not only provocative (necessary), but determinative (sufficient), insofar as the culture sees violence as an appropriate response for males to make in the face of this kind of provocation. Therefore, unlike the situation in Black culture, the recipient here is not considered to be responsible for having responded violently to verbal provocation.

Black Verbal Dueling

All of what has been said above applies to the social interaction within Black verbal dueling, a game of verbal insult played predominantly by Black males (though females also have been known to play) and learned by Black males at a relatively early age. The difference is that insofar as verbal dueling is a "game," and therefore, a form of play, one might expect that the game rules allow for a temporary suspension of the rules of accountability that normally prevail in real life social situations. And this is so to an extent. Thus the rules of verbal dueling declare that a verbal insult is to be countered with another verbal insult—offense is to be met with offense; consequently, the rules of the game direct individuals away from what for children might be regarded as a "normal" nonplay reaction to verbal provocation, which is either to withdraw from the contest, respond defensively as opposed to offensively, or to fight physically. All of these individual responses would "lose," according to the game rules.

Thus we can see that verbal dueling as play does provide for a relaxation of the rules that would normally prevail for children in real life social interactions, insofar as it affords them an opportunity to escape from the continual need to defend their self-esteem from attack by others; joking relationships among adults also serve this function. But insofar as the rules within verbal dueling also serve to promote the development of attitudes, strategies, and skills that Black culture has established to be necessary to carry on appropriate social interaction in adult nonplay contexts, then one can well regard this form of play to be as much education as sport. In effect, socialization through verbal dueling compels those Black youngsters to learn how to resist the impulse to react defensively to verbal attacks on their self-esteem. As such it also serves to promote and develop the adult Black cultural view of matters relating to talk, fight, and responsibility, discussed above.

For example, the adult Black view is (1) that people should respond in kind, and (2) that "talking" and "fighting" within the context of verbal aggression are culturally nonequivalent. If the normal responses for young children in the face of a verbal attack are either to withdraw, argue, or physically fight, then children are, in verbal dueling, being encouraged to give "talk," in response to "talk," and not "fight" in response to "talk."

Moreover, responding in kind also entails returning the same kind of talk; that is, offensive talk as opposed to defensive talk. This effectively eliminates excuses from the category of equivalent type responses. This socializing process continues until such time as young Black males are returning verbal insults for verbal insults, and in so doing, not only satisfying the rules of the game and the characteristics of their structured play role within it, but also acquiring adult standards for appropriate cultural communication.

Ritual and personal insults. Within verbal dueling, play is clearly marked by the use of ritual insults: those known by all parties present to be untrue of either the recipient or those whom the recipient would normally be obliged to defend (such as the recipient's family, especially the mother; see Labov, 1972a). Kochman (1970, p. 159) provides examples of ritual insults:

Yo mama is so bowlegged, she looks like the bite out of a donut.

Your house is so small the roaches walk single file.

Or from Labov (1972a):

Your mother got baptised in a whiskey bottle.

Your mother sail the seven seas in a sardine can.

As might be expected, ritual insults are an extensive part of the repertoire of younger Black males (ages 10 to 13) primarily for reasons of safety. Males within this age group have not as yet been socialized sufficiently within the verbal dueling game for them to be able to manage the greater tension generated from an exchange of personal insults (that is, they are not able to prevent the structure of the activity from dissolving into defensive denials or physical violence). Older adolescents, however, frequently include personal references in verbal dueling and, of course, even with some of the above ritual insults the themes are never that far removed from real life concerns. Thus Maryland provides an example of both ritual and personal insults in a verbal dueling contest played out in Chicago (there the game is called "signifying").

Cunny (to Pretty Black): Boy, you so Black, you sweat super Permalube Oil . . .

Pretty Black: Reese, what you laughing 'bout? You so square you shit bricked shit . . .

Reese: Square huh, what about your nappy ass hair before it was stewed, that shit was so bad till, when you went to bed at night, it would leave your head and go on the corner and meddle [solicit for customers, as a prostitute].

Pretty Black: On the street meddling, bet Dinky didn't offer me no pussy and I turned it down.

Frank: Reese scared of pussy. (Kochman, 1970, pp. 158ff.)

Here the insults begin to get distinctly personal, hitting upon real failings of the participants. The age of the adolescents here was between 15 and 17, and the tension (as reported by Maryland) intensified as the insults began to get more deeply personal. Finally, between still older Black males, the topics are almost entirely personal, though ritual insults are occasionally interspersed to relieve matters when things begin to get too tense (see Maryland, 1972). Thus we see a progression among

Black males within this activity moving from the ritual (with occasional personal reference) to the personal (with occasional reference to ritualized, obviously untrue personal attributes).

The movement from ritual to personal insults has the effect of increasing tension for the participants primarily by moving what is obviously play in the direction of nonplay, and thereby decreasing the measure of safety for the participants. As with most joking relationships, and with play, there is often the danger of "having gone too far." But it is also important to recognize that this view often is based upon a cultural premise (like that pertaining in White mainstream culture) that would make the initiator of the verbal provocation also responsible for how it might be taken (that is, in terms that we already discussed above, the initiator would be held accountable not only for his own instigating action but also for the recipient's reaction). But in Black culture, as we have pointed out above, the recipient vis-à-vis the initiator is seen to be acting independently, not dependently, which is to say, he is not obliged to respond only along the lines that the initiator has set. Moreover, it is especially through the use of personal insults within sounding that interactants learn this strategic option.

Let me show this by examining more closely a sounding exchange between Black adolescents Boot and David:

(1) David: So your . . . So then I say, "Your father got brick teeth."

(2) Boot: Aw your father got teeth growing out his behind!

(3) David: Yeah, your father, y-got, your father grow, uh, uh, grow hair from, from between his, y'know.

(4) Boot: Your father got calluses growin' up through his ass, and comin' through his mouth.

(5) Boot: Your father look like a grown pig.

(6) David: Least my—at least my father don't be up there talking uh-uh-uh-uh-uh-uh!

(7) Boot: Uh-so my father talks stutter talk what it mean?

(8) Boot: At least my father ain't got a gray head! His father got a big bald spot with a gray head right down there, and one long string . . .

(9) David: Because he' old, he's old, that's why! He's old, that's why! (Labov, 1972a, pp. 296ff.)

Within the above exchange, Boot and David trade both ritual and personal insults. Ritual insults would be between points 1 and 5, personal insults at points 6 and 8. The comments at points 7 and 9 are clearly out of character with the other comments, which all fall within the structure of verbal dueling. They, as Labov points out, are not "sounds"—"sounding" is the name of the game of verbal dueling used by Blacks in Harlem, New York City—but rather defensive denials or mitigations of the previous accusations. They break the structure of the game insofar as the sequencing rule within the game that a "sound" should follow another "sound" is not followed. Insofar as these comments are not "sounds," the game dissolves at those points.

But a question that has great implications for the kind of socializing effect that verbal dueling has on Black males is where precisely the character of the game, like that given above, shifts from verbal dueling (or sounding) to defensive denial. Labov (1972a) argued that the shift in the above contest occurred at 6 and 8, the points at which personal insults were issued. This effectively placed personal insults outside the framework of the game, and, indeed, Labov did formulate his rules for sounding such that only ritual insults qualified as sounds, but not personal insults. However, as my own data showed, and as I illustrated above, personal insults can and do function as part of verbal dueling, even as they did in Labov's example of the exchange between Boot and David.

However, if the insults at points 6 and 8 also function as sounds, then the precise points at which the character of the activity shifts from verbal dueling to quarrelling are at 7 and 9, the points at which the personal insults were respectively denied. And if the structure of verbal dueling places the point at which the game is interrupted and therefore "lost" at the point of denial, then it must also place the principal responsibility for maintaining the game on the recipients, especially upon their ability to continue to behave offensively, by returning one verbal insult with another, notwithstanding the always present temptation to react defensively, as Boot and David did at points 7 and 9.

And this is precisely where verbal dueling makes its contribution to Black male psychosocial growth (especially the ability of Black males to manage intensely expressive presentations of self, whether as presenter or receiver). By also placing personal insults (along with ritual insults) within the framework of verbal dueling, the rules of the game work to decrease the safety of the contestants still further, thereby forcing them to manage the tension that comes from the increasing sense of risk that neither opponent will be able to continue to take personal insults unseriously, that is, as "play." And being regularly challenged to manage that tension within the context of play then socializes Blacks to develop the high defense that eventually enables them to receive potent stimuli in nonplay situations, too, without becoming overwhelmed or overly antagonized by them.

Summary

This chapter identifies a few of the more salient features of race, language, and culture that could be regarded as ethnic with regard to Blacks and which serve to give Blacks in the United States their special identity as a distinctive social group. I distinguish emblematic from nonemblematic criteria, further differentiating between emblematic criteria those "objective" (ascribed) criteria that are known to both outsiders and insiders from the more subjectively based performance criteria that are part of the Black inside group boundary. The latter, known only to Black ingroup members themselves, includes the ability and willingness to display distinctively Black intonation patterns and expressively intense behavior in ingroup social contexts. Nonemblematic cultural patterns include Black boasting and the distinctively Black cultural strategies surrounding accusations and denials.

The second part of the chapter dealt with the socialization of Black ethnic patterns, specifically, the acquisition of those skills needed to manage expressively intense presentations of either oneself or others. The chapter focused on the Black cultural concept of "talk," the boundaries of play and nonplay within the framework of "talk" and the larger cultural boundary between "talk" and "fight," to show how adolescents begin to acquire adult cultural norms through play structures. Special attention was given to the attitudes, sensibilities, interactional capacities, and strategies that are developed through the Black speech genre "verbal dueling."

12

Historical Sociocultural Premises and Ethnic Socialization

ROGELIO DIAZ-GUERRERO

This chapter outlines the role of historical sociocultural premises in children's socialization as a basis for the understanding of ethnic group differences. Historical sociocultural premises (HSCPs) are implicit assumptions regarding the nature of personal and social interactions that characterize the value system of a culture and guide individual behavior. Empirical data evaluating the impact of these HSCPs on individual development and cross-cultural interactions will be reviewed in this chapter; in the case of Mexican Americans three dimensions or coping styles underlie the development of these HSCPs. Assessment of these dimensions among subcultural and cross-cultural groups allows us to describe differences among cultures.

Historical Sociocultural Premises: Mexico and the United States

Historical sociocultural premises (HSCPs) can be defined as cultural traditions concerning values, beliefs, and behaviors (Diaz-Guerrero, 1963, 1967, 1972a, 1972b). Every culture develops HSCPs. For example, in the United States there is pressure for one to be individualistic, autonomous, independent, detached, and competitive. HSCPs are taken for granted largely and often are not verbalized, but may be more verbalized in some societies than in others. In this sense, we can say that

239

often they are unconscious or only semiconscious for the individual. The job of social scientists is to articulate HSCPs and empirically assess them.

HSCPs can be defined operationally as beliefs and values held by more than 50% of the individuals of a given culture. Although HSCPs are defined as a disposition to feel, think, or act in a predetermined way, the HSCPs are not attitudes; they are cognitive rather than affective or behavioral constructs. They are historically permanent and supraindividual. They are most clearly demonstrated when articulated, but they will be evident as they affect thinking, feeling, and behavior within the cultural ecosystem (Diaz-Guerrero, 1963, 1982a). They provide absolute affirmations to help the developing person compare his or her own cognitive and behavioral experiences to cultural belief systems.

To operationalize HSCPs, I began with hundreds of common sayings, proverbs, maxims, morals, dictums, and so on, of the Mexican people. In the last 12 years several factor analyses have been executed with items derived from these sayings. Currently, nine factors or nine sets of beliefs shared among Mexicans have been derived from empirical studies (Diaz-Guerrero, 1982a). Once having obtained HSCPs, we can then measure the distance or variations in the norms across cultures as well as within cultural groups. The HSCPs for Mexicans are listed below. My empirical research with Mexicans, Mexican Americans, and Anglo-Americans shows how these HSCPs allow us to compare subgroups within a culture as well as examine cross-national differences. We should expect that each HSCP will be endorsed most strongly by Mexicans, second most by Mexican Americans, and least by Anglo-Americans.

I studied 60 Mexican and 60 Mexican American mothers and 60 each of 15 to 16-year-old adolescents, 11 to 12-year-old preadolescents, and 5 to 6-year-old children, with both sexes almost equally represented. These families were recruited from two sites: Monterrey, Mexico, and San Antonio, Texas. All families belonged to the same social class (as measured by education and occupation of the father). I administered the Short Scale of HSCPs of the Mexican Family and compared the scores of these groups on each of the following factors.

(1) Machismo. The meaning of this factor is provided by high scores in statements such as "Submissive women are best"; "It is far better to be a man than to be a woman"; "Men are more intelligent than women."

On this scale, as expected, mothers of the Mexican and Mexican American sociocultures endorsed machismo more with their preadolescent than their adolescent children. There was, however, a clearly significant difference, with the Mexican mothers and preadolescents obtaining higher scores in Machismo than their Mexican American counterparts. United States norms are not supportive of the Mexican Machismo HSCPs. As a matter of fact, there may be contrasting Anglo-American HSCPs stating something like "Independent women are best"; "It is just as good to be a man as to be a woman"; and "Men and women are equally intelligent." No significant difference appeared for the adolescents, which may reflect strong acquisition of gender appropriate role behaviors during this developmental period.

(2) Affiliative Obedience. This factor is defined by high scores in statements similar to "One should never question the word of a mother." On Affiliative Obedience Mexican Americans are less obedient to the cultural figures of authority, the father, the mother, the teacher, than the Mexicans. Again, United States norms are at odds with the Mexican. It may be assumed that Anglo-American HSCPs would prescribe "It is bad to blindly obey the mother, father, teacher or any adult."

(3) Value of Virginity. This factor is defined by items such as "To be a virgin is of much importance for single women." The scale of Virginity was applied in this study only to the mothers. Although the scale has been widely given in Mexico to adolescents and preadolescents, previous experiences predicted great turmoil if applied in the United States, suggesting another cultural difference. As expected, Mexican mothers endorsed virginity significantly more often. It may have to be assumed that the pertinent Anglo-American HSCPs would prescribe: "Nonvirgins make as good wives and mothers as virgins."

(4) Abnegation. This factor is identified by high scores in beliefs such as "Women suffer more during their life than men." The Abnegation scale showed that mothers in both places agree that women suffer more in their lives than men. However, the older the child, also in both subcultures, the less the agreement.

(5) Fear of Authority. This factor is defined by high scores on beliefs such as "Many children fear their parents." The Fear of Authority scale portrayed all groups agreeing that most children fear their parents, with Mexican adolescents endorsing this more than any other group.

(6) Family Status Quo. This factor is identified by high scores on "A good wife should always be faithful and loyal to her husband," or "Most little girls would prefer to be like their mothers." For the Family Status Quo scale all groups, almost equally, agreed that women should be faithful and loyal to their husbands.

(7) Respect over Love. This factor is defined by high scores in statements similar to "It is more important to obey a father than to love him." In the factor scales of Respect over Love all three Mexican groups score higher than their Mexican American counterparts. The latter appeared neutral regarding whether it is better to love or to respect a parent. The Anglo-American HSCP may be "It is more important to love than to respect a parent."

(8) Family Honor. This factor is defined by items that imply a disposition to defend, even to extremes, the reputation of the family; for example "A woman who dishonors her family should be punished severely," and "A married women should dance only with her husband." The mothers in both samples agreed less with these than did the children and adolescents, but more Mexican than Mexican American mothers agreed with them.

(9) Cultural Rigidity. This factor refers to strict parents and restrictions on independent work and free courting for women. It is defined by agreement with items such as "The stricter the parents, the better the children"; "Young women should not go out alone at night with men"; and "It is not advisable for married women to work outside their homes." Although both groups of mothers reject these premises, the Mexican mothers reject them less than the Mexican Americans. There are strong differences in preadolescence and adolescence, showing that Mexican youth still favor strictness in the parents and restrictions for women.

The original HSCP questionnaires, as well as the factorized version, have been applied extensively in Mexico across ages, sexes, socioeconomic classes, regional, and racial groups (Diaz-Guerrero, 1982a). Although presently there are no published data regarding their acquisition, it appears that mothers play a fundamental role in transferring these norms nonverbally to children at early stages of development. I hypothesize that later these traditions are learned as direct statements from parents, brothers, extended family, teachers, and other significant adults. Data from preadolescents and adolescents in the school system show that age or grade is highly significant, the individual becoming more self-assertive or differentiated with age and less strict in endorsing and behaving in accordance with the HSCPs. However, data on mothers and other adults suggest that the HSCPs grow stronger in adulthood. In most of these factorial dimensions preadolescents are closer to their mothers' beliefs than are the adolescents, thus confirming the importance of the mother in this socialization process.

Adult Indian groups in Taxcala and Puebla appear in as strong or stronger agreement with the HSCPs as Mexico City preadolescents. Subjects in provincial cities are generally more in favor of the HSCPs than subjects in Mexico City. There are also sex differences in the acquisition of HSCPs. In factors such as Machismo that clearly discriminate against women, women score significantly below the males. In others, like affiliative obedience, women score higher.

As discussed below, these premises are embedded in broader economic and historical-political contexts. The tendency for Mexican Americans to endorse these HSCPs less than Mexicans may be because the Mexican Americans have greater economic resources and opportunities. It is not necessarily reflective of changes due to contact with Anglo-American HSCPs. I hypothesize that both economic and socialization factors affect the drift in HSCPs among this group. In several studies in Mexico, years of education have been found to be negatively related to backing of the HSCPs.

Coping Styles:
Mexico and the United States

The HSCPs are not only prescriptive of thoughts and feelings but are reflected in behaviors (Diaz-Guerrero, 1963). I examined the various HSCPs in a search of an underlying coherence that would encompass the values, attitudes, and behaviors of a given culture in regards to the style of facing stress. I hypothesized that cultures vary in the ways in which they resolve the problem of dealing with life stress. These differences, termed *cultural coping styles,* vary along three dimensions: (1) active, internal control versus passive, external control; (2) affiliative obedience versus active self-assertion; and (3) interdependence versus autonomy.

My research, extending over a period of more than 20 years, has documented a number of clear and consistent differences between the two model cultures: Mexican and Anglo-American. Although different studies have used differing constructs and methodologies, the results support the idea of underlying dimensions that differentiate cultural groups. This research will be reviewed in terms of these dimensions as they are revealed in a variety of studies.

Active, Internal Control Versus
Passive, External Control

This dimension defines two alternative coping styles, or ways of perceiving and dealing with the environment. Active, internal control implies perceiving problems as existing outside the individual in the physical, interpersonal, and social environment; the best way to resolve problems is to modify the environment. The individual is seen as being in control of events. Passive, internal control implies that although problems may be posed by the environment, the best way to cope with them is through self-modification, adapting the self to the events. The external environment is seen as exerting control over the individual (Diaz-Guerrero, 1963, 1973).

Early evidence for cultural differences on this dimension derive from a series of studies begun in the early 60s. The *Filosofia de Vida* (Views of Life) test was initiated in seminars with American students in Austin, Texas, and Mexican students in Mexico City. It consisted of 60 pairs of statements in a forced-choice format, originally constructed to produce maximal discrimination between Mexicans and Americans. Items such as "Man can change the world to suit his own needs," and "When I do well in a test in the school it is usually because I studied for the test," were contrasted with opposite statements.

A later longitudinal cross-cultural study of Mexican and Anglo-American school children was carried out, using similar measures (Holtzman, Diaz-Guerrero, & Swartz, 1975). The results from the factor analysis and from additional measures used in the same study show clear cultural differences on the active-passive dimension. American children tended to be more actively independent and to struggle for a mastery of problems and challenges in their environment, whereas Mexican children were more passively obedient and adapted to stresses in the environment rather than trying to change them.

The internal-external dimension, however, is complex and cannot differentiate consistently between Mexicans and Americans. Anglo-Americans, probably unconsciously, are as externally controlled by their culture as are Mexicans. This dimension has both similarities and differences with Rotter's (1966) internality-externality dimension. Thus items on preference for cooperation over competition cluster on the active internal style for Mexicans and on the passive external for Americans. The illustrations of this dimension below refer more often to the active-passive aspects than to the internality-externality aspect of this dimension.

In a major cross-national study (Peck & Stenning, 1967; Peck et al., 1972-1974, 1973) a story completion measure was used to study ways of coping with work, authority, interpersonal relations, anxiety, and aggression. Ten stories were used—five with a male hero, five with a female hero. The stem for one of the stories for coping with interpersonal relations read as follows:

> Helen and her friend began to play a game. Helen said it should be played one way, her friend said it should be played in a different way. Helen . . .

A total of 40 story completions each from Brazil, Mexico, and the United States were content analyzed for six dimensions, including the active-passive dimension (Peck & Stenning, 1967). A high score was given if the action in the story was initiated by the stimulus person; a low score was given when the action was initiated by some other individual. Scores between these extremes were given to stories with jointly initiated action, depending on the degree of contribution. Significant differences on nine of the ten stories showed that the Mexican children scored most passive of all three nations.

In a more recent study (Diaz-Guerrero, 1982b), Mexican and Anglo-American high school boys were given the Semantic Differential (Diaz-Guerrero & Salas, 1975; Osgood, May, & Miron, 1975; Osgood, Suci, & Tannenbaum, 1957). Of special interest in the present context are the distance measures between ratings of I Myself and Most People and each of 27 occupations. For Mexicans, the concept of I Myself was closest in affective meaning to Most People (.6), Storekeeper (.9), Peasant (1.0), Servant (1.0), Teacher (1.0), and Artist (1.0) and was most unlike Beggar (3.9) and Student (2. 4). In contrast, for Americans, the concept of I Myself was closest in affective meaning to Soldier (.4), Worker (.6), Student (.7), and Policeman (1.0) and most unlike Beggar (5.6) and Artist (3.4).

These results suggest an aspect of cultural differences expressed by Mexican poet Octavio Paz (1961, p. 70), who, in speaking of the Mexican, said: "There is nothing simpler, therefore, than to reduce the whole complex groups of attitudes that characterize us—especially the problem that we constitute for ourselves—to what may be called the 'servant mentality' in opposition to the 'psychology of the master' and also that of modern man, whether proletarian or bourgeois."

Holtzman (1980) elaborates further on the differences in activity level between the two cultures. "From studies with inkblots, it was learned that Mexican children see less movement and have longer reaction times in test situations than the Anglo-American child. Time passes more slowly for the Mexican than the Anglo-American. Activity has a different meaning for the Anglo-American than for the Mexican."

A passive internal coping style also is associated with fatalism and pessimism, that is, a sense that potential problems cannot be avoided. A parent attitude survey completed by mothers in the two cultures (Holtzman et al., 1975) showed Mexican mothers to be more pessimistic in their outlook and Anglo-American mothers to be more optimistic.

Emmite and Diaz-Guerrero (1983) and Diaz-Guerrero and Emmite (in press) have shown that an active, internally oriented coping style relates significantly more often to a good self-concept and better school grades, and is inversely related to trait anxiety across Mexican Americans, Blacks, Anglo-Americans, and Mexican high school students.

Though the data presented imply a negative view of the passive, externally controlled individual, it is important to stress that before unchangeable events such as death, chronic illness, or disability, Mexicans, feeling that life is to be endured rather than enjoyed, will find it easier to cope than Anglo-Americans. On the other hand, a rapidly changing environment may be easier for Anglo-Americans to cope with.

Affiliative Obedience Versus Active Self-Assertion

This dimension reflects the distribution of interpersonal power in a culture; the ends of the continuum represent the extent to which one is obedient versus self-assertive toward authority figures. In the *Filosofia de Vida* test referred to above (Peck et al., 1972-1974), items that loaded on this factor contrasted statements of absolute obedience to the father, the mother, and the teacher with statements establishing a well-reasoned alternative not to obey. The results of the study demonstrate that Mexican children show far more affiliative obedience than Anglo-American children.

These results are reported by Holtzman, Diaz-Guerrero, and Swartz (1975). A total of 400 14-year-old Mexican children of two social classes were compared with 400 Anglo-American children each in Austin, Texas, and Chicago, Illinois, on a variety of measures. The results show

Mexican children to be higher in affiliative obedience than American children; in addition, children in Austin were more affiliative than those in Chicago. Across all three geographical samples, lower-class children showed more affiliative obedience than middle-class children.

Using the story completion measure from the Peck et al. (1972-1974) study, Reyes de Ahumada and Stenning (1967) found that help in solving a problem was sought from an authority figure, such as mother, father, brother, or police officer significantly more often in the Mexican than in the Anglo-American sample. This dimension thus suggests not only obeying authority figures, but also seeking guidance from them.

There is a trend over time toward active self-assertion and away from affiliative obedience. These tendencies are illustrated empirically in cross-cultural and intracultural studies (Diaz-Guerrero, 1976, 1977a, 1977b; Holtzman et al., 1975). In Mexico, active self-assertive coping style is related consistently to higher scores in cognitive, perceptual, and reading tests, as well as achievement scores; to higher social class; to dominant, autonomous, and aggressive personality traits (Diaz-Guerrero, 1976, 1977a); to vocational choice (Diaz-Guerrero & Emmite, in press); and to field independent cognitive style (Diaz-Guerrero & Castillo Vales, 1981; Reyes-Lagunes, 1982). However, health for the individual and the culture are enhanced where flexibility is valued; that is, where persons are capable of affiliative obedience or active self-assertion depending on the situation.

Interdependence Versus Autonomy

This dimension refers to the affective interactions between people in a society, with closeness and love at one extreme and independence and detachment at the other. Items in the *Filosofia de Vida* Test that define interdependence are contrasted with the following items for autonomy: "Work first, friendship second," "I am self-confident," and "I do not need the approval of other people."

The Interdependence versus Autonomy dimension is revealed in the way family relationships are structured. Mexicans tend to be more family centered, and Anglo-Americans are more individual centered. Families in Mexico tend to stretch out in a network of relatives and compadres that often runs into scores of individuals. Mexicans tend to see themselves achieving by standing on the shoulders of their fathers and mothers or other family members, and Anglo-Americans see themselves as achieving primarily by virtue of their own independent efforts. Interdependence is a major feature of the Mexican culture. Any fear or anxiety concerning the taking of an examination in school on the part of the Mexican child is not so much fear of individual failure as it is a fear of failing to support the interdependent system in which the family plays a central role.

On the *Filosofia de Vida* Test, one item consists of the following pair of statements from which to choose one: "One must fight when the rights of the family are threatened," or "One must fight when the rights of the individual are threatened." The majority of Anglo-Americans selected the individual-centered alternative, and the reverse occurred for the Mexicans.

Interdependence as a characteristic of Mexican culture is shown also in the literature on cooperation versus competition. In two of the items of the *Filosofia de Vida* Test, cooperation and competition are contrasted as ways of dealing with problems set by the environment. Mexicans select a significantly greater number of cooperative alternatives, and Anglo-Americans select more competitive responses (Diaz-Guerrero, 1982a). Experimental studies comparing Mexican and Anglo-American children by Kagan and Madsen (1971) also show that Mexican children tend to be highly cooperative in experimental games, and Anglo-Americans are highly competitive, even when such competition is dysfunctional.

Similarly, in the Reyes de Ahumada and Stenning (1967) study, there was a clear preference for the American children of both social classes and both sexes to solve the interpersonal conflict without help. In the story example cited, the American children were significantly more likely than the Mexican children to say that nobody was called to help solve the conflict, or that Helen and her friend solved the conflict alone. The solution proposed by Helen's friend or by other friends was accepted significantly more often in Mexico than in the United States.

To summarize the findings, Mexicans can be broadly differentiated from Anglo-Americans in these ways:

(1) Anglo-Americans tend to be more active than Mexicans in their style of coping with life's problems and challenges.

(2) Anglo-Americans tend to be more technological, dynamic, and external than Mexicans.

(3) Anglo-Americans tend to be more complex and differentiated in cognitive structure than Mexicans.
(4) Mexicans tend to be more family centered and Anglo-Americans more individual centered.
(5) Mexicans tend to be more cooperative in interpersonal activities and Anglo-Americans more competitive.
(6) Mexicans tend to be more fatalistic and pessimistic in outlook on life than Anglo-Americans.

In times of ideological turmoil, it is provocative to contrast the family centeredness of the Mexican (and most traditional Third World societies) with the intense individualism in most capitalistic countries and the collectivism of communist societies. At least from a mental health viewpoint, it appears better to base a society on the family than on either the individual or the collectivity.

Economic Dimensions

In order to understand the basis for the cultural differences that have been identified, I have examined economic factors as they relate to coping styles. Within an evolving culture two critical economic characteristics exist: (1) the amount of material resources and opportunities available, and (2) the efficiency in the utilization of these opportunities. The economic characteristics of the culture affect and are shaped by the historically established coping style of the culture (Diaz-Guerrero, 1973, 1979, in press).

As resources and opportunities decrease, there will be a corresponding increase in the number of contingencies favoring the development of a passive, affiliative-obedient, coping style, with all its cognitive and personality developmental consequences, at the level of the individual. When resources and opportunities decrease at the larger social system level, there will be a corresponding increase in the number of contingencies favoring the development of an interdependent, group-oriented coping style in the individual and congruent HSCPs for the society. As the efficacy (constructiveness) in the use of resources and opportunities increases at any level of the social system, there will a corresponding increase in the number of contingencies favoring the development of an active internal control coping style in the individual and in the HSCPs for the society.

The differences between Mexican and American children's coping styles (Holtzman et al., 1975) reflect dramatically different historical sociocultural premises held by the mothers in the two cultures. Many of these differences are epiphenomena; the basic economic differences between the countries led to different HSCPs. For example, in this case, per capita income in the two nations at large was roughly seven times greater in the United States than in Mexico at the time of the study. There is however evidence that personal and cultural values are more important than economic values for the quality of life in Mexico (Diaz-Guerrero, in press).

The amount and the variety of educational opportunities have long been recognized as being decisive for children's intellectual development (Dave, 1964; Wolf, 1964, 1965). Holtzman et al. (1975) reported large differences in the variety and the extent of intellectually stimulating objects and activities favoring American over Mexican homes. Bradley, Caldwell, and Elardo (1977) found correlations of up to .79 between the Stanford Binet I.Q. of 3-year-olds and scales in Home Observation for Measurement of the Environment Inventory (HOME), a question-naire for measuring environmental objects and processes that may stimulate the intellect.

The amount of raw resources available within the culture as defined earlier appears easy to assess. Efficacy, which we have termed *constructiveness in the use of resource opportunities,* is far more difficult to define operationally. I hypothesize that efficacy in societies varies in proportion to the material wealth of the society, whether traditional, communist, or capitalist. These factors are not empirically validated at this time.

Conclusion

Plotting cultural beliefs and assumptions as exemplified in the HSCPs and the dimensions described above remains the systematic basis for studying cross-cultural differences and intercultural interactions. Human realities are, fundamentally, subjective cognitive reality. The job of the behavioral scientist is to systematize and map this reality. However, such subjective reality must be examined within the context of structural and economic factors operating in the culture.

PART IV

The Study of Ethnicity: Emerging Themes and Implications

The last part of the book deals with the study of ethnicity and its implications in today's world. Schofield and Anderson's chapter deals with special problems involved in studying ethnicity, with a focus on the ways in which qualitative and quantitative research methods can be combined. They point out that these two methods are not fundamentally different, irreconcilable approaches to research; the distinction between them is rather one of degree. Both approaches have subjective elements, and neither is necessarily more valid than the other. Given the complexity of the issues involved in studying ethnicity in children, research that combines the two methods may ultimately provide the clearest answers to the many unanswered questions. They conclude their chapter with specific suggestions of ways in which quantitative methods may be introduced into basically qualitative studies dealing with ethnicity.

The final chapter integrates the material presented in the other chapters and reviews four underlying themes that are central to understanding children's ethnic socialization: the impact on development of ethnic group differences; the role of developmental change; the differing influence of ethnicity on minority and majority group children; and the impact of the sociocultural and historical contexts. This chapter discusses the implications of these themes for researchers interested in studying children. It also spells out specific implications for educators, counselors, health and social workers, and others who deal with children, suggesting ways of increasing awareness of and sensitivity to the role of ethnicity in development, in order to promote a better understanding of ethnicity and optimal outcomes for children of all ethnic groups.

13

Combining Quantitative and Qualitative Components of Research on Ethnic Identity and Intergroup Relations

JANET WARD SCHOFIELD
KAREN ANDERSON

The last 15 years have seen a remarkable burgeoning of interest in qualitative research methods in areas of study that heretofore had ignored or even scorned such methods. The most striking change has occurred in educational research. Sociologists, anthropologists, and psychologists concerned with the study of education have all remarked on this change (Bogdan & Biklen, 1982; Reichardt & Cook, 1979; Rist, 1980; Spindler, 1982; Wolcott, 1980). Other fields have also begun to appreciate the potential contribution of the qualitative approach. For example, although qualitative methods occasionally were employed in evaluation research as much as twenty years ago, only in the last decade have calls for their utilization become both widespread and influential (Filstead, 1979; Ianni & Orr, 1979; Knapp, 1979; Patton, 1980). The use of qualitative methods in the study of organizations also has gained increasing attention. Van Maanen (1982, p. 13) comments that the market for textbooks on qualitative research is "booming."

AUTHORS' NOTE: The preparation of this chapter was funded by the University of Pittsburgh's Learning Research and Development Center, which receives funding from the National Institute of Education. However, no endorsement of the contents of the chapter by NIE is implied or intended.

Reactions to the rapid gain in popularity of qualitative methods have been mixed. Naturally, those who engage in this sort of research are pleased with its growing visibility and acceptance, although some are concerned that this sudden spurt of interest combined with the surface simplicity of most qualitative research methods has attracted untrained researchers who claim to do such research without really understanding the complexity of the process or the discipline it requires (Fetterman, 1982; Rist, 1980; Wolcott, 1980). Those identified with more traditional quantitative research have tended to be less positive, in part because of concerns over the apparent subjectivity of many qualitative data-gathering and analysis techniques. However, there is a growing tendency, even on the part of some researchers strongly identified with quantitative research methods, to accept or even to advocate the utilization of qualitative methods.

Exemplifying this trend is the shift in the position of Donald Campbell. Campbell and Stanley's (1966, p. 6) widely used book on quasi-experimental design written about 20 years ago contended that the "one-shot case study," which is the model for much of today's qualitative research, has "such a total absence of control as to be of almost no scientific value." However, more recently Campbell (1979, p. 52) wrote a paper to "correct some of [his] own prior excesses in describing the case study approach" in which he takes the, for many, rather startling position that when qualitative and quantitative results conflict, "the quantitative results should be regarded as suspect until the reasons for the discrepancy are well understood."

This growing appreciation of qualitative techniques is a positive development because it broadens the range of approaches researchers are likely to consider in deciding which of the many available methods is most appropriate for the problems they are studying. Additionally, and equally important, the increasing acceptance of qualitative research opens up the possibility of integrating elements of qualitative and quantitative methods when this is desirable for the problem at hand. Although such integration is an exciting possibility, it is not as yet common.

The purpose of this chapter is to take some initial steps in suggesting ways in which this possibility can be realized. To introduce the body of the chapter, we will explain what we mean by the terms *quantitative* and *qualitative* research. Then, we consider why it makes sense to integrate these approaches, at least under some circumstances. Finally, in an extended illustration of one approach to the broad question of how qualitative and quantitative methods can be combined, we will turn to an analysis of just when and how qualitative research can fruitfully employ quantitative components.

In writing a paper on the integration of quantitative and qualitative approaches to research, one has two basic choices—to write a "domain-less" purely methodological piece, or to anchor one's observations in a particular substantive domain. We chose this latter route, primarily because it suggests a literature to work from and adds a useful concreteness to the analysis. The substantive focus chosen to provide a basis for the methodological analysis is a broad one—really two interconnected ones—the areas of ethnic identity and intergroup relations. We have chosen this focus for three reasons. First, enough research of both a quantitative and a qualitative nature has been done in these areas to provide a literature that can be examined. Second, the first author's extensive personal experience in directing a qualitative study that utilized numerous quantitative techniques to explore ethnic identity and intergroup relations in an educational setting serves as a useful resource. Third, and most important, the related areas of ethnic identity and intergroup relations seem especially likely to profit from an attempt to integrate quantitative and qualitative approaches. Although there is a rich tradition in anthropology of taking a qualitative approach to the study of ethnic identity, most of the work performed by psychologists in this area has fallen within the quantitative tradition (see Aboud, this volume). Similarly, the traditional approach taken by psychologists interested in examining intergroup relations in desegregated schools has been almost exclusively quantitative (Gerard & Miller, 1975; Miller & Brewer, 1984; Patchen, 1982; St. John, 1975; Stephan & Feagin, 1980). Much has been learned from this research. However, we would argue that the related areas of ethnic identity and intergroup relations are ripe for qualitative investigation and for further quantitative work that is enriched by fuller acquaintance with the qualitative tradition.

Although we see no necessary link between paradigm and methodology, qualitative researchers tend to emphasize understanding perceptions and feelings, the ways in which groups create systems of meaning, and the behavior patterns that typify groups. The study of ethnic identity could greatly profit from such an orientation because ethnic identity is preeminently a socially constructed system of meaning that includes both rules about how ethnicity is to be determined and what affiliation with a particular group entails. Likewise, intergroup relations is an area in which social meanings and nuances, often the focus of qualitative research, can be of extraordinary importance. For example, Triandis, Vassiliou, Vassiliou, Tanaka, and Shanmugam (1972) argue that one cause of friction in intergroup relations is the fact that members of different cultures interpret specific behaviors quite differently. Because certain behaviors have different meanings to different participants in an intergroup interaction, the individuals may react in ways that mystify, irritate, or annoy each other. A clear example of this phenomenon emerged in a study of peer relations in a desegregated middle school (Sagar & Schofield, 1980). An experiment designed to reveal students' perceptions of various ambiguously aggressive acts, such as bumping into another student in the hallway, found that White boys considered some of these acts as markedly more mean and threatening than did their Black peers, who, in contrast, saw them as more playful. At the conclusion of her extensive review of the literature on the impact of school desegregation on the children involved, St. John (1975) states:

> The most needed type of research at this juncture is probably not a mammoth longitudinal testing program. . . . Far more illuminating would be small-scale studies involving anthropological observations of the process of interracial schooling across [diverse] settings. (pp. 122-123)

In summary, then, qualitative work on ethnic identity and on intergroup relations yields the promise of illuminating important aspects of these subjects. For this reason, it seems desirable to consider both how qualitative components could enrich primarily quantitative work in this area and how future qualitative work could be performed in a manner that capitalizes on the strengths associated with that approach but also profits from incorporating quantitative components when they would be useful.

Qualitative and Quantitative Approaches to Research: A Brief Overview and an Illustrative Example

We will use the term *qualitative research* to refer to a wide array of increasingly popular techniques often referred to as qualitative research, naturalistic research, or even ethnography, and described in detail elsewhere (Bauman, 1972; Bogdan & Biklen, 1982; Bogdan & Taylor, 1975; Erickson, 1979; Reichardt & Cook, 1979; Spindler, 1982; Wilcox, 1982; Wilson, 1977; Wolcott, 1973). Research that is designated by these diverse terms generally (a) is conducted in natural settings, such as schools or neighborhoods; (b) utilizes the researcher as the chief "instrument" in both data gathering and analysis, a procedure often criticized by quantitative researchers as unduly subjective; (c) emphasizes "thick description," that is, obtaining "real," "rich," "deep," data that illuminate everyday patterns of action and meaning from the perspective of those being studied (Ryle, cited in Geertz, 1973); (d) tends to focus on social processes rather than primarily or exclusively on outcomes; (e) employs multiple data-gathering methods, especially participant-observation and interviews; and (f) uses an inductive approach to data analysis, extracting its concepts from the mass of particular detail that constitutes the data base. Qualitative methods generally are considered to be relatively high on internal validity, but low on reliability (see LeCompte & Goetz, 1982, for a thorough review).

In contrast to the holistic and contextual approach taken by qualitative research, quantitative research generally focuses on the testing of specific hypotheses that are smaller parts of some larger theoretical perspective. This approach follows the traditional natural science model more closely than qualitative research, emphasizing experimental design and statistical methods of analysis. Quantitative research emphasizes standardization, precision, objectivity, and reliability of measurement as well as replicability and generalizability of findings. Thus quantitative research is characterized not only by a focus on producing numbers but on generating numbers that are suitable for statistical tests. The quantitative researcher is assumed to take a maximally objective approach to data gathering and analysis. Additionally, the situations studied generally are assumed to be a stable, rather than changing, reality.

The differences and similarities between the quantitative and qualitative approaches can be illustrated by a brief discussion of research on ethnic self-identification and ethnic identity. As Aboud's (this volume) chapter points out, the typical procedure for measuring a child's ethnic or racial self-identity in studies within the tradition of quantitative psychology has been to present individuals with a number of pictures of others and to ask them to select the peer who "looks most like you."

Another common procedure is to ask children to sort pictures of individuals, including themselves, into piles based on their ethnicity. As Aboud notes, "If the self stimulus is placed in the correct pile, ethnic self-identity is accurate" (this volume).

These common approaches to the measurement of ethnic identification share a number of attributes typical of quantitative research. For example, they generally are utilized within controlled experimental situations designed to permit statistical analysis of differences between children of different ages, different ethnic groups, or the like. In addition, these methods both tend to assume that there is a "correct" social group membership that the researcher can ascertain objectively. In fact, the focus of the research is frequently on the question of whether the subjectively evidenced identity, as measured on the tasks described above, is the same as the objectively determined "correct" identity, as determined by the appearance of the research participants, or by reliance on official school records. Furthermore, these approaches do relatively little to probe the subjective significance of correct self-identification or the psychological meaning of "incorrect" identification.

In the qualitative approach to the study of ethnicity, the issue of basic self-identification, that is, of one's ability to label or to categorize oneself in accordance with some external indicators or records of one's group membership, has not been a focus of much attention. Anthropologists, whose work still heavily influences qualitative work in psychology and sociology, have traditionally studied foreign, and often rather isolated, homogeneous communities, in which the question of correct self-identification was not relevant. More important, qualitative researchers emphasize the social construction and meaning of various categories and distrust "objectively" defined categories. A good example of this emphasis on the fluid, subjective, social nature of the concept of ethnic identity can be found in Pitt-Rivers' (1977) account of the concept of Raza in Latin America. The Guatemalan census of 1940 classified the population into five groups based on an objective physical concept of race. However, these classifications were so at odds with the functionally important categories in that society that the next census simply dichotomized the population as Indian or Latino—a "nonIndian" category that included Blacks, Chinese, and even Mormon missionaries. Of course, the problem of defining what was meant by Indian still arose. Because the criteria that were crucial in identifying a person as Indian varied dramatically from one community to the next, the census takers were finally instructed to consider individuals *Indian* if that classification was generally applied to them within their own communities. Genetic phenotype was found to be correlated with the categories to which communities assigned individuals, but it was by no means the determining factor.

The Need for a Rapprochement Between Qualitative and Quantitative Research Methods

Although qualitative and quantitative research clearly differ in numerous ways, a number of important recent statements argue against the traditional view that qualitative and quantitative work are based on fundamentally different paradigms and are thus competing and irreconcilable ways of approaching research (Cook & Reichardt, 1979). Scholars of this persuasion argue that the distinction between qualitative and quantitative research is a matter of degree rather than of a basic difference (Campbell, 1979; Filstead, 1979; Spindler, 1982).

One of the most lucid and persuasive statements of this position can be found in a paper by Reichardt and Cook (1979). They argue that the characterization of quantitative research as objective and of qualitative research as subjective ignores important aspects of subjectivity that enter the quantitative research process at virtually every stage. Similarly, this characterization ignores the fact that there are many procedures commonly utilized in qualitative research to create a "disciplined subjectivity" (Erickson, 1973) that contribute substantially to the reliability and validity of qualitative research findings (LeCompte & Goetz, 1982). In the same vein, Reichardt and Cook point out that qualitative data have no corner on internal validity, raising participant observation of a visual illusion as a case in which quantitative methods would lead to more valid conclusions about the stimuli than qualitative ones.

A brief discussion of the differences between the approach of quantitative and qualitative researchers to the issues of ethnic self-identification and ethnic identity can illustrate Reichardt and Cook's contention that qualitative and quantitative approaches differ in degree rather than in fundamental nature. For example, interest in the subjective meaning of group membership is not exclusively the province of qualitative researchers. As Aboud (this volume) makes clear, the early classic studies of ethnic self-identification of Black children in the United States included questions ("Who's the good doll?") designed to assess children's feelings about and images of the groups in question, as have many of the later studies modeled on them (Clark & Clark, 1947; Greenwald & Oppenheim, 1968; Hrabra & Grant, 1970; Kircher & Furby, 1971; Morland, 1966; Rice, Ruiz, & Padila, 1974). Additionally, studies of Black adults' identity development that utilize traditional quantitative techniques have probed issues of meaning and change (Cross, this volume). Similarly, qualitative researchers have not completely eschewed study of the issues of ethnic self-identification as evidenced by Ogbu's (1974) work in this area.

In fact, it is just those cases in which researchers of one school have begun work on issues generally dealt with by researchers of the other school that show how these contrasting approaches can profit from interchange. For example, Ogbu (1974) utilized school records, which often are used by quantitative researchers to define the actual group membership of children, in a way undoubtedly influenced by the qualitative researchers' emphasis on subjectivity and social meaning. He compared such records to the ethnic identity reported in lengthy interviews in which respondents both indicated their own ethnic identity and talked about what that categorization meant to them.

At least two of Ogbu's observations have relevance in quite different ways for quantitatively oriented researchers. First, he found that some of the individuals classified by the school as Black preferred to call themselves Negro. Although they did not dispute the fact that they belonged to the social category "Black," they felt that the specific words used to designate this category implied a set of social attitudes as well as a certain genetic phenotype. Such an observation certainly suggests that children using different labels to identify themselves may feel differently about their own group and other groups even if those labels are merely different descriptions referring to the same phenotypic category. A study by Lampe (1982) suggests this is the case, as does the work of Buriel (this volume).

Second, Ogbu reported that some individuals classified officially as Anglo regarded themselves as Black or, much more commonly, as Mexican. It seems reasonable to assume that Ogbu's respondents, who were adults, had some objective basis for their self-reported ethnic identity that was missed in the official classification process, rather than that they misperceived themselves as Mexican when they were "really" White. If this is the case, standard procedures for measuring ethnic self-identification in their children, such as comparing the results of a matching or categorization test with the child's "real" ethnicity based on school records, or even possibly on observed physical characteristics, could lead to classifying them mistakenly as misperceiving their actual ethnic group membership. The arbitrariness of many classification procedures and the possibility for gaps between subjective sense of ethnic group membership and official classification is made clear when one considers the lengths that countries like South Africa, and the United States in the not too distant past, have gone in order to decide just who should be considered Black. Of course, quantitative researchers do not always accept official records at face value, as is shown by careful discussions of the types of errors that are likely to be found in such records (DeFleur, 1975; Kitsuse & Cicourel, 1963; Morgenstern, 1963). However, researchers with different backgrounds are likely to be sensitive to different types of errors and thus each perspective has something to gain from the other.

In the last decade, a number of scholars have argued not only that quantitative and qualitative approaches *can* be utilized jointly but that they *should* be so utilized (Campbell, 1979; Cook & Cook, 1977; Eisner, 1977; Erickson, 1977; Fetterman, 1982; Filstead, 1979; Light & Pillemer, 1982; McClintock, Brannon, & Maynard-Moody, 1979; Sieber, 1973; Spindler, 1982; Tikunoff & Ward, 1978), because they tend to have complementary strengths. Experimental or quasi-experimental methods coupled with quantitative data analysis are well-suited to reducing the ambiguity about causal connections between variables. However, they also have some drawbacks. First, they are not generally used in ways that illuminate the processes accounting for the effects they document. Second, they are far from ideal for exploring the impact of contextual factors that cannot be clearly specified in advance. Furthermore, they tend to be rigid because change of course in midstream in response to new information is difficult when experimental designs are being utilized (Campbell, 1979). Although quantitative studies have the advantage of presenting precise numerical data, often such studies do little to give the reader a "picture" of what is going on. For example, Finkelstein and Haskins (1983), Sagar, Schofield, and Snyder (1983), Schofield and Francis (1982), and Singleton and Asher (1977) have all studied peer interaction in children in racially mixed schools using traditional quantitative observational strategies. The reader is presented with statistical evidence regarding same-race and cross-race interactions. This is certainly useful information; however, the inclusion of qualitative data could strengthen these papers. For example, descriptions of behavioral incidents actually observed could serve to give the reader a more concrete, vivid, and memorable idea of the types of interactions that occurred. Similarly, in other situations, adding open-ended interview responses could effectively illustrate what the numerical data conclude.

Qualitative research, on the other hand, is weak where experimental and other quantitative designs are often strong and strong where such designs are frequently weak. Qualitative research is not generally able to specify causal connections as clearly as many quantitative strategies can. However, it can suggest ideas about social processes, explore the context in which the phenomena under investigation occur, and capture with both vividness and subtlety the perceptions of the individuals being studied (see Ramsey, this volume). Some studies combining quantitative and qualitative strategies can be found (Fetterman, 1982; LeCompte, 1969; Tikunoff, Berliner, & Rist, 1975; Trend, 1978; Wilcox, 1982). However, they are not as common as one might expect when one considers the volume of the chorus calling for such integration. There are a number of possible reasons for this. For example, Reichardt and Cook (1979) point out that the joint use of these two strategies is likely to be expensive and time consuming. Furthermore, combining two different types of methodologies obviously requires a much broader range of research skills than using either one by itself.

There is another important but largely unrecognized obstacle to the integration of these two approaches. There is a vast literature on traditionally quantitative research methodology and a smaller, but still substantial, literature on qualitative methodologies, but there is extremely little guidance available on how to combine these two approaches and use them jointly. Knowing how to handle these two research strategies separately does not necessarily imply being able to handle their interaction, as indicated in Light and Pillemer's (1982) paper on utilizing both types of data in literature reviews. Indeed, Trend (1978) provides a fascinating discussion of the difficulties encountered when the analysis of qualitative data from a participant observer produced conclusions that could not easily be reconciled with those emerging from analysis of the quantitative data gathered at the same research site. Only after considerable difficulty did a new interpretation of the data emerge that accounted convincingly for both sets of findings. Trend (1978, p. 83) concludes, with considerable understatement, that "procedures for using the two [methodologies] together are not well developed."

Unfortunately, Trend, like virtually all others who have advocated the combination of qualitative and quantitative techniques, does not explore how these methods might best be integrated. To date, few have taken up this challenge, especially with regard to the issues of how and when one might usefully incorporate quantitative techniques into qualitative projects. Indeed, a widely used text on qualitative research contends pessimistically that integrating quantitative components into qualitative projects is generally likely to produce little more than "a big headache" (Bogdan & Biklen, 1982, p. 39). One of the major reasons for this is that so little systematic attention has been given to the issues of when and how to perform such integration efficiently and effectively. Numerous volumes on qualitative research are close to silent on such issues (Bogdan & Biklen, 1982; Guba, 1978; Hansen, 1979; Merton, Coleman, & Rossi, 1979; Patton, 1980; Van Maanen, Dabbs, & Faulkner, 1982; Wax, 1971). This chapter takes a first step in the direction of filling this gap. Specifically, we will shortly address the question of how basically qualitative studies can fruitfully incorporate quantitative components. Of course, this topic addresses only one facet of the more general issue of how quantitative and qualitative research can be integrated. Much work is also needed on the ways in which quantitatively oriented research could benefit from familiarity with and utilization of qualitative techniques.

The Utilization of Quantitative Techniques in Qualitative Studies of Ethnicity and Intergroup Relations

The ideas to be presented here on how and when quantitative methods can be utilized by qualitative researchers emerged from four very different types of sources. First, and most obviously, we searched carefully for methodological papers focusing specifically on this topic (Cook & Reichardt, 1979; Sieber, 1973; Spindler, 1982; Zelditch, 1962). Second, we consulted a dozen texts dealing primarily or extensively with qualitative methodology to see what, if anything, they had to say on this topic. Third, we examined nearly 20 relatively well-known book length monographs presenting qualitative research on ethnic identity and/or intergroup relations to see what, if any, basically quantitative techniques had been employed in these studies. Finally, we drew on the first author's experience in directing a 4-year ethnographic research project on social relations between Black and White children in a desegregated school (Schofield, 1982) that included a wide array of quantitative techniques, including experiments (Sagar & Schofield, 1980), quasi-experiments (Schofield & Sagar, 1977; Schofield, 1979), the development and utilization of quantitative observational coding systems (Sagar & Schofield, 1980; Schofield & Francis, 1982) and sociometric and other questionnaires (Schofield, Whitley, & Snyder 1983; Whitley & Schofield, 1984).

The Use of Numbers

The incidental use of a few numbers can hardly be considered a departure from traditional qualitative techniques. Yet it is useful to examine both what sorts of things are frequently quantified in qualitative studies and to what end these numbers are used. Even those ethnographies that make little use of numbers frequently use some incidental quantification in describing the research site and its context, the research participants, and the project methodology (Bossert, 1979; Gans, 1962; Hanna, 1982; Rist, 1978; Valentine, 1978). One of the most typical procedures is to use census data, unemployment rates, and other similar government-generated figures to describe the neighborhood or population studied. Qualitative researchers also frequently present quantitative information of the sort used by most individuals in their everyday lives, such as the amount of time devoted to some task (Rist, 1973; Warren, 1982; Wolcott, 1973). For example, studies of ethnic communities or of the behavior of members of such communities often present quantitative information about the physical attributes of the people studied, such as their age, height, or weight (Liebow, 1967). Also information is commonly presented on the cost of various items, the wages people receive, and so on (Valentine, 1978; Wolcott, 1980).

Several factors seem to account for the usage of quantitative information in the ways described above including (a) the ready availability of government-generated statistics, and (b) the precision and relative objectivity inherent in utilizing numbers rather than words to convey certain types of information. For example, indicating that the classes studied averaged 33 students rather than calling them "quite large" is more precise and avoids the implicit use of a standard that readers may not share.

Two caveats are warranted about even such straightforward and common types of usage of quantitative elements. First, as Bogdan and Biklen (1982, p. 113) point out, the concept of "real rates" is a misnomer because "rates and counts represent a point of view . . . toward people, objects and events." Thus in using at face value numbers generated by others, the researcher implicitly accepts a particular set of definitions and assumptions. In fact Bogdan and Ksander (1980) see all numbers as so dependent on the particular assumptions and social processes involved in their production that they suggest that this dependency itself be the object of study in a field they call enumerology.

This concern about the origins of numbers and of categories that are used in counting is especially crucial in studies of topics such as ethnic self-identification, ethnic identity, and interethnic interaction. The danger of assuming that the official classification of an individual reflects his or her own sense of self rather than the ways in which others perceive that individual is well illustrated by a problem that arose at a school in which the first author was studying relations between Black and White children (Schofield, 1982). Teachers selecting students for a biracial committee set up to improve relations between Blacks and Whites chose a child, whom we will call Tony, as one of the Black participants. Tony regarded himself as "mixed" because one of his parents was White and the other was Black. Both Black and White members of the research team had assumed that he was White because his facial features were basically Caucasian and his skin tone was very light. Many of Tony's peers were angry about the committee's composition, some not realizing that Tony could be considered Black and others arguing that he was behaviorally as well as physically about as White a Black as one could imagine. Thus research that took at face value the official school figures that showed a racially balanced committee would be incomplete at best. Similarly, a study of racial self-identification that compared Tony's responses to supposedly correct responses based on the researchers' initial classification of him as White would have been misleading given his mixed parentage.

Qualitative researchers must also approach the task of quantifying information in a way that benefits from their emphasis on an in-depth understanding of the topics studied. For example, Valentine's (1978) ethnography of a poor Black community concluded that food prices averaged over 20% higher in that neighborhood than in surrounding White ones. However, it then goes beyond this to point out that the quality of the goods in the ghetto markets is often poor relative to similar products in nearby middle-class areas. Thus the difference in value received is even greater than it appears to be based on the quantitative information alone.

Ballparking: The Utilization of Rough
Estimates in Qualitative Research

Valentine's work on food prices is useful as an example of the ways in which ethnographers often collect and present quantified information. First, the information was collected in a fairly systematic way, but not one designed to yield highly reliable, maximally precise conclusions. Second, the presentation is fairly casual, in that numerous fine details about the ways in which the data were collected are omitted.

Both of these common practices in qualitative research are considered serious defects in quantitative research. Yet they are not terribly serious problems in ethnographic works as long as it is absolutely clear to the reader that the ethnographer is engaged in a process that we will call "ballparking," that is, producing a very rough estimate of a particular phenomenon.

Metz (1978), in her ethnographic study of authority in two desegregated high schools, deals explicitly with the issue. More conservative than most, she generally avoids "ballpark" figures and states clearly that the numbers that are presented are only very rough estimates of the actual situation. She writes:

> Since I did not draw random samples of either events or persons, I cannot generalize from the frequency of any event or characteristic in my sample to its frequency in the school. . . . I intentionally use such phrases as "few teachers said this". . . . If I were to report that "three out of fifteen teachers" . . . behaved in such and such a way, I would imply that these proportions reflected patterns in the whole school. My sample does not allow such inferences. My quantitative statements are only broad approximations of the situations in these schools. (p. 13)

A somewhat more common position is illustrated by Smith and Geoffrey's (1968) statement that a teacher engages in 767 personal interactions in a morning and Jackson's (1968) observation that a teacher engages in "as many as 1,000 interpersonal interchanges each day." Neither of these authors would have his readers believe that these numbers are precise. Yet both use them skillfully to suggest the order of magnitude of the phenomenon they discuss.

However, ballparking is a potentially dangerous practice because it can easily be mistaken for what we will call specifying, that is, gathering data according to all the canons of methodology designed to increase the likelihood that one's data are reliable and precise. Indeed, it is often unclear to the reader whether the ethnographer is ballparking or specifying. Further, even when it appears that an ethnographer has intended to specify, traditional ethnographic styles of writing make it very difficult for readers to judge whether or not the specifying has been appropriately performed. To illustrate, intercoder reliabilities are generally not provided even when the numbers presented are the end result of fairly complicated decision-making processes. For example, a paper whose first author is a highly respected past president of the Council on Anthropology and Education categorizes classroom activities like "teacher circulating, giving individual attention" and "teacher waiting for class" and presents data on the frequency and duration of such events without even mentioning whether reliability estimates were made or not (Erickson & Mohatt, 1982).

Thus potential problems arise when the conventions that have grown up for ballparking are applied in cases in which the ethnographer is specifying or in which it is unclear which process is occurring. We will illustrate this point by examining the Erickson and Mohatt paper mentioned above. We have chosen this paper because it exemplifies a trend toward utilization of quantitative analysis of videotape and/or audiotape within a rich qualitative context. Being on the cutting edge of such a trend, Erickson and Mohatt make an important contribution by providing a model for similar future work but, simultaneously, they may not have discovered how best to deal with all the issues such a trend raises. Their paper sets out to explore the hypothesis that there are certain cultural differences between Native American culture and that of the dominant White middle class that cause difficulties for Indian children taught by White teachers. Erickson and Mohatt compared the teaching style of two competent and experienced teachers—one Indian and one White. Roughly twelve hours of videotaping was conducted in each classroom. Some of this material was subjected to intense fine-grained analysis focusing on a variety of teacher and student behaviors. The result of this analysis is presented in numerous tables and in statements, such as "Teacher II uses three times as many directives as Teacher I, and issues them at a rate more than twice as fast" (Erickson &

Mohatt, 1982, p. 152). No statistical tests were conducted. The paper concludes that "microethnographic analysis reveals the specific features of cultural organization of social relationships in communication which differ, albeit slightly, from mainstream ways of teaching. . . . These findings have implications for pedagogy in the education of Native American children" (p. 67).

The advantage to an analysis strategy and a quantitative presentational style like that of Erickson and Mohatt is that it allows efficient presentation of data on a great many points that relate to the basic question of whether or not there are cultural differences in teaching style. Further, it provides the reader with a somewhat clearer picture of the magnitude of these differences than would completely qualitative statements to the effect that Teacher I was more or less likely to do certain things than Teacher II. The problem, of course, is that the numbers, once produced, imply a precision and reliability that they may well not have. Often, the reader is told little about precisely how these numbers were generated. An even more basic issue in many ethnographic studies, as implied in the earlier cited quote from Metz, is whether the data have been gathered in a way that makes it reasonable to make even rough statements about the frequency, prevalence, or duration of many phenomena.

Two considerations may account for the frequent practice of omitting detailed information on data gathering and analysis even when ethnographic studies feature quantitative analysis as an important part of their results. First, as indicated above, because statistical tests are performed rarely and the emphasis is often on an overall pattern rather than any one particular finding, such information may seem unnecessary. Second, the sort of detail customary in traditional quantitative reports is quite incompatible with the literary narrative form that makes ethnographies so interesting to read. We would suggest, however, that readers would be well served by extended footnotes or by appendices that would supply such information when quantitative results are featured importantly and/or when they are used to specify rather than to ballpark.

The Use of Sampling Procedures

Many qualitative studies would benefit from paying heed to sampling practices generally associated with quantitative methodology. In general, random sampling is less useful in site selection than at other points in ethnographic research, because ethnographic researchers usually study just one or a very small number of sites. Random selection ensures randomness but nothing more. If an ethnographer randomly selected for study one school from the 20 schools in a particular school system there is no *a priori* reason to believe that that school is representative of that system. A far better approach is one in which the researcher decides what type of study is to be made and then looks for a setting or settings that appear appropriate. Exemplifying this sort of approach is Wilcox's (1982) recent study, aimed at seeing whether students in basically upper-middle-class schools are socialized differently in school than those from lower-middle-class schools. Using the method known in anthropology as controlled comparison (Nader, 1964), Wilcox selected two schools as similar as possible except for the variable of interest, class background of the student body. This seems a reasonable strategy, although when the criteria used for selecting sites produce several possible candidates, one might consider random sampling from these candidates.

Although random selection procedures may not be very useful in site selection, they are clearly underutilized in ethnographic work in choosing areas or individuals within sites for study. Although randomness does not guarantee representativeness, especially when small numbers of subunits are studied, there are reasons to consider random or stratified random procedures here. For example, an ethnographer interested in how ethnicity influences teacher behavior could classify teachers according to ethnicity, classify them again on the basis of other relevant criteria, such as years of experience, and then randomly select from teachers who meet all the criteria for inclusion in the study. Because one always uses *some* procedure in selecting subsites for study, random selection provides a good place to start. One may decide that the teachers' attitude toward the study is sufficiently crucial that randomly selected individuals who appear particularly uncooperative will be replaced by another more cooperative randomly selected individual. Although such a procedure is not consistent with the canons of quantitative research, it is likely to produce a more representative set of subunits than the procedures that are typically used in qualitative studies.

Similarly, stratified random procedures should be considered in choosing individuals within sites. Used judiciously or combined with theoretical sampling (Glaser & Strauss, 1967), such a strategy can increase a study's internal validity without compromising flexibility. Interviewing a random sample of students from classes chosen because they embody characteristics of interest to the researcher gives one the advantages of theoretical sampling and increasing internal validity. This is especially important because research suggests that participant observers may tend to gravitate toward certain types of informants (Vidich & Shapiro, 1955). Although such random selection is sometimes used in qualitative studies (Hanna, 1982; Leacock, 1969; Schofield, 1982), it is frequently not used when it could be. The utilization of random sampling procedures need not function as a straitjacket, precluding the ethnographer from consulting especially insightful or well-informed informants. Rather, the two procedures can supplement each other.

The Use of Questionnaires and Observational Checklists

Qualitative studies often look in depth at some relatively small segment of an educational institution or a community. For example, many studies look at no more than a few classrooms within a school (Erickson & Mohatt, 1982; Rist, 1973; Smith & Geoffrey, 1968). Similarly, qualitative studies of the behavior patterns of various racial and ethnic groups typically are conducted in just one community or, more frequently, in one neighborhood within a larger community (Valentine, 1978). It would certainly lend weight to the findings of such studies if one knew that the patterns found were not unique to the particular classroom or neighborhood studied. Yet in-depth study of a large number of classes or neighborhoods is often impractical. Here, the use of quantitative components, such as survey research or certain types of behavioral checklists, may be appropriate. For example, Wilcox (1982) intensively studied one first-grade classroom in a middle-class school and one in a comparable working-class school. Then, to see whether or not the contrasting behaviors documented were characteristic of behaviors in each school, he conducted much briefer observations in several other classrooms at each site. Although a concern with the generalizability of findings is more typical of quantitative than qualitative work, many qualitative projects could profit from Wilcox's example.

In our own work, questionnaires were used not only to see if patterns apparent in the classrooms studied were characteristic of the school more broadly, but to help interpret the meaning of these patterns. For example, observation in a relatively small number of classrooms suggested that boys interacted more with peers of the other race than did girls. Sociometric questionnaires administered to a much larger number of classes confirmed that this phenomenon was widespread (Schofield,

Whitley, & Snyder, 1983). However, they also demonstrated something that the observation could not. Specifically, the results of the statistical analyses of the sociometric data demonstrated clearly that White girls showed a very strong ingroup preference that Black girls did not. Classroom observation had given us some inkling that this was the case, but did not provide truly convincing evidence to this effect because it was often hard to tell who initiated a specific interaction and even harder to determine who terminated it. Further, later interviews suggested that many Black girls who were open to interacting with Whites were sometimes reluctant to initiate interactions for fear of rejection; thus cross-race initiation rates might not have been very different for Black and White girls even though openness to cross-race interaction differed considerably.

The Use of Content Analysis

Another way to gather data efficiently from a larger number of instances than the ethnographer can study in depth is the utilization of content analysis procedures. For example, if an intensive study of a few neighborhoods suggests that certain values are more important to some ethnic groups than others, a content analysis of local newspapers produced by and for other similar communities would shed light on whether the differences found initially are specific to the particular subcommunities studied or if this conclusion holds true more generally.

Content analysis holds dangers as well as promise in ethnographic work. One serious problem can arise when ethnographers attempt to content analyze field notes. Smith and Geoffrey (1968) have pointed out that the observer is of necessity selective in recording the myriad events in a classroom setting. The same holds true for virtually any social setting. This gives rise to the "two realities" problem, the fact that field notes contain only a portion of the events that occur in the setting observed. *Ex post facto* coding of notes or other material for categories of behavior that may not have been equally likely to have been recorded is likely to lead to spurious conclusions (Goetz & LeCompte, 1982). Unfortunately, one frequently finds reference to the coding of field notes in cases where it is not clear whether or not the items of interest were specified in advance.

Although advance specification substantially reduces the "two realities" problem, it certainly does not alleviate it entirely. For example, behaviors that are more salient will more likely be noticed and hence recorded more consistently than behaviors that are less salient. In spite of the problems inherent in coding field notes, some qualitative studies of schooling and/or ethnicity have used content analysis effectively (Leacock, 1969; Rist, 1978).

The Use of Experimental Techniques

Experimental work generally is seen as the antithesis of qualitative research; however, we believe that it too may have a place in ethnographic studies. Specifically, experimental work can play a useful role within qualitative projects in three special cases: (a) when qualitative techniques would require an unacceptably high degree of inference on the researcher's part; (b) when one wants to isolate a weak but potentially important linkage between two variables that may be masked by the "blooming buzzing confusion" of the setting studied; and (c) when the natural co-occurrence of two events makes it difficult to know which of them is linked causally to a third event.

A discussion of the way in which an experiment was utilized in a basically qualitative study of peer relations in a desegregated school can illustrate these points (Schofield, 1982). One impression that emerged from the first year of this qualitative study was that students tended to react differently to ambiguously aggressive acts on the part of other students depending upon the race of the peer. Specifically, it seemed that mild or ambiguous aggression on the part of Blacks was perceived more negatively than similar behavior on the part of Whites. If true, this idea had important implications because White students complained frequently and angrily about Blacks' aggressiveness, and their concerns about this substantially influenced peer relations.

It was impossible to verify this impression by observation alone, however, because it was possible that minor nuances in the behaviors that an observer could not accurately gauge, such as small differences in facial expression or in the exact amount of pressure exerted when poking a peer, might have been at the root of this phenomenon. Thus the level of inference required was too high to draw firm conclusions based on observational data. Similarly, interview data could not resolve this question because it seemed quite likely that Whites' fears of Black aggression could influence their perceptions of the behaviors themselves. Complicating this whole issue was that of social class. Because most of the Black students were of lower social class than the White students, it was possible that cues connected with social class were responsible for the fear generated by the behavior of Blacks.

Because it was of interest to see if race itself was a sufficient cue to lead to differential interpretation of peer's behavior, an experiment was designed and conducted. Black and White children were shown several sketches depicting common mildly aggressive behaviors, such as one student poking another with a pencil. The sketches shown to different students were identical, except that the race of the perpetrator of the aggressive act and the race of its victim were varied. As anticipated on the basis of classroom observation, a number of these mildly aggressive behaviors were perceived as more mean and threatening when performed by a Black than when performed by a White. Further, regardless of who performed them, certain types of mildly aggressive behavior were perceived differently by Whites and Blacks, with Whites more likely to see them as threatening and Blacks more likely to see them as somewhat playful. These two sets of experimental findings opened up a whole area of investigation that was explored qualitatively in open-ended student interviews and in further classroom observation.

Conclusion

Quantitative and qualitative research methods are not diametrically opposed strategies, but rather somewhat different ways of approaching understanding, each with its own strengths and weaknesses. The potential value of combining these two types of methods appears to be particularly promising for those studying the related areas of ethnic identity and intergroup relations. Although care must be taken to avoid certain pitfalls in the use of quantitative methods in qualitative studies, there are numerous instances in which quantitative components can be appropriately incorporated into qualitative research projects.

First, systematic random sampling procedures can aid the ethnographer in choosing both research sites and individuals or subunits within that site for study. A reliance on random or stratified-random sampling techniques can avoid or minimize certain biases in the selection of sites (or individuals) for study that can undermine the reliability and validity of qualitative data. Second, the use of questionnaires or other more typically quantitative instruments can enhance or amplify an idea or hypothesis suggested by ethnographic field notes. Third, the use of formal content analysis procedures can help to focus and confirm an impression received from observations or to see whether or not conclusions developed in one milieu hold in others. Finally, the use of traditional experimental techniques in larger qualitative projects can be extremely valuable under certain conditions.

Although such methods have been used successfully by a small number of qualitative researchers, their potential has not been fully tapped in the broad range of situations in which they could be appropriately employed. This may be because little guidance is available for the qualitative researcher interested in the use of quantitative methods. We have tried to outline some useful techniques for the qualitative researcher and the occasions on which their use may be especially fruitful. Because the potential benefits of combining the two method types are substantial, we hope that the ideas presented in this chapter will stimulate other qualitative researchers to devote more thought to such methodological issues.

14

Children's Ethnic Socialization: Themes and Implications

JEAN S. PHINNEY
MARY JANE ROTHERAM

From the theoretical and empirical work discussed in this book, there emerge four unifying themes that serve as a basis for our understanding of children's ethnic socialization: (1) Ethnic group differences in appearance, behaviors, attitudes, and values have a significant impact on development. (2) The impact of ethnicity varies with the child's age. (3) Ethnic socialization has different implications depending on the particular group to which children belong. (4) The role of ethnicity in development is affected by the immediate environment and the sociocultural and historical context. This chapter reviews these themes and examines their implications for educators, counselors, health care and social work professionals, and those doing research with children.

Unifying Themes

(1) **Important differences in attitudes, values, and behaviors distinguish ethnic groups; these differences affect the socialization of children within their own group and their attitudes and responses to other groups.**

Ethnic group differences go beyond the more obvious perceptual differences that children notice first, such as skin color, food, or language, to include variation in values, attitudes, and rules of social interaction. An understanding of the variations among groups can help adults work more effectively with children from diverse groups. But because ethnic characteristics are defined in terms of the group, not the individual, they must be treated with caution when dealing with individual children.

Ethnic differences as perceived by children serve as a basis for learning the characteristics of their own and other groups. Children's developing awareness of contrasts between groups may result in tension and negative attitudes toward other groups. There is, therefore, need for deliberate efforts to promote understanding and positive interactions. Children's exposure to cultural differences in pluralistic societies also means that some degree of biculturalism is likely. Biculturalism may create stress due to conflicting values, particularly for minority group children, but it does not appear to have a negative effect on self-esteem. It may in fact increase flexibility and promote competence to function in two cultures.

(2) The impact of ethnicity on children and the way children understand and deal with it vary significantly with age and developmental level.

As children develop, their mental and physical growth, together with their widening experience of the world, bring about changes in their cognitions, attitudes, and self-awareness with regard to ethnicity. Children's early understandings are inconsistent, concrete, and idiosyncratic. With increasing cognitive abilities children develop more stable, differentiated, and abstract conceptions of ethnicity. Children's sense of their own ethnic group membership (that is, their ethnic identity) also undergoes clear developmental changes. In young children, the development of ethnic identity can be conceptualized as learning what they are based on objective criteria (for example, the ethnicity of their parents). However, beginning in early adolescence, children become aware of choices that they can make in terms of the extent to which they identify with their own group and its attributes. Ethnic identity in adolescents includes both the objective criteria of ethnicity learned in childhood and subjective criteria reflecting the individual's choice of reference group. Attitudes and preferences toward ethnic groups likewise undergo developmental changes, but these shifts are more difficult to pinpoint in relation to age. Although attitudes appear to stabilize with increasing age, older children are also more aware of the constraints of social desirability; thus their attitudes are more difficult to assess accurately.

(3) **The process of ethnic socialization differs in important ways depending on the particular group children belong to, and on whether that group is the majority group or a minority group in the society.**

The impact of ethnicity on children's development is related to whether they are members of a minority or a majority group. Children who are in the minority are more aware of their own ethnicity, and their ethnicity is more evident to other children. Minority children will inevitably be exposed to differences between their own and the majority group. Majority children, on the other hand, may be shielded from an awareness of such differences, or may see such differences only stereotypically, as presented by the media or in comments by adults. Majority group children are more likely to be ethnocentric in the sense of being unaware of, or convinced of the inferiority of, attitudes and values different from their own. In most situations, for example in schools, the norms of the majority prevail, and minority children are expected to follow these norms or rules. Minority group children are thus more often faced with a conflict between the values of their own group and those of the majority culture.

The terms *minority* and *majority* as used above refer to numbers in the society. However, the definition of these terms varies depending on the frame of reference. In the world as a whole, Whites are in the minority. This may also be true at the local level; a few White children in a predominantly Black school experience minority status in that setting.

(4) **Children's ethnic socialization is a function of both the immediate environment and the sociocultural context; social and historical change is continually altering the relationships among groups and the meaning of ethnicity for children.**

The context influences ethnic socialization on many levels, including immediate family, school, community, and the entire culture, as Bronfenbrenner (1979) has outlined for development generally. Children's awareness of ethnicity and its salience in describing themselves or others depends largely on the proportion of own-group and other-group members in the environment. Children's sense of their ethnicity is influenced also by the broad social structure, including the way ethnic groups are defined, the coherence of a group and the supports it provides (such as social organizations, churches, or language schools), the relative status of groups, and the tensions that exist among them. But the social structure itself changes over time. Recent social movements and an increased focus on cultural pluralism have made minority group children more aware of their own cultural heritage and have made majority children more conscious of diversity in the society.

Each of these themes has important implications for those who work with or study children. In the following sections we outline these implications for the fields of education; counseling, health care, and social services; and research.

Implications for Education

Educating Children About
Ethnic Differences

Multicultural education refers to materials and programs that foster understanding and appreciation of ethnic diversity and promote positive interethnic relations. Some such programs involve special units on each of a variety of ethnic groups. Others aim to include information about minority cultures in all subjects, for example, art, music, literature, and history (Banks, 1981; Craft, 1984; Ramsey, 1987). Other programs attempt to promote positive interactions between groups with different values, attitudes, and behaviors (Pusch, 1979) or to enhance cultural awareness (Pasternak, 1979). In spite of the general endorsement of multicultural programs, it is not clear how widespread the use of such programs actually is in schools, nor has there much evaluation of their effectiveness in meeting their goals of fostering understanding and positive interaction.

Furthermore, multicultural programs can be controversial. Recognition and discussion of differences may lead to stereotyping and increased prejudice between groups (Adam, 1978). Some writers, including Allport (1954), feel that programs to promote intergroup relationships should stress similarities among groups rather than differences. However, Stephan and Stephan (1984) state that "knowledge and understanding of differences as well as similarities among groups is important in reducing prejudice" (p. 238). They found that the more that Anglo children knew about Chicano culture, the more favorable were their attitudes toward Chicanos.

To be successful, multicultural education programs need to be tailored to the developmental level and interests of children. Because of the concrete thinking and experiential learning of young children, the best approach in early childhood is personal experience with members of other groups, including the opportunity to share the food they eat, learn about their customs and holidays, and discuss the observable physical differences. In ethnically isolated areas, where cross-group contact is not feasible, children can vicariously experience ethnic differences through photographs, artifacts, foods, and celebrations. With the increased cognitive competence of the elementary school years, children can explore the geographic origins, cultural history, and the contributions to society of different groups. As children enter adolescence and develop the capacity to understand more abstract issues, they can examine the treatment of different ethnic groups in literature, films, and television, and begin to deal with the topics of stereotypes, prejudice, and discrimination.

Multicultural education programs also need to recognize the different needs and perspectives of majority and minority children. Majority group children are likely to be more ethnocentric and less aware of ethnic differences than minority group children. Thus they particularly need accurate information about other groups and an understanding of the value of diversity in enriching a society. Minority children are typically already familiar with the majority culture, but often their own culture has been ignored or disparaged in the curriculum. For them, a better understanding of the strengths and achievements of their own culture is important. For example, several studies by Ramirez and colleagues (cited in Ramirez & Castaneda, 1974) found that Mexican American children who received lessons on their Mexican American heritage showed enhanced self-esteem scores.

Educating Children from
Different Ethnic Groups

Schools in the United States, as in most Western countries, traditionally have been White middle-class institutions that propagate the values and attitudes of the dominant group. As such, they often have not served the needs of children coming from different backgrounds. Minority group children show significantly poorer school achievement (Scarr, Caprulo, Ferdman, Tower, & Caplan, 1983) and have a substantially higher drop-out rate than majority children. In the Los Angeles school district, the high school drop-out rate for Hispanic students is 45%, versus 17% for Anglo students (Savage, 1985). Gallimore, Boggs, and Jordan (1974) see the classroom in a pluralistic community as "an interface of cultures, in which the learning process is disrupted because teachers and pupils have incongruent expectations, motives, social behaviors, and language and cognitive patterns" (p. 251). The cognitive characteristics and interaction patterns of minority group children that may interfere with school success are beginning to be documented (Buriel, 1983; Shade, 1982).

The work of Gallimore and his colleagues working with native Hawaiian children provides a number of examples of how an understanding of a culture can be used to promote positive educational outcomes. In terms of the dimensions discussed earlier in this volume, Hawaiian culture is characterized by an emphasis on the group rather than the individual. Hawaiian children grow up with a strong orientation to their family and community. Although they have been described as lacking in achievement motivation, Gallimore et al. (1974) point out that these children are motivated to achieve in order to gain access to others and to maintain affiliative ties, rather than to attain personal goals. Therefore, teachers introduce a team approach into the classroom, so that students work together and receive group rewards. As a result, low achieving Hawaiian children show significant increases in academic performance (MacDonald & Gallimore, 1971). For those tasks that cannot be carried out effectively in a team, such as reading, they found that good work habits were promoted by rewarding completion of an assignment with the opportunity to socialize with peers.

In addition, in Hawaiian culture children's relationship to authority figures differs from the attitudes teachers expect. Hawaiian children, as a result of the sibling caretaking system, learn to attend only selectively to adults, primarily when the adult's behavior is positive and receptive. By having teachers increase the number of positive and supportive statements directed at children behaving appropriately, MacDonald and Gallimore (1971) were able to effect a significant increase in children's attention to the teacher's instruction.

However, the development of programs for minority children introduces what Bullivant (1981) calls the pluralistic dilemma in education: How can the legitimate special needs of minority group children be reconciled with the need for all children, regardless of ethnic background, to learn common skills as citizens of a nation? He suggests that programs devoted to minority language and culture may detract from learning skills more important for later success in jobs. One approach to this dilemma emphasizes helping all children draw on the advantages of each culture. As noted earlier in this volume, cultures may vary on field dependence and independence. The research of Ramirez and Castaneda (1974) on cognitive styles demonstrated that the typical classroom, because it is structured to promote the development of field independence, may interfere with the learning of Mexican American children, who are predominantly field dependent. Ramirez and Casta-neda propose that although Mexican American children can benefit from learning to become more field independent, all children profit from developing "bicognitive functioning," that is, the ability to use both field independent and field dependent styles as appropriate. The authors provide specific guidelines for a learning environment that encourages bicognitive development, for example, by using both abstract and personalized presentations of material and by allowing children to work on both individual and group projects.

Another approach to meeting the particular needs of minority children derives from an understanding of developmental changes across childhood. Young children, with their egocentric thinking and inability to handle multiple perspectives, need unconditional acceptance and understanding of themselves and their language and customs. Adult Mexican Americans cite the humiliation they felt in school when they were scolded and punished for speaking Spanish. Young children are unable to distinguish between lack of acceptance for their culture and for themselves. As they grow older, children can begin to understand other perspectives and learn that their own culture may differ from the majority culture without being "deficient." They can develop the skills necessary for academic and professional achievement in the majority culture and can then make conscious choices about their lifestyle and orientation toward their own and other groups, rather than being limited in their options by lack of skills or information.

Yet the resolution of the pluralist dilemma is not a purely logical process of making rational choices. As ethnic minority adolescents and young adults move from high school into higher education, they may face the emotional choices of retaining close ties with family members or developing new ties to quite different values (Rodriguez, 1982). This can be particularly difficult for college students, many of whom are the first members of their family to attend college.

Promoting Positive Interactions
in Multiethnic Settings

Desegregation does not automatically result in improved interethnic relations. According to the contact hypothesis, contact between groups leads to improved relations only under specified conditions: (1) equal status within the situation, (2) opportunity to disconfirm stereotypes about the other group, (3) mutual interdependence in achieving group goals, and (4) social norms that favor group equality (Miller & Brewer, 1984). A number of programs have been developed to address each of these conditions. Perhaps the most studied are teaching methods that promote mutual interdependence. For example, Johnson and Johnson (1981) divided a fourth-grade class into ethnically mixed four-person teams that worked together to complete social studies assignments. Students in this class engaged in more cross-ethnic interactions during free time than students in a comparable class using traditional individual assignments. In a more comprehensive study with seventh and tenth graders, extending over a year (Weigel, Wiser, & Cook, 1975), four- to six-member multiethnic teams cooperated on assignments and projects; activities involved working toward common goals and required mutual interdependence among group members. Teachers reported that cross-ethnic conflict was significantly less frequent and cross-ethnic helping significantly more frequent in classes using this method, compared to traditional classes. A variation of the cooperative learning approach is the "jigsaw" method (Aronson & Bridgeman, 1979), in which each student learned part of the required material and taught it to groupmates. Students who worked together in this way showed greater liking for groupmates than for other classmates.

Social norms favoring equality, another condition of the contact hypotheses, are to a large extent a product of the attitudes and actions of teachers and school administrators. Intergroup acceptance is enhanced when school personnel explicitly express and promote egalitarian norms (Cook, 1984). An additional condition of the contact hypothesis, equal status within the situation, may be particularly difficult to achieve given the inequality in academic achievement among ethnic groups (Cohen, 1984). Cohen suggests that social power, that is, the successful exercise of interpersonal influence, is one area in which Black children may have equal status with Whites. Social power can be used to help balance academic status and prevent dominance by Whites, for example in cooperative learning teams. However, Brewer and Miller (1984) point out that even when the conditions of the contact hypothesis are met, other factors influence the outcome of cross-ethnic contact, including individual characteristics of the children and prior experiences.

In addition, cross-ethnic interactions will be influenced by the developmental level of the children. Although preschoolers notice and comment on ethnic differences and may even verbalize negative ethnic attitudes, they readily play with and choose friends from among children of other groups. At this age, bringing together children of different groups in a positive atmosphere with many opportunities for cooperative play provides a base for good intergroup relations, especially when combined with multicultural education programs. In elementary school, when peer groups naturally divide along sex lines, it may be particularly valuable to encourage cross-ethnic contact within the same-sex groupings typical of this age (Rogers, Hennigan, Bowman, & Miller, 1984). With adolescence and the increased interest in heterosexual relationships, cross-ethnic social contacts may be problematic (Schofield, 1982). Friendships are more likely to develop between same-sex peers who share interests and aptitudes; the opportunity for such contacts may be provided best through activities such as debate groups, theater and musical productions, and sports.

Training Teachers and School Personnel

Programs that deal successfully with ethnicity depend on trained teachers and school personnel. Many teachers lack an awareness of the impact of ethnicity in the classroom, are unwilling to admit the reality of racism (Milner, 1983), or even state specifically that it should be ignored (Schofield, 1981). Thus teachers may avoid mentioning a student's ethnicity in discussing him or her with a colleague. This "colorblind" stance, that assumes that color or ethnicity does not matter, does not help students or teachers deal with real differences that exist. Teachers also may be ignorant of cultural patterns that influence their interactions with children. During a recent study in an elementary school, the authors heard a teacher comment on the "sullen and devious" behavior of Mexican American children, who would not look her in the eye when being scolded; in fact, Mexican American children are taught to show respect by looking down when being addressed by an authority.

Thus teachers need training in order to understand and deal effectively with the issues surrounding ethnicity. Levy (1983) outlines competencies in three areas that should be goals of such training programs. The three areas and examples of competencies in each are as follows: (1) theory: know various views of cultural diversity, for example, cultural deprivation versus cultural differences; (2) society: know some similarities and differences between the majority and minority cultures and the potential conflicts and opportunities they create for social groups; and (3) classroom: know the potential effects of cultural and socioeconomic variables on students' school-related attitudes, values, and behavior, and demonstrate sensitivity to cultural differences among students, parents, and instructional personnel.

But even if there is awareness and understanding of ethnic differences, there remains the problem of prejudice and differential expectations toward children from various groups. Washington (1982) found that both Black and White teachers had more negative perceptions of Black children than of White children. Teachers' expectations of poorer performance from minority children often are reflected in children's poor attitudes and achievement (Gallimore et al., 1974). Teachers are likely to deny having ethnically based expectations, because the tendency to respond differently to children in terms of their ethnicity is generally unconscious, or, if conscious, is considered socially unacceptable. If schools are to be successful in working with all children, training programs need to increase teachers' awareness not only of ethnic differences but also of their own attitudes and expectations regarding ethnicity.

Implications for Counseling, Health Care, and Social Work

Identifying and Defining Problems

Ethnic differences in types and frequency of problems consistently have been found for both physical health (Harwood, 1981) and mental health (Wolkind & Rutter, 1985). The observed variations can be attributed to many factors, such as biases in assessment instruments; biases on the part of medical and psychiatric evaluators; varying access of ethnic groups to treatment; genetic predispositions; or risk factors such as poverty, poor nutrition, or exposure to pathogenic agents.

Biases can be seen in the negative ethnic stereotypes that emerge as a function of standardized psychometric assessments and clinical judgments (Snowden & Todman, 1982). To combat this problem, multicultural assessment methods have been developed to address a pluralistic orientation.

SOMPA, the System of Multicultural Pluralistic Assessment (Mercer & Lewis, 1978), is perhaps the most widely accepted and popular approach. Parents and children are interviewed as informants to evaluate social, peer, and family interactions, physical health, and acculturation; standardized measures of behavioral, perceptual, motor, visual, auditory, and cognitive functioning are also used. However, despite the intentions of the researchers, the battery has been attacked for failing to distinguish between cultural and social environments and failing to control for conceptual and functional equivalence of test items with cross-cultural and subcultural samples (Snowden & Todman, 1982).

Behavioral approaches, in particular, have been suggested as a strategy that is likely to be less biased than traditional assessment procedures (Franklin, 1982). The data are generally descriptive and less a reflection of the assessor's biases. For example, although Asian Americans are typically characterized as somewhat less assertive than Whites, Sue, Ino, and Sue (1983) demonstrated that this was only evident when self-report measures were employed. Behavioral assessments demonstrated equal assertiveness between Asian and White American adolescents. Even these techniques have been assailed, however. The evaluation of a behavior as assertive or nonassertive is in the eye of the beholder (Rich & Schroeder, 1976; Rotheram, 1984) and there are clear cultural differences in the application of this label and value assumptions on whether such a characteristic is desirable or undesirable.

Serving Children from Different Ethnic Groups

Services to children in the areas of counseling, health care, and social work generally are provided through the family and community. Children do not independently seek services, but are referred by parents and teachers. Initial contact is usually with a parent, and effective solutions involve working with the family unit; thus an understanding of the cultural context is essential.

Medical journals are beginning to recognize the importance of culture for optimal health care (for example, Clark, 1983; Hartog & Hartog, 1983). In the field of nursing, Leininger (1978, 1984) has introduced the concept of transcultural nursing, defined as study and practice focused on comparative analysis of different cultures and subcultures with respect to health and illness beliefs, values, and practices. For example, cultures vary in the way symptoms are perceived, evaluated, and acted upon; in the perception of pain; and the threshold at which illness leads an individual to seek professional help (Mechanic, 1968). Detailed information on characteristics of specific groups relative to health care is available in recent books aimed at physicians (Harwood, 1981) and nurses (Leininger, 1978).

Similarly, in the field of mental health there is increasing recognition of the impact of ethnicity. Minorities' cultural values and beliefs, differences in behaviors, language and worldview, and past power experiences with the larger society influence the success or failure of mental health consultations (Gordon & Steele, 1984). Because the definition of what is normal and what constitutes a problem varies among groups (Draguns, 1980), therapists may fail to see the problems experienced by minority groups, or may define as problems behaviors and attitudes that are considered normal by the ethnic group. Kitano (1982) shows how the differential importance of shame in Japanese-American families influences whether or not the family will seek help from mental health professionals and when. Several recent books provide information on the characteristics of a variety of ethnic groups for therapists (Atkinson, Morten, & Sue, 1983; McGoldrick, Pearce, & Girodano, 1982; Pedersen, Draguns, Lonner, & Trimble, 1981). Similarly, there is increasing recognition of the impact of ethnicity in the field of social work (Davis, 1984).

It is not clear to what extent culture conflict is a particular source of stress for minority children. Ekstrand (1977) suggests that culture conflict is a relatively infrequent cause of disturbance in children. Szapocnik and Kurtines (1980) discuss the special adjustment problems in immigrant families that may result from intergenerational gaps in acculturation. These are particularly common between a highly acculturated adolescent boy and an underacculturated parent, usually mother, who strives to maintain traditional values. In the Cuban immigrants that these authors have studied, acculturation per se is not the cause of problems; rather, the lack of bicultural involvement causes a disequilibrium that is maladjustive. "Individuals who either underacculturate (fail to learn how to interact with the Anglo-American context) or overacculturate (reject skills necessary to interact with the Hispanic-American context) do not have the flexibilty to cope with their entire cultural milieu" (p. 146). La Fromboise and Rowe (1983) have demonstrated that an assertiveness training intervention can be effective in improving bicultural competence and reducing cultural conflict in American Indian children.

Ethnic groups also vary in the quantity and quality of care that they receive. A recent report from the Department of Health and Human

Services documents the disparity between the health of minorities and Whites (Cimons, 1985). In the area of mental health, minorities are underrepresented in counseling programs, are diagnosed differently from Anglos, have higher drop-out rates, and tend to receive inferior quality services (Atkinson et al., 1983; Sue, 1977). Blacks are more likely to be offered custodial care and medication, rather than psychotherapy (Hollingshead & Redlich, 1958). Kitano (1982) suggests that the reasons for these differences include the segmentation of minorities from mainstream culture and barriers such as language differences, fear of bureaucracies, and a concern for the stigma of seeking help. Residential segregation leads people to utilize local services that are generally of poorer quality (Kain, 1975). An additional problem may be noncompliance with medical directives, which approaches 70% with some groups (Harwood, 1981).

On the other hand, DeVos (1980) points out the special strengths of some groups in handling problems. He sees the family integration and community cohesiveness that typify Japanese Americans as a deterrent to psychiatric disturbances. This view is consistent with the creation of psychologies specific to each ethnic group, for example, an African psychology (Khatib & Nobles, 1977) and La Raza for Hispanic Americans (Martinez, 1977).

Professionals who work with children also must take into consideration both developmental changes and the differing needs for services among various groups. The young minority child, as Spencer (this volume) shows, is at risk primarily due to poverty and associated health and nutritional problems. As they get older, there is increasing chance of behavior problems as children from ethnic minorities deal with a school system and society geared to majority norms. For example, Black boys with a diagnosis of conduct disorder are overrepresented in inpatient and outpatient facilities (Wolkind & Rutter, 1985). Minority adolescents may face the stress of limited opportunities for employment, as well as personal identity issues associated with their attempt to deal simultaneously with their own ethnicity and the majority culture. However, it should be noted that adjustment can vary significantly with the setting. Children and adolescents may have adjustment problems at school but function effectively with their peers and at home or vice versa. Assessments of functioning in several settings could provide a better understanding of the way cultural differences may be causing difficulties for an individual.

Training Professionals to Work
with Diverse Ethnic Groups

The first issue is to make professionals aware of ethnicity in their work with children. Gordon and Steele (1984) note that of all the literature they reviewed on mental health consultation, only 2.9% dealt with minorities, although these groups comprise more than 23% of the nation's population. Thus most of the writing ignores the special needs of minorities. In addition, there are difficulties of putting into practice the insights concerning cultural factors, even when they are understood. A generalized awareness of the characteristics of various ethnic groups does not translate easily into applications, for a number of reasons. Often cited are problems such as poor communication, lack of trust, and stereotyping between professionals and clients from different ethnic groups (Atkinson et al., 1983). According to Erickson and Shultz (1982), the relationship between a counselor and client who represent different groups is inevitably problematic. For example, Hispanics prefer and expect a relaxed, personalized style of interaction that often conflicts with the impersonality and time consciousness typical of mainstream professionals.

These problems raise the question of whether or not anyone can understand fully the experiences of members of another ethnic group. Minority group members in particular question the ability of the majority group to understand and deal sensitively with their concerns. To begin to meet the needs of all groups, it is obviously necessary to recruit and train more minority group members in the helping professions. Also valuable would be the use of multiethnic teams to work together in health care and community settings.

However, because minorities are still underrepresented in these professions, a further need is for better training of majority group members to work with ethnic minority groups. There has been far more extensive writing on cross-cultural training (typically for people who work, do business, or study in foreign countries) than on cross-ethnic training within a country. Techniques from cross-cultural psychology (Brislin, Landis, & Brandt, 1983) could profitably be applied to interethnic relations. Approaches such as the culture assimilator (Fiedler, Mitchell, & Trandis, 1971) could be adapted for use in training professionals to function more effectively in multiethnic settings with children.

Implications for Research

The problems and potential benefits of research on ethnicity are much the same as those of cross-cultural psychology. Psychology in the United States has tended to be insular and has failed to become more sensitive to the "powerful, multiform variable of culture" (Kennedy, Scheier, & Rogers, 1984). But attempts to study other cultures often are impeded by the difficulties of understanding cultural conceptions that are fundamentally different from one's own. According to Shweder and Bourne (1982), observers often have interpreted patterns of behavior in other cultures in evolutionary terms (that is, lower on the evolutionary scale than their own) or universal terms (that is, not really different, but only a variation on a universal characteristic). These authors suggest a third, relativistic, interpretation of such differences that preserves the integrity of different groups; that is, each culture must be understood in the context of its own conceptions of the world. This perspective applies equally to the study of ethnicity.

Much of the early research on ethnicity was highly ethnocentric, paying little attention to minority perspectives. Carried out primarily by majority researchers, it typically considered White middle-class children as the norm to which minority children were compared, generally unfavorably (Howard & Scott, 1981). Research with White children was generalized to children from very different backgrounds. Although awareness of ethnic perspectives is increasing, majority values and perspectives continue to dominate research, and publications devoted to minority issues have relatively little prestige. In order for ethnic groups to be understood on their own terms, there is a need for more ethnic minority researchers and more multiethnic research teams, and wider recognition of work by minority researchers. It is also essential that majority researchers increase their understanding of other ethnic groups and their awareness of the assumptions they bring to research from their own backgrounds.

Ethnicity as a Variable
in Research with Children

Because of a history of discrimination and prejudice in political, social, and economic domains, the study of ethnicity is a sensitive issue that presents special problems to the researcher. Parents and other adults responsible for children are often reluctant to give permission for studies that raise questions about ethnic identity and attitudes. Although parents and administrators can be given assurance that the research will not be harmful to the children involved, it is more difficult to control the use to which research findings are put, as shown by the bitter debate over differences in IQ among ethnic groups (Kamin, 1974). Although social scientists cannot condone censorship of research with important social implications, neither can they ignore the implications of their work. An approach that could help diffuse criticism of research involving minorities is to formulate positive questions about such groups (Scarr, 1985). For example, what are the strengths of Black families? How do minority group values differ from that of the mainstream, such as a group rather than individual orientation? In addition, it is the responsibility of social scientists to present findings carefully, emphasizing the limitation to interpretation of the results in terms of particular groups studied.

Methodological Issues

In studying ethnicity with children, the researcher must first determine a child's ethnic group membership. If one considers children as belonging to their parents' ethnic group, one should determine the ethnicity of the parents before assigning a child to a group. However, this procedure often is not followed; most researchers use either appearance or school records to determine ethnicity. But as Schofield (this volume) documents, there often is considerable discrepancy between official records and children's or parents' views of their ethnic group membership. Buriel (this volume) points out the difficulties in assigning Mexican American children to ethnic groups, because the label used reflects both attitudes and degree of assimilation. He notes that almost a quarter of a sample of eighth-grade children of Mexican descent considered themselves American rather than Mexican American. Although such children presumably know that they are of Mexican descent, their ethnic identity may not include a sense of belonging to that group. As noted above, subjective aspects of ethnic identity become more important as children get older. Researchers therefore need to consider seriously when to rely on appearance, school records, or parental report to determine ethnicity, and when to rely on subjects' self-report of their own sense of group membership. A conservative approach would be to use several measures of ethnicity and select as subjects only those for whom the measures converge.

An important methodological problem posed by research on ethnicity involves controlling for differences in socioeconomic status. Because of the correlation between ethnic minority status and SES, many studies have confounded these variables. SES differences are often greater than ethnic group differences, and many reported ethnic differences may in fact be differences between lower-class minority children and middle-class White children. An important issue for research in this area is to untangle the confounded effects of class and ethnicity.

The differences among ethnic groups in patterns of social interaction may result in a response style that complicates data collection. For example, the tendency of Mexican American children to attend more to people stimuli than to task variables and to be deferent to authority figures can mean that their responses reflect primarily a desire to please the examiner (Cedillos, Smith, & Rotheram, 1983). A variety of approaches needs to be tried to elicit responses from such children, including more open-ended, qualitative techniques administered by supportive same-ethnic examiners.

A final measurement issue is the complexity of the constructs of identity, awareness, and attitudes and the need to consider their perceptual, cognitive, affective, and behavioral components. Recent research in this area is increasingly using multiple measures to probe the multidimensionality of these constructs and to examine their inter-relationships (Van Parys & Bernal, 1985). In addition, given the possibility of biculturalism, measures should allow children to express separate identifications with more than one group, rather than use a forced-choice format that assumes that all children are monocultural.

Variables Related to Changes in Age and Context

Most discussions of research with children stress the need for more longitudinal studies; the study of ethnic socialization is no exception. Increased attention needs to be devoted both to the changing meaning of ethnic awareness, attitudes, and identity with age, and to the changes in the ways these constructs can be measured over time. These processes have been studied mainly in young children. Katz (this volume) urges extending the range of studies both downward and upward. Although attitudes and preferences toward other ethnic groups undergo important developmental shifts, there have been few attempts to design measures developmentally. There is a need to bridge the gap between the doll and picture choice methods used with young children and the distance measures used with adults. In addition, attempts to measure attitudes in middle childhood and adolescence are hampered by children's increasing awareness of socially desired attitudes. There is a need for more qualitative investigations, through interviews and projective tests, of attitudes during these years.

There has been almost no research on the way children acquire, during childhood and adolescence, the values, attitudes, and behavior patterns associated with ethnic group membership. Although young children absorb ethnic attitudes unconsciously through normal socialization processes, older children become more aware of ethnic differences and the possibility of choices. The extent to which this process is conscious, the kinds of choices children make at different ages, and the bases for these choices all remain areas in need of investigation.

Virtually all the chapters of this book stress the role of the environmental context as a factor in ethnicity, yet few studies directly address this issue. Studies of school desegregation are beginning to examine some of the contextual factors that influence intergroup attitudes, such as the structure of the classroom, power relationships among groups, and attitudes of school personnel (Miller & Brewer, 1984). Also likely to be important but less studied are the proportion of various ethnic groups in a classroom or school, the age at which children first experience desegregation, and the length of time spent in desegregated schools. Few studies include the variable of neighborhood balance, or, perhaps more important, the impact of a changing ethnic balance in a neighborhood. Cross-ethnic relations may be particularly problematic where a new ethnic group is rapidly moving into a formerly stable ethnic community (Rotheram & Phinney, 1983).

Finally, because of the impact of the changing social structure on children's ethnic socialization, research needs to consider variation among cohorts, such as those discussed by Cross (this volume) and Vaughan (this volume). Changes are accelerating as a result of increased immigration, population shifts, and improved communication, all of which are likely to foster increased group consciousness and ethnic awareness. Particularly lacking are studies of how majority group children respond to their own and others' ethnicity, as diversity increases and pluralism becomes more accepted.

Comparable to the benefits of cross-cultural psychology (Triandis & Brislin, 1984), research on ethnic socialization can expand the range of theories invoked to explain behavior, help to unconfound the complex variable of culture, and contribute to our understanding of coping. It can elucidate both the unique processes of development within particular ethnic groups and the ways in which ethnicity influences the socialization of children generally. Finally, it can lead to an understanding and acceptance of children from differing backgrounds and provide guidelines for structuring environments to promote the optimal development of all children.

References

Aboud, F. E. (1977). Interest in ethnic information: A cross-cultural developmental study. *Canadian Journal of Behavioral Science, 9*, 134-146.

Aboud, F. E. (1979). Self: An identity, a concept or a sense? In L. H. Strickland (Ed.), *Soviet and Western perspectives in social psychology*. Oxford: Pergamon.

Aboud, F. E. (1980). A test of ethnocentrism with young children. *Canadian Journal of Behavioral Science, 12*, 195-209.

Aboud, F. E. (1984). Social and cognitive bases of ethnic identity constancy. *Journal of Genetic Psychology, 145*, 227-229.

Aboud, F. E., & Christian, J. D. (1979). Development of ethnic identity. In L. Eckensberger, Y. Poortinga & W. J. Lonner (Eds.), *Cross-cultural contributions to psychology*. Lisse, Holland: Swets & Zeitlinger.

Aboud, F. E., & Mitchell, F. G. (1977). Ethnic role taking: The effects of preference and self-identification. *International Journal of Psychology, 12*, 1-17.

Aboud, F. E., & Skerry, S. A. (1983). Self and ethnic concepts in relation to ethnic constancy. *Canadian Journal of Behavioral Science, 15*, 14-26.

Aboud, F. E., & Skerry, S. A. (1984). The development of ethnic attitudes: A review. *Journal of Cross-Cultural Psychology, 15*, 3-34.

Abrahams, R. D. (1972a). Joking: The training of the man of words in talking broad. In T. Kochman (Ed.), *Rappin' and stylin' out: Communication in urban Black America*. Urbana: University of Illinois Press.

Abrahams, R. D. (1972b). The training of the man of words in talking sweet. *Language in Society, 1*, 15-29.

Abrahams, R. D. (1974). Black talking on the streets. In R. Bauman & J. Sherzer (Eds.), *Exploration in the ethnography of speaking*. London: Cambridge University Press.

Adam, B. D. (1978). Inferiorization and "self-esteem." *Social Psychology, 41*, 47-53.

Adorno, T. W., Frenkel-Brunswik, E., Levinson, D. J., & Sanford, R. N. (1950). *The authoritarian personality*. New York: Harper & Row.

Aellen, C., & Lambert, W. E. (1969). Ethnic identification and personality adjustments of Canadian adolescents of mixed English-French parentage. *Canadian Journal of Behavioural Science, 1*, 69-86.

Aiello, M., Jr., & Jones, C. (1971). Field study of the proxemic behavior of young school children in 3 subcultural groups. *Journal of Personality and Social Psychology, 19*, 351-356.

Akoodie, M. A. (1980). Immigrant students: A comparative assessment of ethnic identity, self-concept and locus of control amongst West Indian, East Indian and Canadian students. *Dissertation Abstracts International, 41*, 2565.

Alejandro-Wright, M. N. (1985). The child's conception of racial classification: A socio-cognitive model. In M. B. Spencer, G. K. Brookins, & W. R. Allen (Eds.), *Beginnings: Social and affective development of Black children*. Hillsdale, NJ: Erlbaum.

Allen, I. L. (1983). *The language of ethnic conflict: Social organization and lexical culture*. New York: Columbia University Press.

Allport, G. W. (1954). *The nature of prejudice*. Cambridge, MA: Addison-Wesley.

Amir, Y. (1976). The role of intergroup contact in change of prejudice and ethnic relations. In P. Katz (Ed.), *Towards the elimination of racism* (pp. 245-308). New York: Pergamon.

Argyle, M., Furnham, A., & Graham, J. (1981). *Social situations.* New York: Cambridge University Press.

Argyle, M., & Little, B. R. (1972). Do personality traits apply to social behavior? *Journal for the Theory of Social Behavior, 2,* 1-35.

Arkoff, J. (1967). *Psychological needs and cultural systems: A case study.* Princeton, NJ: Van Nostrand.

Arnopoulos, S. (1982). *Hors du Québec: Point de salut?* Montreal: Editions Libre Expression.

Aronson, E., & Bridgeman, D. (1979). Jigsaw groups and the desegregated classroom: In pursuit of common goals. *Personality and Social Psychology Bulletin, 5,* 438-446.

Asch, S. (1956). Studies of independence and conformity: A minority of one against the unanimous majority. *Psychological Monographs, 10,* 516.

Asher, S. R., & Allen, V. L. (1969). Racial preference and social comparison processes. *Journal of Social Issues, 25,* 157-167.

Asher, S. R., Singleton, L. C., & Taylor, A. R. (1982). *Acceptance versus friendship: A longitudinal study of racial integration.* Paper presented at the annual meeting of the American Educational Research Association, New York.

Atkinson, D., Morten, G., & Sue, S. (1983). *Counseling American minorities: A cross-cultural approach.* Dubuque, IA: W. C. Brown.

Baldwin, J. (1979). Theory and research concerning the notion of black self-hatred: A review and reintepretation. *Journal of Black Psychology, 5,* 51-78.

Ballard, B. (1976). Development of racial awareness: Task consistency, reliability and validity. *Journal of Genetic Psychology, 129,* 3-11.

Ballard, R. (1976). Ethnicity: Theory and experience. *New Community, 5,* 196-202.

Baltes, P. B., & Willis, S. C. (1979). Life-span developmental psychology, cognitive functioning, and social policy. In M. R. Riley (Ed.), *Aging from birth to death* (pp. 15-25). Washington, DC: Westview.

Bandura, A. (1969). *Principles of behavior modification.* New York: Holt, Rinehart & Winston.

Bandura, A., & Walters, R. H. (1959). *Adolescent aggression.* New York: Ronald Press.

Banks, J. (1981). *Multiethnic education: Theory and practice.* Boston: Allyn & Bacon.

Banks, W. (1972). The differential effects of race and social class in helping. *Journal of Clinical Psychology, 28,* 90-92.

Banks, W. C. (1976). White preference in Blacks: A paradigm in search of a phenomenon. *Psychological Bulletin, 83,* 1179-1186.

Barker, R. C. (1968). *Ecological psychology.* Palo Alto, CA: Stanford University Press.

Barnes, E. J. (1980). The Black community as the source of positive self-concept for black children: A theoretical perspective. In R. L. Jones (Ed.), *Black Psychology.* New York: Harper & Row.

Barnlund, D. C. (1975). *Public and private self in Japan and the U.S.* Tokyo: Simul.

Barnlund, D. C. (1975). Communicative styles in two cultures: Japan and the U.S. In T. Williams (Ed.), *Socialization and communication in primary groups* (pp. 399-428). The Hague: Mouton.

Baron, H. M. (1971). The demand for Black labor. *Radical American, 5,* 1-46.

Barrera, M. (1980). *Race and class inequality in the Southwest.* West Lafayette, IN: University of Notre Dame Press.

Barry, H., Bacon, M., & Child, I. L. (1975). A cross cultural survey on some sex differences in socialization. *Journal of Abnormal and Social Psychology, 55,* 327-332.

Barth, F. (1966). *Models of social organization.* Occasional Paper No. 23. London: Royal Anthropological Institute.

Barth, F. (1969). *Ethnic groups and boundaries.* Boston: Little, Brown.

Batchold, L. (1982). Children's social interactions and parental attitudes among Hupa Indians and Anglo-Americans. *Journal of Social Psychology, 116,* 9-17.

Batchold, L. (1984). Antecedents of caregiver attitudes and social behavior of Hupa Indian and Anglo-American preschoolers in California. *Child Study Journal, 13,* 217-233.

Bauman, R. (1972). An ethnographic framework for the investigation of communicative behavior. In R. D. Abraham and C. Troike (Eds.), *Language and cultural diversity in American education.* Englewood Cliffs, NJ: Prentice-Hall.

Bauman, R., & Sherzer, J. (Eds.). (1974). *Explorations in the ethnography of speaking.* Cambridge: Cambridge University Press.

Baxter, J. (1970). Interpersonal spacing in natural settings. *Sociometry, 33,* 444-456.

Beg, V. (1966). Value orientations of Indian and American students: A cross-cultural study. *Psychologia, 9,* 111-119.

Benedict, R. (1934). *Patterns of culture.* Boston: Houghton Mifflin.

Berle, B. (1980). *Eighty Puerto Rican families in New York City.* New York: Columbia University Press.

Berlyne, D. E. (1960). *Conflict, arousal and curiosity.* New York: McGraw-Hill.

Berrien, F. K. (1966). Japanese and American values. *International Journal of Psychology, 1,* 129-141.

Berry, J. W. (1967). Independence and conformity in subsistence level societies. *Journal of Personality and Social Psychology, 7,* 415-418.

Berry, J. W. (1979). Social and cultural change. In H. L. Triandis & R. Brislin (Eds.), *Handbook of cross-cultural psychology* (Vol. 5). Boston, MA: Allyn & Bacon.

Berrry, J. W. (1980). Acculturation as varieties of adaption. In A. M. Padilla (Ed.), *Acculturation: Theory, models, and some new findings.* Boulder, CO: Westview.

Berry, J. W., & Annis, R. C. (1974). Acculturative stress. *Journal of Cross-Cultural Psychology, 5,* 382-406.

Berry, J. W., & Blondel, T. (1982). Psychological adaptation of Vietnamese refugees in Canada. *Canadian Journal of Community Mental Health, 1.*

Bhatnager, J. K. (1980). Linguistic behavior and adjustment of immigrant children in French and English schools in Montreal. *International Review of Applied Psychology, 29,* 141-157.

Biaggio, A. (1969). Internalized versus externalized guilt: A cross-cultural study. *Journal of Social Psychology, 78,* 147-149.

Black Coalition (1984). *The people's platform.* Washington, DC: National Black Leadership Roundtable.

Block, J. H. (1973). Conceptions of sex role: Some cross-cultural and longitudinal perspectives. *American Psychologist, 28,* 512-526.

Bochner, S. (Ed.). (1982). *Cultures in contact: Studies in cross-cultural interaction.* London: Pergamon.

Bogatz, G. A., & Ball, S. (1971, November). *The second year of Sesame Street: A continuing evaluation.* Princeton, NJ: Educational Testing Service.

Bogdan, R., & Ksander, M. (1980). Policy data as a social process: A qualitative approach to quantitative data. *Human Organization, 39,* 302-309.

Bogdan, R., & Biklen, S. K. (1982). *Qualitative research for education: An introduction to theory and methods.* Boston, MA: Allyn & Bacon.

Bogdan, R., & Taylor, J. (1975). *Introduction to qualitative research methods: A phenomenological approach to social science.* New York: John Wiley.

Bolton, F. G., Jr. (1980). *The pregnant adolescent: Problems of premature parenthood.* Beverly Hills, CA: Sage.

Bond, H. M. (1928). Self respect as a factor in racial advancement. *Annals of American Academy of Political and Social Science, CXXX,* 21-25.

Bond, M. (1983). How language variation affects inter-cultural differentiation of values by Hong Kong bilinguals. *Journal of Language and Social Psychology, 2,* 57-66.

Bond, M., & Tornatzky, L. (1973). Locus of control in students from Japan and the United States: Dimensions and levels of response. *Psychologia, 16,* 209-213.

Boney, J. (1971). An analysis of the participation of racially integrated guidance groups. *Journal of Negro Education, 40,* 390-393.

Bossert, S. T. (1979). *Tasks and social relationships in classrooms: A study of instructional organization and its consequences.* Cambridge, MA: Cambridge University Press, ASA Arnold and Caroline Rose Monograph Series.

Bottomley, G. (1975). Some Greek sex roles: Ideals, expectations and action in Greece and Australia. *Australian and New Zealand Journal of Sociology, 10,* 8-16.

Bottomley, G. (1976). Ethnicity and identity among Greek Australians. *Australian and New Zealand Journal of Sociology, 12,* 118-125.

Bottomley, G. (1979). *After the Odyssey. A study of Greek Australians.* St. Lucia, Queensland: University of Queensland Press.

Bourhis, R., Giles, H., & Rosenthal, D. A. (1981). Notes on the construction of a "subjective vitality questionnaire" for the development of ethnolinguistic groups. *Journal of Multilingual and Multicultural Development, 2,* 145-155.

Bourne, E. (1978a). The state of research on ego identity: A review and appraisal (Part I). *Journal of Youth and Adolescence, 7,* 223-251.

Bourne, E. (1978b). The state of research on ego identity: A review and appraisal (Part II). *Journal of Youth and Adolescence, 7,* 371-392.

Bradley, D. (1982, May). Black and American, 1982. *Esquire,* pp. 58-71.

Bradley, R. H., Caldwell, B. M., & Elardo, R. (1977). Home environment, social status and mental test performance. *Journal of Educational Psychology, 69,* 697-701.

Branch, C., & Newcombe, N. (1980). Racial attitudes of black preschoolers as related to parental civil rights activism. *Merrill-Palmer Quarterly, 26,* 425-428.

Brand, E. S., Ruiz R. A., & Padilla, A. M. (1974). Ethnic identification and preference: A review. *Psychological Bulletin, 81,* 860-890.

Breton, R. (1964). Institutional completeness of ethnic communities and the personal relations of immigrants. *American Journal of Sociology, 70,* 193-205.

Brewer, M. (1979). Ingroup bias in the minimal intergroup situation: A cognitive-motivational analysis. *Psychological Bulletin, 86,* 307-324.

Brewer, M., & Miller, N. (1984). Beyond the contact hypothesis: Theoretical perspectives on desegregation. In N. Miller and M. Brewer (Eds.), *Groups in contact: The psychology of desegregation.* New York: Academy Press.

Briggs, J. (1971). Strategies of perception: The management of ethnic identity. In R. Paine (Ed.), *Patrons and brokers in the East Arctic* (pp. 55-73). Toronto: University of Toronto Press.

Brim, O., & Kagan, J. (Eds.). (1980). *Constancy and change in human development.* Cambridge, MA: Harvard University Press.

Brislin, R., Landis, D., & Brandt, M. (1983). Conceptualization of intercultural behavior and training. In D. Landis & R. Brislin (Eds.), *Handbook of intercultural training, Vol I.* (pp. 1-35). New York: Pergamon.

Bronfenbrenner, U. (1979). *The ecology of human development.* Cambridge, MA: Harvard University Press.

Broughton, J. (1980). The divided self in adolescence. *Human Development, 24,* 13-32.

Brown, C. (1972). The language of soul. In T. Kochman (Ed.), *Rappin' and stylin' out: Communication in urban Black America.* Urbana: University of Illinois Press.

Brown, P., & Levinson, S. (1978). Universals in language usage: Politeness phenomena. In E. Good (Ed.), *Questions and politeness.* Boston: Cambridge University Press.

Brown, W. A. (1931). The nature of race consciousness. *Social Forces, 10,* 90.

Bruner, J. S., Goodnow, J., & Austin, G. A. (1956). *A study of thinking.* New York: John Wiley.

Bullivant, B. (1981). *The pluralist dilemma in education.* London: George Allen & Unwin.

Burger, H. (1973). Cultural pluralism and the schools. In C. Brembeck & W. Hill (Eds.), *Cultural challenges to education.* Lexington, MA: D. C. Heath.

Buriel, R. (1975). Cognitive styles among three generations of Mexican-American children. *Journal of Cross-Cultural Psychology, 6,* 417-429.

Buriel, R. (1982). *Acculturation and biculturalism among three generations of Mexican-American and Anglo-American school children.* (ERIC Document Reproduction Service, No. ED 207741)

Buriel, R. (1983). Teacher-student interactions and their relationship to student achievement: A comparison of Mexican-American and Anglo-American children. *Journal of Educational Psychology, 75,* 889-897.

Buriel, R. (1984). Integration with traditional Mexican American culture and sociocultural adjustment. In J. J. Martinez, Jr., & R. H. Mendoza (Eds.), *Chicano psychology* (2nd ed.). New York: Academic Press.

Buriel, R., Calzada, S., & Vasquez, R. (1982). The relationship of traditional Mexican American culture to adjustment and delinquency among three generations of Mexican-American adolescents. *Hispanic Journal of Behavioral Science, 4,* 41-55.

Buriel, R., & Vasquez, R. (1982). Stereotypes of Mexican descent persons: Attitudes of three generations of Mexican Americans and Anglo-American adolescents. *Journal of Cross-Cultural Psychology, 13,* 59-70.

Buriel, R., & Vasquez, R. (1983). *Affiliation preference of three generations of Mexican Americans and Euro-American adolescents.* Unpublished manuscript, Pomona College, Psychology Department, Claremont, CA.

Burns, R. B. (1979). *The self concept: Theory, measurement, development and behaviour.* New York: Longman.

Bulter, R. (1976). Black children's racial preferences: A selected review of the literature. *Journal of Afro-American Issues, 4,* 168-171.

Callan, V. J., & Gallois, C. (1982). Language attitudes of Italo-Australian and Greek-Australian bilinguals. *International Journal of Psychology, 17,* 345-358.

Callan, V. J., & Gallois, C. (1983). Ethnic stereotypes: Australian and southern European youth. *Journal of Social Psychology, 119,* 287-288.

Callan, V. J., & Gallois, C. (in press). Sex-role attitudes and attitudes to marriage among urban Greek-Australian and Anglo-Australian youth. *Journal of Comparative Family Studies.*

Campbell, B. (1981). Race of interviewer effects among southern adolescents. *Public Opinion Quarterly, 45,* 231-244.

Campbell, D. T. (1967). Stereotypes and the perceptions of group differences. *American Psychologist, 22,* 817-829.

Campbell, D. T. (1979). Degrees of freedom and the case study. In T. D. Cook & C. S. Reichardt (Eds.), *Qualitative and quantitative methods in evaluation research.* Beverly Hills, CA: Sage.

Campbell, D. T., & Stanley, J. (1966). *Experimental and quasi-experimental designs for research.* Chicago: Rand McNally.

Cantor, G. N. (1972). Use of a conflict paradigm to study race awareness in children. *Child Development, 43,* 1437-1442.

Caplan, N. (1970). The new ghetto man: A review of recent empirical studies. *Journal of Social Issues, 26,* 59-73.

Carlos, M. L., & Padilla, A. M. (1974). *Measuring ethnicity among Mexican-Americans: A preliminary report on the self-identity of a Latino group in the U.S.* Bogota, Colombia: Inter-American Congress of Psychology.

Carter, A. (1974). *An analysis of the use of contemporary Black literature and music and its effects upon self-concept in group counseling procedures.* Unpublished doctoral dissertation, Purdue University, IN.

Castonguay, C. (1977). Les transferts linguistiques au foyer. *Recherches Sociographiques, 18,* 431-450.

Cazden, C. (1986). Classroom discourse. In M. Wittrock (Ed.), *Handbook of research on teaching.* New York: Macmillan.

Cedillos, A., Smith, C., & Rotheram, M. (1983, August). *Assessing social relationships of Black, Hispanic, and White children.* Paper presented at the American Psychological Association Annual Convention, Anaheim, California.

Chapman, J. W., & Nicholls, J. G. (1976). Occupational identity status, occupational preference, and field dependence in Maori and Pakeha boys. *Journal of Cross-Cultural Psychology, 7,* 61-72.

Cheek, D. (1976). *Assertive Black . . . puzzled White.* San Luis Obispo, CA: Impact.

Child, I. L. (1943). *Italian or American? The second generation in conflict.* New Haven, CT: Yale University Press.

Children's Defense Fund (1984). *Children having children*. Washington, DC.

Choquette, R. (1975). *Language and religion: A history of English-French conflict in Ontario*. Ottawa: University of Ottawa Press.

Christian, J., Gadfield, N. J., Giles, H., & Taylor, D. M. (1976). The multidimensional and dynamic nature of ethnic identity. *International Journal of Psychology, 11*, 281-291.

Churchill, S. (1976). National linguistic minorities: The Franco-Ontarian educational renaissance. *Prospects, 5*, 439-449.

Ciaccio, N. (1978). Erikson's theory in cross-cultural perspective: Social class and ethnicity in Third World communities. In K. Riegel & M. Meacham (Eds.), *The developing individual in a changing world* (Vol. 1). The Hague: Mouton.

Cichello, A. (1984). *The meeting of two cultures: Ethnic identification and psychosocial development in Italian-Australian adolescents*. Unpublished bachelor of arts (honors) thesis, University of Melbourne.

Cicourel, A. (1973). *Cognitive sociology*. London: Penguin.

Cicourel, A. (1975). Discourse and text: Cognitive and linguistic processes in studies of social structure. *Versus, 12*, 33-84.

Cicourel, A. (1978). Language and society: Cognitive, cultural and linguistic aspects of language use. *Sozialwissenschaftliche Annalen*, Band 2, B25-58, Wien.

Cicourel, A. (1980). Three models of discourse analysis: The role of social structure. *Discourse Processes, 3*, 101-132.

Cimons, M. (1985, October 17). Minorities suffer from health gap. *Los Angeles Times*, Part I, p. 5.

Clark, A., Hocevar, D., & Dembo, M. H. (1980). The role of cognitive development in children's explanations and preferences for skin color. *Developmental Psychology, 16*, 332-339.

Clark, C. (1971). General systems theory and Black studies: Some points of convergence. In C. Thomas (Ed.), *Boys, no more* (pp. 28-47). Encino, CA: Glencoe.

Clark, K. B., & Clark, M. P. (1939a). The development of consciousness of self and the emergence of racial identification in Negro preschool children. *Journal of Social Psychology, 10*, 591-599.

Clark, K. B., & Clark, M. P. (1939b). Segregation as a factor in the racial identification of Negro preschool children. *Journal of Experimental Education, 8*, 161-163.

Clark, K. B., & Clark, M. P. (1940). Skin color as a factor in racial identification and preference in Negro children. *Journal of Negro Education, 19*, 341-358.

Clark, K. B., & Clark, M. P. (1947). Racial identification and preference in Negro children. In T. M. Newcomb & E. L. Hartley (Eds.), *Reading in social psychology* (pp. 169-178). New York: Holt, Rinehart & Winston.

Clark, K. B., & Clark, M. P. (1950). Emotional factors in racial identification and preference in Negro children. *Journal of Negro Education, 19*, 341-350.

Clark, M. (1983). Cultural context of medical practice. *Western Journal of Medicine, 139*, 806-810.

Clausen, J. (1968). *Socialization and society*. Boston, MA: Little, Brown.

Clift, D., & Arnopoulos S. (1979). *Le fait anglais au Quebec*. Montreal: Editions Libre Expression.

Cohen, E. (1984). The desegregated school: Problems in status power and interethnic climate. In N. Miller & M. Brewer (Eds.), *Groups in contact: The psychology of desegregation*. New York: Academic Press.

Coleman, J. S. (1974). *Youth: Transition to adulthood*. Chicago: University of Chicago Press.

Collins, J. (1982). Discourse style, classroom interaction and differential treatment. *Journal of Reading Behavior, 14*, 429-437.

Connell, W. F., Stroobant, R. E., Sinclair, K. E., Connell, R. W., & Rogers, K. W. (1975). *12 to 20: Studies of city youth*. Sydney: Hicks, Smith.

Cook, S. (1978). Interpersonal and attitudinal outcome in cooperating racial groups. *Journal of Research and Development in Education, 12*, 97-113.

Cook, S. (1984). Cooperative interaction in multiethnic contexts. In N. Miller & M. Brewer (Eds.), *Groups in contact: The psychology of desegregation*. New York: Academic Press.

Cook, S. (1985). Experimenting on social issues: The case of school desegregation. *American Psychologist, 40*, 452-460.

Cook, T. D., & Cook, F. L. (1977). Comprehensive evaluation research and its dependence on both humanistic and empiricist perspectives. In R. S. French (Ed.), *Humanistic and policy studies: Relevance revisited. Curriculum development in the humanities* (No. 3). Washington, DC: George Washington University, Division of Experimental Programs.

Cook, T. D., & Reichardt, C. S. (1979). *Qualitative and quantitative methods in evaluation research.* Beverly Hills, CA: Sage.

Corenblum, B., & Wilson, A. E. (1982). Ethnic preference and identification among Canadian Indian and White children: Replication and extension. *Canadian Journal of Behavioural Science, 14,* 50-59.

Craft, M. (Ed.). (1984). *Education and cultural pluralism.* London: Falmer Press.

Crawford, T., & Naditch, M. (1970). Relative deprivation, powerlessness and militancy: The psychology of social protest. *Psychiatry, 33,* 208-223.

Crooks, R. C. (1970). The effects of an interracial preschool program upon racial preference, knowledge of racial differences, and racial identification. *Journal of Social Issues, 26,* 137-144.

Cross, W. (1971). The Negro to Black conversion experience. *Black World, 20,* 13-27.

Cross, W. (1978). The Thomas and Cross models of psychological nigrescence: A review. *Journal of Black Psychology, 5,* 13-31.

Cross, W. (1980). Models of psychological nigrescence: A literature review. In R. L. Jones (Ed.), *Black psychology* (pp. 81-98). New York: Harper & Row.

Cross, W., (1981). Black families and black identity development. *Journal of Comparative Family Studies, 12,* 19-50.

Cross, W. (1983). The ecology of human development for Black and White children: Implications for predicting racial preference patterns. *Critical Perspectives of Third World America, 1,* 177-189.

Cross, W. (1985). Black identity: Rediscovering the distinction between personal identity and reference group orientation. In M. Spencer, G. K. Brookins, & W. R. Allen (Eds.), *Beginnings: Social and affective development of Black children.* Hillsdale, NJ: Erlbaum.

Dalby, D. (1972). The African element in American English. In T. Kochman (Ed.), *Rappin and stylin out: Communication in urban Black America.* Urbana: University of Illinois Press.

Damico, S. B., Bell-Nathaniel, A., & Green, C. (1981). Effects of school organizational structure on interracial friendships in middle schools. *Journal of Educational Research, 74,* 388-395.

Damon, W. (1983). *Social and personality development.* New York: Norton.

Damon, W., & Hart, D. (1982). The development of self-understanding from infancy through adolescence. *Child Development, 53,* 841-864.

Dasen, P. R. (1972). Cross-cultural Piagetian research: A summary. *Journal of Cross-Cultural Psychology, 3,* 23-39.

Dave, R. H. (1964). *The identification and measurement of environmental process variables that are related to educational achievement.* Unpublished doctoral dissertation, University of Chicago.

Davey, A. G., & Mullin, P. N. (1980). Ethnic identification and preference of British primary school children. *Journal of Child Psychology & Psychiatry, 21,* 241-251.

Davidson, F. H. (1976). Ability to respect persons compared to ethnic prejudice in childhood. *Journal of Personality & Social Psychology, 34,* 1256-1267.

Davis, L. (1984). *Ethnicity in social group work practice.* New York: Haworth.

DeFleur, L. B. (1975). Biasing influences on drug arrest records: Implications for deviance research. *American Sociological Review, 40,* 88-103.

De la Serna, M. (1982). Competitive behaviors among urban Mexican-Americans and Anglo-American children. *Revista Interamericana de Psicologia, 16,* 70-76.

Derbyshires, R. L. (1968). Adolescent identity crisis in urban Mexican-Americans in East Los Angeles. In E. B. Brody (Ed.), *Minority group adolescents in the United States.* Baltimore: Williams & Wilkins.

Despres, L. (Ed.). (1975). *Ethnicity and resource competition in plural societies.* The Hague: Mouton.

Detweiller, R. (1979). Over the ages an age-old problem: A categorization perspecitve on children's and adults' intercultural difficulties. *International Journal of Group Tensions, 9,* 134-148.

DeVos, G. A. (1980). Ethnic adaptation and minority status. *Journal of Cross-Cultural Psychology, 11,* 101-124.

DeVos, G., & Romanucci-Ross, L. (Eds.). (1982). *Ethnic identity: Cultural continuities and change.* Chicago: University of Chicago Press.

Diaz-Guerrero, R. (1955). Neurosis and the Mexican-American family structure. *American Journal of Psychiatry, 112,* 411-417.

Diaz-Guerrero, R. (1963). Sociocultural premises, attitudes and cross-cultural research. *Anuario de Psicologia II* (pp. 31-46). Mexico: Facultad de Filosofia y Letras, U.N.A.M.

Diaz-Guerrero, R. (1967). The active and the passive syndrome. *Revista Interamericana de Psicologia, 1,* 263-272.

Diaz-Guerrero, R. (1972a). Una escala factorial de premisas historico-socioculturales de la familia Mexicana. *Revista Interamericana de Psicologia, 6,* 235-244.

Diaz-Guerrero, R. (1972b). *Hacia una teoria historico-bio-psico-socio-cultural de comportamiento humano.* Mexico: Trillas.

Diaz-Guerrero, R. (1973). Interpreting coping styles across nations from sex and social class differences. *International Journal of Psychology, 8,* 191-203.

Diaz-Guerrero, R. (1975). *Psychology of the Mexican.* Austin: University of Texas Press.

Diaz-Guerrero, R. (1976). *Hacia una psicologia social del tercer mundo* (Cuadernos de Humanidades No. 5). Mexico: Universidad Nacional Autonoma de Mexico, Departmento de Humanidades, Difusion Cultural.

Diaz-Guerrero, R. (1977a). A Mexican psychology. *American Psychologist, 32,* 934-944.

Diaz-Guerrero, R. (1977b). Culture and personality revisited. *Annals of the New York Academy of Sciences, 285,* 119-130.

Diaz-Guerrero, R. (1979). Origines de la personnalité humaine et des systemes sociaux. *Revue of Psychologie Appliquée, 29,* 139-152.

Diaz-Guerrero, R. (1982a). The psychology of the historic-sociocultural premise, I. *Spanish Language Psychology, 2,* 383-410.

Diaz-Guerrero, R. (1982b). El Yo del Mexicano y la piramide. In R. Diaz-Guerrero (Ed.), *Psicologia de Mexicano,* Mexico: Trillas.

Diaz-Guerrero, R. (1982c). *Psicologia del Mexicano.* Mexico: Trillas.

Diaz-Guerrero, R. (in press). *El ecosistema sociocultural y la calidad de la vida.* Mexico: Trillas.

Diaz-Guerrero, R., & Castillo Vales, V. M. (1981). El enfoque cultura-contracultura y el desarrollo cognitivo y de la personalidad en escolares yucatecos. *Ensenanza e Investigacion en Psicologia, 7,* 5-26.

Diaz-Guerrero, R., & Emmite, P. L. (in press). *Innovaciones en educacion. Un analisis de sistemas de las habilidades basicas en la educacion.* Mexico: Imprenta Universitaria, U.N.A.M.

Diaz-Guerrero, R., & Salas, M. (1975). *El diferencial semantico del idioma Español.* Mexico: Trillas.

Diss, R. (1979). An ethnographic study of interactional factors affecting access of Black kindergarten children to participation structures and reading information. *Dissertation Abstracts International, 41,* 1742-1743.

Doczy, A. G. (1966). *The social assimilation of adolescent boys of European parentage in the metropolitan area of Western Australia.* Unpublished doctoral dissertation, University of West Australia.

Doczy, A. G. (1968). Life problems of young adolescent immigrant boys in Australia. *International Migration, 6,* 12-19.

Doi, T. (1973). *Anatomy of dependence.* New York: Harper & Row.

Doise, W. (1976). *Groups and individuals: Explanations in social psychology.* London: Cambridge University Press.

Dore, R. (1958). *City life in Japan.* Berkeley: University of California Press.

Douvan, E., & Adelson, J. (1966). *The adolescent experience.* New York: John Wiley.

Draguns, J. (1980). Psychological disorders of clinical severity. In H. Triandis & J. Draguns (Eds.), *Handbook of cross-cultural psychology* (Vol. 6). Boston, MA: Allyn & Bacon.

Driedger, L. (1975). In search of cultural identity factors: A comparison of ethnic students. *Canadian Review of Sociology and Anthroplogy, 12,* 150-162.

Driedger, L. (1976). Ethnic self-identity: A comparison of ingroup evaluations. *Sociometry, 39,* 131-141.

DuBois, W.E.B. (1971). *An ABC of color*. New York: International Publishing.

Eisenberg, A. (1984, March). *The role of question routines in the linguistic socialization of Mexican American children*. Paper presented at the meeting of the Southwestern Society for Research in Human Development, Denver.

Eiser, J. R., & Stroebe, W. (1972). *Categorization and social judgement*. London: Academic Press.

Eisner, E. W. (1977). Critique. *Anthropology and Education Quarterly, 8*, 71-72.

Ekstrand, L. (1977, January). Migrant adaptation: A cross-cultural problem. *Educational and Psychological Interactions, 59* (whole issue).

Elder, G. H., Jr. (1974). *Children of the Great Depression*. Chicago: University of Chicago Press.

Elkind, D. (1974). *Children and adolescents: Interpretive essays on Jean Piaget* (2nd ed.). New York: Oxford University Press.

Elkind, D., & Bowen, R. (1979). Imaginary audience behavior in children and adolescents. *Developmental Psychology, 15*, 38-44.

Emmite, P. L., & Diaz-Guerrero, R. (1983). Cross-cultural differences and similarities in coping style, anxiety and success-failure on examinations. In C. D. Spielberger & R. Diaz-Guerrero (Eds.), *Cross-Cultural Anxiety, Vol. 2*. Washington DC: Hemisphere Publishing.

Empey, D., Phinney, J., & Rotheram, M. J. (1984, March). *Ethnic differences in children's social expectations*. Paper presented at the meeting of the Southwestern Society for Research in Human Development, Denver.

Eppink, A. (1979). Socio-psychological problems of migrant children and cultural conflicts. *International Migration, 17*, 87-117.

Epstein, Y.M., Krupat, E., & Obudho, C. (1976). Clean is beautiful: Identification and preference as a function of race and cleanliness. *Journal of Social Issues, 32*, 109-118.

Erickson, F. (1973). What makes school ethnography "ethnographic"? *Anthropology and Education Quarterly, 4*(2), 10-19.

Erickson, F. (1976). Gate-keeping encounters: a social selection process. In P. Sanday (Ed.), *Anthropology and the public interest* (pp. 11-145). New York: Academic Press.

Erickson, F. (1977). Some approaches to inquiry in school-community ethnography. *Anthropology and Education Quarterly, 8*(2), 58-69.

Erickson, F. (1979). *Mere ethnography: Some problems in its use in education practice*. East Lansing, MI: Institute for Research on Teaching.

Erickson, F., & Mohatt, G. (1982). Cultural organization of participation structures in two classrooms of Indian students. In G. Spindler (Ed.), *Doing the ethnography of schooling: Educational anthropology in action*. New York: Holt, Rinehart & Winston.

Erickson, F., & Shultz, J. (1982). *The counsellor as gatekeeper: Social interaction in interviews*. New York: Academic Press.

Erikson, E. H. (1959). *Identity and the life cycle: Selected papers*. (Psychological Issues Monograph Series, I, no. 1). New York: International Universities Press.

Erikson, E. H. (1963). *Childhood and society*. New York: Norton.

Erikson, E. H. (1968). *Identity: Youth and crisis*. New York: Norton.

Fairchild, H. H., & Cozens, J. A. (1981). Chicano, Hispanic, or Mexican American? What's in a name. *Hispanic Journal of Behavioral Sciences, 3*, 191-198.

Festinger, L. (1954). A theory of social comparison processes. *Human Relations, 7*, 117-140.

Fetterman, D. M. (1982). Ethnography in educational research: The dynamics of diffusion. *Educational Researcher, 11*, 17-22.

Fiedler, F., Mitchell, T., & Triandis, H. (1971). The culture assimilator: An approach to cross-cultural training. *Journal of Applied Psychology, 55*, 95-102.

Filstead, W. J. (1979). Qualitative methods: A needed perspective in evaluation research. In T. D. Cook & C. S. Reichardt (Eds.), *Qualitative and quantitative methods in evaluation research*. Beverly Hills, CA: Sage.

Finkelstein, N. W., & Haskins, R. (1983). Kindergarten children prefer same-color peers. *Child Development, 54*, 502-508.

Fisher, L. (1976). Dropping remarks and the Barbadian audience. *American Ethnologist, 3*, 227-242.

Fitzgerald, T. K. (1971). Education and identity: A reconsideration of some models of acculturation and identity. *New Zealand Council of Educational Studies*, 45-57.

Flavell, J. H. (1977). *Cognitive development*. Englewood Cliffs, NJ: Prentice-Hall.

Forgas, J. (1979). *Social episodes*. New York: Academic Press.

Fox, D. J., & Jordan, V. D. (1973). Racial preference and identification of Black, American Chinese, and White children. *Genetic Psychology Monographs, 88*, 229-286.

Frake, C. (1969). The ethnographic study of cognitive systems. In S. A. Tyler (Ed.), *Cognitive anthropology*. New York: Holt, Rinehart & Winston.

Frake, C. (1964). A structural description of Subanum "religious" behavior. In W. Goodenough (Ed.), *Explorations in cultural anthropology*. New York: McGraw-Hill.

Franklin, A. (1982). Therapeutic interventions with urban Black adolescents. In E. Jones & S. Korchin (Eds.), *Minority mental health*. New York: Praeger.

Frazier, E. F. (1941). *Negro youth at the crossroads*. Washington, DC: American Council on Education.

Freedle, R. (1977). Introduction. In R. O. Freedle (Ed.), *Discourse production and comprehension*. Norwood, NJ: Ablex.

Freud, A. (1958). Adolescence. In *Psychoanalytic study of the child, Vol. 13*. New York: International Universities Press.

Freud, S. (1918). *Totem and taboo*. New York: New Republic.

Friedman, P. (1980). Racial preferences and identifications of white elementary school children. *Contemporary Educational Psychology, 65*, 256-265.

Fromm, E., & Maccoby, M. (1970). *Social character in a Mexican village*. Englewood Cliffs, NJ: Prentice-Hall.

Fu, V., Hinkle, D., & Korslund, M. (1983). A developmental study of ethnic self concept among adolescent girls. *Journal of Genetic Psychology, 142*, 67-73.

Gal, S. (1984, March). *Discourse style and language attrition: The interaction of usage and structure*. Paper presented at the Fifth Annual Ethnography and Education Forum, University of Pennsylvania.

Gallimore, R., Boggs, J., & Jordan, C. (1974). *Culture, behavior and education*. Beverly Hills, CA: Sage.

Gans, H. J. (1962). *The urban villagers: Group and class in the life of Italian Americans*. New York: Free Press.

Garbarino, J. (1982). *Children and families in the social environment*. New York: Aldine.

Garcia, H.D.C. (1980). *Chicano social class, assimilation, and nationalism*. Unpublished doctoral dissertation, Yale University.

Garcia, J. (1981). Yo soy Mexicano. . . : Self-identity and sociodemographic correlates. *Social Science Quarterly, 62*, 88-98.

Garcia, J. (1982). Ethnicity and Chicanos: Measurement of ethnic identification, identity and consciousness. *Hispanic Journal of Behavioral Sciences, 4*, 299-314.

Gardner, R. C. (1973). Attitudes and motivation: Their role in second language acquisition. In J. Oller & J. Richards (Eds.), *Focus on the learner* (pp. 235-245). Rowley, MA: Newbury House.

Gecas, V. (1973). Self-conceptions of migrant and settled Mexican-Americans. *Social Science Quarterly, 54*, 579-595.

Geertz, C. (1973). *The interpretation of cultures*. New York: Basic Books.

Genesee, F. (1978). Second language learning and language attitudes. *Working Papers on Bilingualism, 16*, 19-41.

Genesee, F., Tucker, G. R., & Lambert, W. E. (1978). The development of ethnic identity and ethnic role-taking skills in children from different school settings. *International Journal of Psychology, 13*, 39-57.

Genishi, C. (1981). Codeswitching in Chicano six-year-olds. In R. Duran (Ed.), *Latino language and communicative behavior* (pp. 133-152). Norwood, NJ: Ablex.

George, D. M., & Hoppe, R. A. (1979). Racial identification, preference, and self concept. *Journal of Cross-Cultural Psychology, 10*, 85-100.

Gerard, H., & Miller, N. (1975). *School desegregation*. New York: Plenum.

Gerlach, L., & Hine, V. (1970). *People, power, and change: Movements of social transformation*. Indianapolis: Bobbs-Merrill.

Giannopolous, G. (1978). Beyond the generation gap: A Greek perspective. *Australian Journal of Early Childhood, 3*, 37-40.

Gibbs, J. (1973). Black students/white university: Different expectations. *Personnel and Guidance Journal, 51*, 463-469.

Gibbs, J. (1980). The interpersonal orientation in mental health consultation: Toward a model of ethnic variations in consultation. *Journal of Community Psychology, 8*, 195-207.

Giggs, J. A. (1977). The mental health of immigrants in Australia. In M. Bowen (Ed.), *Australia 2000: The ethnic impact*, Armidale, N.S.W.: University of New England Publishing Unit.

Giles, H. (1977). *Language, ethnicity and intergroup relations*. London: Academic Press.

Giles, H., Bourhis, R. Y., & Taylor, D. M. (1977). Towards a theory of language in ethnic group relations. In H. Giles (Ed.), *Language, ethnicity and intergroup relations*. London: Academic Press.

Giles, H., & Johnson, P. (1981). The role of language in ethnic group relations. In J. C. Turner and H. Giles (Eds.), *Intergroup behaviour*. Oxford: Blackwell.

Giles, H., Llado, N., McKirnan, D. H., & Taylor, D. M. (1979). Social identity in Puerto Rico. *International Journal of Psychology, 14*, 185-201.

Giles, H., Rosenthal, D. A., & Young, L. (1985). Perceived ethnolinguistic vitality: The Anglo- and Greek-Australian setting. *Journal of Multilingual and Multicultural Development, 6*, 253-269.

Giles, H., & St. Clair, R. (Eds.). (1979). *Language and social psychology*. Baltimore, MD: University Park Press.

Giles, H., Taylor, D. M., & Bourhis, R. Y. (1973). Towards a theory of interpersonal accommodation through speech: Some Canadian data. *Language in Society, 2*, 117-192.

Giles, H., Taylor, D. M., & Bourhis, R. Y. (1977). Dimensions of Welsh identity. *European Journal of Social Psychology, 7*, 29-39.

Giles, H., Taylor, D. M., Lambert, W. E., & Albert, G. (1976). Dimensions of ethnic identity: An example from Northern Maine. *Journal of Social Psychology, 100*, 11-19.

Glaser, B. G., & Strauss, A. L. (1967). *The discovery of grounded theory: Strategies for qualitative research*. Chicago: Aldine.

Goetz, J. P., & LeCompte, M. D. (1982). Ethnographic research and the problem of data reduction. *Anthropology and Education Quarterly, 12*(1), 51-65.

Goffman, E. (1974). *Frame analysis*. New York: Harper Colophon.

Goldstein, C., Koopman, E., & Goldstein, H. (1979). Racial attitudes in young children as a function of interracial contact in the public schools. *American Journal of Orthopsychiatry, 49*, 88-99.

Goodman, M. E. (1946). Evidence concerning the genesis of interracial attitudes. *American Anthropologist, 48*, 624-630.

Goodman, M. E. (1964). *Race awareness in young children* (rev. ed.). New York: Collier. (Original work published 1952)

Goodwin, M. H. (1980). He-said-she-said: Formal cultural procedures for the construction of a gossip dispute activity. *American Ethnologist, 7*, 674-694.

Goodwin, M. H. (1982). Processes of dispute management among urban Black children. *American Ethnologist, 9*, 76-79.

Gordon, C. (1968). Self-conceptions: Configurations of content. In C. Gordon & K. Gergen (Eds.), *The self in social interaction*. New York: John Wiley.

Gordon, M. (1964). *Assimilation in American life: The role of race, religion and national origins*. New York: Oxford University Press.

Gordon, M. (1978). *Human nature, class, and ethnicity*. New York: Oxford.

Gordon, S., & Steele, R. (1984). Consultation and the mental health of minority communities: An examination of the literature from 1973 through 1983. *American Psychological Association Division of Community Psychology Newsletter, 17*(2), 4-6.

Gordon, V. (1980). *The self-concept of Black Americans*. Lanham: University Press of America.

Gottfried, A. W., & Gottfried, A. E. (1974). Influence of social power vs. status envy modeled behaviors on children's preferences for models. *Psychological Reports, 34*, 1147-1150.

Gouch, H., Harris, D. B., Martin, W. E., & Edwards, M. (1972). Children's ethnic attitudes: I. Relationships to certain certain personality factors. In A. Brown (Ed.), *Prejudice in children*. Springfield, IL: Charles C Thomas.

Graves, N., & Graves, T. (1976). Inclusive versus exclusive behavior in New Zealand school settings: Polynesian-Pakeha contracts in learning styles. *South Pacific Research Institute Report No. 12*. Aukland, New Zealand.

Grebler, L., Moore, J. W., & Guzman, R. C. (1970). *The Mexican-American people*. New York: Free Press.

Greco, T., Vasta, E., & Smith, R. (1977) "I get these freaky feelings like I'm splitting into a million pieces." Cultural differences in Brisbane, Australia. *Ethnic Studies, 1*, 17-29.

Greenberg, B. S. (1972). Children's reactions to T.V. Blacks. *Journalism Quarterly, 49*, 5-14.

Greenwald, H. J., & Oppenheim, D. B. (1968). Reported magnitude of self-misidentification among Negro children: Artifact? *Journal of Personality and Social Psychology, 8*, 49-52.

Grossman, B. (1982). Ethnic identity and self-esteem. A study of Anglo, Chicano, and Black adolescents in Texas. *Dissertation Abstracts International, 42*, 3423.

Guba, E. G. (1978). *Toward a methodology of naturalistic inquiry in educational evaluation*. (CSE Monograph Series in Education Evaluation, Vol 8). Los Angeles, CA: University of California, Center for the Study of Education.

Gumperz, J. (1972). The speech community. In P. Giglioli (Ed.), *Language in social contexts* (pp. 381-386). Harmondsworth: Penguin.

Gumperz, J. (Ed.). (1982a). *Language and social identity*. London: Cambridge.

Gumperz, J. (1982b). *Discourse strategies*. London: Cambridge.

Gumperz, J., & Hymes, D. (Eds.). (1972). *Directions in sociolinguistics: The ethnography of communication*. New York: Holt, Rinehart & Winston.

Gumperz, J., & Roberts, C. (1980). *Developing awareness skills for interethnic communication* (Occasional Paper No. 12). Singapore: Seameo Regional Language Center.

Gutierrez, A., & Hirsch, H. (1973). The militant challenge to the American ethos: "Chicanos" and "Mexican-Americans." *Social Science Quarterly, 53*, 830-845.

Haiman, F. S. (1972). The fighting words doctrine: From Chaplinsky to Brown. *Iowa Journal of Speech, 3*, 1-31.

Hall, W., Cross, W., & Freedle, R. (1972). Stages in the development of Black awareness: An exploratory investigation. In R. Jones (Ed.), *Black psychology* (1st ed.). New York: Harper & Row.

Hallinan, M. T. (1982). Classroom racial composition and children's friendships. *Social Forces, 61*, 56-72.

Hallinan, M. T., & Tuma, N. (1978). Race differences in children's friendships. *Sociology of Education, 51*, 270-282.

Halpin, A., Glennelle, G., & Gerald, F. (1980). The relationship of perceived parental behaviors to locus of control and self-esteem among American Indian and White children. *Journal of Social Psychology, 111*, 189-195.

Hanna, J. L. (1982). Public social policy and the children's world: Implications of ethnographic research for desegregated schooling. In G. Spindler (Ed.), *Doing the ethnography of schooling: Educational anthropology in action*. New York: Holt, Rinehart & Winston.

Hansen, J. F. (1979). *Sociocultural perspectives on human learning: An introduction to educational anthropology*. Englewood Cliffs, NJ: Prentice-Hall.

Harre, R. (1980). *A theory for social psychology*. Totowa, NJ: Rowan & Littlefield.

Harrell, J. P. (1979). Analyzing black coping styles: A supplemental diagnostic system. *Journal of Black Psychology, 5*, 99-108.

Harris, J. (1980). *Identity: A study of the concept in education for a multicultural Australia* (Education Research and Development Committee Report No. 22). Canberra: Australian Government Publishing Service.

Harris, R. McL. (1979). Fever of ethnicity: The sociological and educational significance of the concept. In P. R. de Lacey and M. E. Poole (Eds.), *Mosaic or melting pot: Cultural evolution in Australia*. Sydney: Harcourt Brace Jovanovich.

Harrison, P. C. (1972). *The drama of Nommo*. New York: Grove.

Harter, S. (1982). The Perceived Competence Scale for Children. *Child Development, 53,* 87-97.

Hartog, J., & Hartog, E. (1983). Cultural aspects of health and illness behavior in hospitals. *Western Journal of Medicine, 136,* 910-916.

Harwood, A. (1981). *Ethnicity and medical care.* Cambridge, MA: Harvard University Press.

Hechter, M. (1975). *Internal colonialism.* Berkeley: University of California Press.

Heider, F. (1958). *The psychology of interpersonal relations.* New York: John Wiley.

Heller, M. (1982a). *Language, ethnicity and politics in Quebec.* Unpublished doctoral dissertation, University of California, Berkeley.

Heller, M. (1982b). "Bonjour, hello?": Negotiations of language choice in Montreal. In J. Gumperz (Ed.), *Language and social identity* (pp. 108-118). Cambridge: Cambridge University Press.

Heller, M. (1984). Language and ethnic identity in a Toronto French-language school. *Canadian Ethnic Studies, 16,* 1-14.

Heller, M., Bartholomot, J. P., Levy, L., & Ostiguy, L. (1982). *Le processus de francisation dans une enterprise montréal-aise: Une analyse sociolinguistique.* Quebec: l'Editeur Officiel.

Heller, M., & Freeman, S. (in press). First encounters: The role of conversation in the medical intake process. In M. Heller & S. Freeman (Eds.), Discourse as organizational process [Special issue]. *Discourse Processes.*

Helson, H. (1964). *Adaptation-level theory: An experimental and systematic approach to behavior.* New York: Harper & Row.

Hewstone, M. J., Jaspars, J., & Lalljee, M. (1982). Social representation. *European Journal of Social Psychology, 12,* 241-269.

Hills, M. D. (1973). *Culture conflict in Australia: Reactions to integration disparity in second-generation immigrants and Australian adolescents.* Unpublished doctoral thesis, Australian National University.

Hitch, P. (1983). Social identity and the half-Asian child. In G. M. Breakwell (Ed.), *Threatened identities* (pp. 107-127). Chichester: John Wiley.

Hodgson, J. W., & Fischer, J. L. (1979). Sex differences in identity and intimacy development in college youth. *Journal of Youth and Adolescence, 8,* 37-50.

Hofman, J. E. (1982). Social identity and the readiness for social relations between Jews and Arabs in Israel. *Human Relations, 35,* 727-741.

Hofman, J. E., & Rouhana, N. (1976). Young Arabs in Israel: Some aspects of a conflicted social identity. *Journal of Social Psychology, 99,* 75-86.

Hofstede, C. (1984). *Culture's consequences: International differences in work-related values.* Beverly Hills, CA: Sage.

Hollingshead, A., & Redlich, F. (1958). *Social class and mental illness.* New York: John Wiley.

Holtzman, W. H., Diaz-Guerrero, R., & Swartz, J. D. (1975). *Personality development in two cultures.* Austin: University of Texas Press.

Horowitz, E. L. (1936). The development of attitudes toward the Negro. *Archives of Psychology, 194.*

Horowitz, E. L. (1940). Some aspects of the development of patriotism in children. *Sociometry, 3,* 329-341.

Horowitz, R. E. (1939). Racial aspects of self-identification in nursery school children. *Journal of Psychology, 7,* 91-99.

Howard, A., & Scott, R. (1981). The study of minority groups in complex societies. In R. Munroe, R. Munroe, & B. Whiting (Eds.), *Handbook of cross-cultural human development.* New York: Garland.

Hraba, J. (1972). The doll technique: A measure of racial ethnocentrism? *Social Forces, 50,* 522-527.

Hraba, J., & Grant, G. (1970). Black is beautiful: A reexamination of racial preference and identification. *Journal of Personality and Social Psychology, 16,* 398-402.

Huerta, A. (1980). The acquisition of bilingualism: A code-switching approach. In R. Bauman & J. Sherzer (Eds.), *Language and speech in American society.* Austin, TX: Southwest Educational Development Laboratory.

Hunsburger, B. (1978). Racial awareness and preference of White and Indian Canadian children. *Canadian Journal of Behavioral Science, 10,* 176-179.

Hwang, C. H., & Morland, J. (1981). Racial/ethnic identity of preschool children: Comparing Taiwan, Hong Kong and the U.S. *Journal of Cross-Cultural Psychology, 12,* 409-424.

Hyman, H., & Singer, E. (1968). *Readings in reference group theory research.* New York: McGraw-Hill.

Hymes, D. (1980). Foreword. In S. B. Shimanoff (Ed.), *Communication rules: Theory and research.* Beverly Hills, CA: Sage.

Ianni, F., & Orr, M. (1979). Toward a rapprochement of quantitative and qualitative methodologies. In T. D. Cook & C. S. Reichardt (Eds.), *Qualitative and quantitative methods in evaluation research.* Beverly Hills, CA: Sage.

Inhelder, B., & Piaget, J. (1964). *The early growth of logic in the child: Classification and seriation.* New York: Harper & Row. (Original work published 1959)

Inkeles, A., & Levinson, D. (1969). National character: The study of model personality and socio-cultural systems. In G. Lindzey & E. Aronson (Eds.), *The handbook of social psychology* (Vol. 4). Reading, MA: Addison-Wesley.

Irvine, J. (1974). Strategies of status manipulation in the Wolof greeting. In R. Bauman & J. Sherzer (Eds.), *Explorations in the ethnography of speaking* (pp. 167-181). Cambridge, MA: Cambridge University Press.

Isaacs, H. R. (1968). Group identity and political change: The role of color and physical characteristics. In J. H. Franklin (Ed.), *Color and race.* Boston, MA: Houghton Mifflin.

Isajiw, W. W. (1974). Definitions of ethnicity. *Ethnicity, 1,* 111-124.

Jackson, B. (1976). *The function of black identity development theory in achieving relevance in educational.* Unpublished doctoral dissertation, University of Massachusetts at Amherst.

Jackson, D. N., & Paunonen, S. V. (1980). Personality structure and assessment. *Annual Review of Psychology, 31,* 503-551.

Jackson, P. (1968). *Life in classrooms.* New York: Holt, Rinehart & Winston.

Jacobs, J. H. (1978). Black-White interracial families: Marital process and identity development in young children. *Dissertation Abstracts International, 38,* 5023.

Jenkins, A. (1982). *The psychology of the Afro-American: A humanistic approach.* New York: Pergamon.

Johnson, C. S. (1941). *Growing up in the black belt.* Washington, DC: American Council on Education.

Johnson, D. (1983). *Racial attitudes and biculturality in interracial preschoolers.* Unpublished master's thesis, Cornell University.

Johnson, D., & Johnson, R. (1981). Effects of cooperative and individualistic learning experiences on interethnic interaction. *Journal of Educational Psychology, 73,* 444-449.

Johnson, K. R. (1972). The vocabulary of race. In T. Kochman (Ed.), *Rappin and stylin out: Communication in urban Black America.* Urbana: University of Illinois Press.

Johnson, N. B., Middleton, M. R., & Tajfel, H. (1970). The relationship between children's preference for and knowledge about other nations. *British Journal of Social and Clinical Psychology, 9,* 232-240.

Johnston, R. (1972). *Future Australians: Immigrant children in Perth, Western Australia.* Canberra: Australian National University Press.

Jones, J. (1983, August). *The concept of race in the history of social psychology.* Paper presented at the annual meeting of the American Psychological Association, Anaheim, CA.

Joy, R. (1972). *Languages in conflict.* Toronto: McClelland & Stewart.

Jupp, T., Roberts, C., & Cook-Gumperz, J. (1982). Language and disadvantage: The hidden process. In J. Gumperz (Ed.), *Language and social identity* (pp. 232-256). New York: Cambridge University Press.

Kagan, S. (1977). Social motives and behavior of Mexican-American and Anglo-American children. In J. Martinez (Ed.), *Chicano psychology.* New York: Academic Press.

Kagan, S., & Carlson, J. (1975). Development of adaptive assertiveness in Mexican and United States children. *Developmental Psychology, 11,* 71-78.

Kagan, S., & Endler, P. B. (1975). Maternal response to success and failure of Anglo-American, Mexican-American, and Mexican children. *Child Development, 46,* 452-458.

Kagan, S., & Knight, G. (1981). Social motives among Anglo-American and Mexican-American children: Experimental and projective measures. *Journal of Research in Personality, 15,* 93-106.

Kagan, S., Knight, G., Martinez, S., & Santa, P. (1981). Conflict resolution style among Mexican children. *Journal of Cross-Cultural Psychology, 12,* 222-232.

Kagan, S., & Madsen, M. C. (1971). Cooperation and competition of Mexican, Mexican-American and Anglo-American children of two ages under four instructional sets. *Developmental Psychology, 5,* 32-39.

Kain, J. (1975). Race, ethnicity, and residential location. In *Urban planning: Policy analysis and administration* (discussion paper). Cambridge, MA: Harvard University, Department of City and Regional Planning.

Kalin, R. (1979). Ethnic and multicultural attitudes among children in a Canadian city. *Canadian Ethnic Studies, 11,* 9-81.

Kamin, L. (1974). *The science and politics of IQ.* Potomac, MD: Erlbaum.

Kantrowitz, N. (1969). The vocabulary of race relations in a prison. *Publications of the American Dialect Society, 51,* 23-34.

Katz, P. A. (1973a). Perception of racial cues in preschool children: A new look. *Developmental Psychology, 8,* 295-299.

Katz, P. A. (1973b) Stimulus predifferentiation and modification of children's racial attitudes. *Child Development, 44,* 232-237.

Katz, P. A. (1976). The acquisition of racial attitudes in children. In P. A. Katz (Ed.), *Towards the elimination of racism.* New York: Pergamon.

Katz, P. A. (1982). A review of recent research in children's racial attitude acquisition. In L. Katz (Ed.), *Current topics in early childhood education* (pp. 17-54). Norwood, NJ: Ablex.

Katz, P. A. (1983). Development of racial and sex-role attitudes. In R. Leahy (Ed.), *The child's construction of social inequality.* New York: Academic Press.

Katz, P. A., Sohn, M., & Zalk, S. R. (1975). Perceptual concomitants of racial attitudes in urban grade-school children. *Developmental Psychology, 11,* 135-144.

Katz, P. A., & Zalk, S. R. (1974). Doll preferences: An index of racial attitudes? *Journal of Educational Psychology, 66,* 663-668.

Katz, P. A., & Zalk, S. R. (1978). Modification of children's racial attitudes. *Developmental Psychology, 14,* 447-461.

Keenan, E. (1974). Norm-makers, norm-breakers: Uses of speech by men and women in a Malagasy community. In R. Bauman and J. Sherzer (Eds.), *Explorations in the ethnography of speaking* (pp. 125-143). Cambridge: Cambridge University Press.

Keil, C. (1966). *Urban blues.* Chicago: The University of Chicago Press.

Keiser, R. L. (1969). *The vice lords: Warriors of the streets.* New York: Holt, Rinehart & Winston.

Keller, A., Ford, L. H., Jr., & Meacham, J. (1978). Dimensions of self-concept in preschool children. *Developmental Psychology, 14,* 483-487.

Kelman, H. (1970). A social-psychological model of political legitimacy and its relevance to Black and White student protest movements. *Psychiatry, 33,* 224-246.

Kendler, T. S. (1961). Concept formation. *Annual Review of Psychology, 12,* 447-472.

Kennedy, S., Scheirer, J., & Rogers, A. (1984). The price of success: Our monocultural science. *American Psychologist, 39,* 996-997.

Kerlinger, F. (1951). Decision making in Japan. *Social Forces, 30,* 36-41.

Keyes, C. F. (1976). Towards a new formulation of the concept of ethnic group. *Ethnicity, 3,* 202-213.

Khatib, S. M., & Nobles, W. W. (1977). Historical foundations of African psychology and their philosophical consequences. *Journal of Black Psychology, 4,* 91-101.

Kircher, M., & Furby, L. (1971). Racial preferences in young children. *Child Development, 42,* 2076-2078.

Kitano, H. (1982). Mental health in the Japanese-American community. In E. Jones & S. Korchin (Eds.), *Minority mental health.* New York: Praeger.

Kitsuse, J., & Cicourel, A. (1963). A note on the uses of official statistics. *Social Problems, 12,* 131-137.

Klein, P. S., Levine, E., & Charry, M. M. (1979). Effects of skin color and hair differences on facial choices of kindergarten children. *Journal of Social Psychology, 107,* 287-288.

Klineberg, O. (1940). *Social psychology*. New York: Holt, Rinehart & Winston.

Knapp, M. S. (1979). Ethnographic contributions to evaluation research: The experimental schools programs evaluation and some alternatives. In T. T. Cook & C. S. Reichart (Eds.), *Qualitative and quantitative methods in evaluation research*. Beverly Hills, CA: Sage.

Knight, G., & Kagan, S. (1982). Siblings, birth order and cooperative-competitive social behavior: A comparison of Anglo-American and Mexican-American children. *Journal of Cross-Cultural Psychology, 13*, 239-249.

Knight, G., Nelson, W. Kagan, S., & Gumbiner, J. (1982). Cooperative-competitive social orientation and school achievement among Anglo-American children. *Contemporary Education Psychology, 7*, 97-106.

Knudson, K. (1979). The relationships among affective role-taking, empathy, and prosocial behavior in a sample of Mexican-American and Anglo-American children of two ages. *Dissertation Abstracts International, 39*(8)B, 1042.

Koch, H. L. (1946). The social distance between certain racial, nationality, and skin-pigmentation groups in selected populations of American school children. *Journal of Genetic Psychology, 68*, 63-95.

Kochman, T. (1970). Toward an ethnography of Black American speech behavior. In N. E. Whitten, Jr., & J. Szwed (Eds.), *Afro-American anthropology*. New York: Free Press.

Kochman, T. (1976). Perceptions along the power axis: A cognitive residue of inter-racial encounters. *Anthropological Linguistics, 18*, 261-274.

Kochman, T. (1981). *Black and white styles in conflict*. Chicago: University of Chicago Press.

Kochman, T. (1983). The boundary between play and nonplay in Black verbal dueling. *Language in Society, 12*, 239-337.

Kohlberg, L. (1976). Moral stages and moralization: The cognitive-development approach. In T. Lickona (Ed.), *Moral development and behavior*. New York: Holt, Rinehart & Winston.

Kohlberg, L. (in press). *Psychosexual development in children: A cognitive interpretation*. New York: Holt, Rinehart & Winston.

Kosslyn, S. M., & Kagan, J. (1981). "Concrete thinking" and the development of social cognition. In J. H. Flavell & L. Ross (Eds.), *Social cognitive development*. New York: Cambridge University Press.

Kourakis, M. (1983). *Biculturalism: The effect upon personal and social adjustment*. Unpublished master's thesis, University of Adelaide.

Koutsounadis, V. (1979). *Cross-cultural conflict between Greek children and their parents*. Paper presented at the First Pan-Australian Greek Welfare Conference, N.S.W.

Kozhanov, A. A. (1976). External appearance as a factor in ethnic identification. *Soviet Sociology, 16*, 35-48.

Kuhn, T. (1962). *The structure of scientific revolutions*. Chicago: University of Chicago Press.

Kuhn, M., & McPartland, T. (1954). An empirical investigation of self-attitudes. *American Sociological Review, 19*, 68-76.

Kurakawa, M. (1971). Mutual perceptions of racial images: White, Black, and Japanese Americans. *Journal of Social Issues, 27*, 213-235.

Labov, W. (1972a). Rules for ritual insults. In T. Kochman (Ed.), *Rappin and stylin out: Communication in urban Black America*. Urbana: University of Illinois Press.

Labov, W. (1972b). *Sociolinguistic patterns*. Philadelphia: University of Pennsylvania Press.

Lachapelle, R., & Henripin, J. (1980). *La situation demolinguistique au Canada*. Montreal: Institute for Research on Public Policy.

La Fromboise, T., & Rowe, W. (1983). Skills training for bicultural competence: rationale and application. *Journal of Counseling Psychology 30*, 589-595.

Lamare, J. W. (1982). The political integration of Mexican American children: A generational analysis. *International Migration Review, 16*, 159-188.

Lambert, W. (1967). A social psychology of bilingualism. *Journal of Social Issues, 23*, 91-109.

Lambert W. (1972). *Language, psychology and culture*. Stanford, CA: Stanford University Press.

Lambert, W. E., Hamers, J. F., & Frasure-Smith, N. (1979). *Child-rearing values. A cross-national study*. New York: Praeger.

Lambert, W. E., & Klineberg, O. (1967). *Children's views of foreign peoples.* New York: Appleton-Century Crofts.

Lambert, W. E., Giles, H., & Picard, O. (1975). Language attitudes in a French-American community. *International Journal of the Sociology of Language, 4,* 127-152.

Lambert, W. E., & Tan, A. (1979). Expressive styles and strategies in the aggressive actions of children of six cultures. *Ethos, 7,* 19-36.

Lambert, W. E., & Tucker, G. R. (1972). *Bilingual education.* Reading, MA: Newbury House.

Lampe, P. E. (1975). Mexican American self-identity and ethnic prejudice. *Cornell Journal of Social Relations, 10,* 223-237.

Lampe, P. E. (1977). Student acceptability of "Black" and "Chicano" as ethnic labels. *Urban Education, 12,* 223-228.

Lampe, P. E. (1978). Ethnic self-referent and the assimilation of Mexican-Americans. *International Journal of Comparative Sociology, 50,* 259-270.

Lampe, P. E. (1982). Ethnic labels: Naming or name calling? *Ethnic and Racial Studies, 5,* 542-548.

Landis, D., & Brislin, R. (Eds.). (1983). *Handbook of intercultural training: Area studies in intercultural training* (Vol. 3). New York: Pergamon.

Landreth, C., & Johnson, B. C. (1953). Young children's responses to a picture and inset test designed to reveal reactions to persons of different skin color. *Child Development, 24,* 63-79.

Lasker, B. (1929). *Race attitudes in children.* New York: Holt, Rinehart & Winston.

Leacock, W. B. (1969). *Teaching and learning in city schools: A comparative study.* New York: Basic Books.

LeCompte, M. (1969). *The dilemmas of inner city school reform: The Woodlawn experimental school project.* Unpublished master's thesis, University of Chicago.

LeCompte, M. D., & Goetz, J. P. (1982). Problems of reliability and validity in ethnographic research. *Review of Educational Research, 52,* 31-60.

Lee, D., & Lapointe, J. (1979). The emergence of Franco-Ontarians: New identity, new boundaries. In J. Elliott (Ed.), *Two nations, many cultures: Ethnic groups in Canada* (pp. 99-113). Toronto: Prentice-Hall.

Leininger, M. (1978). *Transcultural nursing.* New York: John Wiley.

Leininger, M. (1984). Transcultural nursing: An overview. *Nursing Outlook, 32,* 76-77.

Lemaine, G. (1974). Social differentiation and social originality. *European Journal of Social Psychology, 4,* 17-52.

LeVine, E., & Padilla, A. (1980). *Crossing cultures in therapy: Pluralistic counseling for the Hispanic.* Monterey, CA: Brooks/Cole.

LeVine, E., & Ruiz, R. (1978). An exploration of multi-correlates of ethnic group choice. *Journal of Cross-Cultural Psychology, 9,* 179-190.

LeVine, R. (1982). *Culture, behavior and personality.* New York: Aldine.

LeVine, R., & Campbell, D. (1972). *Ethnocentrism: Theories of conflict, ethnic attitudes and group behavior.* New York: John Wiley.

Levy, J. (1983). Developing intercultural competence in bilingual teacher-training programs. In D. Landis & R. Brislin (Eds.), *Handbook of intercultural training* (Vol. III). New York: Pergamon.

Lewin, K. (1948). Self-hatred in Jews. In K. Lewin (Ed.), *Resolving social conflicts.* Newe York: Harper & Row.

Lewis, D. K. (1975). The Black family: Socialization and sex roles. *Phylon, 36,* 221-237.

Lewis, M., & Brooks, J. (1975). Infant's social perception: A constructivist's view. In L. B. Cohen & P. Salapatek (Eds.), *Infant perception: From sensation to cognition* (Vol. 2). New York: Academic Press.

Liebow, E. (1967). *Tally's corner: A study of Negro street corner men.* Boston: Little, Brown.

Light, R. J., & Pillemer, D. B. (1982). Numbers and narrative: Combining their strengths in research reviews. *Harvard Educational Review, 25,* 41-48.

Little, J. (1983). *An exploration of the relationship among reference group orientation, self-esteem and reference group dilemmas.* Unpublished doctoral dissertation, Cornell University.

Longshore, D. (1982). Race composition and white hostility: A research note on the problem of control in desegregated schools. *Social Forces, 61,* 3-78.

Longstreet, W. S. (1978). *Aspects of ethnicity*. New York: Teachers College Press.

Lonner, W. (1980). The search for psychological universals. In H. Triandis & J. Berry (Eds.), *Handbook of cross-cultural psychology*. Boston: Allyn & Bacon.

Loomis, C. P. (1974). A backward glance at self-identification of Blacks and Chicanos. *Rural Sociology, 39,* 96.

Loomis, C. P., Loomis, Z. K., & Gullahorn, J. E. (1966). *Linkage of Mexico and the United States* (Research Bulletin 14). East Lansing: Michigan Agricultural Experiment Station.

Lyman, S. M., & Douglass, W. A. (1973). Ethnicity: Strategies of collective and individual impression management. *Social Research, 40,* 344-365.

Lynn, R. (1971). *Personality and national character*. Oxford: Pergamon.

Lynn, R. (1973). National differences in anxiety and the consumption of caffeine. *British Journal of Social and Clinical Psychology, 12,* 92-93.

Lynn, R., & Hampson, S. L. (1975). National differences in extraversion and neuroticism. *British Journal of Social and Clinical Psychology, 14,* 223-240.

Madsen, M. (1971). Development and cross-cultural differences in the cooperative and competitive behavior of children. *Journal of Cross-Cultural Psychology, 2,* 365-371.

Madsen, M., & Lancy, D. (1981). Cooperative and competitive behavior. Experiments related to ethnic identity in Papua New Guinea. *Journal of Cross-Cultural Psychology, 12,* 387-408.

Maccoby, E. (1966). *The development of sex differences*. Stanford, CA: Stanford University Press.

MacDonald, S., & Gallimore, R. (1971). *Battle in the classroom: Innovations in classroom techniques.* Scranton: Intext.

Mackey, J., & Appleman, D. (1983). The growth of adolescent apathy. *Educational Leadership, 40,* 30-33.

Magnusson, D. (1971). An analysis of situational dimensions. *Perceptual and Motor Skills, 32,* 851-867.

Magnusson, D. (1974). *The person and the situation in the traditional measurement model* (Reports from the Psychological Laboratories, 426). University of Stockholm.

Magnusson, D., & Ekehammar, B. (1973). An analysis of situational dimensions: A replication. *Multivariate Behavioral Research, 8,* 331-339.

Mahler, R. (1974). A comparative study of locus of control. *Psychologia, 17,* 135-138.

Maltz, D., & Borker, R. (1982). A cultural approach to male-female miscommunication. In J. Gumperz (Ed.), *Language and social identity* (pp. 195-216). Cambridge, MA: Cambridge University Press.

Marcia, J. E. (1966). Development and validation of ego identity status. *Journal of Personality and Social Psychology, 3,* 551-558.

Marrett, C., & Leggon, C. (1979). *Research in race and ethnic relations* (Vol. 1). Greenwich, JT: Jai.

Martinez, J. (1977). *Chicano psychology*. New York: Academic Press.

Marvin, R. (1973). *Attachment, exploratory and communicative behavior of two, three, and four-year-old children.* Unpublished doctoral dissertation, University of Chicago.

Maryland, J. (1972). Shoe-shine on 63rd. In T. Kochman (Ed.), *Rappin' and stylin' out: Communication in urban Black America*. Urbana: University of Illinois Press.

Maxwell, T. (1977). *The invisible French: The French in Metropolitan Toronto*. Waterloo, Ontario: Wilfrid Laurier University Press.

May, J. W., & May, J. G. (1983). Effects of age on color preference for black and white by infants and young children. *Perceptual and Motor Skills, 56,* 323-330.

McAdoo, H. (1970). *An exploratory study of racial attitude change in Black preschool children.* Unpublished doctoral dissertation, University of Michigan.

McAdoo, H. (1977). The development of self-concept and racial attitudes in Black children: A longitudinal study. In W. Cross (Ed.), *The 3rd conference on empirical research in Black psychology* (pp. 47-60). Washington, DC: NIE (HEW).

McClelland, D. C. (1975). *Power: The inner experience*. New York: Irvington.

McClelland, D. C. (1968). *The achieving society*. New York: Van Nostrand.

McClintock, C. C., Brannon, D., & Maynard-Moody, S. (1979). Appling the logic of sample surveys to qualitative case studies: The case cluster method. *Administrative Science Quarterly, 24,* 612-629.

McClure, E. (1981). Formal and functional aspects of the code-switched discourse of bilingual children. In R. Duran (Ed.), *Latino language and communicative behavior* (pp. 69-94). Norwood, NJ: Ablex.

McDougall, W. (1943). *Social psychology* (25th ed.). London: Methuen. (Original work published 1908)

McFee, M. (1968). The 150% man, a product of Blackfeet acculturation. *American Anthropologist, 70,* 1096-1103.

McGhee, J. D. (1984). *Running the gauntlet: Black men in America.* Unpublished report, National Urban League.

McGoldrick, M., Pearce, J., & Giordano, J. (Eds.). (1982). *Ethnicity and family therapy.* New York: Guilford.

McGuire, W. J., McGuire, C. V., Child, P., & Fujioka, T. (1978). Salience of ethnicity in the spontaneous self-concept as a function of one's ethnic distinctiveness in the social environment. *Journal of Personality and Social Psychology, 36,* 511-520.

McGuire, W. J., & Padawer-Singer, A. (1976). Trait salience in the spontaneous self-concept. *Journal of Personality and Social Psychology, 33,* 743-754.

McMichael, R. E., & Grinder, R. E. (1964). Guilt and resistance to temptation in Japanese and White Americans. *Journal of Social Psychology, 64,* 217-233.

McRoy, R. G. (1981). A comparative study of the self-concept of transracially and interracially adopted black children. *Dissertation Abstracts International 42*(03), Sec. A. 1318.

McWilliams, C. (1968). *North from Mexico.* New York: Greenwood.

Mead, G. H. (1934). *Mind, self, and society.* Chicago: University of Chicago Press.

Meade, R. D., & Whitaker, J. D. (1967). A cross-cultural study of authoritarianism. *Journal of Social Psychology, 72,* 3-7.

Means, R. (1980). Fighting words on the future of the earth. *Mother Jones, 5*(10), 10-38.

Mechanic, D. (1968). *Medical sociology: A selective view.* New York: Free Press.

Mediax, (1980, June). *Accept my profile: Perspectives for headstart profiles of program effects on children* (Volume I). Washington, DC: Department of Health, Education and Welfare. (Contract No: HEW-105-77-1006).

Meichenbaum, D. (1983, December). *The relationships between cognition, emotion, and behavior: Implications for treatment.* Paper presented at the meeting of the World Congress on Behavior Therapy, Washington, DC.

Meier, M. S., & Rivera, F. (1981) *Dictionary of Mexican American history.* Westport, CT: Greenwood.

Mehan, H. (1979). *Learning lessons.* Cambridge, MA: Harvard University Press.

Mehan, H. (1983). The role of language and the language of role in institutional decision-making. *Language in Society, 12,* 187-212.

Mennell, S. (194). *Sociological theory: Uses and unities.* London: Nelson.

Mercer, J., & Lewis, L. (1978). *System of multicultural pluralistic assessment.* New York: Psychological Corporation.

Merton, R. K., Coleman, J. S., & Rossi, P. H. (Eds.). (1979). *Qualitative and quantitative social research: Papers in honor of Paul F. Lazarsfeld.* New York: Free Press.

Metz, M. H. (1978). *Classrooms and corridors.* Los Angeles: University of California Press.

Michaels, S. (1981). "Sharing time": Children's narrative styles and differential access to literacy. *Language in Society, 10,* 423-442.

Miller, A. (1973). Integration and acculturation of cooperative behavior among Blackfoot Indian and non-Indian Canadian children. *Journal of Cross-Cultural Psychology, 4,* 374-380.

Miller, M. V. (1976). Mexican Americans, Chicanos, and others: Ethnic self-identification and selected social attributes of rural Texas youth. *Rural Sociology, 41,* 234-247.

Miller, N., & Brewer, M. (Eds.). (1984). *Groups in contact: The psychology of desegregation.* New York: Academic Press.

Milner, D. (1983). *Children and race* (2nd ed.). Harmondsworth: Penguin.

Milliones, J. (1974). *Construction of the development inventory of Black consciousness.* Unpublished doctoral dissertation, University of Pittsburgh.

Mitchell-Kernan, C. (1972). Signifying, loud-talking and marking. In T. Kochman (Ed.), *Rappin' and stylin' out: Communication in urban Black America.* Urbana: University of Illinois Press.

Mock, R., & Tuddenham, R. (1971). Race and conformity among children. *Developmental Psychology, 4,* 349-365.

Moerman, M. (1965). Ethnic identification in a complex civilization: Who are the Lue? *American Anthropologist, 67,* 1215-1230.

Mohr, D. M. (1978). Development of attributes of personal identity. *Developmental Psychology, 14,* 427-428.

Montijo, J. A. (1975). The relationships among self-esteem, group pride, and cultural group identification. *Dissertation Abstracts International, 35,* 4189.

Moore, C. L. (1976). The racial preferences and attitude of preschool Black children. *Journal of Genetic Psychology, 129,* 37-44.

Moore, S. M., & Rosenthal, D. A. (1984). Balance versus main effects androgyny: Their relationship to adjustment in three ethnic groups. *Psychological Reports, 54,* 823-831.

Moos, R. H. (1968). Situational analysis of a therapeutic community milieu. *Journal of Abnormal Psychology, 73,* 49-61.

Morgenstern, O. (1963). *On the accuracy of economic observation* (2nd ed.). NJ: Princeton University Press.

Morland, J. K. (1958). Racial recognition by nursery school children in Lynchburg, Virginia. *Social Forces, 37,* 132-137.

Morland, J. K. (1962). Racial acceptance and preference of nursery school children in a southern city. *Merrill-Palmer Quarterly, 8,* 271-280.

Morland, J. K. (1966). A comparison of race awareness in Northern and Southern children. *American Journal of Orthopsychiatry, 36,* 22-31.

Morland, J. K., & Hwang, C. (1981). Racial ethnic identity of preschool children: Comparing Taiwan, Hong Kong and the United States. *Journal of Cross-Cultural Psychology, 12,* 409-424.

Morner, M. (1967). *Race mixture in the history of Latin America.* Boston: Little, Brown.

Moscovici, S., & Paicheler, G. (1978). Social comparison and social recognition: Two complementary processes of identification. In H. Tajfel (Ed.), *Differentiation between social groups* (pp. 251-266). New York: Academic Press.

Mougeon, R., & Canale, M. (1979). Maintenance of French in Ontario: Is education in French enough? *Interchange, 9,* 30-39.

Muga, D. (1984). Academic sub-cultural theory and the problematic of ethnicity: A tentative critique. *The Journal of Ethnic Studies, 12,* 1-51.

Mussen, P. (1953). Differences between the TAT responses of Negro and White boys. *Journal of Consulting Psychology, 17,* 373-376.

Mussen, P. (1983). *Handbook of child psychology.* New York: John Wiley.

Mussen, P. H., Conger, J. J., Kagan, J., & Huston, A. C. (1984). *Child development and personality.* New York: Harper & Row.

Nader, L. (1964). *Talea and Juquila: A comparison of Zapotec social organization.* Berkeley: University of California Press.

Nagata, J. (1974). What is a Malay? Situational selection of ethnic identity in a plural society. *American Ethnologist, 1,* 331-350.

Nagata, J. (1979). *Malaysian mosaic.* Vancouver: University of British Columbia Press.

Napper, G. (1973). *Blacker than thou.* Grand Rapids, MI: Eerdmans.

National Black Coalition. (1984). *The people's platform.* Washington, DC: Author.

National Urban League. (1986). *The state of Black America.* New York: Author.

Negandhi, A. R., & Prasad, S. P. (1971). *Comparative management.* New York: Appleton-Century-Crofts.

Nevius, J. (1982). School participation and culture in play groups of young children. *Journal of Social Psychology, 116,* 291-292.

Newman, B., & Newman, P. (1978). *Infancy and childhood.* New York: John Wiley.

Nobles, W. (1973). Psychological research and the Black self-concept: A critical review. *Journal of Social Issues, 29,* 11-31.

Novakovic, J. (1977). *The assimilation myth revisited: Rejection of home culture by second generation Yugoslav immigrant children as a function of age, friendship and sex.* Unpublished bachelor's honors thesis, University of New South Wales.

Offer, D. (1969). *The psychological world of the teenager.* New York: Basic Books.

Offer, D., Ostrov, E., & Howard, F. I. (1981). *The adolescent: A psychological self-portrait.* New York: Basic Books.

Ogbu, J. (1974). *The next generation: An ethnography of education in an urban neighborhood.* New York: Academic Press.

Ogbu, J. (1981). Origins of human competence: A cultural ecological perspective. *Child Development, 52,* 413-429.

Ogbu, J. (1982). Socialization: A cultural ecological approach. In K. Borman (Ed.), *The social life of children in a changing society.* Hillsdale, NJ: Erlbaum.

Ogbu, J. (1983). Crossing cultural boundaries: A comparative perspective on minority education. In *Race, class, socialization and the life cycle.* Symposium presentation in honor of Allison Davis, John Dewey Professor Emeritus, University of Chicago.

Osgood, C. E., May, W. H., & Miron, M. S. (1975). *Cross cultural universals of affective meaning.* Urbana: University of Illinois Press.

Osgood, C. E., Suci, G. J., & Tannenbaum, P. H. (1957). *The measurement of meaning.* Urbana: University of Illinois Press.

Padilla, A. (Ed.). (1980). *Acculturation: theory, models, and some new findings.* Boulder, CO: Westview Press.

Parkham, T., & Helms, J. (1981). The influence of Black students' racial identity attitudes on preferences for counselor's race. *Journal of Counseling Psychology, 28,* 250-257.

Parsons, O. A., & Schneider, J. M. (1974). Locus of control in university students from Eastern and Western societies. *Journal of Consulting and Clinical Psychology, 42,* 456-461.

Parsons, T., & Shils, A. (1951). *Toward a general theory of action.* Cambridge, MA: Harvard University Press.

Pasternak, M. (1979). *Helping kids learn multicultural concepts.* Champaign, IL: Research Press.

Patchen, M. (1982). *Black-white contact in schools.* Lafayette, IN: Purdue University Press.

Patton, M. Q. (1980). *Qualitative evaluation methods.* Beverly Hills, CA: Sage.

Paz, O. (1961). *The labyrinth of solitude.* New York: Grove.

Peck, R. F., Angelini, A. L., Diaz-Guerrero, R., Miller, K. M., Hayde, W., Weinert, F., Piquardt, R., Zorman, L., Tolicic, I., Cesa-Bianchi, M., Havighurst, R. J., & Kubo, S. (1972-1974). *Coping style and achievement: A cross national study of school children* (4 vols.). Austin: University of Texas, Research and Development Center in Teacher Education.

Peck, R. F., Angelini, A. L., Diaz-Guerrero, R., Miller, K. M., Hayde, W., Weinert, F., Piquardt, R., Zorman, L., Tolici, I., Cesa-Bianchi, M., Havighurst, R. J. & Kubo, S. (1973). *A replication study of coping patterns in eight countries* (Vols. 5a and 5b, *Coping styles and achievement: A cross national study of school of school children).* Austin: University of Texas, Personality Research Center. (ERIC Document Reproduction Service No. EDO78342).

Peck, R. F., & Stenning, W. (1967). Intercountry comparisons. *Proceeding of the Xth Interamerican Congress of Psychology* (pp. 259-268). Mexico: Trillas.

Pedersen, P., Draguns, J., Lonner, W., & Trimble, J. (1981). *Counseling across cultures.* Hawaii: University of Hawaii Press.

Pettigrew, T. F. (1967). Social evaluation theory: Convergences and application. *Nebraska Symposium of Motivation, 15,* 241-318.

Pettigrew, T. F. (1978). Placing Adam's argument in a broader perspective: Comment on the Adam paper. *Social Psychology, 41,* 58-61.

Pfefferbaum, A., & Dishotsky, N. (1981). Racial intolerance in a correctional institution: An ecological view. *American Journal of Psychiatry, 138,* 1057-1062.

Phinney, J., Rotheram, M. J., & Romero, A. (1985, August). *Ethnic behavior patterns among Black and Mexican-American school children.* Paper presented at a meeting of the American Psychological Association, Los Angeles.

Piaget, J. (1951). *The child's conception of the world.* New York: Humanities.

Piaget, J. (1960). *The child's conception of physical causality.* Patterson, NJ: Littlefield, Adams.

Piaget, J. (1963). *The origins of intelligence in children.* New York: Norton. (Original work published in 1936)

Piaget, J. (1965). *The moral development of the child.* New York: Free Press.

Piaget, J., & Weil, A. M. (1951). The development in children of the idea of the homeland and of relations with other countries. *International Social Science Bulletin, 3,* 561-578.

Pierce, C. (1982). *Personal communication.*

Pinderhughes, C. (1968). The psychodynamics of dissent. In J. Masserman (Ed.), *The dynamics of dissent* (pp. 56-79). Orlando, FL: Grune & Stratton.

Pinderhughes, E. (1982). Afro-American families and the victim system. In M. McGoldrick, J. Pearce, & J. Giordano (Eds.), *Ethnicity and family therapy.* New York: Guilford Press.

Pitt-Rivers, J. (1977). Race in Latin America: The concept of *Raza.* In J. Stone (Ed.), *Race, ethnicity and social change.* Belmont, CA: Wadsworth.

Poplack, S. (1980). Sometimes I'll start a sentence in English y termino en espanol: Towards a typology of code-switching. *Linguistics, 18,* 581-618.

Porter, J.D.R. (1971). *Black child, white child: The development of racial attitudes.* Cambridge, MA: Harvard University.

Porter, J., & Washington, R. (1979). Black identity and self-esteem: A review of studies of Black self-concept, 1968-1978. *Annual Review of Sociology, 5,* 53-74.

Postman, N. (1982). *The disappearing child.* New York: Delacorte.

Powell, G. J. (1973). Self concept in White and Black children. In C. V. Willie, B. M. Kramer, & B. S. Brown (Eds.), *Racism and mental health.* PA: University of Pittsburgh Press.

Powell, G. J. (1983). Coping with adversity: The psychological development of Afro-American children. In G. J. Powell (Ed.), *The psychological development of minority group children* (pp. 49-76). New York: Brunner/Mazel.

Preston, J. (1972). A study of the behavior of Negro and white preschool children in social groups with variations in the object environment. *Dissertation Abstracts International, 32*(7)B, 4260.

Proshansky, H. (1966). The development of intergroup attitudes. In L. W. Hoffman & M. L. Hoffman (Eds.), *Review of child development research* (Vol. 2). New York: Russell Sage.

Pugh, R. W. (1972). *Psychology and the Black experience.* Monterey, CA: Brooks/Cole.

Pusch, M. (Ed.). (1979). *Multicultural education: A cross-cultural training approach.* La Grange Park, IL: Intercultural Network.

Putnins, A. L. (1981). *Latvians in Australia: Alienation and assimilation.* Canberra: Australian National University Press.

Ramirez, M., III (1969). Identification with Mexican-American values and psychological adjustment in Mexican-American adolescents. *International Journal of Social Psychology, 15,* 151-156.

Ramirez, M., III (1977). Recognizing and understanding diversity, multiculturalism and the Chicano movement in psychology. In J. Martinez (Ed.), *Psychology of the Chicano.* New York: Academic Press.

Ramirez, M., III (1983). *Psychology of the Americas: Mestizo perspectives on personality and mental health.* New York: Academic Press.

Ramirez, M., III, & Castaneda, A. (1974). *Cultural democracy, bicognitive development, and education.* New York: Academic Press.

Ramirez, M., III, & Price-Williams, D. (1974). Cognitive styles of children of three ethnic groups in the United States. *Journal of Cross-Cultural Psychology, 5,* 212-219.

Ramsey, P. G. (1982). *Racial difference in young children's descriptions and contacts with peers.* Paper presented at the annual meeting of the American Psychological Association, Washington, DC.

Ramsey, P. G. (1983, April). *Young children's responses to racial differences: Sociocultural perspectives.* Paper presented at the biennial meeting of the Society for Research in Child Development, Detroit.

Ramsey, P. G. (1985, April). *Early ethnic socialization in a mono-racial community.* Paper presented at the biennial meeting of the Society for Research in Child Development, Toronto, Ontario.

Ramsey, P. G. (1987). *Teaching and learning in a diverse world: Multicultural education for young children*. New York: Teachers College.

Reichardt, C. S., & Cook, T. D. (1979). Beyond qualitative *versus* quantitative methods. In T. D. Cook & C. S. Reichardt (Eds.), *Qualitative and quantitative methods in evaluation research*. Beverly Hills, CA: Sage.

Reid, P. T. (1984). Feminism vs. minority group identity: Not for Black women only. *Sex Roles, 10*, 247-256.

Reisman, K. (1974). Noise and order. In W. W. Gage (Ed.), *Language in its social setting*. Washington, DC: Anthropological Society of Washington.

Reitz, H. G., & Groff, G. K. (1974). Economic development and belief in locus of control in 4 countries. *Journal of Cross-Cultural Psychology, 5*, 344-355.

Reyes-Lagunes, I. (1982). *Actitudes de los maestros hacia la profesion magisterial y su contexto*. Mexico: Tesis de Doctorado, Facultad De Psicologia, U.N.A.M.

Reyes de Ahumada, I., & Stenning, W. (1967). El rol desempenado por la autoridad en los desacuerdos interpersoples. Un estudio comparativo en estudiantes Mexicanos y Northeamericanos (Contribucion No. 10). *Memorias del XI Congreso Interamericano de Psicologia, Vol. 1*. Mexico: Universidad Nacional Autonoma de Mexico.

Reynolds, C. R. (1980). Differential construct validity of a preschool battery for Black, White, males and females. *Journal of School Psychology, 18*, 112-125.

Rice, A. S., Ruiz, R. A., & Padilla, A. M. (1974). Person perception, self-identity, and ethnic group preference in Anglo, Black and Chicano preschool and third-grade children. *Journal of Cross-Cultural Psychology, 5*, 100-108.

Rich, A. R., & Schroeder, H. E. (1976). Research issues in assertiveness training. *Psychological Bulletin, 83*, 1081-1096.

Riegel, K. F. (1976). Dialectics of human development. *American Psychologist, 31*, 689-700.

Riley, M. W. (1979). Introduction: Life course perspectives. In M. W. Riley (Ed.), *Aging from birth to death*. Washington, DC: Westview.

Rist, R. C. (1973). *The urban school: A factory for failure*. Cambridge: MIT Press.

Rist, R. C. (1978). *The invisible children*. Cambridge, MA: Harvard University Press.

Rist, R. C. (1980). Blitzkreig ethnography: On the transformation of a method into a movement. *Educational Researcher, 9*(2), 8-10.

Rist, R. C. (1982). Foreword. In R. C. Bogdan & S. K. Biklen (Eds.), *Qualitative research in education: Theory and methods*. Boston: Allyn & Bacon.

Robeck, M. C. (1978). *Infants and children: Their development and learning*. New York: McGraw-Hill.

Rodriguez, R. (1982). *Hunger of memory*. Boston: Godine.

Rogers, M., Hennigan, K., Bowman, C., & Miller, N. (1984). Intergroup acceptance in classroom and playground settings. In N. Miller & M. Brewer (Eds.), *Groups in contact: The psychology of desegregation*. New York: Academic Press.

Rohrer, G. K. (1977). Racial and ethnic identification and preference in young children. *Young Children, 32*, 24-33.

Rokeach, M. (1973). *The nature of human values*. New York: Free Press.

Rosch, E., Mervis, C. B., Gray, W. D., Johnson, D. M., & Boyes-Braem, P. (1976). Basic objects in natural categories. *Cognitive Psychology, 8*, 382-439.

Rosen, H., & Frank, J. D. (1962). Negros in psychotherapy. *American Journal of Psychiatry, 119*, 456-460.

Rosenberg, M. (1979). *Conceiving the self*. New York: Basic Books.

Rosenberg, M., & Simmons, R. (1970). *Black and White self-esteem: The Black urban child* (Rose Monograph Series). Washington, DC: American Sociological Association.

Rosenthal, B. G. (1974). Development of self-identification in relation to attitudes toward the self in the Chippewa Indians. *Genetic Psychology Monographs, 90*, 43-141.

Rosenthal, D. A. (1984). Intergenerational conflict and culture: A study of immigrant and non-immigrant adolescents and their parents. *Genetic Psychology Monographs, 109*, 53-75.

Rosenthal, D. A., Gurney, R. M., & Moore, S. M. (1981). From trust to intimacy: A new inventory for examining Erikson's stages of psychosocial development. *Journal of Youth and Adolescence, 10,* 525-537.

Rosenthal, D. A., & Hrynevich, C. (1985). Ethnicity and ethnic identity: A comparative study of Greek-, Italian-, and Anglo-Australian adolescents. *International Journal of Psychology, 20,* 723-742.

Rosenthal, D. A., Moore, S. M., & Taylor, M. J. (1983). Ethnicity and adjustment: A study of the self-image of Anglo-, Greek-, and Italian-Australian working-class adolescents. *Journal of Youth and Adolescence, 12,* 117-135.

Ross, L. (1981). The "intuitive scientist" formulation and its developmental implications. In J. H. Flavell & L. Ross (Eds.), *Social cognitive development.* New York: Cambridge University Press.

Rotheram, M. J. (1984). Therapeutic issues in assertiveness training. *Psychology: A Journal of Research, 21,* 28-33.

Rotheram, M. J. (1985, April). *Ethnic identity in adolescence.* Bernice Ryerson MacEvoy Foundation and CIBA Geigy Inc. Lecture Series.

Rotheram, M. J., & Phinney, J. (1983, May). *Intercultural attitudes and behaviors of children.* Paper presented at the meeting of the Society for Intercultural Evaluation, Training and Research, San Germignano, Italy.

Rotheram, M., & Phinney, J. (1984, April). *Behavioral reciprocity among preschool friends.* Paper presented at the meeting of the Eastern Psychological Association, Baltimore.

Rotheram, M. J., & Phinney, J. (1985, April). *Ethnic behavior patterns as an aspect of identity.* Paper presented at a meeting of the Society for Research in Child Development, Toronto.

Rotter, J. B. (1966). Generalized expectancies for internal versus external control of reinforcement. *Psychological Monographs, 80* (Whole No. 609).

Rovner, R. A. (1983). Theory and measurement of the relationship between ethnic identity and self-esteem. *Dissertation Abstracts International, 44,* 956-957.

Royce, A. P. (1982). *Ethnic identity: Strategies of diversity.* Bloomington: Indiana University Press.

Ryan, E., & Giles, H. (Eds.). (1982). *Attitudes towards language variation: Social and applied contexts.* London: Arnold.

Ryan, W. (1971). *Blaming the victim.* New York: Pantheon Books.

Sacks, H., & Schegloff, E. (1973). Opening up closings. *Semiotica, 8,* 289-327.

Sacks, H., Schegloff, E., & Jefferson, G. (1974). A simplest systematics for the organization of turn-taking in conversation. *Language, 50,* 696-735.

Sagar, C., Brayboy, T., & Wayenberg, B. (1972). Black patient-White therapist. *American Journal of Orthopsychiatry, 42,* 415-423.

Sagar, H. A., & Schofield, J. W. (1980). Racial and behavioral cues in Black and White children's perceptions of ambiguously aggressive acts. *Journal of Personality and Social Psychology, 39,* 590-598.

Sagar, H. A., Schofield, J. W., & Snyder, H. N. (1983). Race and gender barriers: Preadolescent peer behavior in academic classrooms. *Child Development, 54,* 1032-1040.

Salagaros, S., Humphris, G., & Harris, R. McL. (1974). Cultural tension in Greek families in Adelaide. *Greek-Australian Review,* 27-28.

Sanches, M., & Blount, B. (Eds.). (1975). *Sociocultural dimensions of language use.* New York: Academic Press.

Sanchez, F. S. (1984). The Chicano English dilemma: Deficit or dialect? *La Red/The Net: Newsletter of the National Chicano Council on Higher Education, 79,* 2-8.

Sanders, M., Scholz, J., & Kagan, S. (1976). Three social motives and field-dependence in Anglo-American and Mexican American children. *Journal of Cross-Cultural Psychology, 7,* 451-461.

Sankoff, G. (1980). *The social life of language.* Philadelphia: University of Pennsylvania Press.

Savage, D. (1985, May 7). Door still revolves in inner city: High school dropouts. *Los Angeles Times,* Part I, p. 1.

Scarr, S. (1979). From evolution to Larry P., or "What shall we do about IQ tests?" *Intelligence 2,* 325-342.

Scarr, S. (1985, August). *Race and gender as experimental variables: Ethical questions.* Paper presented at the meeting of the American Psychological Association, Los Angeles.

Scarr, S., Caparulo, B., Ferdman, B., Tower, R., & Caplan, J. (1983). Developmental status and school achievement of minority and non-minority children from birth to 18 years in a British Midlands town. *British Journal of Developmental Psychology, 1,* 31-48.

Schacter, S., & Singer, J. (1962). Cognitive, social, and physiological determinants of emotional state. *Psychological Review, 69,* 379-399.

Schegloff, E. (1972). Sequencing in conversational openings. In J. Gumperz and D. Hymes (Eds.), *Directions in sociolinguistics* (pp. 346-380). New York: Holt, Rinehart & Winston.

Scheidlinger, S., Sarcka, A., & Mendes, H. (1971). A mental health consultation service and neighborhood organizations in a ghetto area. *Community Mental Health Journal, 7,* 264-271.

Scheidlinger, S., Struening, E., & Rabkin, J. (1970). Evaluation of a mental health consultation service to a ghetto area. *American Journal of Psychotherapy, 24,* 485-493.

Schenkel, S., & Marcia, J. E. (1972). Attitudes toward premarital intercourse in determining ego identity status in college women. *Journal of Personality, 3,* 472-482.

Schieffelin, B. (1979). Getting it together: An ethnographic approach to the study of the development of communicative competence. In E. Ochs and B. Schieffelin (Eds.), *Developmental pragmatics* (pp. 73-110). New York: Academic Press.

Schofield, J. W. (1979). The impact of positively structured contact on intergroup behavior. Does it last under adverse conditions? *Social Psychology Quarterly, 42,* 280-284.

Schofield, J. W. (1981). Complementary and conflicting identities: Images and interactions in an interracial school. In S. R. Asher & J. M. Gottman (Eds.), *The development of children's friendships.* New York: Cambridge University Press.

Schofield, J. W. (1982). *Black and white in school: Trust, tension or tolerance?* New York: Praeger.

Schofield, J. W., & Francis, W. D. (1982). An observational study of peer interaction in racially-mixed "accelerated" classrooms. *Journal of Educational Psychology, 74,* 722-732.

Schofield, J. W., & Sagar, H. A. (1977). Peer interaction patterns in an integrated middle school. *Sociometry, 40,* 130-138.

Schofield, J. W., Whitley, B. E., Jr., & Snyder, H. N. (1983). Peer nomination versus rating scale measurement of children's peer preferences. *Social Psychology Quarterly, 46,* 242-251.

Schutz, A. (1970). *Reflections on the problem of relevance.* In R. M. Zaner (Ed.). New Haven, CT: Yale University Press.

Scotton, C. M. (1976). Strategies of neutrality: Language choice in uncertain situations. *Language, 52,* 919-941.

Scotton, C. M. (1983). The negotiation of identities in conversation: A theory of markedness and code choice. *International Journal of the Sociology of Language, 44,* 115-136.

Scourby, A. (1980). Three generations of Greek Americans: A study in ethnicity. *International Migration Review, 14,* 43-52.

Seagoe, M. V. (1970). Children's play as an indicator of cross-cultural and intra-cultural differences. In G. Luschen (Ed.), *Cross-cultural analysis of sports and games.* Champaign, IL: Stipes.

Seagoe, M. V. (1971). A comparison of children's play in 6 modern cultures. *Journal of School Psychology, 9,* 61-72.

Seagoe, M. V., & Murakami, K. (1961). Comparative study of children's play in America and Japan. *California Journal of Educational Research, 12,* 124-130.

Sears, R. R., Maccoby, E. E., & Levin, H. (1957). *Patterns of childrearing.* Evanston, IL: Row, Peterson.

Selman, R. (1980). *The growth of interpersonal understanding.* New York: Academic Press.

Semaj, L. (1976). *Race and sex effects of spatial behavior in a naturalistic setting.* Unpublished master's thesis, Rutgers University.

Semaj, L. (1979). Reconceptualizing the development of racial preference in children: The role of cognition. In W. Cross & A. Harrison (Eds.), *4th conference on Empirical Research in Black Psychology.* Washington, DC: Center for Minority Group Mental Health Programs (MIMN), 180-198.

Semaj, L. (1981). The development of racial-classification abilities. *Journal of Negro Education, 50, of Black Psychology, 6*, 59-79.

Semaj, L. (1981). The development of racial-classification abilities. *Journal of Negro Education, 50,* 41-47.

Seymour, S. (1975). Child rearing in India: A case study in change and modernization. In Williams (Ed.), *Socialization and communication in primary groups* (pp. 41-58). The Hague: Mouton.

Shade, B. (1982). Afro-American cognitive style: A variable in school success? *Review of Educational Research, 52*, 219-244.

Sherif, M., & Sherif, C. (1969). *Social psychology.* New York: Harper & Row.

Sherif, M., & Sherif, C. (1970). Black unrest as a social movement toward an emerging self-identity, *Journal of Social and Behavioral Sciences, 15*, 41-52.

Shibutani, T. (1955). Reference groups as perspectives. *American Journal of Sociology, 60*, 562-569.

Shibutani, T., & Kwan, K. (1965). *Ethnic stratification.* New York: Macmillan.

Shimanoff, S. B. (1980). *Communications rules: Theory and research.* Beverly Hills, CA: Sage.

Shireman, J., & Johnson, P. (1980). *Adoption: Three alternatives* (2nd Progress Report). Chicago: Chicago Child Care Society.

Shweder, R., & Bourne, E. (1982). Does the concept of the person vary cross-culturally? In A. Marsella & G. White (Eds.), *Cultural conceptions of mental health and therapy.* Dordrecht, Holland: Riedel.

Sieber, S. (1973). The integration of fieldwork and survey methods. *American Journal of Sociology, 78*, 133-159.

Silverstein, B., & Krate, R., (1975). *Children of the dark ghetto.* New York: Praeger.

Simmons, R. G. (1978). Blacks and high self-esteem: A puzzle. *Social Psychology, 41*, 54-57.

Singleton, L. C., & Asher, S. R. (1977). Peer preferences and interaction among third-grade children in an integrated school district. *Journal of Educational Psychology, 69*, 330-336.

Singleton, L. C., & Asher, S. R. (1979). Racial integration and children's peer preference: An investigation of developmental and cohort differences. *Child Development, 50*, 936-941.

Slaby, R. G., & Frey, K. S. (1975). Development of gender constancy and selective attention to same-sex models. *Child Development, 46*, 849-856.

Slaughter, D. T., & McWhorter, G. (1985). Social origins and early features of the scientific study of Black American families and children. In M. B. Spencer, G. K. Brookins, & W. R. Allen (Eds.), *Beginnings: Social and affective development of Black children.* Hillsdale, NJ: Erlbaum.

Slavin, R. E. (1983). *Cooperative learning.* New York: Longman.

Smith, L. M., & Geoffrey, W. (1968). *The complexities of an urban classroom.* New York: Holt, Rinehart & Winston.

Smolicz, J. J. (1976). Ethnic cultures in Australian society: A question of cultural interaction. In S. Murray-Smith (Ed.), *Melbourne studies in education, 1976.* Melbourne: Melbourne University Press.

Smolicz, J. J., & Seacombe, M. J. (1979). Cultural interaction in a plural society. In P. R. de Lacey and M. E. Poole (Eds.), *Mosaic or melting pot: Cultural evolution in Australia.* Sydney: Harcourt Brace Jovanovich.

Snowden, L., & Todman, P. (1982). Psychological assessment of Blacks. In E. Jones & S. Korchin (Eds.), *Minority mental health.* New York: Praeger.

Snyder, M. (1974). Self-monitoring of expressive behavior. *Journal of Personality & Social Psychology, 30*, 526-537.

Soares, A. T., & Soares, L. M. (1969). Self-perceptions of culturally disadvantaged children. *American Educational Research Journal, 6*, 31-45.

Sommerlead, E., & Bellingham, W. (1972). Cooperation-competition: A comparison of Australian, European and aboriginal school-children. *Journal of Cross-Cultural Psychology, 3*, 149-157.

Sotomayor, F. (1983). A boxful of labels. In *Southern California's Latino Community.* A series of articles reprinted from the *Los Angeles Times.*

Sotomayor, M. (1977). Language, culture and ethnicity in developing self concept. *Social Case Work, 58*, 195-203.

Spencer, M. (1977). *The socio-cognitive and personality development of the Black preschool children: An exploratory study of developmental process*. Unpublished doctoral dissertation, University of Chicago.

Spencer, M. B. (1982). Preschool children's social cognition and cultural cognition: A cognitive developmental interpretation of race dissonance findings. *Journal of Psychology, 112*, 275-296.

Spencer, M. B. (1983). Children's cultural values and parental child rearing strategies. *Developmental Review, 4*, 351-370.

Spencer, M. B. (1984a). Black children's race awareness, racial attitudes and self concept: A reinterpretation. *Journal of Child Psychology and Psychiatry, 25*, 433-441.

Spencer, M. B. (1984b, September). *Resilence and vulnerability: Black children's evolving self and society*. Paper presented at the Congressional Black Caucus Foundation Research Conference, Washington, DC.

Spencer, M. B. (1985). Cultural cognition and social cognition as identity factors in Black children's personal-social growth. In M. B. Spencer, G. K. Brookins, & W. R. Allen (Ed.), *Beginnings: social and affective development of Black children*. New York: Erlbaum.

Spencer, M. B., Brookins, G. K., & Allen, W. R. (1985). *Beginning: Social and affective development of Black children*. New York: Erlbaum.

Spencer, M. B., & Horowitz, F. D. (1973). Effects of systematic social and token reinforcement on the modification of racial and color concept attitudes in Black and White preschool children. *Developmental Psychology, 9*(2), 246-254.

Spicer, E. (1971). Persistent identity systems. *Science, 4011*, 795-800.

Spiegel, J. (1982). An ecological model of ethnic families. In M. McGoldrick, J. Pearce, & J. Giordano (Eds.), *Ethnicity and family therapy*. New York: Guilford.

Spiegel, J., & Papajohn, J. (1975). *Transactions in families*. San Francisco, CA: Jossey-Bass.

Spindler, G. (Ed.). (1982). *Doing the ethnography of schooling: Educational anthropology in action*. New York: Holt, Rinehart & Winston.

Spindler, G., & Spindler, L. (1982). Roger Harker and Schonhausen: From the familiar to the strange and back again. In G. Spindler (Ed.), *Doing the ethnography of schooling: Educational anthropology in action*. New York: Holt, Rinehart & Winston.

Spradley, J. (1979). *The ethnographic interview*. New York: Holt, Rinehart & Winston.

St. John, N. (1975). *School desegregation: Outcomes for children*. New York: John Wiley.

St. John, N. H., & Lewis, R. G. (1975). Race and the social structure of the elementary classroom. *Sociology of Education, 48*, 346-368.

Staples, R. (1976). *Introduction to Black sociology*. New York: McGraw-Hill.

Starc, S. (1980). A personal dilemma. In R. Burns (Ed.), *Teacher education in and for a multicultural society*. Melbourne: La Trobe University, Center for Comparative and International Studies in Education.

Steinberg, J., & Hall, V. (1981). Effects of social behavior on interracial acceptance. *Journal of Educational Psychology, 73*, 51-56.

Steinkalk, E. (1983). *The adaptation of Soviet Jews In Victoria: A study of adolescent immigrants and their parents*. Unpublished doctoral thesis, Monash University.

Stember, C. H. (1976). *Sexual racism: The emotional barrier to an integrated society*. New York: Elsevier.

Stephan, W. (1978). School desegregation: An evaluation of predictions made in Brown vs. Board of Education. *Psychological Bulletin, 85*, 217-238.

Stephan, W., & Feagin, J. (Eds.). (1980). *School desegregation: Past, present, and future*. New York: Plenum.

Stephan, W., & Stephan, C. (1984). The role of ignorance in integroup relations. In N. Miller & N. Brewer (Eds.), *Groups in contact: The psychology of desegregation*. New York: Academic Press.

Stevenson, H. W., & Stewart, E. C. (1958). A developmental study of racial awareness in young children. *Child Development, 29*, 399-409.

Stewart, E. (1972). *American cultural patterns: A cross-cultural perspective*. Chicago: Intercultural Press.

Stoddard, E. R. (1973). *Mexican Americans.* New York: Random House.

Stone, P. J. (1972). Child care in twelve countries. In A. Szalai (Ed.), *The use of time.* The Hague: Mouton.

Stonequist, E. V. (1935). The problem of a marginal man. *American Journal of Sociology, 41,* 1-12.

Stonequist, E. V. (1964). The marginal man: A study in personality and culture conflict. In E. Burgess and D. J. Bogue (Eds.), *Contribution to urban sociology.* Chicago: University of Chicago Press.

Storm, P. (1971). An investigation of self-concept, race image and racial preference in racial minority and majority children. *Dissertation Abstracts International, 31* (10-B), 6246-6247-B.

Sudarkasa, N. (1983). Race, ethnicity and identity: Some conceptual issues in defining the Black population in the United States. Conference presentation at the University of Michigan, Ann Arbor.

Sue, D. (1973). Ethnic identity: The impact of two cultures on the psychological development of Asians in America. In S. Sue and N. Wagner (Eds.), *Asian-Americans: Psychological perspectives.* Ben Lomond, CA: Science and Behavior Books.

Sue, D., Ino, S., & Sue, D. (1983). Nonassertiveness of Asian Americans: Inaccurate assumption. *Journal of Counseling Psychology, 30,* 518-588.

Sue, S. (1977). Community mental health services to minority groups. *American Psychologist, 32,* 616-624.

Sue, S., & Wagner, N. (Eds.). (1973). *Asian-Americans: Psychological perspectives.* Ben Lomond, CA: Science and Behavior Books.

Szapocznik, J., & Kurtines, W. (1980). Acculturation, biculturalism, and adjustment among Cuban Americans. In A. Padilla (Ed.), *Acculturation: Theory, models, and some new findings.* Boulder, CO: Westview.

Taft, R. (1965). *From stranger to citizen.* Perth: University of Western Australia Press.

Taft, R. (1973). Beyond the third generation: The ethnic identification of Jewish youth. In P. Medding (Ed.), *Jews in Australian society.* Melbourne: Macmillan.

Taft, R. (1974). Ethnically marginal youth and culture conflict: A problem in cross-cultural sciences. In J.L.M. Dawson and W. J. Lonner (Eds.), *Readings in cross-cultural psychology.* Hong Kong: Hong Kong University Press.

Taft, R. (1977). Coping with unfamiliar cultures. In N. Warren (Ed.), *Studies in cross-cultural psychology.* London: Academic Press.

Taft, R., & Johnston, R. (1967). The assimilation of adolescent Polish immigrants and parent-child interaction. *Merrill-Palmer Quarterly, 13,* 111-120.

Tajfel, H. (1970). Experiments in intergroup discrimination. *Scientific American, 223,* 96-102.

Tajfel, H. (1973). The roots of prejudice: Cognitive aspects. In P. Watson (Ed.), *Psychology and race.* Chicago: Aldine.

Tajfel, H. (1978). *Differentation between social groups: Studies in the social psychology of intergroup relations.* London: Academic Press.

Tajfel, H. (1981). *Human groups and social categories: Studies in social psychology.* London: Cambridge University Press.

Tajfel, H., & Jahoda, G. (1966). Development in children of concepts and attitudes about their own and other nations: a cross-national study. *Proceeding of the XVIIIth International Congress of Psychology* (pp. 17-33). Moscow: Nauka.

Tannen, D. (1982). Ethnic style in male-female conversation. In J. Gumperz (Ed.), *Language and social identity* (pp. 217-321). Cambridge, CA: Cambridge University Press.

Taylor, D. M., Bassili, J., & Aboud, F. E. (1973). Dimensions of ethnic identity: An example from Quebec. *Journal of Social Psychology, 89,* 185-192.

Taylor, D. M., Simard, L. M., & Aboud, F. E. (1972). Ethnic identification in Canada: A cross-cultural investigation. *Canadian Journal of Behavioral Science, 4,* 13-20.

Taylor, R. (1976). Psychosocial development among Black children and youth: A reexamination. *American Journal of Orthopsychiatry, 46,* 4-19.

Teske, R.H.C., Jr., & Nelson, B. H. (1973). Two scales for the measurement of Mexican American identity. *International Review of Modern Sociology, 3,* 192-203.

Thomas, C. W. (Ed.). (1971). *Boys no more*. Encino, CA: Glencoe.

Thomas, C. W., & Thomas, S. W. (1971). Something borrowed, something Black. In C. W. Thomas (Ed.), *Boys no more*. Encino, CA: Glencoe.

Thomas, D. R. (1974). Social distance in Fiji. *Journal of Social Psychology, 93,* 181-185.

Thomas, D. R. (1975). Cooperation and competition among Polynesian and European children. *Child Development, 46,* 948-953.

Tikunoff, W. J., Berliner, D. C., & Rist, R. C. (1975). *Special study A: An ethnographic study of the forty classrooms of the BTES known sample.* San Francisco: Far West Laboratory for Educational Research and Development.

Tikunoff, W. J., & Ward, B. A. (1978). *Conducting naturalistic research on teaching: Some procedural considerations.* San Francisco: Far West Laboratory for Educational Research and Development.

Toldson, I., & Pasteur, A., (1975). Developmental stages in Black self-discovery: Implications for using Black art forms in group interactions. *Journal of Negro Education, XLIV,* 130-138.

Torres-Metzgar, J. V. (1975). *The ethnic sensitivity of Spanish New Mexicans.* Paper presented at a meeting of the Western Social Science Association, Denver, Colorado.

Trend, M. G. (1978). On the reconciliation of qualitative and quantitative analysis. *Human Organization, 37,* 345-354.

Triandis, H. (1971, August). *Some psychological dimensions of modernization.* Paper presented at the 17th Congress of Applied Psychology, Liege, Belgium.

Triandis, H. (1972). *The analysis of subjective culture.* New York: John Wiley-Interscience.

Triandis, H. (1977). *Interpersonal behavior.* Monterey, CA: Brooks/Cole.

Triandis, H., & Berry, J. (Eds.). (1980). *Handbook of cross-cultural psychology* (Vol. 2). Boston, MA: Allyn & Bacon.

Triandis, H., & Brislin, R. (1984). Cross-cultural psychology. *American Psychologist, 39,* 1006-1016.

Triandis, H., Vassiliou, V., Vassiliou, G., Tanaka, Y., & Shanmugam, A. (1972). *The analysis of subjective culture.* New York: John Wiley.

Tsounis, M. P. (1975). Greek communities in Australia. In C. Price (Ed.), *Greeks in Australia.* Canberra: Australian National University Press.

Turner, J. (1971). Black nationalism: The inevitable response. *Black World, 20,* 4-13.

Turner, J. (1978). Social categorization and social discrimination in the minimal group paradigm. In H. Tajfel (Ed.), *Differentiation between social groups* (pp. 101-140). New York: Academic Press.

Tzuriel, D., & Klein, M. M. (1977). Ego identity: Effects of ethnocentrism, ethnic identification, and cognitive complexity in Israeli, Oriental and Western ethnic groups. *Psychological Reports, 40,* 1099-1110.

United States Department of Commerce. (1981, February). 1980 Census population totals for racial and Spanish origin groups in U.S. announced by Census Bureau. *U.S. Department of Commerce News.* Washington, DC: Government Printing Office.

Valentine, B. (1978). *Hustling and other hard work: Life styles in the ghetto.* New York: Free Press.

Van Maanen, J. (1982). Introduction. In J. Van Maanen, J. Dabbs, & R. Faulkner (Eds.), *Varieties of qualitative research.* Beverly Hills, CA: Sage.

Van Maanen, J., Dabbs, J., & Faulkner, R. (Eds.). (1982). *Varieties of qualitative research.* Beverly Hills, CA: Sage.

Van Parys, M. (1983, April). *Preschool children's understanding and use of race and gender.* Paper presented at the biennial meeting of the Society for Research in Child Development, Detroit.

Van Parys, M., & Bernal, M. (1985, August). *Ethnic identity in young Mexican American children.* Paper presented at a meeting of the American Psychological Association, Los Angeles.

Vasta, E. (1975). *Adolescents in conflict: A sociological study of the personal and social adjustment of second generation Italian immigrants.* Unpublished bachelor's (honors) thesis, University of Queensland.

Vasta, E. (1980). The second generation Italian adolescent at home and at school. *New Education, 2,* 95-102.

Vaughan, G. M. (1963a). Concept formation and the development of ethnic awareness. *Journal of Genetic Psychology, 103,* 93-103.

Vaughan, G. M. (1963b). The effect of the ethnic grouping of the experimenter upon children's responses to tests of an ethnic nature. *British Journal of Social and Clinical Psychology, 2,* 66-70.

Vaughan, G. M. (1964a). Ethnic awareness in relation to minority group membership. *Journal of Genetic Psychology, 105,* 119-130.

Vaughan, G. M. (1964b). The development of ethnic attitudes in New Zealand school children. *Genetic Psychology Monographs, 70,* 135-175.

Vaughan, G. M. (Ed.). (1972). *Racial issues in New Zealand.* Auckland: Akarana Press.

Vaughan, G. M. (1978a). Social change and intergroup preferences in New Zealand. *European Journal of Social Psychology, 8,* 297-314.

Vaughan, G. M. (1978b). Social categorization and intergroup behavior in children. In H. Tajfel (Ed.), *Differentiation between social groups: Studies in the social psychology of intergroup relations* (pp. 339-360). London: Academic Press.

Vaughan, G. M., Tajfel, H., & Williams, J. (1981). Bias in reward allocation in an intergroup and an interpersonal context. *Social Psychology Quarterly, 44,* 37-42.

Verna, G. B. (1981). Use of a free-response task to measure children's race preferences. *Journal of Genetic Psychology, 138,* 87-93.

Verna, G. B. (1982). A study of the nature of children's race preferences using a modified conflict paradigm. *Child Development, 53,* 437-445.

Vidich, A. J., & Shapiro, G. (1955). A comparison of participant observation and survey data. *American Sociological Review, 20,* 28-33.

Wagley, C., & Harris, M. (1958). *Minorities in the new world: Six case studies in New York.* New York: Columbia University Press.

Wallace, A.F.C. (1970). *Culture and personality* (2nd ed.). New York: Random House.

Ward, S., & Braun, J. (1972). Self-esteem and racial preference in Black children. *American Journal of Orthopsychiatry, 42,* 644-647.

Ware, H. (1981). *A profile of the Italian community in Australia.* Hawthorn, Victoria: Citadel Press.

Warren, R. L. (1982). Schooling, biculturalism, and ethnic identity: A case study. In G. Spindler (Ed.), *Doing the ethnography of schooling: Educational anthropology in action.* New York: Holt, Rinehart & Winston.

Washington, V. (1982). Racial differences in teacher perceptions of first and fourth grade pupils on selected characteristics. *Journal of Negro Education, 51,* 60-72.

Waterman, C. K., & Nevid, J. S. (1977). Sex differences in the resolution of the identity crisis. *Journal of Youth and Adolescence, 6,* 337-342.

Wax, R. (1971). *Doing fieldwork: Warning and advice.* Chicago: University of Chicago Press.

Weigel, R., Wiser, P., & Cook, S. (1975). The impact of cooperative learning experiences on cross-ethnic relations and attitudes. *Journal of Social Issues, 31,* 219-244.

Weiland, A., & Coughlin, R. (1979). Self-identification and preferences: A comparison of White and Mexican American first and third graders. *Journal of Cross-Cultural Psychology, 10,* 356-365.

Wetherell, M. (1982). Cross-cultural studies of minimal groups: Implications for the social identity theory of intergroup relations. In H. Tajfel (Ed.), *Social identity and intergroup relations* (pp. 207-240). England: Cambridge University Press.

White, R. (1974). Strategies of adaptation: An attempt at systematic description. In G. V. Coelho, D. A. Hamburg, & J. E. Adams (Eds.), *Coping and adaptation.* New York: Basic Books.

Whiting, B. B. (1963). *Six cultures: Studies of child rearing.* New York: John Wiley.

Whiting, B. B., & Edwards, C. P. (1973). A cross-cultural analysis of sex differences in the behavior of children aged 3-11. *Journal of Social Psychology, 91,* 171-188.

Whiting, B. B., & Whiting, J. W. (1975). *Children of six cultures: A psycho-cultural analysis.* Cambridge, MA: Harvard University Press.

Whitley, B. E., Jr., & Schofield, J. W. (1984). Peer preference in desegregated classrooms: A round robin analysis. *Journal of Personality and Social Psychology, 46,* 799-810.

Wicker, A. (1969). Attitudes versus action: The relationship of verbal and overt behavioral response to attitude objects. *Journal of Social Issues, 25,* 41-78.

Wilcox, K. (1982). Ethnography as a methodology and its applications to the study of schooling: A review: In G. Spindler (Ed.), *Doing the ethnography of schooling: Educational anthropology in action*. New York: Holt, Rinehart & Winston.

Williams, J. E., Best, D. L., & Boswell, D. A. (1975). The measurement of children's racial attitudes in the early school years. *Child Development, 46*, 494-500.

Williams, J. E., & Morland, J. K. (1976). *Race, color, and the young child*. Chapel Hill: University of North Carolina Press.

Williams, R. (1975). Race and ethnic relations. In Alex Inkles et al. (Eds.), *Annual Review of Sociology*. Palo Alto, CA: Annual Reviews.

Wilson, S. (1977). The use of ethnographic techniques in educational research. *Review of Educational Research, 47*, 245-265.

Winbush, R. A. (1977). A quantitative exploration into the theoretical formulations of Erik Erikson concerning Black identity. *Dissertation Abstracts International, 37B*, part 5.

Winn, M. (1984) *Children without childhood*. New York: Penguin.

Wiseman, R. (1971). Integration and attainment of immigrant secondary school students in Adelaide. *Australian Journal of Education, 15*, 253-268.

Wish, M., Deutsch, M., & Kaplan, J. (1976). Perceived dimensions of interpersonal relationships. *Journal of Personality and Social Psychology, 33*, 409-420.

Witkin, H. A. (1979). Socialization, culture, and ecology in the development of group and sex differences in cognitive style. *Human Development, 2*, 358-372.

Witkin, H. A., & Berry, J. W. (1975). Psychological differentiation in cross-cultural perspectives. *Journal of Cross-Cultural Psychology, 6*, 4-87.

Wolcott, H. (1973). *The man in the principal's office*. New York: Holt, Rinehart & Winston.

Wolcott, H. (1980). How to look like an anthropologist without really being one. *Practicing Anthropology, 3*, 39.

Wolf, R. (1964). *The identification and measurement of environmental process variables related to intelligence*. Unpublished doctoral dissertation, University of Chicago.

Wolf, R. (1965). The measurement of environments. In C. W. Harris (Ed.), *Proceedings of the 1964 Invitational Conference on Testing Problems* (pp. 93-106). Princeton, NJ: Educational Testing Service.

Wolfson, N., & Manes, J. (1979). Don't dear me. *Working papers in socio-linguistics* (No. 53). Austin, TX: Southwest Educational Development Laboratory.

Wolkind, S., & Rutter, M. (1985). Sociocultural factors. In M. Rutter & L. Hersov (Eds.), *Child and adolescent psychiatry*. Oxford: Blackwell.

Womack, W.M., & Fulton, W. (1981). Transracial adoption and the Black preschool child. *Journal of the American Academy of Child Psychiatry, 20*, 712-724.

Wynn, E. A. (1978, January). Behind the discipline problem: Youth suicide as a measure of alienation. *Phi Delta Kappan*, 305-315.

Yamamoto, J., & Kubota, M. (1983). The Japanese-American family. In G. J. Powell (Ed.), *The psychosocial development of minority group children* (pp. 237-247). New York: Brunner/Mazel.

Zajonc, R. B. (1976). Family configuration and intelligence. *Science, 192*, 227-236.

Zajonc, R. B. (1980). Feeling and thinking: Preferences need no inferences. *American Psychologist, 35*, 151-175.

Zea, L. (1974). *Dependencia liberaction en la cultura Latino American*. Mexico, D. F.: Editorial Joaquin Mortiz, S. A.

Zelditch, M., Jr. (1962). Some methodological problems of field studies. *American Journal of Sociology, 67*, 566-567.

Zentella, A. (1981). "Ta bien, you could answer me en cualquier idioma": Puerto Rican codeswitching in bilingual classrooms. In R. Duran (Ed.), *Latino language and communicative behavior* (pp. 109-131). Norwood, NJ: Ablex.

Zigler, E. (1982, April). *Human rights and the American family*. Symposium presentation at Emory University, Atlanta, GA.

Zinser, O., Rich, M. C., & Bailey, R. C. (1981). Sharing behavior and racial preference in children. *Motivation and Emotion, 65*, 179-187.

INDEX

Contributors

Frances E. Aboud: Department of Psychology, McGill University, Montreal, Quebec, Canada.

Karen M. Anderson: Department of Psychology, University of Pittsburgh, Pittsburgh, PA 15260.

Raymond Buriel: Department of Psychology, Pomona College, Claremont, CA 91711.

William E. Cross, Jr.: Africana Studies, Cornell University, Ithaca, NY 14853.

Rogelio Diaz-Guerrero: Department of Psychology, Universidad Autonoma de Mexico, Cuernavaca, Mexico.

Monica Heller: Ontario Institute for Studies in Education, Toronto, Ontario, Canada.

Phyllis A. Katz: Institute for Research on Social Problems, 520 Pearl Street, Boulder, CO 80302.

Thomas Kochman: Department of Communication and Theatre Arts, University of Illinois, Chicago Circle, P.O. Box 4348, Chicago, IL 60680.

Jean S. Phinney: Department of Family Studies, California State University, Los Angeles, CA 90032.

Patricia G. Ramsey: Department of Psychology and Education, Mt. Holyoke College, South Hadley, MA 01075.

Doreen A. Rosenthal: Department of Psychology, University of Melbourne, Parkville, Victoria 3052, Australia.

Mary Jane Rotheram: Division of Child Psychiatry #60, Columbia University, 722 W. 168th Street, New York, NY 10032.

Janet Ward Schofield: Learning Research and Development Center, University of Pittsburgh, Pittsburgh, PA 15260.

Margaret Beale Spencer: Division of Educational Studies, Emory University, Atlanta, GA 30322.

Graham M. Vaughan: Department of Psychology, University of Auckland, Auckland, New Zealand.